PROSPERITY FOR ALL

PROSPERITY FOR ALL

Consumer Activism in an Era of Globalization

MATTHEW HILTON

Cornell University Press
Ithaca and London

First published 2009 by Cornell University Press
First printing, Cornell Paperbacks, 2009

Printed in the United States of America

Library of Congress Cataloging-in-Publication Data

Hilton, Matthew.
    Prosperity for all : consumer activism in an era of globalization /
Matthew Hilton.
        p. cm.
    Includes bibliographical references and index.
    ISBN 978-0-8014-4644-3 (cloth : alk. paper) —
ISBN 978-0-8014-7507-8 (pbk. : alk. paper)
    1. Consumer protection—Political aspects.   2. Consumption
(Economics)—Political aspects.   3. Consumer satisfaction—
Political aspects.   4. Consumer behavior—Political aspects.
5. Globalizaion—Political aspects.   I. Title.

    HC79.C63H55 2009
    381.3'4—dc22
                                                        2008032878

Cornell University Press strives to use environmentally responsible
suppliers and materials to the fullest extent possible in the publishing of its books. Such materials include vegetable-based, low-VOC
inks and acid-free papers that are recycled, totally chlorine-free, or
partly composed of nonwood fibers. For further information, visit
our website at www.cornellpress.cornell.edu.

Cloth printing   10 9 8 7 6 5 4 3 2 1
Paperback printing   10 9 8 7 6 5 4 3 2 1

For Heather

CONTENTS

Acknowledgments   ix

Introduction: The Wealth of Access   1

1. The Fear of Fortune: The Uneasy Consumer in an Age
   of Affluence   21

2. Cold War Shoppers: Consumerism As State Project   51

3. Poverty amid Prosperity: Consumer Protest beyond
   the Affluent West   75

4. Consumers of the World Unite: Consumption and the
   New Global Order   98

5. The All-Consuming Network: The Politics of Protest
   in an Age of Consumption   126

6. Backlash: The Corporate Critique of Consumerism   153

7. Choose Life: Consumer Rights versus Human Rights   185

8. Shopping for Justice: The Freedom of Free Trade   214

Conclusion: The Poverty of Choice   241

Notes   255

Index   307

ACKNOWLEDGMENTS

The politics of living in a consumer society is a global politics. This book is concerned with both the rich and the poor, the North and the South, those living within and those living outside the world of capitalist consumption. It is about access, participation, and collective needs as much as it is about choice, greed, and individual wants. What I am trying to get across is that consumer society constitutes a world that concerns everybody rather than just those citizens fortunate enough to enjoy its more extravagant pleasures. In its focus on consumer activists, the book is fortunate to have as a case study a social phenomenon that allows me to tackle these global politics of consumption.

So far, the debates about consumer society have not generally appreciated the globalized nature of consumption, in the sense that those excluded are of as fundamental importance as those included. Instead, the literature has been dominated by an Anglo-American scholarship, particularly one inspired by a liberal critique that perennially worries itself with the problems of having too much: the "anxieties of affluence" as one writer has so aptly put it. Originally conceived, this book was merely going to continue these debates. It was intended as a comparative study of consumer movements and consumer politics in Western Europe and North America. It was to be about how the affluent dealt with consumption and how they sought protection regimes to defend their roles as consumers.

But in tracing the campaigns raised by consumer activists the world over, this book soon began to adopt a transnational rather than comparative approach. In so doing, it has not performed detailed analyses of consumer politics in different national contexts. Instead it has examined consumer activism beyond the nation-state, focusing in on national movements only when they have high-lighted or explained a wider global trend: somewhat problematically, therefore, Poland stands in for the experience of the Soviet bloc, while Malaysia serves as the case study for the developing world. Readers who have participated in or supported the consumer movement will regret many of the omissions I have been forced to make, not only of national contexts but of core consumer campaigns. But in order to maintain the global approach I have focused in on those issues that I consider to be key moments and emblematic events that cast light on broader histories of globalization, social movement activism, global civil society, and so on.

As I have moved from place to place, and issue to issue, it means that my acknowledgements are to individuals and institutions spread all around the world as I have traced consumer politics in not only Europe and North America, but also in Africa and Asia. I am indebted to all the historians, consumer experts, colleagues, friends, and activists who have assisted me in my work over the last few years. While all errors remain my own, I am grateful to all the participants in a huge number of presentations and seminars from Montreal to Penang, from Tartu to Dar-es-Salaam. I am also indebted to the collaborations I have entered into, many of the ideas from which have shaped this book. I am grateful to all the participants at the *Au nom du consommateur* colloquium in Paris in 2004, especially to my co-organizers, Marie-Emmanuelle Chessel and Alain Chatriot. The work on Poland was only possible because of the research undertaken by Malgorzata Mazurek, and my work in Malaysia was helped enormously by the unpublished research of Jeremy Seabrook. Much of the comparative work on consumer protection regimes owes a debt to the meetings organized in Paris, Chicago, and Oxford with Iselin Theien and Gunnar Trumbull.

I could not have undertaken the research or the writing of this book without the help of a number of institutions. The award of a Philip Leverhulme Prize in 2002 kick-started this project and gave me the freedom to explore new areas well beyond my usual areas of expertise. The Department of Modern History at the University of Birmingham generously supported this prize with a period of extended leave, backed up with a further sabbatical to write up the results of the research. I am extremely grateful to the Nuffield Foundation for awarding me a small research grant and to the Arts and Humanities Research Council for providing matching funds for my sabbatical.

The Center for European Studies at Harvard University provided a wonderful base from which to undertake the U.S. research. Colleagues there and at a number of other universities across the United States and Canada assisted with many ideas, tips, and sources. I am especially grateful to Dirk Bonker, Lizabeth Cohen, Gary Cross, Karl Gerth, Larry Glickman, Carolyn Goldstein, Robert Herrmann, Gabriele Lingelbach, Robert Mayer, Malcolm Mckinnon, Kathy Pence, Jarrett Rudy, Jurgen Ruckerberle, Daniel Schönpflug, and Norman Silber. In addition, staff at the Schlesinger Library at Harvard University, Tony Crawford and Pat Patton at the Kansas State University Archives, and Kevin

Manion at the Consumer Movement Archive, Yonkers, New York, were all supremely helpful.

The consumer movement itself assisted greatly in the field work for this book. Julian Edwards provided many contacts and made the archives of Consumers International open to me. His own thoughts on the development of consumerism were also crucial, as were those of many others who have participated in international consumer groups, especially Rhoda Karpatkin. In Kuala Lumpur, the hospitality provided by Indrani Thuraisingham, Josie Fernandez, Kamal Ali, and Marimuthu Nadason will be appreciated always. To them and their colleagues at ERA and FOMCA I owe so much, as I do to a countless number of activists and advocates in Malaysia: Mohd Hamdan Adnan, Jomo KS, M. Nadarajah, Sothi Rachagan, the late Bishan Singh, Mohamed Yunus Yasin, and all the staff at the CI-ROAP offices. In Penang, Anwar Fazal was an extraordinary host, as were the staff at CAP and Universiti Sains Malaysia. I am indebted to Kumariah Balasubramaniam, S. M. Mohamed Idris, Francis Loh, Meena Rahman, Sarojini Rengam, Foo Gaik Sim, and Khoo Boo Teik.

Colleagues at Birmingham have yet again provided a marvelous place to work. I am grateful to so many of them for their friendship and support, especially those who, along with others across the United Kingdom, have taken time to read various drafts of chapters. I owe a big thank you to Francesca Carnevali, Martin Daunton, Michael Heale, Conrad James, Helen Laville, Jerzy Lukowski, Graeme Murdock, Dan Scroop, Leslie Sklair, Pat Thane, and all of the DANGO team: Nicholas Crowson, Sarah Davies, James McKay, and Jean-Francois Mouhot. I am particularly indebted to Corey Ross, who read through the entire manuscript and offered his perceptive comments on so many aspects of the book. Thanks too must extend to Alison Kallet and Peter Potter at Cornell University Press who not only helped to see the book through to completion but offered some of the soundest editorial advice I have come across. I am grateful to the comments of two readers, especially to Larry Glickman who identified himself and provided invaluable comments on both the detail and the organizing framework of the book.

Finally, through all of this, Heather Widdows has encouraged, supported—and provoked(!)—me all the way. Through so many unpredictable and stimulating paths of the last few years, Heather has always been there. Together, we have pursued our own interests, which have on so many occasions come neatly together: intellectually, professionally, and personally. At the end of this project, Clara Rose joined us. It is to Heather that I dedicate this book.

INTRODUCTION

The Wealth of Access

There is much more to the history of consumer society than just shopping. Ever since the eighteenth century consumers have protested against the abuses of the market. They have boycotted products, offered alternative moral economies, sought to politicize the act of consumption, and promoted different notions of fair and honest trade. In certain instances they have been driven by the hunger in their stomachs. On occasion, they have been motivated by politics, especially when goods have come to hold symbolic meanings for wider ideological struggles. And at times, their focus has not been on the plight of consumers, but on the conditions endured by workers, the inequities experienced by citizens, and the disenfranchisement suffered by would-be voters. Consumers have challenged the shape of the economy and have questioned the direction of the society being built in their name.

When consumers have organized as consumers they have fought for greater access to the world of goods, not only for themselves but for all. They have offered visions of consumer society in which participation, access, and enjoyment have been key inspirations for those who have sought a more prosperous way of life. To be sure, they have not usually been prone to utopian dreaming or revolutionary action, and certain consumer actions can be as much prejudiced as progressive. But usually consumers have been concerned with the core aspects of the very meaning of the market. In food riots the world over, alternative plans for the organization of the capitalist economy have been developed. In the millions who have joined consumer co-operative societies, an ideal of a "co-operative commonwealth" has lurked in the back of the minds of many an activist. In the number of products that have symbolized the inequities of the system of manufacture and distribution—from global slavery to American racial segregation, South African apartheid, and colonial and post-colonial oppression—consumers have mobilized around consumption to make a wider political point. And for those who have been able to participate in the affluent world of goods there has always existed a concern to relieve the plight of those on whom their comfort rests; be they the consumers' leagues of late nineteenth-century continental Europe and North America, the social wings of the established faiths, or the supermarket shoppers of today directing their purchases to fair trade labeled products. The point is that individual material advantage is only one consideration of being a consumer and that for much of our recent history movements of consumers have appeared, which draw collectively on these wider motivations.

That said it is undoubtedly the case that the common understanding of the meaning of consumer society is now far removed from these political goals of participation, access, and improved standards of living for all. Indeed, there is any number of critiques of our current consumerist condition. All generally point to its principal characteristics as being marked by greed, individualism, and ever-spiraling wants and desires. It has come to be associated with the economic and political reforms of the 1980s, especially those of Ronald Reagan in the United States and Margaret Thatcher in the United Kingdom, in which, arguably, a society of citizens was replaced with an aggregation of individual shoppers. Today, so the critique continues, we have been left with a world dominated by the brand, by celebrity, and by material excess, and this has been tied to a global economic system geared toward meeting the ever higher rates of demand of those who can participate in the "good life." Consumerism, a term once used to cast aspersions on the consumer movement associated with Ralph Nader, has come to mean either a belief in the economic benefits of progressively increasing rates of consumption or the general adherence of society to materialistic values.

In this world the key goal of the consumer has come to be about the satisfaction of individual choice, and it seems choice alone has come to be the defining element of consumer society. Indeed, freedom of choice has been raised to a higher ideological purpose. In the weeks following the attacks of 11 September 2001, President George W. Bush urged Americans to keep on shopping: consumption, through its boost to the economy, was one means by which to win the "war on terror." Similarly, the then prime minister of Canada Jean Chrétien insisted that we must consume to keep the travel and tourism industries alive, noting also that interest rates had fallen to their lowest levels in years. "So it is time to go out and get a mortgage, to buy a home, to buy a car," he argued. And Tony Blair in Britain also urged everyone to "go about their daily lives: to work, to live, to travel and to shop."[1] Such linkages of consumption with democracy are not in themselves new. But what is different is that little was said about those who could not afford to shop, about those who were not in a position to exercise their freedom of choice. Although the liberal-left critics of consumption are coming from a very different political perspective to that of Bush and Blair, what unites all is an unwillingness to discuss those excluded from the society of consumption.

This has not always been the case. Consumers themselves have urged the creation of a world in which all—rather than the lucky few—can participate in the good life. For the period when consumer society is generally believed to have reached its full maturity—that is, the half century of economic reconstruction after World War II—organizations of consumers emerged all over the world concerned with creating a more equitable marketplace. Initially, and even primarily, much of the work of these groups has been geared to providing information resulting from the comparative testing of different branded commodities to individual shoppers, but they have gone on to articulate a politics of consumption that has been as much about ensuring that the market serves the interests of everybody as well as the individual. Moreover, they operated within a political climate in which the improvement of the standard of living became a key goal of governments that often equated consumer society with modern citizenship. The poor and the marginal have arguably been ignored in practice by administrations the world over, but this does not deny the appeal of the rhetoric by which politicians have sought to legitimate their power through the promise of participation in consumer society. Moreover, within this context, consumer activists have been able to argue that access was just as important as choice. As consumer movements emerged in the West, they applied notions of equitability in markets collectively as well as individually. In the latter half of the twentieth century, as the consumer movement expanded across the developing world, this theme was adopted more forcefully. Successive generations of activists have sought to ensure that the poor and the disadvantaged would be likewise able to participate in the world of goods.

How the definition of consumer society has shifted from a focus on access to one of choice is the subject of this book. Admittedly, the goals are not incompatible, and consumer activists, national politicians, and international diplomats have promoted both greater access and greater choice. But the activities of the organized consumer movement cast light on the change in the relative weighting placed on access and choice that has taken place over the last half century. This represents a redefinition of consumerism, which reflects more broadly on the dilemmas we all face as consumers: Do we want more stuff and more prosperity for ourselves? or do we want others less fortunate to be able to enjoy the same opportunities and standard of living as we do? Should the politics of consumer society be tied to wider questions of social welfare or simply to the satisfaction of individual desire? These conflicting goals have manifested themselves within a consumer movement that stretches from the affluent suburbs of North America to the impoverished slums found all across Africa and Latin America: a global consumer movement has had to trade off these competing interests of the rich and poor alike. Nevertheless, beyond these dilemmas and possibly contradictory goals, the story found in this book is one in which the vision of consumer society provided by organized consumers gave way to one promoted by organized business and the institutions of global governance in the latter decades of the twentieth century. By the end of the millennium global consumer society had been reoriented so that the relatively greater weighting attached to social welfare over individual gain, or access over choice, had been reversed. Increasingly, consumer society has been geared to serve only those who can already afford it.

I

To understand the meaning of consumer society we need to understand its origins and growth. The "birth of a consumer society" was first identified in eighteenth-century England.[2] Subsequently, others have gone on to identify similar consumer "revolutions" in North America and Western Europe, but it is the nature of this consumer society that is key.[3] The essence of the English consumer revolution was that it brought more stuff to more people for more of the time: "More men and women than ever before in human history enjoyed the experience of acquiring material possessions. Objects that for centuries had been the privileged possessions of the rich came, within the space of a few generations, to be within the reach of a larger part of society than ever before, and, for the first time, to be within the legitimate aspirations of almost all of it."[4] This was the century that witnessed the popularization of coffee and sugar, tulips and calicoes, jewelry and silver plate, luxury food and clothing, paintings and travel guides, and a whole host of fashionable items marking out a new and expanding middle class. The English consumer revolution was followed in the nineteenth century by a retailing revolution and a technological revolution that enabled cheap, mass-produced, and pre-packaged commodities to be sold to all. By the first two decades of the twentieth century, many of the world's most famous brands had become items of mass consumption: Coca-Cola, Marlboro, Kodak, Kellogg's, Nestlé, Heinz, Shell.

The point about this consumer society was that its varied advocates never meant it to be confined to just one section of the population. The very dynamism of capitalist growth meant that all were to be embraced by the market and that all would eventually participate in its pleasures. Attendant to the seemingly inexorable rise of the society of consumption was an accumulation of rights and interests attached to the consumer. If, in the eighteenth and nineteenth centuries, consumption had been a matter for the economy, society, and culture, by the twentieth century it became important to politics too. Unlike in previous centuries, when consumption could serve mainly as a theoretical and practical rallying point for economists and consumers, in the twentieth century, consumers were recognized as political entities to which governments must respond: defending the consumer-citizen and working to protect his or her standard of living became a typical populist manifesto of politicians of all persuasions.

Markets and commodities can be identified in any number of periods and places. What makes the twentieth century distinct is the modern domination of society by the market, when social life itself became intricately bound up with commodity exchange and styles of consumption.[5] Attendant to this social and economic phenomenon, though, was the presence of the consumer as a political entity, in which consumer politics emerged during—in U.S. terms—the Progressive Era that preceded World War I. The attempts to protect consumers in the market, or to appeal to their needs and desires, marks the last century and a half from earlier moments of politicized consumption, when consumers did not constitute a more general, abstract political presence. This is not to say that discussions of the consumer did not take place, but the consumer remained a fragmented being selectively interpreted as a cultural entity, a political being, an economic agent, and a social actor. By the twentieth century, in speaking for the consumer, commentators, politicians, bureaucrats, professional experts, and consumers themselves were more aware of the different dimensions of consumption that could play a role in modern citizenship.[6]

Regulations that have protected the consumer are by no means specific to the last hundred years. A leader of the international consumer movement has often invoked the Hittites of Anatolia from the eighteenth-century BC as the earliest defenders of the consumer interest. Somewhat stretching a point, he has claimed that Hittite laws on the poisoning and "bewitching" of oil were essentially consumer protection measures against adulteration and misleading marketing practices.[7] Similar claims have also been made for medieval sumptuary legislation and the codes and practices prescribed by guilds.[8] But it was in the late nineteenth century that changes in the provision of basic goods required intervention by legislatures that had some bearing on the consumer. Urbanization in particular encouraged the municipalization of utilities and the related promotion of public health legislation in regard to the water supply. Citizens were seen to identify themselves as consumers to demand either the more widespread or the more equitable distribution of gas and electricity, while politicians could invoke the consumer as a new populist measure since in providing a basic commodity for all the older political notion of "the public" became synonymous with the new emphasis on "the consumer".[9]

Likewise, campaigns for pure food and drink resulted in legislation against adulteration, the expansion of health inspectorates, and the development of weights and measures regulations.[10] By all means, adulteration measures could be just as much about making certain business practices legitimate rather than being a defense measure for the consumer, but often the impact on consumers could be far-reaching not only in terms of the practical impact on their lives but in the precedents set for further state infringements into consumer sovereignty. For instance, the French law on fraud and falsifications in food adopted in 1905 was the product of various campaigns for public hygiene, scientific investigations, the standardization movement, and the competing interests of producers and distributors. Yet it was also the model for all subsequent French legislation dealing with frauds as well as a partial inspiration for the European Codex Alimentarius.[11] In the United States, the 1906 Pure Food and Drug Act has subsequently been heralded as one of the first pieces of social legislation specifically designed to improve the welfare of the general public.[12] Together with the Meat Inspection Act of the same year, influenced by Upton Sinclair's novel on the Chicago meat-packing industry, *The Jungle*, the legislation inspired consumer groups to campaign for further consumer regulations.[13]

War provided a crucial impetus to political consumerism. The penetration of government into so many aspects of people's lives necessarily affected their roles as consumers. The French state, worried about political instability arising from shortage during World War I, introduced a comprehensive system of food control in 1917.[14] This recognition of the citizen as a consumer was similarly witnessed in Britain, where a Consumers' Council was established toward the end of the War to foster communication between the general public and state institutions dealing with food supply.[15] During World War II, states were far more organized in the administration of rationing schemes, controlling prices and systems of provision, and analyzing consumer needs. They also had to rely on the expertise and input of scientists, women's groups, producers, retailers, and a whole range of other spokesbodies for the consumer if detailed studies were to be made of nutritional levels, rationing requirements, and the supply systems needed to meet these. In Switzerland, for example, the politics of nutrition involved a dialogue among dieticians, housewives' organizations, patriotic groups concerned with the purification of Swiss customs, businessmen, co-operators, journalists, and legislators, all of whom sought to speak for the consumer.[16]

The mobilization of the state around issues of consumption created opportunities for those who saw in the consumer a citizen around which modern welfare regimes could be built. In the United States, liberals such as John Kenneth Galbraith and Lewis Mumford were attracted to institutions such as the Office of Price Administration because they saw in these state interventions a more social democratic citizenship and one that satisfied their moral dilemmas over abundance. They urged frugality and "chastened consumption" in the present in order to enjoy indulgence in the future.[17] While many of these institutions were fiercely opposed, not least by big business, wartime state consumerism offered a "fair shares" politics of consumption that was attractive at the ballot box in the subsequent years of austerity and reconstruction.[18]

However, consumerism as a state project was not simply the product of emergency measures of wartime. The consumer as a political subject was also the focus of a developing professionalization of expertise and the changing roles of governance by both private and public bodies and forms of knowledge. The consumer increasingly became the subject of inquiry of a host of professions, from behavioral psychology to marketing to industrial design, a process bound up with the modern creation of the self and all the terms that cluster around it: autonomy, identity, individuality, and choice.[19] In economic thought, the consumer had long been subordinate to the producer. Indeed, it was felt that the unproductive purchases of the average consumer too often reduced rather than added to wealth. But toward the end of the nineteenth century, greater attention was given to consumer choice, the theory of marginal utility in particular divorcing value from production costs and equating it instead with the satisfaction it provided the consumer. The consumer had earlier been ignored for as much moral as economic reasons, because his or her unproductive consumption detracted from value. By redefining value, this shifted the focus from supply to demand and enabled social scientists to observe the consumer in a non-moralistic manner. Figures such as Thorstein Veblen and Simon Patten retained a critique of the acquisitive shopper and the conspicuous consumer, but they could also write of how the economic system exploited consumers and failed to free up their potential contribution to the economy. By releasing the potential of demand, the consumer provided the spur to industry: if this demand could be spent efficiently rather than wastefully, then abundance would eventually be brought to all.[20]

Such consumer-oriented economics reflected a more widespread attention to the consumer within expert thought. The burgeoning advertising industry and market research professions attempted to dissect and to know the consumer in all of his or her manifestations, reducing him or her to an individual unit to whom products could be sold and distributed. By privileging their own professional expertise in knowing the consumer, they also positioned themselves as the representatives of the consumer in general, a tactic that became institutionalized in the new professional bodies of advertisers and salesmen which, in turn, promoted their own interests and understandings of consumption at the level of the state.[21] The definition of the consumer as an atomized purchaser was therefore replicated in government offices that promoted trade, especially in the U.S. Bureau of Foreign and Domestic Commerce, which set up in 1912 and worked to promote U.S. business abroad. Moreover, U.S. advertising agencies—for example, J. Walter Thompson—opened up their own European branches.[22]

The professionalization of consumer knowledge by the advertising and marketing industry was replicated in, for instance, the home economics movement, which similarly posited itself as the expert voice on consumer affairs. In the United States this was symbolized most clearly in the attempt to incorporate the consumer into the state during the period of the New Deal. The consumer was to stand in for the public in general, acting as a bulwark against other economic interests and legitimating state intervention on behalf of all citizens while holding on to the basic premises of the capitalist economy.[23] Consumers came up against other, better organized, and better funded interest groups, which meant their effectiveness was severely curtailed. Such consumer representation established an important principle: that consumers could have a say in the running of the economy, which legitimated demands for further consumer involvement in subsequent decades.[24]

Other countries adopted similar piecemeal tactics to represent and contain consumer criticism. As democratic states equated consumers with the public, regimes of a more authoritarian nature also attempted to direct consumers toward official goals. The women's associations of the Weimar Republic underwent a process of Nazification in 1930s Germany as they were subject to the control of the state, ultimately being replaced by the Women's Bureau Division of Political Economy-Home Economy in 1935. This sought not to empower women as shoppers but to teach them to respect the needs of producers and retailers and to undertake housewifery under a national socialist fashion.[25] Nazi Germany also claimed to be raising standards of living in line with fascist ideology. This meant placing great emphasis on key products such as automobiles and radios, although in practice it required consumers to engage in virtual consumption, because their savings set aside for such goods were actually channeled toward rearmament.[26] Indeed, nationalism for a long time had been a rallying cry for consumer political action. It had played a role in consumer movements of the past but in the 1930s it was promoted by the state to shape particular forms of consumption. For example, Fascist Italy sought to define beauty and fashion in opposition to U.S. styles.[27] Moreover, consumption was a central tactic of Chinese and Korean nationalists in their struggle against the Japanese, and the *swadeshi* movement politicized homespun cloth for generations of Indian nationalists inspired, in particular, by Mahatma Gandhi.[28]

Following World War II, consumer society was championed as the bright future to which the ravaged economies must direct themselves. Most obviously in the United States, mass consumption was not to be a "personal indulgence, but rather a civic responsibility designed to provide 'full employment and improved living standards for the rest of the nation.'"[29] Through greater state spending on infrastructure, the expansion of credit facilities, the encouragement of home ownership in the new suburbs, and the creation of personal opportunities symbolized by the GI Bill (Serviceman's Readjustment Act) in 1944, all Americans were being invited to participate in the "consumers' republic." Arguably, this model of an all-embracing consumer culture was exported through the Marshall Plan, but Roosevelt's "freedom from want" was mirrored in Beveridge's welfarism in Britain and in social democracy in Europe. Sociologist Jean Fourastié elaborated on a long-standing commitment to planning in French political economy, extolling the virtues of consumption as a civilizing process that would drag citizens from older modes of living. During *les trente glorieuses,* he took it to be his mission to educate the French that technological progress leads to greater productivity, which in turn leads to higher standards of living for all.[30] In Germany, the social market economy espoused by the Minister of Economics, Ludwig Erhard, presented its own model of a future consumer society. Erhard embraced an alliance with consumers in the rebuilding exercise and, riding the crest of the economic miracle, was able to announce "prosperity for all."[31]

This rhetorical construct of a future consumer society shared and participated in by everybody contrasts with a spirit of consumerism concerned solely with individual choice and acquisition. If "consumer democracy" as a term is perhaps only truly applicable to the United States, so all-pervasive was the idea that state policy, mass consumption, and universal standards of living were bound up with one another, that the rhetoric crossed the Iron Curtain to the Soviet bloc. Although an ethical critique has always persisted about the luxurious elements of consumption, after World War II luxury and necessity were combined in a notion of consumer society that promised a morally neutral and politically shared commitment to providing affluence and the good life for everybody. Even Stalin spoke of the need to pay attention to the production of consumer goods and, according to the most thoroughgoing study of twentieth-century consumer economies, the Cold War became a "struggle over which system more effectively satisfied standards for the good life, with each spelling out, in opposition to the other, a definition of mass consumption suited to its resources and legacy of development."[32]

The two competing systems almost literally clashed in the kitchen at the 1959 U.S. Trade and Cultural Fair in Moscow. U.S. vice president Richard Nixon and Soviet premier Nikita Khrushchev, walking around the model homes engaged in a teasing dialogue about the relative merits of capitalism and communism in bringing more goods, better homes, and higher incomes to more people.[33] Across both sides of the Iron Curtain, therefore, it seemed the expansion of consumption and the promotion of consumer society to everybody were defining features of the role of the modern state.

II

It would be a mistake to believe that the regimes of consumption developed by states were top-down initiatives that paid little attention to the actual voices of consumers themselves. The focus of this book is on the global organized consumer movement since World War II, but this is not to deny the presence of formidable social movements geared around consumption prior to this. They played a leading role in articulating diverse consumer demands to which governments were in many ways forced to respond. The co-operative movement had a strong claim to being the oldest, most established, and most successful consumer organization over the previous century. Beginning in the North of England in the 1840s, the dividend-on-purchase, consumer co-operative ethos of the "Rochdale Pioneers" spread throughout Europe as an alternative to the capitalist marketplace. By the outbreak of World War I, there were literally thousands of local societies in the United Kingdom, Austria, Germany, France, Russia, and across Scandinavia.[34] In the United States, the co-operative movement was never so strong.[35] There existed instead a long tradition of workers' involvement in cost of living campaigns and the fights for a living wage. As U.S. workers conceptualized the pay packet in terms of how it was spent, as well as

how it was earned, their struggles were about "pocketbook politics" that combined both their producer and consumer roles.[36] Trade unionists often joined
with other philanthropic, women's, and faith-based organizations to bring consumers together in defense of workers' rights. "White lists" were compiled by
anti-sweating campaigners and groups, such as the U.S. Knights of Labor and
the British Christian Social Union, to guide middle-class shoppers toward stores
with union-approved working conditions.[37] In 1890, a Consumers' League was
formed by the Women's Trade Union League in New York, which soon inspired
equivalent organizations across Western Europe all of which campaigned
against poor labor conditions behind the manufacture of goods sold in the main
high street stores.[38]

More radical women's activism has also leapt to the defense of the worker.
The League of Women Shoppers in the United States maintained close links with
the Communist party and embarked on a series of high-profile progressive
causes, especially over the cost of living.[39] Its opposition to certain forms of
consumption fits in with a longer, if sporadic, form of protest—the boycott—
around which women have in particular mobilized. Rising food prices, rent
hikes, shortages, and perceptions of profiteering have persistently brought
women onto the streets, occasionally resulting in more sustained forms of action, at other times petering out as the specific problem was resolved.[40] In
Berlin, for instance, during World War I, housewives gave up on their earlier
commitment to assisting the government and joined their husbands in attacking a system that no longer catered to their basic needs. The activism of women
consumers was a key means by which ordinary grievances were understood as
the legitimate complaints of citizens.[41] Likewise, the civil rights movement mobilized consumers around race, triggering more radical interventions by the
consumer movement as a whole.[42] And the boycott of South African products
inspired by the anti-apartheid movement fed through into the modern fair trade
movement and the rise of ethical consumption.[43]

Since the mid-twentieth century, the history of consumer activism has been
intimately tied in with the growth of the comparative testing movement. Beginning in 1929, when Consumers' Research was incorporated in the United
States, the publication of magazines devoted to the provision of product information, as well as indicators of "best buys," has proved tremendously popular
with the affluent middle classes all around the world. In 1936, a rival organization, Consumers Union, was established in America, which ultimately became the more successful of the two and the model for organized consumerism
as it took off in Europe after World War II. By the end of the 1960s, comparative testing consumerism had a presence in every country of the North Atlantic
community, its reach extended all around the world and, through the establishment of the International Organisation of Consumers Unions (IOCU) in
1960, it had a global federation that meant consumerism had a political presence on the world stage. Just a few years later, organizations had appeared in
the developing world too. In the 1970s, consumerism was present in most of

the countries of Southeast Asia. It would be followed by similar growth in Latin America and, from the end of the 1980s, into the former Soviet bloc and Africa as well. For years IOCU has been able to rightly claim that it is a genuinely global non-governmental organization—in 2008 there are many hundreds of groups affiliated to it from over one hundred different countries.

What needs to be emphasized about organized comparative testing consumerism is that it was not simply about publishing consumer advice. It was a social movement. Undoubtedly, for the many millions of subscribers to *Consumer Reports* in the United States, *Which?* in the UK, *Que Choisir* in France, and *Test* in Germany, the magazines were simply the publications of organizations that could be regarded as advice bureaus to help shoppers obtain better value for money in their household purchases. But to truly understand the nature of consumer organizing it is more appropriate to regard modern consumer groups as the latest manifestation of a longer history of consumer activism. They have protested against abuses in the marketplace, they have politicized consumption for many millions of consumers, they have lobbied and campaigned to have a profound impact on late twentieth-century government, they have captured the attention of the mass of consumers at key periods, and they have persistently put forward a definition of consumer society that has tried to position the modern economy more deliberately in line with the interests of consumers.

These organizations of consumers have not been normally regarded as either activist bodies or the institutional expression of a grassroots social movement. Yet if we were to discuss a global organization that consisted of many hundreds, if not thousands, of similar local and national bodies all around the world; if we knew that the leaders of some of these organizations had been arrested and detained without trial; that they had campaigned—with many successes—on issues such as the use of pesticides, the inappropriate marketing of breast milk substitutes, the safety of basic consumer staples such as crops subjected to genetic modification and the dumping of pharmaceuticals on the developing world; that they had launched wide-ranging critiques of the power of multinational firms and the institutions of global economic governance; that they championed the rights of the "little man" in an apparently dehumanizing world then we might more readily identify them as a social movement. Certainly, these characteristics all apply to the organized consumer movement that has largely been associated with the comparative testing of different branded goods. As early as 1939, some observers were prepared to regard consumerism as a social movement, one that emerged from "the transition from a producer's economy to a consumer's economy; from an economy of scarcity to one of plenty."[44] Yet in the literature emerging in reaction to the rise of new social movements of the 1960s, consumerism has not widely entered the "pantheon of protest." Although definitions of what constitutes a social movement have broadened in recent years, the movements of the 1960s generation—civil rights, the women's movement, environmentalism, student revolt, the peace movement—are still held to be the exemplars of social protest in an age no longer dominated by class-based politics.[45] Unfortunately, this definition of social movements excludes as much as it includes; to the extent that the personal political bias of the author can determine what and who is included in the notion of activism.[46]

Yet the investigations into the subscriber base of comparative testing magazines demonstrate popularity among a social milieu, which also flocked to protest organizations more regularly associated with the 1960s. Activism took place on a broader front than those constituting the vanguard of any street-based demonstration. It included the rise of faith-based international development agencies and the campaigns against child poverty and discrimination based on age and disability. The 1960s witnessed the flourishing of voluntary action and the establishment of charitable foundations dealing with a whole variety of specific social ills, and which were prepared to provide advice to citizens in all aspects of their lives: as immigrants, as taxpayers, as prisoners, as drug addicts, as the homeless, and as consumers.[47] "Expressive groups" campaigned on moral issues from abortion to gun control to animal rights to sexuality to human rights; issues that traversed the conventional political spectrum but that nevertheless constituted a more general social phenomenon than that recognized by the leftism of a 68-inspired literature.[48] The irony is that at the time, counterculturalists often poured scorn on consumer activists whose radicalism might stretch to a Vance Packard or a Ralph Nader but never to a Herbert Marcuse or Jean-Paul Sartre. Yet, in the longer term, the individualism inherent to the anti-establishment and identity-based politics of the 1960s possibly offered a more direct link to the individualism of contemporary capitalism than any acquisitive materialism identified in the membership of a consumer organization.[49]

If the notion that activism has to involve outright rebellion is rejected, then in the more reformist agendas of organized consumerism and other political actors a more integrative social and political space can be identified, which broadens out the definition of social movement.[50] As the capitalist West shifted from an industrial to a post-industrial society, becoming a society based on consumption rather than production, then so too did the emotional life of citizens become geared toward how they spent—rather than how they earned—their income. As chapter 1 shows, in the comparative testing organizations of Europe, North America, and Australasia, there existed a social movement concerned with the desire of the newly affluent to play a part in the society being constructed in their name. Certainly, they sought for themselves the more "local" advantage of better value for money, but by being organized they developed into a movement concerned not only "for itself" but "embedded in broader processes of social change."[51] Consumerism always had the potential to be just about getting more stuff—and for hundreds of thousands of subscribers it was to be nothing more than that—but it warrants an identification as a movement since it came to be about not just fighting for the individual, but fighting for all individuals to be able to participate equally in the good life. If comparative testing organizations never demanded a redistribution of wealth, they did at least demand that all consumers be respected in the marketplace and that all citizens were to have the opportunities to enjoy that respect. It could hardly be identified as an anti-capitalist organization, but in the diffuse and shifting demands it made of the marketplace it ensured its place alongside other social movements of the affluent society. Moreover, politicians and statesmen recognized the existence of a new social phenomenon: witness the incredible growth of consumer protection systems all around the world at the same time (see chapter 2).

What must also be appreciated about organized consumerism as a social movement is its global reach and global impact. Consumer activism was not confined to affluent capitalist society but was also prominent all over the developing world. From the 1960s consumer activists emerged across Southeast Asia and Latin America, inspired by figures such as Ralph Nader, and also drawing on their own traditions and political contexts. Using a case study of Malaysian consumer activism, chapter 3 sets out the development of a consumer agenda that focused as much on the rights of the poor to basic needs— food, shelter, water, energy, and medicine—as on the problems of the affluent in obtaining value for money. As many newly independent former colonial societies sought to promote economic development, consumer activism appealed to those educated urban professionals who embraced the world of goods but remembered too a childhood of poverty that they did not want to see persist for large numbers of their fellow citizens left behind in the developmental process. Moreover, in the unevenness of economic growth, consumerism afforded an opportunity for everyday concerns about access to the market and citizen participation in the economy to be addressed in a relatively non-confrontational manner. It meant that the definition of consumer rights was transformed, access to basic needs coming to occupy a central place in the consumer movement's definition of the consumer society.

In adopting a politics of consumption that emphasized the standards of living of the majority of the world's poor, the consumer movement tied itself to an internationalist agenda as set out in the Universal Declaration of Human Rights. Indeed, the history of the global consumer movement is largely one of its attempts to influence the policies and agendas of the United Nations. As we will see in chapter 4, consumer activists soon gained recognition by several UN agencies, especially those connected to the Economic and Social Council. As a general issue organization, the work of IOCU was recognized by the UN and it was awarded a high category status enabling it, alongside other non-governmental organizations (NGOs) such as the trade union and women's movement, to have an influential role in UN debates. By the 1980s, then, not only had consumerism become a worldwide movement concerned as much with the poor as with the rich, but it was able to adopt something of a leadership role in global civil society thanks to its prominent position in UN committees. In its promotion of market society it was granted a degree of respectability that opened many doors for its lobbyists at the international level, while the radicalism fostered by its grassroots basic needs agenda ensured it led the way on many specific issues addressed by a whole cross-section of civil society actors. For all of these reasons, it is appropriate to regard organized consumerism as a social movement. Although it has never espoused an agenda quite as radical or as utopian as many of the new social movements associated with the 1960s counterculture, and although it never experienced as high a media profile as enjoyed by equivalent NGOs working more directly in the sphere of human rights and environmentalism, it was nevertheless a movement of social activists.

III

Encapsulated within the consumer movement are many of the central dilemmas that have faced consumer societies as a whole since the mid-twentieth century: between trading off the competing demands of the poor and the affluent; in deciding the extent to which the developed and the developing world should participate in the modern marketplace; and in negotiating the extent to which we are free to consume in our own interests and likewise obliged to take into consideration the myriad of political and moral questions that are inherent to every decision we make to purchase a good. For these reasons, an examination of the global consumer movement is an ideal device for examining consumer society itself. This is especially the case when the consumer movement has seemed to represent the attitudes of consumers in general. In the 1950s and 1960s, as European, Australian, and North American consumers as a whole wanted to participate in the society being built in their name, consumerism seemed to offer the helping hand that many newly affluent shoppers craved. In the 1970s and 1980s, the developing world consumer movement likewise represented a broader shift in consumer attitudes. This is evidenced not only in the astonishing popularity of some consumer publications in specific developing world contexts but in the extent to which consumer politics became a rallying point for the international community as a whole. The successes of IOCU at the UN and the degree to which other NGOs connected with consumers on specific issues attests to the wider relevance of the movement at this time.

Today, it is questionable whether the politics of consumption associated with comparative testing quite holds the consumer's imagination as it did in earlier decades. Undoubtedly, subscription rates are still very high in some parts of the world, but usually providers of consumer information now find themselves competing with other commercial and private firms who have offered their own evaluation of products. Moreover, state institutions have been established—such as ombudsmen, information bureaus, watchdogs, and regulatory authorities—that actually police the market in a way in which consumer groups have campaigned for. Indeed, it might even be argued, as some veteran consumer activists like to claim, that a potential reason for any perceived decline in the movement's fortunes is due precisely to the successes it has obtained. It can generally be assumed that products will not explode in their user's face, that if they break certain forms of redress are available, and that agencies will intervene on behalf of the collective mass of consumers to protect them from the systematic abuses and inequities of the marketplace. In the developing world these are still clear and present issues, but as in the provision of consumer information in the capitalist West, consumer groups operate in a more competitive marketplace. The exponential growth in national and international NGOs since the 1980s has meant many of the issues that the consumer movement has pioneered have now been taken up by other groups either more narrowly focused and better equipped to deal with the problem or else sufficiently robust to operate independently of the consumer movement's resources.

Undoubtedly, organized consumerism was a product of affluence and much of its success came in a period of increasing economic growth that could afford to tolerate regulatory and protective mechanisms in the defense of the consumer. Nevertheless, the theme running throughout this book is that, through the consumer movement and the national and international bodies that responded to it, a definition of consumer society has been promoted at odds with the one that tends to predominate today. Simply put, this was a vision of consumer society that emphasized access and the collective right of all to participate rather than choice and individual gain. In the decades following World War II consumer activists articulated a vision of a fairer marketplace that not only improved the individual's ability to make supposedly wiser purchases, but improved the operation of the market for everybody. In addition to personal advice the consumer protection reforms they campaigned for and obtained were the complementary goals of their movement. Part of the reason they enjoyed such success was due to the agendas of national governments that had to be seen to be promising prosperity for all. As the consumer movement spread throughout the developing world, this focus on standards of living only increased as the concerns of the poor were made more central to the international organization's campaigning agenda. The right to basic needs became the defining principle of the consumer movement for much of the second half of the twentieth century.

That the consumer movement did so well in these decades of growing prosperity was also due to its moderate and reformist politics that bound its global agendas to those of the international community. Almost from its inception, IOCU adopted a rights-based perspective to the consumer interest, setting out its operating philosophy through a list of rights: to information, to choice, to representation, to redress, to safety, to education, to a healthy environment, and to basic needs. As we will see in chapter 7, these conformed broadly with the economic and social rights of the Universal Declaration of Human Rights, especially when the right to basic needs tied the consumer movement to the developmental agendas of the UN. Indeed, the declaration of a New International Economic Order appeared, initially, to suggest a reorientation of global geopolitics to the concerns of the Third World, which the consumer movement was ideally placed to capitalize on thanks to its impressive growth in the region at the same time. The consumer movement was able to unite the Western liberal rights-based approach with the concerns of the developing world's poor not only through the declaration of the right to basic needs—a broad-ranging right that imposes on the declarer a duty to address a whole range of issues about economic and social justice—but through its campaign tactics. From the late 1970s, the consumer movement pioneered the use of transnational advocacy networks, whereby pre-existing organizations from diverse political backgrounds came together on specific issues to share knowledge and resources, to coordinate tactics, and to make stronger demands on national and international governmental bodies. As we will see in chapter 5, networks are everywhere in global civil society, but because the consumer movement was able to present itself as a politically neutral body, it took the initiative in bringing together North and South, radical and reformist, religious and atheist in a series of networks dealing with subjects such as pesticides, breast milk substitutes, tobacco, dangerous goods, and pharmaceuticals.

The notion of consumer society that was promoted by the consumer movement and others was therefore one that emphasized the poor as much as the rich. It also promoted a regulatory environment in national legislatures and in the control of global commerce where it touched on the issues raised by the networks. It is this regulatory tendency that ultimately played a crucial part in the eclipse of the participatory consumer agenda. Amid the global economic problems of the 1970s, consumer protection became a luxury that many business leaders felt they could no longer afford. Chapter 6 traces the rise of an anti-regulatory agenda, first in the United States through the attacks on the most prominent consumer leader, Ralph Nader, and then on the international stage. The opponents of regulation—usually big businesses but backed up by a revitalized radical right—achieved a symbolic defeat of the American consumer movement as it campaigned and failed to obtain a consumer protection agency in the 1970s.

Once the Reagan administration came into power, what might loosely be identified as an anti-regulatory movement associated with those "neoconservative" institutions such as the Heritage Foundation and the American Enterprise Institute began to attack the agendas of the consumer movement at the UN. Through the networks, the consumer movement obtained a number of measures that sought to curb some of the more disreputable activities of multinational corporations, especially in the marketing of dangerous and inappropriate goods. By the mid-1980s, however, the anti-regulatory agenda was being articulated so forcefully by the U.S. mission to the UN that the consumer movement witnessed a number of specific setbacks. Moreover, the nature of these setbacks was particularly impressive. For not only did the consumer movement see many of its specific campaigns fail, but the whole nature of global economic governance changed. As we will see in chapter 8, the entire regulatory impulse of the UN infrastructure was bypassed through the Uruguay Round of trade negotiations. This promoted instead the liberalization of markets, culminating in the establishment of the World Trade Organization (WTO) in 1994. Unlike the UN, the WTO gave short shrift to NGOs such as the consumer movement. Consequently, the ability of global civil society to restrict the business practices of multinational corporations was severely curtailed.

It might well be argued that the consumer movement had reached is natural peak, the national and international consumer protection initiatives it had campaigned for and won by the 1980s representing the furthest it could take its consumerist agenda. Yet protection for consumers as shoppers was only one half of its agenda, especially because an ascendant developing world consumerism continued to emphasize basic needs and further curbs on the operation of the global economy. By this time, however, the organized multinational business community was not prepared to have the same series of restrictions imposed on its international trading activities as it had conceded in various domestic settings. The key to understanding the reversal in the consumer movement's fortunes in the 1980s, therefore, has as much to do with the opposition it faced as with its own internal contradictions that had for many decades delicately balanced the competing demands of the poor and the affluent.

Moreover, other spokesbodies for the consumer have emerged in more recent years, which have articulated a very different notion of consumer society from that espoused by the consumer movement and its allies. Implicit in the trade rules governed by the WTO, but also in the structural adjustment programs administered by the International Monetary Fund and the World Bank, a notion of the consumer interest has been put forward that claims, in neo-classical economic terms, that individual satisfaction is obtained through greater choice. Indeed, ensuring that some consumers are provided with greater choice and lower prices are perhaps the guiding principles of the governance of the global economy today. This is a notion of consumer society that pays much less attention to those who cannot afford choice or those whose primary motivation is to satisfy their demand for necessity. Choice was only one aim of the consumer movement and of those who had sought to reconstruct the consumer societies after World War II: to reduce the definition now to choice represents an impoverished notion of the participatory dimensions that lay behind the consumer movement's vision of consumer society. Defeat, as well as dilemma, must therefore operate as the two primary narratives of this book, because together they encapsulate the losses the consumer movement faced since the 1980s as well as the difficulties it faced in representing a tremendously diverse global constituency.

Simply stated, then, the argument of this book is that the changing fortunes of the consumer movement offer insights into and help explain the changing dominant meanings of global consumer society. By the 1990s, the movement was no longer as prominent as it had been in the early 1980s. First, its competing list of consumer rights saw a reorientation as it reigned itself in from the global South (where much of its expansion had previously been), thereby narrowing its own philosophy and field of action. Second, though, it was subjected to a number of defeats within the international political arena that curtailed its effectiveness as a potential leader of global civil society.

Taken together, the consumer movement chose to place less emphasis on basic needs while other spokesgroups for the consumer assumed an ascendancy that emphasized individual choice over collective action. In so doing, the more democratic and social justice elements of consumer society have been eclipsed by that which prioritizes individual choice. This is not to claim that the politics of consumption is no longer a contested field, that the consumer movement no longer has a say in global affairs, or that new generations of consumer activist have not emerged to offer new challenges to the meaning of consumer society, but it is to claim that consumer society today is a very different place from what it was thirty, forty, or fifty years ago.

IV

This is not a story so far told by other scholars and critics of consumer society. Instead, the dominant narrative has been to present consumer society as a rather monolithic entity that is somehow troublesome for our modern selves. Rather than worrying about the consequences of too little for the world's poor consumers, most discussions of consumer society by those liberal critics living in the affluent West have worried about the consequence of too much. Undoubtedly there are the champions of consumer society, but this only means that the debate on affluence is geared around a polemical discussion as to whether consumption is the cause or the cure of society's ailments. If ever-increasing standards of living were championed as the rewards of consumerist democracy, others have subsequently worried over affluence's social and psychological consequences: witness the "anxieties of affluence" expressed not in any U.S.-bashing old regime of Europe or a newly assertive global South, but in the United States itself as critics as varied as John Kenneth Galbraith, Vance Packard, Daniel Bell, Christopher Lasch, and Jimmy Carter have all bit their nails over the consequences of having too much stuff.[52] What is not appreciated are the ambivalent attitudes to affluence felt by many consumers. Affluence has been embraced as it offers a route from the past but it has also been feared as it promises an uncertain future. The resolution of such feelings more often lies between the two extremes rather than in a systematic embrace or rejection of its dubious rewards.

Individual responses to affluence have been presented in problematic and negative terms. Affluence has been said to unsettle our sense of self, to breed impatience and to undermine well-being. Because affluence is driven by novelty, it creates new wants that ultimately "undermine the capacity to enjoy them." As we constantly seek out the new, we give up on those forms of commitment that do not provide immediate gratification. And the more these commitments decline the less we are rooted in the world around us, an unsettled imbalance that can only further fuel the compensatory desire for greater novelty and commodified pleasure. Affluence therefore results in a loss of self-control, manifested most clearly in addiction and obesity, if not the entire fabric of societies built on family life and the careful, committed rearing of children.[53]

Such a critique has extended to find popular expression in well-publicized books, magazines, and TV documentaries. They include the phenomenally successful attack on corporate branding, *No Logo*, by the anti-globalization journalist Naomi Klein, the diagnosis of society's ills as one of "affluenza," the celebration of seemingly radical countercultural and situationist-inspired "culture jamming," as well as the ascetic retreat from consumption by downsizers, environmentalists, and pursuers of the "new American dream."[54] For historians, the debate about consumer society has been somewhat different. On the one hand, present-day consumer capitalism is invoked negatively while an earlier rose-tinted version of the past is recalled. For decades critics of consumption have often posited an earlier stage in consumer society's growth as more appropriate to the fulfillment of human happiness. On the other hand, historians have championed, uncovered, and told the story of so many instances of consumer activism in the past, be these philanthropically minded women, cost-of-living campaigners connected to the labor movement, or consumer co-operators seeking to build an alternative society and economy. Too often these initiatives have been minority pursuits, especially when compared to the many millions who have subscribed to testing magazines all over the world and who have been broadly sympathetic to the tens of thousands of consumer activists, at the local and global level, who have spearheaded the modern organized consumer movement. Instead, because of its work in testing, the consumer movement of the latter half of the twentieth century has been overlooked, else dismissed as an agent of acquisitive individualism that has contributed to the demise of our present consumer-oriented world.

The intention of this book is neither to assume that the consumer is the radical opponent of market capitalism nor the alienated atomized being that has fallen into the trap of consuming too much, too often, and too fast. Instead, it seeks to show how consumers have embraced a vision of consumer society but one that is not solely about satisfying individual gain. It seeks to uncover the history of those everyday political dimensions of consumer society by showing how an understandable desire to participate in the world of goods also led to a desire to reform the marketplace to ensure that it served the collective interest of all those it claimed to represent. For generations of consumer activists, across the developing and the developed world, the politics of consumer society was not about declaring it good or bad, but about ensuring it worked, and that it worked for all.

To this extent, the history of the consumer movement serves as an entry point for many of our thoughts and interactions with the commercial world around us. As the recent rise of ethical shopping and fair trade demonstrates, there exists a perennial concern to take into account the lives of others in our everyday purchasing decisions. At the same time, we also consume to satisfy purely selfish urges. The point is that the material world is incredibly rich and diverse. It is the very stuff of life and it is only to be expected that our interactions with it reflect a whole host of concerns. In promoting more choice for those who could afford it and more stuff for those who could not, the consumer movement embarked on a series of seemingly contradictory campaigns. These have been contradictions that have threatened to split the consumer movement and they are contradictions, as we shall see in the discussion of rights in chapter 7, that have been resolved in ways that have not always satisfied the interests of a tremendously varied constituency. But they are contradictions that are the result of our complicated attitude toward goods. To assume that we either celebrate or oppose consumer society does not do justice to all that we bring to our acts of consumption. There is a politics to consumer society but it is one that is neither ideologically consistent nor easily labeled as radical or reformist. The consumer movement has been all of these things, just as we see in ourselves radical, reactionary, ethical, and amoral approaches to our own acts of consumption.

It is in this diversity of consumer demand and consumer politics that this book challenges a definition of consumer society based on choice. Consumption is about so many things that to highlight one element above all others is to impoverish our understanding of it. Since the middle of the twentieth century what we have witnessed is a consumer politics fraught with many tensions but one that has become increasingly decoupled from the social welfare issues so central to the reconstruction policies after World War II. Instead, a focus on choice, only one of eight central demands of the consumer movement, shifts the focus of consumer society on to those who can afford to participate. For those left behind in the world's rising standards of living, choice has little to say. Yet this is precisely what is occurring on a global stage. A focus on basic needs might not address all that confronts us as consumers. It says little about the very real dangers of overconsumption both for flawed individuals and for the environment. Yet it does at least highlight some of the problems of poverty and provide a vision of consumer society to which the world's poor might subscribe. Cutting them out of the race from the beginning provides them with little to see in consumer society of immediate benefit to themselves and contradicts one of the basic goals that is central to the reconstitution of the world order around the United Nations and the Universal Declaration of Human Rights after World War II. Rather than providing the emblem of success for the regime of consumption, choice—when reified as the ultimate definition of consumer society—offers only an impoverished version of the goals of so many consumer activists since the mid-twentieth century.

The Fear of Fortune

The Uneasy Consumer in an Age of Affluence

In 1956, Colston E. Warne, a professor of economics at Amherst College, Massachusetts, sought to spread the gospel of consumerism throughout the Western, capitalist world. Warne had been president of the U.S. comparative testing organization, Consumers Union since its establishment in 1936. After completing his dissertation on the U.S. co-operative movement at the University of Chicago, he had gone on to campaign for workers' rights and civil liberties and became associated with the "people's lobby" of the socialist Benjamin Marsh. At Consumers Union, he had overseen its struggles with difficult financial issues and internal personality clashes, he had helped it overcome the acrimony from its rivals at Consumers' Research (CR), from which it had split twenty years earlier, and he had helped fend off charges of communism leveled against it several times by the House Un-American Activities Committee.[1] Although Consumers Union remained a relatively small organization immediately after World War II, as the European economies gradually shifted from austerity to affluence it proved an inspiration to many thousands of middle-class consumers who embraced the new world of goods yet faced with trepidation the challenges confronting them in a more complex and technological marketplace.

Recognizing the growing interest in comparative testing as a means of assisting consumers in making informed choices, Consumers Union took a special interest in European developments and Warne in particular was eager to foster a nascent movement. As early as 1939, he had explored the possibility of developing comparative testing agencies within the European consumer co-operatives and had identified interest in the work of Consumers Union (CU) by bodies such as the Swedish Home Economics group. Soon after World War II, a steady stream of letters reached him at the offices of CU from enterprising European subscribers to *Consumer Reports,* requesting advice on launching parallel organizations and magazines.[2] Consumers Union provided what materials it could to assist fledgling initiatives such as the Union Fédérale des Consommateurs, established in France in 1951 by the Parisian civil servant André Romieu.[3] Warne assumed responsibility at CU for collating these contacts and he was able to report to the United Nations in January 1956 of interest in organized consumerism in around twenty countries from Iceland to Israel as well as further afield in Pakistan, India, and South Africa.[4] Of particular significance was a letter of 9 November 1955 from Dorothy and Ray Goodman, two American graduate students at the London School of Economics, who were eager to create an organization modeled on CU in Great Britain. They prepared a dummy magazine, obtained the support of a number of prominent public figures, including the "social entrepreneur" Michael Young, who would assume the initiative once they returned to the United States, and helped launch the UK Consumers' Association in 1956, which began publishing its own testing magazine *Which?* the following year.[5] The initial assistance provided by Warne and CU was crucial to its success.

Encouraged by such initiatives, Warne decided to visit Europe in the summer of 1956. Beginning with the Goodmans in London, he toured several countries where consumer organizing had already taken place, such as Belgium, Austria, West Germany, and the Netherlands, and sought out further contacts with government officials and concerned citizens interested in providing independent information about products to consumers. It marked the start of the realization of Warne's international vision for organized consumerism, which would later see him travel around most of the Asia-Pacific region and which would result in the creation of a genuinely global consumer movement. But for the 1950s at least, his trip highlighted a growing concern among consumers that in the transition to affluence not all was to be welcomed. As Europeans were given more choice and enjoyed ever higher incomes to make such choices, there were nevertheless fears to be confronted in the new era of fortune. For however much economic reconstruction was being implemented in the name of the consumer, consumers themselves felt alone and overwhelmed in the modern market. Independent tests of branded commodities therefore offered a means by which the power of the advertiser, the retailer, the manufacturer, and the scientist could be matched by the power of the no longer sovereign consumer.

Warne's consumerist mission of 1956 therefore followed in the wake of so many productivity missions that had crossed the Atlantic in the decade following the end of the war. Just as businesses, government officials, economists, and technocrats sought to rebuild Western Europe, so too did Warne seek to create a new generation of rational, value-seeking consumers who could fend for themselves in a more complex marketplace. The Marshall Plan was a diplomatic and economic initiative that sought to reconstruct Europe around a new citizen: the consumer. As the United States built its own "consumers' republic," it sought—through bodies such as the European Recovery Agency—to present to Western European governments the notion of consumer democracy as a positive counterpoint to the failed project of European citizenship offered by fascism and the powerful alternative promoted across the Iron Curtain under communism. Yet any discussion of the consumer was subsumed within a productivist bias that imagined the consumer as an atomized individual who would receive the benefits of increased output only after sacrifices had been made to foster the greater goal of productivity. Once material reward would reach the citizen in the form of higher standards of living and greater choice, the consumer was expected to behave much as he or she had been imagined in economic thought: as a utility maximizing individual only out for personal or familial gain.[6]

The columns of test reports offered by the magazines of the new consumer organizations modeled on CU arguably represented one stage further in the attempt to Americanize Europe after World War II. *Consumer Reports* in the United States, *Which?* in the UK, *Que Choisir* in France, *Test* in Germany, *Test-Achats* in Belgium, and *Consumentengids* in the Netherlands seemingly bolstered the individual consumers' ability to maximize their own well-being and thus support the notion of consumer sovereignty supposedly at the heart of the capitalist market economy. And just as non-state organizations such as marketing professionals and multinational corporations supported and assisted the U.S. government in its international economic diplomacy, so too could CU be seen as promoting the American way of life. After all, CU had come under close attention from the anti-communist witch-hunters such that Warne had overseen a shift away from certain social issues that appeared to associate the organization with more radical agendas. By the 1950s, the focus of CU was on its comparative testing and the spread of this form of consumer organizing seemingly complemented the goal of the Marshall planners: consumers were to be encouraged to debate the end results of the system of supply, but not to question the entire system of provision.

Yet there was much more to organized consumerism than individual gain. If the motivations of European consumers are to be understood in the crucial decades leading up to the flourishing of consumer society by the 1960s, then they cannot be regarded as simply the pawns in somebody else's wider game, be that of Americanization or economic reconstruction in the wider context of the Cold War. Rather, the efforts of tens and hundreds of thousands of consumers to come together in new organizations represented a transnational social movement born of the common element of affluence experienced by ever increasing numbers of middle-class shoppers across Western Europe and the capitalist world.

Unlike their intellectual leaders who fretted over too much stuff, for these consumers affluence was not something to be slavishly embraced or cynically resisted. Rather, affluence was to be controlled. This is precisely what the new organizations of comparative testing consumers sought to do. They represented

Figure 1. *Consumer Reports* tests instant coffees, 1951. Consumers Union publicity card. Courtesy, Consumers Union Archive, Yonkers, New York.

a desire by many consumers to live in a world of plenty but who feared the uncertainties that this world offered. Consumer sovereignty might well be the goal of those who promoted productivity and economic reconstruction, but as a lived concept it could prove meaningless—if not hollow and irrelevant—amid the competing messages of advertisers, manufacturers, and the new products themselves. Consumer organizing was not the end-of-the-line auxiliary to a process of Americanization, nor was it simply about creating the sovereign consumers that the market so imperfectly imagined. Instead, it represented the real challenge of affluence faced by many ordinary shoppers eager to navigate their way toward the future. In doing so, these consumers created a global social movement of the affluent whose reach would extend far beyond that enjoyed by many more prominent social movements drawn from a similar social milieu. And they would trigger, as will be seen in later chapters, a wider set of demands for consumer protection and consumer participation that attested to a far broader social goal of organized consumerism. Indeed, during the last decades of the twentieth-century, the demands of the citizen-consumer, so often originating in the testing magazines of these rational buyers, would have profound consequences on the shape of the market and the structures of political power at both the national and the global level.

I

The tremendous growth in consumer organizing in Western Europe and the wider capitalist world was truly remarkable. Warne's initial reconnaissance trip in 1956 met with varying stages of organized consumerist development, with many countries still containing just a few committed enthusiasts. By 1969, however, the comparative testing magazine had become a feature of most advanced capitalist economies. *Consumer Reports* led the way with sales of over one and a half million, though by this time sales of *Which?* by the UK Consumers' Association had topped half a million. In Belgium, there were 190,000 members of the two competing consumer groups (Association des Consommateurs and the Union Féminine pour l'Information et la Défense du Consommateur), over a quarter of a million subscribers to *Consumentengids* in the Netherlands (representing one in ten households), and while the number of actual subscribers to *Test* in Germany reached only 67,000, total sales of the magazine from the newsstands brought that figure to 190,000. Most impressive were the Scandinavian countries: although their consumer magazines were published by the state rather than by private testing organizations, subscriptions ran into six figures, with Norway claiming the greatest number of sales relative to households in the world.[7] While a comparative testing magazine had failed to establish itself in the mainstream in France, sales of *Que Choisir* took off in the early 1970s, reaching 300,000 subscribers in 1975.[8] Table 1 gives the circulation figures for some of the leading comparative testing magazines: these figures would continue to rise steadily into the late 1980s. As early as 1969, though, one survey had calculated that there were twenty-two organizations engaged in comparative testing in all of the principal countries of the North Atlantic community. Collectively, they operated on a budget of $20 million (rising to $30 million just three years later), could claim a subscriber base of 3 million, and a readership of many millions more.[9]

The explanation for such a growth is not difficult to determine. Comparative testing as a publishing phenomenon emerged in direct relation to rising levels of consumption. The more branded, technological goods a nation consumed, the more likely would there be a robust consumer testing organization. More specifically, organized consumerism developed in those countries where an expanding middle class bought more of the luxury and semi-luxury items associated with the age of affluence: cars, refrigerators, televisions, stereos, washing machines, vacuum cleaners. The marketplace fundamentally altered in the quarter century following the war. For instance, at the beginning of the

TABLE 1.1.
Circulation figures of leading comparative testing magazines in 1969 and 1975

Magazine	Date started	Country	Organization	Sales in 1969	Sales in 1975
Consumer Reports	1936	USA	Consumers Union (CU) 1936	1,800,000	2,300,000
Consumentengids	1953	Netherlands	Consumentenbond 1953	256,000	470,000
Forbruker Rapporten	1953	Norway	Consumers Council 1953 (Forbrukerrådet)	169,000	235,000
Which?	1957	UK	Consumers Association (CA) 1956	600,000	700,000
Råd och Rön	1957	Sweden	Institute for Consumer Information (Statens Institut för Konsumenfrågor) 1957	104,718	n.a.
Test-Achats	1959	Belgium	Association des Consommateurs/ Verbruikersunie (AC/V) 1957	102,235	240,000
Choice	1959	Australia	Australian Consumers' Association (ACA) 1959	67,204	120,000
Råd og Resultater	1961	Denmark	Home Economics Council (Statens Husholdningsråd) 1935	28,100	n.a.
Que Choisir	1961	France	Union Fédérale des Consommateurs (UFC) 1951	15,000	300,000
Konsument	1961	Austria	Association for Consumer Information (Verein für Konsumenteninformation, VKI) 1960	25,000	n.a.
Canadian Consumer	1963	Canada	Consumers Association of Canada (CAC) 1947	43,000	n.a.
Taenk	1964	Denmark	Danish Housewives Consumer Council (Danske Husmødres Forbrugerråd) 1947	48,000	n.a.
Il Consumatore (Le Scelte del Consumatore)	1965	Italy	Union Nationale Consumatori 1955	100,000	n.a.
Test	1966	Germany	Stiftung Warentest 1964	68,000	250,000
50 Millions de Consommateurs	1970	France	Institut National de la Consommation 1967	0	300,000

Source: Hans B. Thorelli and Sarah V. Thorelli, *Consumer Information Systems and Consumer Policy* (Cambridge, MA: Ballinger, 1977), appendix E, 327–60.

1960s there were just a handful of supermarkets in the Netherlands. By the end of the decade there were over 500. Similarly, in Belgium, the number of supermarkets rose from 19 to 456 in the same decade, a figure even further eclipsed by the massive jump from 49 to 1,833 that occurred in France.[10]

The precise patterns of growth in standards of living across Western Europe remain contested, and the market penetration rates of different goods varies across countries. Such detailed explanations require attention to the specific attributes of products and the cultures within which they have been consumed.[11] But the overall trend is clear. New products, previously only available to the very rich, had become items of mass consumption by the end of the 1960s. The refrigerator slowly made its appearance into European homes in the 1950s, but thereafter consumption expanded exponentially. By the mid-1970s, it was rare to find a home that did not have its own fridge, as nine out of ten households possessed one in the richer European states.[12] The sheer pace of change could only have provoked anxiety among startled consumers. In the mid-1950s in France, 76 percent of all households still did not have running hot water, and nine out of ten did not have a washing machine or a refrigerator.[13] By the end of the 1960s, the average French citizen would automatically have expected to be able to purchase such items, alongside a car, a television, and all the other goods we see as standard consumer durables. Indeed, the popularity of the television set was embraced across all of Europe. In France, in 1955, there were just a quarter of a million television sets, but over 10 million by the end of the 1960s. In Germany over the same period, the figures rose from a little over 100,000 to nearly 16 million. Across the rest of Europe, television sets only began to appear in the mid-1950s, yet millions of licenses were issued in every country by 1969.

Perhaps the most archetypal consumer commodity of all was the motor car. As perhaps the ultimate status symbol of consumer society it has attracted a considerable amount of attention, not only for its manufacture, but for the images with which it has been sold and for the meanings it has acquired in popular culture.[14] Yet as an emblem of the affluent society it also cannot be surpassed. In absolute terms, there were nearly 40 million private motor vehicles in use in the society of the automobile, the United States, just after the war. By the end of the 1960s, this figure had doubled to the massive figure of 87 million. Yet such a growth rate was unimpressive compared to that which occurred in Europe. In Britain, the number of vehicles in use increased from just over 2 million in 1950 to over 11 million in 1960. In Germany there were only half a million vehicle owners in 1950, but nearly 13 million in 1969. Across the same period, car ownership in Italy increased from 350,000 to 9 million, in France from 1.6 million to 12.4 million, and in Sweden from a quarter of a million to over 2 million.

If we are to take the car as the representative commodity of the new consumer society, what also needs to be noted is the sheer degree of consistency between those countries with a high vehicle ownership rate and those with a high subscriber base to their testing magazine. Table 2 lists in descending order the countries with the greatest number of vehicles in use per head of population and puts this alongside a similar list of countries ranked by subscriptions per head to consumer testing bodies in 1969. There is not a direct equivalence but the correlation is reasonably consistent: the greater the degree of car ownership, the greater the reliance of that population on comparative testing. Certainly, such results were to be expected. Consumer organizations were well aware of the demand for tests of cars from their subscribers. The purchase of a car could be the first or second most significant act of consumption in an individual's life

TABLE 1.2.
Ranked list of vehicles per head of population and
subscriptions to comparative testing magazine per head
of population for the year 1969

Vehicles (per head)	Subscriptions (per head)
Australia	Norway
United States	Netherlands
Canada	Denmark
Sweden	Sweden
France	United Kingdom
United Kingdom	Australia
West Germany	Belgium
Denmark	United States
Belgium	Austria
Switzerland	Canada
Norway	Italy
Netherlands	West Germany
Italy	France
Austria	Switzerland
Ireland	
Spain	
Portugal	
Greece	

Source: B. R. Mitchell, *International Historical Statistics: Europe, 1750–2000,* 5th ed. (Basingstoke: Palgrave, 2003); B. R. Mitchell, *International Historical Statistics: The Americas, 1750–1993* (4th ed. (Basingstoke: Macmillan, 1998); Hans B. Thorelli and Sarah V. Thorelli, *Consumer Information Systems and Consumer Policy* (Cambridge, MA: Ballinger, 1977).
Note: There are a number of anomalies hidden by these rankings: they do not take into account the huge growth in subscriptions to comparative testing organizations in France immediately after 1969; there is an element of double counting for Belgium due to the popularity of two consumer groups; some consumers in one country could purchase and utilize the magazine from another country (especially Canada). Figures also represent Europe, the Americas, and Australia; they exclude Japan. The rankings are in descending order.

(depending on the extent to which home ownership was pursued). It was perhaps the most important consuming decision to be made and one that was not entered into lightly. Information was sought from family, friends, the press, the industry and, once a size had been reached to justify the costs of testing, from the comparative testing agencies.

Such a close correlation between the national consumption figures of a particular commodity and the popularity of consumer testing magazines is unlikely to be replicated quite so closely for other consumer durables. There are simply too many factors impinging on the demand for any one commodity in any one economic, cultural, social, and political context. But the point about the car could be made to stand in for the age of affluence in general and we could expect similar results for analyses of other consumer durables associated with the affluent society. Consumers looked with eagerness on the new branded commodities but they did so with a degree of trepidation and sought refuge in the new organized consumer movement. Comparative testing offered a means to control the unease felt in the market as the odds stacked against the supposedly sovereign consumer were simply too overwhelming. If a consumer wanted to purchase a new object, and to do so following the model of perfect competition found in the textbooks, then he or she would be bewildered by the sheer array of brands out there. In January 1969, the German consumer organization, Stiftung Warentest was able to report in its magazine, *Test,* on thirty-two different types of "ordinary" 60-watt light bulbs. In the same year, a French consumer group counted over one thousand different types, models, and brands of refrigerator. Here was not freedom put paralysis in purchasing, the overwhelming weight of choice becoming too great a burden for the individual to bear. Left alone, as early activists liked to proclaim, the consumer became a frightened and confused animal, an innocent deer caught in the neon strip lights of commodity capitalism. Despite that it has been promoted by governments, and catered to the interests of the individual rather than the interests of society as a whole, organized consumerism emerged out of the genuine fears over fortune expressed by a society of consumers who could not keep up the pace with those who claimed to be constructing a society in their name. It is of little surprise then that the work of the Consumers Union was so admired around the world in the 1950s and 1960s and Colston Warne was welcomed with open arms as he first toured Europe in the late 1950s.

II

U.S. comparative testing predated its European followers by two decades. Although Consumers Union (CU) was not established until 1936, it owed it existence to the earlier formation of CR, set up at the end of the 1920s. American consumer activists have usually identified the interwar period as marking the second stage in the development of consumerism. The third started in the 1950s and saw the mass proliferation of consumer activism across the United States, culminating in the rise to prominence of Ralph Nader and his aggressive, anti-corporate, pro-regulation consumer campaigns. Likewise, an earlier period, usually associated with the Progressive Era that preceded World War I, was marked by anti-trust initiatives and the protection of workers' rights and conditions through boycotts and organized buying initiatives, as in the "white lists" of union-approved firms published by the National Consumers' League. The second period, however, has been associated with the creation of CR and CU and was marked, as in Europe in the period of economic reconstruction, by rapid social change and economic dislocation. The establishment of a newly affluent middle class, the mass production of cheap branded commodities and a wider, disruptive economic context created a set of similar circumstances for an affluent minority worried about navigating their way through a less familiar marketplace.[15]

Out of the apparent flux and chaos of commodity capitalism, pro-consumer scientists, engineers, and professionals sought to place order and stability. For some time, the accountant and popular writer Stuart Chase had written extensively about the inefficiencies and wastefulness of the economy. He was inspired not only by earlier critiques of consumption provided by John Ruskin and Thorstein Veblen, but by the effectiveness of government planning, standards, and intervention during World War I. He wrote, in *The Challenge of Waste* (1922) and *The Tragedy of Waste* (1925), of the need to rationalize both production and consumption, so that profits would be improved and the social ills that attended the purchase of inappropriate products would be eliminated.[16] In 1925 he collaborated with the engineer Frederick J. Schlink, who had worked with both the American Standards Association and the U.S. National Bureau of Standards, in a series of articles for the *New Republic,* later collected together in their 1927 best seller *Your Money's Worth.*[17] Chase and Schlink railed against the misinformation of commercial advertising and suggested instead a more skeptical attitude on the part of consumers, the greater use of standards, and the independent testing of advertisers' and manufacturers' claims about their products. Emboldened by the success of the book, Schlink chose to expand a small consumers' club he had established in 1926 in White Plains, New York, and it published its first ratings guide in 1927 in a new magazine, *Consumers' Research Bulletin.* Advertising for new members in January 1928 led to a huge increase in popularity and Consumers' Research was incorporated in 1929. By 1935, CR was employing fifty people of its own staff and around two hundred outside consultants. Its subscription list topped 50,000 and it had moved its offices first from White Plains to New York City and then to larger premises in Washington, New Jersey. The popularity of Chase's and Schlink's earlier collaboration was followed by another consumer exposé of the dangers in everyday food, drugs, and cosmetics in 1933, with *100,000,000 Guinea Pigs* written by Schlink and his successor at the American Standards Association, Arthur Kallett, who had joined the CR Board in 1930.[18]

Efficiency perhaps best summarized the goals of CR. It offered no wide-ranging social critique or ideological solution to the travails of the consumer. Instead, it claimed that rigorous scientific testing would lead to better consumer choices that would in turn improve the workings of the economy. As Schlink increasingly assumed control of CR, he paid little attention to the concerns of earlier generations of consumer activists, specifically the conditions of workers—an omission reflected in the labor relations he adopted at the organization. A poor manager, he filled the CR Board with family and friends, inspired little loyalty in his employees, and frequently fired engineers, clerks, and typists. Moreover, he persistently opposed the establishment of a trade union among his staff, an attitude that came to a head in 1936 when a strike was declared by the newly formed Consumers' Research Chapter of the Technical, Editorial, and Office Assistants Union. The strike became increasingly bitter as Schlink and his supporters on the Board—his wife Mary Phillips and the former communist and Methodist missionary J. B. Matthews—used strikebreakers, minders, private detectives, and legal injunctions against their staff, inspiring a series of strike songs which wished them "to hell" as "liars" and "scabs."[19] More significant, sympathetic Board members such as Arthur Kallet resigned and instead threw their weight behind the strikers resulting in the formation of a breakaway consumer group, Consumers Union, which would ultimately succeed CR as the U.S. most popular and well-known consumer organization.[20]

As CU emerged from an industrial dispute and therefore owed its existence as much to the older politics of production as to the new politics of consumption, it understandably embraced a consumerism as dedicated to the interests of the worker as to the interests of the consumer. In the very first editorial of *Consumer Reports,* in May 1936, CU informed its subscribers that its charter committed it to the maintenance of "decent living standards for ultimate consumers." The emphasis on living standards—as opposed to choice or value for money—was significant. CU recognized that the consumer interest could "never be maintained simply by reporting on the quality and the price of products" and that for the poor consumer especially, if they were to be able to purchase food, clothing, and household supplies, then "the only way in which any organization can aid them materially as consumers is by helping them, in their struggle as workers, to get an honest wage."[21] The distinction between CR and CU in these early years was clear. The former adopted a scientific-focused approach to the testing of goods, while the new upstart continued these traditions though adding a feature of labor conditions into its reports. The rivalry was as much political as institutional and, by turns, personal and individual, creating an acrimonious and bitter relationship, which lasted the better part of the century and set precedents for the political intimidation of CU that had long-term consequences (to be explored in chapter 6).[22]

The more upbeat and attractive layout of *Consumer Reports,* though, meant it soon surpassed *Consumers' Research Bulletin* as the most popular consumer subscription journal in the United States. By 1939, membership reached 85,000, a sufficient base from which to cope with the restricted development to be experienced during the forthcoming war. As it gave evidence before government committees, participated in labor movement protests, and sought to spread the gospel of consumerism to the poor, *Consumer Reports* attracted a liberal readership and a respected reputation. Yet there was perhaps a ceiling to such a cause in terms of membership and Arthur Kallet realized that this wider social vision of consumer politics had detracted from the quality of CU's testing procedures. At the end of the decade, CU courted the attention of the scientific community and realized that future expansion would come through attracting subscriptions among the middle class. Their own market research showed that only 12 percent of poorer families had even heard of consumer activism, in contrast to almost half of all those in the higher income brackets, while those on incomes of less than $1,000 per annum made up just 3.1 percent of the membership.[23] Politics therefore had to be tempered by business sense and increasingly CU came to recognize that its strength lay in the basic service it provided to its members in giving independent and reliable rational information on products.[24]

CU emerged from World War II weakened but ready to guide shoppers in the new "consumers' republic." As servicemen returned home and to family life, *Consumer Reports* proved a useful buying guide to newly prosperous suburban home dwellers. In 1944, membership of CU had fallen to just 55,000. But as soon as hostilities finished, subscriptions shot up: to 150,000 by the end of 1946 and half a million by the beginning of the 1950s.[25] Arthur Kallet's vision of CU as a service organization for its members had increasingly won out during this expansion, frustrating people like Warne who persisted in promoting CU's political and lobbying activities. These differences would eventually culminate in further internal divisions within the consumer movement, but for Warne it meant that his vision of consumerism as a social movement could not be realized. As his own agenda was tempered by Kallett's dominant and commercially oriented approach, it is unsurprising that Warne welcomed the opportunities to develop consumerism abroad. Frustrated at home, the international developments of the 1950s were a release valve for Warne's wider consumer goals. It meant that the CU Board was happy for Warne to concentrate some of his efforts on international development, enabling CU to focus on its business approach, yet also creating a receptive and helpful institution for those fledgling consumer organizations appearing in Western Europe and the wider capitalist world.

III

When Warne visited Europe in 1956 and became more heavily involved in international development for the rest of the decade, he found that consumer organizing had already taken off. While consumption had become a political issue for all Western European governments, the demand for independent testing of branded goods was being felt everywhere. Warne's strongest initial links were with the Goodmans and the British Consumers' Association (CA). Launched in 1956, this proved an immediate success with 10,000 subscribers in the first few weeks and rapid expansion thereafter to a quarter of a million members by 1961.[26] Both the British and the U.S. magazines have formed the backbone of the international consumer movement, enjoying the greatest financial muscle thanks to the extremely high sales of *Which?* and *Consumer Reports*.

If not all consumer organizing was to take the exact form of CU and CA (that is, independence from business and government, membership/subscriber based) consumer testing nevertheless existed in most European countries. The earliest attempt to develop comparative testing in Western Europe came with the

French Union Fédérale des Consommateurs (UFC), launched in 1951. Although it lacked the resources or the stability to launch its own testing magazine, *Que Choisir,* until 1961, relying instead on state subsidies, it nevertheless attracted the support of a growing number of professionals and civil servants who were able to publish a monthly guide to better buying.[27] Two years later Consumentenbond was established in the Netherlands and immediately began publishing *Consumentengids,* which soon reached one of the highest penetration rates of any consumer publication. Consumentenbond sought a government subsidy, which was refused and the Dutch organization—when Warne first came across it—was admired for all that it had achieved on voluntary effort.[28] In Belgium, Louis Darms established the Union Belge des Consommateurs (later Association des Consommateurs) in 1957 that launched *Test Achats* in 1959 and was particularly keen to collaborate with other European testing agencies.[29] Beyond Europe, the Australian Consumers' Association was also able to exist as an entirely independent consumer organization. Thanks to the efforts of a retired Labour Party feminist Ruby Hutchinson, *Choice* magazine was launched in 1959. By the beginning of the 1960s it had attracted over 25,000 member/subscribers.[30] In 1960, the Australian, American, British, Dutch, and Belgian consumer movements would come together to found the International Organisation of Consumers Unions.[31]

Surprisingly, West Germany had not by this stage created its own independent consumer group. Consumer organizations did appear in Germany in the early 1950s but these were very soon coordinated by the regional governments and federated in 1953 in the Working Group of Consumer Associations (Arbeitsgemeinschaft der Verbraucherverbände, AgV). AgV engaged in product testing, but only intermittently published the results because German consumerism preferred to work with business and government agencies. In 1962 Germany's Association of Branded Products took AgV to court for product defamation. AgV's activities were concentrated on lobbying for consumers, providing advice on price movements and liaising with governments on general consumer concerns such as tariff policy, fair trade, and advertising. A mass circulation testing magazine did not appear until 1961, when the editor of *Der Spiegel,* Walmar Schweitzer, began putting results in his monthly (later weekly) publication *DM* (*Deutsche Mark*). Sales of *DM* peaked at 800,000 by 1964 but declined thereafter and the magazine faced persistent problems because of threats of legal action launched by firms to which it gave low ratings. It was also run as a commercial enterprise unlike the non-profit members' organization favored by CU and CA. Also in 1964 what would become Germany's principal consumer body was established following pressure from the labor movement and the Social Democratic Party, as well as the groundswell of public opinion evidenced in the high sales of *DM*. Stiftung Warentest began publishing *Test* in 1966, a magazine that enjoyed immediate success and by 1972 its circulation reached 100,000.[32]

Other, less successful and shorter lived comparative testing consumer groups also emerged in this decade. In Iceland, the Consumers Union of Reykjavik (Neytendasamtok Reykjavikur) appeared in 1953, attracting 2,000 individual members by 1956.[33] In Israel, a Consumers' Association was founded in 1955 by the International Women's Zionist Organization, although its limited funding meant it was unable to undertake tests itself and had to concentrate on consumer representation and the raising of standards.[34] Likewise, in southern Europe, lower standards of living, political indifference, and the comparative smaller size of an affluent class prevented the existence of sustainable independent groups. In Spain a consumer movement was unable to develop under Franco, while in Italy the Union Nationale Consumatori was founded in 1955 and in 1960 launched its own magazine, *Comprare. Comprare* contained few actual test reports and it reached a low subscriber base. Greater success was achieved with the subsequent launch of *Il Consumatore* in 1965, whose subscriptions reached 100,000 within just two years.[35]

In contrast, in Northern and Central Europe, governments were particularly keen to develop consumer organizations and consumer testing. Although this made superfluous the need for independent, grassroots consumer bodies, the popularity of the publications produced by these state-sponsored initiatives attests to the same range of fears and tribulations influencing consumers in these countries as much as in Western Europe. In Austria, two main consumer bodies were launched by labor organizations in the 1950s, though both were subsumed by the new Association for Consumer Information (Verein für Konsumenteninformation, VKI) in 1960, funded by the state, the trade unions and the chambers of commerce for both manufacturing and farming. Its testing magazine *Konsument* was launched the following year and has received regular state funding since. In Norway, the Consumers Council (Forbrukerrådet) was established by the state in 1953 as an independent body made up of the co-operative, trade union, women's and farmers' movements. Its quarterly magazine *Forbruker Rapporten* had achieved a circulation of 50,000 by the beginning of the 1960s and by the end of the decade was estimated to reach more households per head of population than in any other country.[36] In Sweden, the Institute for Consumer Information (Statens Institut för Konsumenfrågor) was established in 1945 by home economists and housewives. It was taken over by the state in 1957 and test results from its own laboratories began to be published in its magazine *Råd och Rön* (*Advice and Discovery*), whose circulation reached 18,000 by 1962. In addition, it was available in libraries and its tests were reprinted in newspapers and magazines.[37] In Denmark, one part of the state structure for consumer protection was the Danish Housewives Consumer Council (Danske Husmødres Forbrugerråd). As in Sweden, this was originally an independent body formed in 1947, but was later brought within the state apparatus and began publishing its consumer magazine *Taenk* (*Think*) in 1964.[38]

By the end of the 1950s, comparative testing consumerism could claim to be a transnational phenomenon. Undoubtedly, it had its stronghold in the English-speaking world with the success of CU, CA, and the Australian Consumers' Association—as well as in Canada[39]—where the independent, non-profit, member/subscriber model was followed. This became the benchmark for other national consumer movements in Western Europe, but political intervention, the absence of economies of scale in smaller linguistic populations, and the established role of the state meant that testing was conducted through a variety of institutional forms. No matter how the information on goods was provided, though, it was eagerly utilized by those newly affluent consumers who felt they needed more careful guidance through the world of goods. By 1969, it was estimated that in fifteen countries of Europe and North America where consumer testing had developed, the total number of subscribers to reports was over three million, rising to over four and a half million by 1975. These subscriptions translated into penetration rates of 2 percent of all households in 1969 and 3 percent in 1975. To make these figures more real, it also has to be acknowledged that a consumer magazine was likely to be read by more than one person or household: copies were kept and heavily used in libraries, while others were circulated among friends and family. The actual readership of the magazines has been estimated to have been anywhere between two and six times the figure for subscriptions. Here, then, was a phenomenon if of very little relevance to the poor, of enormous significance to the affluent across North America, Western Europe, and Australasia in the decades following economic reconstruction.[40]

IV

This growth in comparative testing consumerism raises the question of whether there was a further dimension to the processes of Americanization influencing European societies, economies, and cultures.[41] Just as U.S. consumer goods penetrated European markets and just as U.S. diplomacy promoted capitalist democracy, did the organized consumer movement represent another—non-state—platform promoting the "irresistible empire" of the United States? Did comparative testing promote a model of the rational, sovereign consumer as a necessary auxiliary to the operation of the free market? Certainly, the Marshall Plan, economic assistance and productivity missions extended beyond the official visits and interventions of state bureaucrats and politicians. The "market empire" of the United States pushed itself not only through commercial and political pressure but through the export of voluntary associations, non-governmental organizations, and social-scientific knowledge. According to a 2005 study, these all shared a unity of purpose with government. U.S. foreign trade and democracy went hand in hand, establishing benchmarks not only for the operation of business but a whole range of voluntary, intellectual, and professional organizations.[42] Freedom of choice was therefore promoted not only by politicians, but by marketing executives who accompanied productivity missions, by social scientists concerned with the standard of living, and by nongovernmental organizations who worked within a rights-based framework so central to liberal democracies. Rather than resisting such trends—so all pervasive did the U.S. "way of doing things" become—that Europeans found themselves naturally attracted to U.S. institutions.

There is some evidence to suggest that U.S. consumer testing was bound up with a wider process of promoting consumer democracy and the free market. It had links with international organizations tied up with the wider processes of Americanization. In 1948, the Organization for European Economic Cooperation (OEEC; later the Organization for Economic Cooperation and Development) was established to assist in the administration of the Marshall Plan. Its European Productivity Agency (EPA) was inextricably bound up with the U.S. government's "politics of productivity," which sought to integrate Western Europe and free it from scarcity through increased production.[43]

In November 1957, almost two years after Colston Warne had first reported to the United Nations on fledgling consumer initiatives in Europe, the EPA organized a meeting of representatives of European consumer associations in order to survey their activities.[44] In 1959, the OEEC expressed further interest in assisting consumer organizations in developing an international movement and one or two outcomes emerged from this dialogue between consumerism and productivism. The French Union Fédérale des Consommateurs received some limited financial assistance from its own productivity council and a member of CU's National Advisory Committee who worked in Paris under the Marshall Plan was able to secure funds for consumer testing in Denmark, which ultimately led to the creation of the Danish Housewives Consumer Council and the publication of *Taenk*.[45]

In addition to fostering these international links, CU provided direct support to testing organizations around the world. After Warne's early communications with European consumer activists, more tangible forms of help were offered.[46] First, copies of CU literature and *Consumer Reports* were sent out to interested individuals; then, following specific requests, financial assistance was provided. In October 1957, Warne persuaded the CU Board to offer the British Consumers' Association a $7,000 grant to fund its early activities.[47] A further $7,000 was made available to the Israeli consumer movement and similar grants were given to Consumentenbond in the Netherlands and the Association des Consommateurs in Belgium.[48] After the International Organisation of Consumers Unions was established in 1960, CU—along with the British CA—continued to be the main financial backer for three decades.

It could be argued that by the late 1950s CU not only promoted consumerism around the world after its own image, but that the model it presented was one that had been tempered by the dictates of Cold War propaganda. Yet the development of consumer organizing cannot be seen as a U.S. project, because there was a more general transatlantic dialogue among consumers, and the official bodies connected to U.S. diplomacy were reluctant to be linked too closely with CU. Funding and assistance came not only from the United States. The British CA worked with CU to help Australian consumerism and when the Belgians fell into financial trouble, British loans bailed them out.[49] Mutual assistance has been the norm for consumer organizations, irrespective of state policies.

CU and the Canadian Association of Consumers have developed publishing and testing agreements, as have the French and Belgian consumer groups. European organizations have collaborated formally on testing procedures and, indeed, for all of Warne's committed internationalism, the impetus for the establishment of an international consumer organization came from the Dutch and the Belgians rather than the Americans.[50] During Warne's trip to Europe in 1956, Aldo Diani of the Italian Unione Nazionale Consumatori and Romieu in France both mooted the idea of an international organization and certain overtures were made to UNESCO for assistance.[51] Moreover, CU was never closely aligned with the organizations of the Marshall Plan. In the late 1950s, Warne solicited the direct assistance of the OEEC. Initially, the OEEC was willing to support an international consumer conference in 1959, but later the EPA refused to fund it.[52] Instead, the EPA sought out other spokesmen for consumers, ones who could be relied on to imagine a citizen-consumer more in line with the requirements of production. At the end of 1959, the International Chamber of Commerce conducted its own study of consumer organizing in Europe, which was passed on to the EPA and resulted in no further action.[53] Rather than tying itself to a consumer movement that could be highly critical of many manufacturers, the EPA preferred to work with other "organizations set up by businesses to inform consumers objectively on the quality of products."[54]

CU may well have provided the benchmark for consumer organizing around the world but this did not constitute Americanization. The relationship with business has always been a contentious one for consumer groups and part of the attraction of the independent, membership-based model has been its rigorous desire not to be linked with any commercial interests. It was difficult for consumer groups to work with bodies such as the International Chamber of Commerce, even within the context of an official reconstruction policy to which they—outwardly at least—adhered. Likewise, the close relationships and ideological affinities identified between state and non-state actors such as commercial associations in the midst of the Cold War, did not extend to consumer groups. They remained mistrusted by the proponents of productivity at the international level and consumers themselves wished to retain their distanced, objective, independent angle of vision on the branded commodity. It is better, then, to see in organized consumerism a transnational social movement born of the shared experiences of consumers across America, Western Europe, and the wider capitalist world. The affluent subscribers to the various testing magazines required the same type of guidance in similar economic contexts. The institutional setting for comparative testing may have differed according to the political-economic context of each nation, but the desire for greater information represented a shared desire which, as we will see in subsequent chapters, would eventually be expressed globally. If there was an ideology of consumerism that emerged through comparative testing, it was one that spoke to the needs of the middle classes on both sides of the Atlantic rather than being the imposition of a specifically U.S. model of the consumer as activist or shopper.

V

The similarities in activities among the emerging consumer groups affirm the transnational exchange of ideas. Throughout the 1950s and 1960s consumer groups expanded their testing facilities and increased the number of products reported on in their magazines. By the end of the 1960s, CU and CA employed hundreds of staff, many of them dedicated solely to laboratory work. While other European groups tendered out testing work to private companies and government agencies, most of the main groups were employing ever larger numbers. But what is apparent is that the principal testing organizations increasingly engaged in other activities. These extended the notion of consumerism from the individual assessment of tested and ranked goods to something resembling a more genuine social movement. Testing organizations sought not only to assist individual shoppers but to propagate more generally the benefits of wise spending and the rights and duties of being a modern consumer. The remit of the organizations extended far beyond the subscribers to the magazines leading consumerism to be about assisting all citizens as consumers in all aspects of their consuming lives. To this extent, comparative testing consumerism was truly democratic: not only did it promote freedom of choice, but it pursued the democratic aim of ensuring that everybody was treated fairly and could participate in the marketplace.

All testing organizations attempted to spread the message of consumerism in general. All held lectures, talks, and seminars, arranged public meetings, and spoke directly to women's groups, religious organizations, and sections of the labor and co-operative movements. Pamphlets were published on issues affecting all consumers, such as credit facilities, house purchasing, and guides to buying high ticket items, especially cars. Some used their connections to broadcast radio and television programs, occasionally publicizing the results of tests but more often reporting on more general consumer problems. By the late 1960s, Stiftung Warentest in Germany not only could secure its own TV program, but its tests were taken up by a variety of other radio and television programs. It enjoyed a more prominent public profile than found in consumer broadcasts in other European countries, especially the "nondescript" *Money Programme* of British broadcasting.[55]

Most testing organizations tried to develop close links with other consumer protection bodies. Sometimes this was formalized, as with the Danish Housewives Consumer Council, which was housed in the same office block as the other government funded body, the Danish Government Home Economics Council, which handled consumer complaints as well as assisted in testing programs.[56] More often, it meant working with other groups on specific projects or lobbying for acts of legislation. In other cases, though, the existence of alternative consumer groups proved more divisive. In Britain, the CA never developed a working relationship with the co-operative movement, even shunning its products in its tests, while the consumer movement in Belgium was weakened by the establishment of an alternative group, the Union Feminine pour L'Information et la Defense du Consommateur (UFIDEC, founded in 1959) made up of socialist, labor, co-operative, women's, and trade union bodies.[57]

European organizations also generated new forms of consumer protection that were then copied elsewhere. Better product labeling has been a persistent demand of consumer groups around the world. Here the lead was taken not by CU but by the Swedish Institute for Informative Labeling (Varudeklarations-nämden, VDN), a state-funded auxiliary of the Swedish Standards Association, which developed a comprehensive and informative voluntary labeling scheme that became the goal of many consumer organizations in the 1960s. Established in 1957, the VDN scheme provided standardized information about a product and signified an approved level of quality. If CU had proved to be the original benchmark for the creation of consumer testing organizations, the Swedish labeling scheme assumed an idealized position as to what quantity and quality of information consumer groups demanded from industry and government.[58] Similarly, in Austria, the Association for Consumer Information (Verein für Konsumenteninformation, VKI) led the way in presenting information to a wider public. The VKI headquarters were located on a main shopping street of Vienna. It was able to devote 1,800 square meters (19,375 square feet) of showroom to a permanent exhibition of home appliances and other consumer durables such as record players, sewing machines, and television sets. In 1969, around 200,000 consumers visited the exhibition, being able to make direct comparisons themselves and receive the impartial advice of the VKI's team of counselors.[59] As with the Swedish VDN scheme, the Vienna experiment proved an inspiration to other testing bodies, which campaigned for the establishment of high street consumer advice centers that would reach those sections of the population their magazines had so far been unable to attract.

Consumer groups also sought representation on official and professional committees where business interests were already present, especially in standards institutes or where codes of practice were drawn up, as in the advertising industry. Eventually many became highly professional representatives, but quite often the first ventures into representative work were met with confusion as amateur activists were overwhelmed on technical committees because they "lacked the expertise, time, confidence, and resources that the spokesmen of the corporate sector could muster."[60] Generally, the aim of such representation was not to seek a battle with the producer, but an alliance.[61] Yet in fighting to maintain their independence from industry, more belligerent positions could be taken. After sales of *Que Choisir* took off in the 1970s, the UFC was able to flex its muscles so that by the end of the decade it had acquired a reputation as "the scourge of French industry."[62] In other organizations, the relationship with business was even closer, though no more so than in Germany's Stiftung Warentest—its board of trustees included five representatives from industry.

Finally, consumer testing organizations lent their support to the establishment of mass-based grassroots organizations. The British CA supported and financed the work of the National Federation of Consumer Groups, a network of local consumer organizations that by 1967 consisted of 100 groups and around 18,000 members.[63] The UFC followed suit in France, creating 170 local unions by 1980 with 50,000 members, although this never matched the 800 "clubs de consommateurs" managed by the Associations populaires familiales, which regularly organized mass consumer protests and boycotts.[64] In Germany, although the testing organizations themselves have eschewed mass mobilization, preferring instead to work with industry within a more corporatist structure, Hugo Schui was able to attract 50,000 members by 1970 to his organization, the Deutscher Verbraucherbund, offering them a copy of his magazine, *Der Wecker* (*The Alarm Clock*), as well as legal support and insurance for their own consumer law suits.[65]

VI

In all of these activities, the ideology or ethos of consumerism extended far beyond that arising from the scientific testing of goods. Admittedly, the original calls for rationality, efficiency, and objectivity present in Chase's and Schlink's publications prior to the formation of Consumers' Research were also fundamental to the outlook of consumer organizations elsewhere around the world. In *Your Money's Worth,*—"the Uncle Tom's cabin of the consumer movement" as the sociologist Robert Lynd put it[66]—Chase and Schlink called for scientific shopping—an activity which, for Schlink in particular, held no wider political connotations. Schlink's own arrival at comparative testing had come from his frustration at his time at the Bureau of Standards when he saw a vast amount of information amassed by the government on the technical aspects of brand name products. This information was not made public, yet Schlink realized it could be used by consumers to make more efficient purchases. In this classical political economic position, Schlink believed wiser purchasing would assist industry by directing production to the most efficient and better quality goods, thereby improving profits and living standards for both agents at either end of the chain of provision. At the time of writing *Your Money's Worth* (1927), Schlink had aligned himself with America's liberal left and had even courted socialist thinking, and he proved willing for CR to adopt a political campaigning role, protesting against the treatment of the consumer by business and government alike. But by the mid-1930s he had drifted—or rather had been guided to—the right, by his ally at CR, J. B. Matthews, whose union-bashing and lack of interest in the plight of workers, as well as their own committed anti-communism from that time on, triggered the strike and the formation of CU.[67]

For Schlink, despite his dabbling with liberal left ideas, comparative testing consumerism was always a movement of efficiency, rational purchasing, and empowered individualism. It might result in the aggressive exposure of fraudulent business practices and the uncovering of dubious commercial enterprises—all in the best muckraking tradition of Progressive Era journalism—but ultimately comparative testing worked on the principle that a good consumer was of benefit to industry. Schlink would later describe himself as a "rugged individualist" committed to repealing New Deal legislation and opposing the price controls of World War II. He proclaimed that the only problem with capitalism was the lack of information available to the consumer. Virtually all that consumers needed, Schlink later claimed, would be met with "the extensive development and increase of all the possible sources of practical information which will tell him the relative technical worth of the manufactured products he wants to use."[68] The ideology of consumerism amounted to "a form of ideal Jeffersonian independence" in which the individual would achieve concurrent freedom in both society and the market.[69]

How such an ideology manifested itself on the page of the consumer magazine was through a reporting style that privileged tables, quantification, and the assessment of the technical aspects of goods. Stripped from this analysis would be individual taste, an appreciation of design and, until the 1990s—thanks to the pioneering efforts of the Dutch Consumentenbond—wider political or ethical issues such as "food miles," "fair trade" credentials, or environmental impact. Comparative testing was to focus purely on the objective: all that was subjective was to be omitted from the magazine and, it seemed at times, from the rational individual calculation of which product to purchase. From this perspective, consumer magazines were often able to recommend "best buys" as though the suitability of a product for a person or a family could be determined independently of practicality, absolute price, and those vague fields of social and cultural practice the French sociologist Pierre Bourdieu later referred to as "habitus."[70] Commodities existed separately from the consumer and could be judged accordingly by the scientist and the engineer.

This ethos is immediately apparent in all the testing magazines of the consumer groups in Europe and the wider world. Despite the attention to the plight of the worker, and the slightly more upbeat visual style, the very first issue of *Consumer Reports* continued to promote the rationalist ethic found at the heart of the *Consumers' Research Bulletin*. Photographs of products appeared divorced from their social context, mirroring the forms of commodity fetishism found in early twentieth-century advertising, which sought to appeal to the mass by emphasizing the product rather than the user.[71] Even a feature on stockings refused to portray any part of the wearer above the knee.[72]

Once consumerism took off in the 1950s, the similarities between the magazines are striking. The only individuals to be regularly portrayed were either male technicians and scientists at work in the laboratory or empowered housewives rationally scrutinizing the array of offered products. The first issue of *Que Choisir* in 1961 had the almost obligatory action shot of the laboratories of the Institut Scientifique D'Hygiène Alimentaire de Paris with front covers regularly portraying slightly confused housewives whose underlying look of steely determination aimed to convince readers that individual rationality would triumph over capitalist chaos.[73] *Which?* in Britain proved particularly effective at translating much of the technological jargon into readable prose, which nevertheless did not detract from a general utilitarian imagery. Its style was clearly influential across the capitalist West as *Consumentengids* in the Netherlands, *Konsument* in Austria, *Test* in Germany, *Choice* in Australia, and *Consumer* in New Zealand interspersed statistical tables and photographs of the tested and the testers with more upbeat cartoons and, as much as possible with chatty articles when dealing with the technical aspects of branded goods.[74] Testing itself was often a feature, as magazines reveled in their own extensive testing activities and explained precisely what had been placed under the microscope or subjected to an accelerated process of general wear and tear.[75]

Yet technical data, statistical tables, and cold hard facts did not only serve to guide the individual shopper; they also represented a moral critique of consumer culture, which underpins much of the modern comparative testing movement. Affluence and greater choice were the positive aspects of the expanding markets of the 1950s, but the magazines also emerged from more negative considerations. Their utilitarian style was a direct riposte to the apparent puffery of advertising and marketing, those techniques of salesmanship that were said to have misled the public in the first place. The tremendous popularity of books such as Vance Packard's *The Hidden Persuaders* (1957) and John Kenneth Galbraith's *The Affluent Society* (1958) were postwar equivalents of older critiques of commodity culture, which had inspired consumer activists in the United States in the 1920s. Chase and Schlink, as did Warne and Kallet, looked particularly to the novels of Edward Bellamy, the journalism of Upton Sinclair, and the economics of Thorstein Veblen. From Sinclair's *The Jungle* (1906), they knew of the sharp practices conducted by the firms in the food trade. They admired Bellamy's *Looking Backward* (1888) and his utopian fantasy where all salesmen, all money, and all advertising had been eliminated and consumers were free to make up their own minds as to what they wanted. And from Veblen's *The Theory of the Leisure Class* (1899) and *The Engineers and the Price System* (1921), they learnt of the distinction between the engineer and the businessman, the former always seeking efficiency and technological improvement while the latter sought product differentiation, restraints on trade, and the molding of consumer desire to commercial interests.[76]

Organized consumerism represented more than just helping individuals. It constituted a transfer of the skills of production into the skills of consumption.

The traditional feminine knowledge of the housewife-consumer was to be supplemented by the male knowledge deriving from work, technology, and social science. The magazines reflected this masculinization of consumption and the productivist tendency of Schlinkian shopping. Comparative testing represented a masculine control of a feminine marketplace, just as, earlier and fictionally, Octave Mouret in Émile Zola's *The Ladies Paradise* (*Au Bonheur des Dames*) (1883) sought to control women shoppers through the mechanized, rigorously controlled processes of his Parisian department store.[77]

However, organized consumerism was also to be the basis for something much broader than individual gain. If Schlink retreated into a cynical and embittered anti-communism, his original collaborator, Chase, more consistently held to his consumer-oriented approach he had sought to popularize in the 1920s. Along with Veblen-inspired economists, sociologists, and writers such as Rexford Tugwell and Robert Lynd, Chase's ultimate intellectual investment was in planning. Through the planned organization of the economy—which comparative testing could only assist by ensuring that people's needs were met by industry—inefficiency and waste would be eradicated in production, distribution, and consumption, leading to the eradication of poverty and the improvement in the standard of living for all. Collectively, these writers—many of whom patronized CR in its initial years—distinguished between a "consumer-oriented economy" in which business merely catered to the needs of consumers as shoppers, and a "consumption-oriented economy" that catered to citizen-consumers. Here, engineers and technicians ensured that aggregate and individual consumption levels continued to rise while businesses still enjoyed profits. Chase added a further Ruskinian emphasis on life over consumption so that consumers' quality of life also improved: the rational organization of society would result in a greater emphasis on leisure and the enjoyment—rather than just the purchase—of the material world.[78]

It was precisely these concerns with planning, efficiency, and the creation of a better world for consumers that inspired the new generation of consumer activist in the 1950s. Writing of England, George Orwell spoke of the "younger sons of the bourgeoisie" whom he predicted would bring about a mild-mannered English revolution: "Most of its directing brains will come from the new indeterminate class of skilled workers, technical experts, airmen, scientists, architects and journalists, the people who feel at home in the radio and ferro-concrete age."[79] As the politics of productivity dominated Europe after the war, productivism as an ethos inspired consumerism. While the link between productivity missions and consumer organizing was only direct in Denmark—where Marshall Plan funds were directed to the establishment of the Danish Housewives Consumer Council, elsewhere civil servants, engineers, scientists, home economists, and academics flocked to the organizing committees of European consumer organizations.[80] Their ideology of consumerism was expressed mainly through the pages of their magazines and the spirit of testing itself. But many consumer leaders pursued a wider goal for the organized move-

Figure 2. *Consumer Reports* tests home permanents, 1938. Consumers Union publicity card. Courtesy, Consumers Union Archive, Yonkers, New York.

Copyright © 1997 by Consumers Union of United States, Inc., Yonkers, NY, 10703, the nonprofit publisher of Consumer Reports® and ConsumerReports.org®. Used with permission for educational use only. No reproduction permitted without written permission from Consumers Union of United States, Inc.

ment beyond the rhetoric of rationality. If they did not quite read the counter-cultural critiques of capitalism emerging throughout the 1960s, they did at least continue to be inspired by the liberal traditions of American consumer activism. The student protests of May 1968 may have passed many consumer activists by, but Ralph Nader's visit to France, one year later, proved extremely popular, coinciding as it did with a huge growth in comparative testing by both the UFC and the Institut National de la Consommation.

While independent, member/subscriber-based organizations sought to assert their political neutrality, many of their original boards and councils contained similar characters to those that had developed consumerism in the United States. The British CA invited and obtained the participation of individuals representing all three of the main political parties but this did not disguise the close affinities between its leadership and the social democratic wing of the Labour Party.[81] The Australian Consumers' Association was established by a Labour Party feminist and attracted the support of trade unionists, while prominent individuals included the critic of multinational corporations, Ted Wheelwright, and the Sydney architect, Henry Epstein, who, until his death in 1968, urged the consumer movement "to search for a quality of life rather than for the aggregation of the quantity of goods we possess."[82] The leadership of the Consumers' Association of Canada likewise paid persistent attention to the broader economic and social questions facing the consumer and European groups often expressed an ideology much broader than their magazines' primary purpose.[83] To the value of sovereignty, the Dutch Consumentenbond has added the more vague but potentially more democratic, "responsibility" and "equality," while placing great emphasis on "access" to public goods such as health care, energy, public transport, water, housing, and education.[84] Whatever the achievements of organized consumerism, its self-selected leaders believed that the new ranks of affluent middle classes could form a new social movement with potentially far-reaching consequences. André Romieu wrote of the "silent revolution" of consumer activism; a grassroots consumer organizer believed consumerism represented "the new force in the land"; while Warne himself, in a private conversation, went so far as to utter the term "religion" while trying to define the role and meaning of consumerism.[85]

VII

According to one study of comparative testing organizations conducted in the early 1970s, subscribers to the new magazines were "information seekers": that is, they were "an elite group," a "cosmopolitan set of consumer sophisticates" who positioned themselves as "opinion leaders, critics and proxy purchasing agents for other consumers."[86] Certainly, the vast majority of subscribers to testing magazines was solely concerned with information. Study after study across Europe and North America found that readers of test reports were far more likely to have a higher income, level of education, and occupational status than other consumers. In the United States, a 1970 investigation into the readership of *Consumer Reports* found that four out of five came from the professional, managerial, or clerical income groups—a statistic almost entirely consistent with a similar investigation conducted in the early 1940s.[87] In Canada, a survey conducted in the late 1970s also found that "consumerists" were better educated and from the middle and higher income brackets, read establishment newspapers and were more likely to buy magazines such as *Time* and *National Geographic*. They were also more likely to adopt a cynical attitude toward advertising and were largely from the same cohort of the population, which supported other progressive causes such as women's rights and environmentalism.[88]

In continental Europe, attempts have been made to posit a non-English speaking temperament or culture to argue that consumers have adopted different approaches and tactics than in Britain and North America. It has been suggested that Latin "personalismo" would produce indifference to "best buys" while Romieu, commenting on the low sales of *Que Choisir* in the 1960s, suggested that Frenchmen were less likely than their Northern European counterparts to want to work hard in spending money after having worked hard earning it.[89] But, in truth, consumerism was popular all over Europe and for much the same reasons as it was in the United States. Consumer organizing was also popular in Italy until the 1970s and, once the UFC had reorganized itself and collaborated with the Belgian *Association de Consommateurs* in 1969, sales of *Que Choisir* increased exponentially.

Consumerism was a transnational social phenomenon attracting consumers affected by similar circumstances across the capitalist world. In Norway, in 1969, 79 percent of *Forbruker Rapportern* subscribers had been educated beyond the legal minimum requirement. In Belgium, in the same year, only 9 percent of *Test Achats* subscribers were from the skilled and unskilled worker groups. In Britain in 1964, while only 14 percent of the population regularly read the "quality" broadsheets of *The Times, Telegraph, Guardian,* and *Financial Times,* among *Which?* subscribers this figure was 67 percent. In the Netherlands, in 1966, 42 percent of the *Consumentengids* readers were from the lower middle class, 39 percent from the middle class and 8 percent from the highest social class. This left just 11 percent from the lowest social classes, a figure that had fallen even further to just 1 percent by the end of the decade. In Sweden, a 1968 survey found that *Råd och Rön* readers were those who simply owned more stuff: while only two-thirds of households possessed an automobile, 74 percent of subscribers did so; similarly, less than half the population owned a freezer, yet they could be found in 69 percent of subscriber households. And in Germany, where some of the most detailed research was conducted in the early 1970s into subscribers to *Test* and *Deutsches Mark,* the typical reader was again found to be a member of the "high-income-education elite," socially—and to some extent politically—conservative, though welcoming of the demands of the student movement and not opposed to more government regulation of business.[90]

The reasons these "elite" consumers attached themselves to the consumer movement arose from the insecurities of coping with the modern marketplace. In one of the first ever cross-European studies of consumer attitudes conducted in 1975, consumers expressed high levels of dissatisfaction with the market. Two years after the oil crisis and amid the beginnings of an economic recession, the market by the mid-1970s presented many of the same challenges that had faced affluent shoppers in the immediate post–World War II decades. Two-thirds of consumers within the European Community believed prices were rising ahead of their incomes. Around 40 percent could recall being cheated in the private sector, while the same number expressed complaints about the public services too. The problem was the lack of information available to them. Around half of all consumers believed there was simply not enough information, while many others felt that the available information was of the wrong kind (for example, 72 percent believed advertising to be misleading). Although over half the European population had by this stage heard of comparative testing, only 15 percent expressed a definite (a further 32 percent expressed a speculative) desire to join a consumer association. Those that did join formed a consumer vanguard, which possessed the time, educational ability, and money to spend more wisely. Nevertheless, there was an understandable response to assume control of a marketplace perennially alien and unwelcoming to them.[91]

VIII

This interpretation is not generally accepted by those who have examined the consumer movement, especially those U.S. scholars who have perhaps too readily overlooked these consumer activists in their overviews of twentieth-century U.S. consumer society. Instead, critics have contended that in seeking greater information, the organized consumer movement has helped its members become ever more selfish acquisitive individualists. It has been argued that organized consumerism "protested the practice, not the ideal, of advanced capitalism."[92] It has offered not an alternative to classical economic theory, but an attempt to realize it in practice, a limitation that has prevented it developing a more adversarial politics or a sustained social movement.[93] Even those commenting from within the consumer movement have accepted the extent to which CU in particular sought a "refuge from ideology through the use of its objective method."[94] For some activists, this was not really a problem. Many have emphasized the commensurability of consumer and business interests, while others have allied consumerism to more conservative tendencies.[95] At a meeting of the American Council on Consumer Interests in 1981, delegates were asked to debate the relationship of the consumer movement to other social movements. Instead, the election of a new Republican government had come to dominate proceedings and one speaker chose to explore consumerism's links with the new Reaganite agenda, concluding, "conservatism and consumerism can be compatible."[96]

Yet all of these analyses—contemporary and historical—fail to explore why consumers first came together as consumers in comparative testing organizations across the capitalist world in the 1950s. The question as to the effectiveness and consequences of the consumer movement is addressed in later chapters, but the initial focus must be on why these organizations emerged in the first place. If, as Marx put it, the nineteenth century saw the alienation of the worker from the means of production as the individual succumbed to the discipline of factory time and was divorced from the overall skills of craft-based artisanship, then the twentieth century saw the alienation of the consumer from the means of consumption. No longer could the housewife-shopper rely on her local knowledge and traditional skills to assess the quality and relative merits of everyday household items. Advertising and packaging metaphorically and literally masked the underlying meaning of any commodity while the complexity of the technology involved in the manufacture of semi-luxury mass-produced household durables created an impenetrable semiotic code that the technologically incompetent shopper could never hope to crack. For the vast majority of consumers these dilemmas were an irrelevance because they lacked the money and the resources to purchase the full range of objects laid before them, while others readily bought into the false consciousness of commodity capitalism and invested their trust in the workings of commerce and its agents.[97] But for those consumers who could afford to buy into the new era of affluence, and who had the time, resources, and education to put effort into their consumption, comparative testing became a means by which to overcome the alienation they felt in the marketplace.

Alienation within consumer culture has not normally been applied to these activist agents. As affluent society continued seemingly unbounded throughout the 1960s, a body of criticism emerged that spoke of the general sense of dissatisfaction and frustration—if not guilt of progressive-minded liberals—felt by many living within commodity culture. Just prior to the recession of the 1970s, it was alleged that consumer society had become the "society of the spectacle," a world in which the image or the sign of the commodity prevailed over any supposedly true meaning of the object. No longer was the issue that exchange values bore no relation to use values or that price did not reflect an item's true worth; in the hyper-reality of capitalism, "sign values" had become divorced from both use and exchange. The meanings of goods were contained now only in their image. Image was everything and images only referred to one another. The consumer no longer played a role in the determination of meaning and consumer society had become an intangible spectacle over which they could only ever gaze and never grasp. Here, it can be suggested, was a neo-Marxist development of the concept of alienation applied to the consumer rather than the worker.[98] But rather than offering the basis for a liberatory politics the commodification of culture trapped its subjects within its own endlessly circulating rhythms. True, later generations of scholars wrote of the ability of consumers to negotiate, appropriate, and reject the meanings of goods placed before them, but these on the whole have only been the minor skirmishes of individuals and subcultures in a broader battle that never took place.[99]

The sense of alienation attributed to consumer culture matches the alienation prevalent in several examinations of globalization. In the "runaway world" of

REPORT: WINTERURLAUB IN TUNESIEN

UNTERKUNFT	GESELLSCHAFT	Preis für 2 Wochen Vollpension während der Wintersaison Flug ab			Zuschlag für 2 Wochen (+ bedeutet: im Preis eingeschlossen)					Ver-länge-rungs-Woche
		Frankfurt	Düsseldorf	Berlin	Dusche	Bad	Balkon od. Terrasse	Meer-blick	Einzel-zimmer	
HAMMAMET										
El Bousten	Aero-Lloyd	518,—	548,—	619,—	+	—	+		30,—	130,—	150,—
	Scharnow	518,—	548,—	619,—	+	—	+		30,—	130,—	150,—
	Touropa	518,—	548,—	619,—	+	—	+		30,—	130,—	150,—
	Hummel	520,—	550,—	621,—	+	—	+		30,—	130,—	150,—
	Otto-Reisen	520,—	550,—	621,—	+	—	+		30,—	130,—	150,—
	Nova-Reisen (IT)	805,—	805,—	919,—	+	70,—	+	—		126,—	133,—
Fourati (Seitenflügel)	Aero-Lloyd	458,—	488,—	559,—	+	—	—	60,—	180,— Seeseite		125,—
	Scharnow	458,—	488,—	559,—	+	—	—	60,—	—		125,—
	Hummel	459,—	489,—	560,—	+	—	—	—	—		125,—
	Touropa	459,—	489,—	560,—	+	—	—	—	—		125,—
Fourati (Hauptgebäude)	Neckermann	498,—	513,—	—	+ oder +		—	—		130,—	150,—
	Scharnow	518,—	548,—	619,—	+	—		+		120,—	150,—
	Hummel	519,—	549,—	620,—	+	—		+		120,—	150,—
	Touropa	519,—	549,—	620,—	+	—		+		130,—	150,—
Hammamet	Touropa	539,—	569,—	640,—	+	50,—	+	—		130,— m. Dusche	160,—
Miramar	Neckermann, Altbau	547,—	562,—	—	+	—	—		140,—		171,—
	Neckermann	598,—	613,—	—	+ oder +	+			160,—		200,—
	airtours (IT)	990,—	990,—	1093,—	—	+	+	z.T.	168,—		224,—
	Berliner Flugring (IT)	991,—	991,—	1094,—	—	+	+	z.T.	168,—		224,—
	Cook (IT)	1234,—	1234,—	1337,—	—	+	+	+	204,40		340,90
Les Orangers	Aero-Lloyd	639,—	669,—	740,—	+	60,—	+	—	200,— m. Bad		200,—
	Scharnow	639,—	669,—	740,—	+	60,—	+	—	140,— m. Bad		200,—
	Hummel	640,—	670,—	741,—	+	60,—	+	—	130,—		200,—
	Berliner Flugring (IT)	963,—	963,—	1066,—	+	70,—	+	—	91,—		217,—
	airtours (IT)	966,—	966,—	1067,—	+	49,—	+	—	91,—		213,50
	Nova-Reisen (IT)	969,—	969,—	1083,—	+	56,—	+	—	91,—		196,—
	IT-touristik international (IT)	1108,—	1108,—	1210,—	+ oder +			168,—		280,—
Park Plage (Bungalows)	Aero-Lloyd	588,—	618,—	689,—	+	70,—	+	—	140,—		185,—
	Scharnow	588,—	618,—	689,—	+	70,—	+	—	140,—		185,—
	Touropa	589,—	619,—	690,—	+	← 70,— →		50,—	140,— nur Dusche	185,—
	Berliner Flugring (IT)	882,—	882,—	985,—	+	35,—	+	49,—	112,—		175,—
	airtours (IT)	885,—	885,—	986,—	+	49,—	+	35,—	112,—		175,—
	Nova-Reisen (IT)	907,—	907,—	1021,—	+	56,—	+	—	112,—		175,—
	IT-touristik international (IT)	1164,—	1164,—	1279,—	+	70,—	+	70,—	224,—		308,—
	Cook (IT)	1279,—	1279,—	1382,—	—	+	+	+	215,60		357,70
Sindbad	Neckermann	528,—	543,—	—	+ oder +	+			130,—	160,—
SOUSSE										
Le Boujaffar	Neckermann	528,—	543,—	—	+	—	—	—	130,—	160,—
	Hotelplan (IT)	781,—	781,—	887,—	+	—	+	—	—	133,—
Justinia	Neckermann	528,—	543,—	—	+	—	—	—	130,—	160,—
	Hotelplan (IT)	821,—	821,—	927,—	+ oder +	+			28,—	154,—
	IT-touristik international (IT)	916,—	916,—	1019,—	+ oder +	+	56,—	140,—		189,—
Marhaba	Neckermann	528,—	543,—	—	+ oder +	+			130,—	160,—
	Hotelplan (IT)	821,—	821,—	927,—	+ oder +	+			105,—	154,—
Riadh	Neckermann	465,—	480,—	—	+	—	+	—	—	120,—
SKANES – MONASTIR										
Esplanade	Neckermann	559,—	574,—	—	+	—	+	—	110,—	169,—
Ribat	Cook (IT)	1089,—	1089,—	1192,—	—	+	+	+	57,40	227,50
Skanes Palace	IT-touristik international (IT)	1294,—	1294,—	1396,—	—	+	+	—	224,—	336,—
	Cook (IT)	1323,—	1323,—	1426,—	—	+	+	+	228,20	340,90
ZARZIS										
Zita	Aero-Lloyd	678,—	708,—	779,—	+	50,—	+	—	130,—	210,—
	Scharnow	678,—	708,—	779,—	+	50,—	+	—	130,—	210,—

Figure 3. The Rosetta Stone of contemporary capitalism? From "Report: Winterurlaub in Tunesien," *Test*, January 1969, 36.

Courtesy of Stiftung Warentest.

late modernity, citizens have become separated from the ever shifting sources of economic and political power. Divisions have been created for those who exist within the network society, those who have been described as a "transnational capitalist class," and those who remain connected to the flows of information occurring ever faster around the globe. For them the world seems smaller, but for the majority, the spaces of power, the flow of capital, and the production of information exist separately from daily life and alienation occurs on a mass scale around the world on a daily basis.

For the citizens of the twenty-first century, there has been a recourse to new forms of social movement—fundamentalist to progressive—to overcome alienation by reconnecting the individual to the production of power.[100] Consumers have also participated in this. The fair trade movement has, at the most basic level, sought to assist developing world farmers and producers from their own alienation, but it has also strove to overcome the alienation of the consumer. The modern shopper is presented only with the final outcomes of the chains of provision, the supermarket shelf offering no glimpses into the systems of production and distribution, which brought it there. Fair trade seeks to reconnect the consumer with the producer, thereby rooting the meaning of a commodity in its social relations and its true exchange value rather than in the ephemeral and transient nature of sign values.

For affluent consumers in the latter half of the twentieth century, living in a similar age of dislocation and insecurity, comparative testing offered a means by which they could escape from their alienation. It offered the opportunity to establish themselves as an elite who would be able to reconnect with the world of goods, leaving behind the massed ranks of consumers who continued to be uninformed and systematically duped on a daily basis. Marx argued that modern capitalism creates a fetish of the commodity, the product becoming a hieroglyphic that we seek to decode to understand labor relations.[101] The publication of endless statistics in comparable tables was precisely an attempt to break that code, though rarely to understand the labor theory of value. Rather, comparative testing consumerism enrolled the skills of the scientist and the engineer to help consumers to reconnect with goods.

We should not therefore end with either an optimistic celebration of consumer modernity or a pessimistic conclusion as to the odds stacked against the consumer. Rather we should acknowledge their legitimate desires to participate in the world of plenty and the tactics they developed to navigate their way through it. Testing stood in defiance of the promotional devices of advertising and literally stripped a product down to its constituent parts to render it knowable, understandable, and meaningful. It was an attempt to establish consumer sovereignty, but it was a sovereignty never fully appreciated in these terms. Sovereignty meant control and participation in the forms of power that gave meaning to goods. It was always more than being free to choose and it is for these reasons that consumerism can be said to have provided an ideology of far wider significance than just assisting the acquisitive shopper.

2

COLD WAR SHOPPERS

Consumerism As State Project

It is all too easy to dismiss the subscribers to the comparative testing magazines as the petty-minded penny-pinchers of commodity capitalism. It cannot be denied that a high proportion of *Which?, Que Choisir, Test,* and *Consumer Reports* readers have only been interested in their own material advantage. Value for money, for them, has related only to their own pockets and not to those of their fellow citizens. Yet, even acknowledging that many were only out for personal gain, they nevertheless showed themselves to be sympathetic to the campaigns of the leaders of consumer activism that have sought to reform the marketplace in ways that benefit everybody. If they wished to ensure that the goods that they had purchased did not break down, did not explode in their faces, and that redress could be sought, then they often required the intervention of regulatory authorities that would ensure the market could be made a fairer place for all.

Moreover, these newly affluent shoppers were operating in a consumer society supposedly being built in their name. In the reconstruction of the war torn economies, if standards of living were to be increased for everybody and the society of the consumer was to be brought to all, then it also stood to reason that politicians had to respond by offering shoppers some protection in this unknown age of affluence. Economic growth might be achieved through macroeconomic policies promoting production, but citizens had to be certain they could operate effectively in their assumed roles as consumers. The regime of the producer and the planner had to exist alongside the new regime of the shopper. Yet this was not the case where consumer sovereignty was to be the model for avoiding the perils of unwise purchasing. If consumers were to behave with confidence, providing the impetus for economic growth and making all the improvements in technology and productivity worthwhile, then they required assistance and support. They needed to be assured that their spending would result in greater utility for themselves and their families. They needed to know that in borrowing heavily to purchase a car, a house and the furniture and appliances for it, they would not lose everything if the house was found to be shoddily built, if the car broke down on every trip, and if the appliances bought for the home harmed those who switched them on. As firms grew in size and complexity, increasing the distance between the consumer and producer, citizens needed to know that constraints and curbs would be placed on businessmen's behavior, that capitalism would be kept in check and that, somehow, if not through the authority of choice but through the authority of government, the market would still serve the interests of those it claimed to represent.

For all the emphasis on productivism, in both the U.S. economy and in Western Europe (through the Marshall Plan), governments around the world attempted to develop regimes of consumer protection to provide consumers with the confidence to enter and participate in the market. While states responded in different ways, what must be emphasized above all is that from the 1960s and especially in the 1970s states did respond: it is with good reason that many consumer activists look back on these decades as the time when they achieved many of their greatest successes. The growth in consumer protection measures was simply incredible, sweeping aside many of the rudimentary consumer representative systems developed during the 1930s and 1940s and replacing almost entirely the now seemingly rudimentary regulations enacted at the end of the nineteenth century. In Germany, there were only 25 new laws relating to consumer protection from 1945 to 1970, but an additional 338 were adopted by 1978. Similarly in France, there were only 37 laws and ministerial decrees before 1970, a total that had grown to 94 by 1978.[1] In Britain, major laws relating to consumer safety, hire purchase, resale price maintenance, and trade descriptions were passed in the 1960s, followed by wider regulations on fair trading, credit, and unsolicited goods and services in the first half of the 1970s.[2] In the United States, a flurry of consumer protection laws was passed in the late 1960s relating to the automobile industry, drug safety, meat quality, package labeling, credit reporting, product safety, and a whole host of other trade practices.[3]

Certainly, organizations of comparative testers were not the only representatives of consumers during this period. While many of the evangelists of the new consumer movement liked to imagine themselves as the true representatives of the consumer, they often found themselves competing with others who also staked their claim on a consumerist agenda. Only in a very few countries where privately organized, independent, comparative testing magazines were especially successful—Britain, the Netherlands, the United States—has consumer politics come to be dominated by the backers of the best buy. And as they argued that the consumer was a universal category, their own appeal to a particular cohort of the population only made more obvious what had long been known—that consumers were a diverse public with a diverse range of spokes-men and spokeswomen, especially in societies where affluence was not arriving uniformly.

The trade unions had long campaigned for reductions in the cost of living. The consumer co-operative movement had always been much more than a re-tail store: indeed, its associational and political wings liked to imagine them-selves as the true voice of the ordinary consumer. Women's groups, too, had a direct interest in family provisioning, with many having established themselves within state infrastructures as the consumer representatives since World War I. And in the periods of austerity experienced by so many throughout the first half of the twentieth century, consumption had always had the potential to be politi-cized, as shoppers might rally behind a boycott of the products of a profiteer-ing corporation or in support of firms which recognized workers' rights and aimed to improve their conditions.

Yet the consumer movement associated with the testing magazines certainly revitalized consumer action as a whole. Moreover, in the 1950s, these maga-zines came to represent the vanguard of a heightened consumer consciousness. This is why in Western Europe, Australia, and North America at least, in the period from the transition to affluence to around the 1970s, the consumer movement was clearly at the forefront of a wider set of consumer demands. This is evidenced not only in the broad support they obtained but also in the will-ingness of politicians and governments to respond to their chief concerns. Elected politicians promised shoppers a better life "just around the corner," constructing welfare regimes that guaranteed basic standards of living for all. State officials liaised with consumer experts in the media and in housewives' or-ganizations to develop informative labeling schemes. Business associations worked in conjunction with consumer representatives to develop quality certi-fication marks. The co-operatives continued their campaigns against the abuses of the marketplace by trusts and cartels. And the trade unions continually sought regulatory solutions to some of the perceived inequities of capitalist de-velopment. Consumer protection, therefore, was to be a further complement to both expanding markets and expanding welfare states.

The point to emphasize is that consumerism as a social movement was not simply confined to the affluent middle classes. Although it drew its support from a relatively narrow cohort of the population, its principal goals in terms of cre-ating a fairer marketplace were shared by many across the political spectrum. Consumer society was being held before citizens as the way forward for all. It is of no surprise, therefore, that seasoned campaigners against consumer injus-tices were revitalized in this period alongside the testing magazines. And it is also not surprising that comparative testing did not enter an empty institutional arena. The renewed attention to the consumer was conducted through estab-lished frameworks of politics and economics, which meant that the consumer protection regimes emerging in the affluent society were incredibly diverse. For all the promotion of the free market by the Marshall Plan, the new consumer society found itself open to question by a wide variety of consumer activists, and prone to the different regulatory traditions and practices of each legally bounded nation.

The first section of this chapter sets out some of the different consumer protection regimes built across the developed capitalist world. Many of these reflected the existing political economic framework of each state and important comparisons can be made between certain ideal types: pluralist, corporatist, social democratic, individualist, and so on. But it is the fact that so many states responded that is the crucial point. Indeed, as is shown in the second section of this chapter, so widespread was this desire to create a society of consumption in which all could have some level of access, that it was not just confined to the capitalist West. It represented a transnational phenomenon that could be observed on either side of the Iron Curtain, though rhetoric rather than reality characterized the consumer protection systems of the Soviet bloc.

The important point to make is that the consumer movement obtained many domestic victories in the decades of postwar reconstruction and economic expansion. Many of the measures and regulations introduced not only protected consumer choice but also consumer redress, information, safety, and representation. However, beyond the success stories of different national contexts, consumer protection was being shaped increasingly according to global norms and agendas. What the existence of consumer lobbies in countries such as Poland and the German Democratic Republic (GDR) demonstrates is the transnational nature of consumer protection systems and ideas. In the capitalist West, officials analyzed and copied the consumer protection measures of other states. However, what such convergence also encouraged was a harmonization of consumer protection measures around certain common denominators. The final section, focusing on the development of supra-state measures in Europe, shows how much of this harmonization has resulted in the promotion of lowest common denominators. In practice, this has meant that since the 1970s the ideology of consumer protection has become focused around choice. This is a theme that is explored at greater length in later chapters. As we will see, the consumer movement came up against opponents and governments that responded more to the consumer movement's goal of choice and less to its more social welfare-style agenda: that is, to its focus on the consumer as individual rather than the consumer as collective social citizen. What this chapter does is provide not only a platform for understanding some of the successes of the consumer movement but also for realizing that consumer protection was a highly contested political site that could be made to serve the interests of several other actors. By the 1980s and 1990s, then, consumer protection in Europe was narrowly conceived having moved far from many of the social democratic goals of those who initially sought to build the consumer societies for all in the 1950s and 1960s.

That said, it should not be forgotten that in responding to a heightened awareness of the consumer as a citizen and as a political being, consumer protection was much more than simply a direct reaction to the rise of comparative testing, a cheap political ploy by government ministers to maintain their popularity, or the imposition of an American-modeled market economy on Europe and elsewhere. Instead, it suggests that consumer society was an amorphous entity in which many organizations had an interest. As the consumer was equated with everybody, it was inadequate to merely champion the rights of one consumer over another. Consumerism as a political project had to be seen to be offering something to all consumers, rich and poor alike; to both "best buy" magazine subscribers and to all those affected by structural market inequities. In short, consumer society came to be about everybody, not just those individuals who could buy into it. In the United States, the "consumer democracy" has been argued to have been at the heart of postwar planning, whereby consumers were able to exercise their citizenship not only at the ballot box but on a daily basis through their participation in the marketplace. Consumer democracy might not capture the full range of consumer regimes that emerged in the latter half of the twentieth century, but there was clearly a widely expressed desire to improve standards of living and to ensure that all could participate in the good life. In the consumer societies built after the war—and in the protection regimes established to look over them—there existed a broad-ranging consumer politics that aimed to bring everybody within its grasp. This might have been challenged, co-opted, and even only half-heartedly followed through in practice, but in the diversity of voices seeking to speak for the consumer, consumption became an activity that was potentially democratic, universal, and open to all.

I

The consumer protection regimes of North America and Western Europe owed their existence not only to the particular legal and political infrastructures of each country but to the traditions of consumer organizing. When consumer representatives began to obtain a voice in state bureaucracies, governments cultivated the support and involvement of a variety of movements. The consumer co-operative movement—although weakened through its own institutional and parochial shortcomings, the interference of totalitarian regimes, and the competition of more dynamic capitalist firms—was still a vociferous presence in Europe and Japan after World War II. Co-operatives played an important role in the establishment of consumer protection systems in Scandinavia, as well as provoking an ongoing debate about their relevance as a third sector alternative to capitalism.[4] Although in Britain they tended to follow rather than lead the new directions in consumerism, in France the consumer co-operative movement built its own testing laboratories as early as 1955 and in Belgium the co-operatives went so far as to help create a second consumer testing organization in 1959, the Union Feminine pour l'"Information et la Défense du Consummateur (UFIDEC), as an alternative to the earlier established Association des Consommateurs.[5]

The labor movement had its own interest in consumer affairs. Some trade unions had already contacted Consumers Union in the 1930s to learn how consumer action could complement the tactics of the workplace and others were quick to mobilize in the 1950s around consumption, recognizing that working-class consumers too had a right to participate in the affluent society. In France, four syndicalist labor groups, representing 2 million workers, established the Organisation Générale des Consommateurs (ORGECO) in 1959, concerned mainly with the implementation of consumer policy at the national level. In the Netherlands, Konsumenten Kontakt was established by the three main trade unions in 1957, working in collaboration with the co-operative movement. Consumentenbond had also earlier refused to allow the trade unions an automatic seat on their board, resulting in the labor movement's successful pressuring of the government to create an alternative testing organization (Stichting Vergelijkend Warenonderzoek). And in Austria, the principal consumer testing organization owed its existence to the labor movement as the Austrian Trade Union and the syndicalist institution, the Chamber of Labour (Arbieterkammer), created the Association for Consumer Information (Verein für Konsumenteninformation) in 1961.[6]

The women's movement too had long had an interest in consumption and its members were prominent representatives of the consumer in the 1950s. Women shoppers had had to suffer the privations of the austerity regimes of the 1940s, and their spokesgroups were keen to speak out on the politics of fair shares and reconstruction. Women in Montreal, for instance, drew on a sense of their entitlements to organize around consumer issues in the immediate postwar years. The experience of rationing and controlled supply and distribution bolstered attitudes that the right to basic needs was a fundamental tenet of modern citizenship.[7] Elsewhere, new groups of women consumers emerged out of the devastation of the economic infrastructure. In Japan, housewives took advantage of the democratic reforms immediately following the end of the war and formed a whole range of women's organizations from many social backgrounds. In October 1945, a protest over inequitable rationing schemes in Osaka led to the formation of the Kansai Federation of Housewives' Associations. In 1948, the seemingly trivial issue of defective matches led to a huge protest rally in Tokyo, so frustrated were consumers with the continuing shortages. This resulted in the establishment of the Federation of Housewives (Shufuren), which by 1949 claimed half a million members in the Tokyo region alone. Led by Oku Mumeo, a feminist and labor activist and later an elected representative with the People's Co-operative Party, the movement focused on women's and consumer issues, moving on to testing, advice, and information by the early 1950s.[8]

Similarly, European women's groups experienced a natural coalescence with consumerism. Progressive women's organizations assisted in the formation of UFIDEC in Belgium, faith-based family groups were central pillars of organized consumerism in France, and women journalists and home economists were invited to contribute to the different consumer groups in the United Kingdom, be they organized by the Consumers' Association or the British Standards Institute.[9] Everywhere else, broad-based and socially diverse women's groups provided the personnel for the renewed mobilization of the consumer. To take just one example, in the Netherlands women's groups took up collective membership of Consumentenbond. The Netherlands Housewives' Society (Nederlandse Vereniging van Huisvrouwen, NVH) established the Institute for Information on Home Economics in 1926, which become increasingly independent of the NVH by the 1960s. Moreover, women's groups joined with the main testing organization, co-operatives, faith-based labor unions and family groups to found the Consumenten Contact Orgaan in 1957.[10]

Decades of consumer protest, the traditional tactics of the labor and co-operative movements, the growth of new women's groups, and the experience of austerity and the politics of reconstruction all created an extremely diverse number of consumer voices and self-appointed representatives of an aspect of citizenship that appears to lack any fundamental coherence. Here was a pluralism of consumer organizations across the world that resulted in varied movements from country to country. The respective strength of each of the consumer spokesgroups helps to explain the relative success of each type of consumer mobilization in each country. It is clear that this diversity further fuelled the growth of organized consumerism in all its manifestations during the era of affluence.

In the United States, grassroots consumerism found its expression not only through the Consumers Union, but in a variety of state and local organizations—consumers' leagues, citizen action groups, public interest organizations, energy and utility groups, and information and advice centers—many placing themselves under the umbrella of the Consumer Federation of America established in 1967.[11] In Japan, Shufuren was soon joined by a whole range of consumer groups—other housewives' organizations, such as Chifuren (the Federation of Regional Women's Organizations), co-operatives, local buying clubs, the radical Consumers Union of Japan, and the state-assisted Consumers' Association—totaling more than 13,000 by the late 1980s.[12]

In France, the comparative testing organization Union Fédérale des Consommateurs struggled to obtain any monopoly on the consumer voice, competing as it was with a tremendous number of activist consumers: women's groups, a large number of family organizations, trade unions, rural pressure groups, co-operatives, and a whole variety of others supported to varying degrees by state financing.[13]

Within the French trade union movement there were several consumer bodies as ORGECO was subject to a number of splits: in 1974 Force Ouvrière broke off to form the Association Force Ouvrière Consommateurs (AFOC); in 1979 the Communist Confédération Générale du Travail (CGT) created its separate Information de Défense des Consommateurs Salariés (INDECOSA-CGT); and, in 1981, the Confédération Francaise Démocratique du Travail (CFDT) broke away to form the Association Etudes et Consommation (ASSECO-CFDT). The different trade union groups, together with all the other representatives of the consumer, could claim 2 million members by the late 1980s.[14]

With such a broad interest in consumer protection it is no surprise that governments responded to the demand for a more regulated marketplace and that these responses varied greatly from country to country. From the 1950s, not just specific acts of legislation but entire bureaucracies were created devoted to protecting the consumer. Across Europe and the United States, official institutions were created to provide information to consumers about products, the operation of the market, and their rights within it. Various types of consumer council emerged that drew on the grassroots consumer movement and utilized their own resources to represent consumers in various ministries that touched on consumer affairs. Some specifically dealt with consumer complaints, taking companies to court on behalf of individual shoppers or consumers as a whole in class action suits. Ombudsmen, trading standards officers, and weights and measures inspectorates were all expanded at national, regional, and local levels to watch over more disreputable manufacturers and traders. Standards institutes and official quality certification schemes were either controlled by the state or heavily funded from the public purse. Moreover, codes of practice, regulatory watchdogs, and independent councils were established to monitor specific aspects of the market, such as advertising, financial services and the utilities, whether supplied by nationalized industries, municipal authorities, or by private corporations.[15]

It is incredibly difficult to draw meaningful comparisons among these different regimes of consumer protection. Most consumer legislation has emerged on an ad hoc basis and on only a few occasions have entire regimes been put in place at once. Inevitably, government intervention into consumer affairs has been shaped by the path-dependent variables of existing political economic structures, but what marks the history of consumer protection is the cross-fertilization of consumerist thought around the world and the development of international standards that have helped traverse national particularities.

The most meaningful attempt at comparison so far has been conducted by a political scientist. Gunnar Trumbull has argued that there have been three broad models of consumer citizenship. First, an economic model of citizenship has regarded consumers as partners in the economy and the challenges facing them as the consequence of market failures and imperfections, be they information asymmetries or the inequities emerging from the abuse of monopolistic power. The solutions sought have revolved around strengthening existing market mechanisms and ensuring the consumer can behave as predicted by economic theory. To some extent, this model has dominated consumer protection policies in countries such as Germany, Britain, Austria, and Japan. In the Scandinavian countries, however, a second, more "associational" model of citizenship has been pursued, whereby consumers have been regarded like other legitimate social interest groups. Rather than finding protections within the market consumers have been given the right to participate in forums dealing with overall structural issues. Having made the assumption that consumers and producers share many interests, associational citizenship seeks to create mechanisms through which different interests can negotiate with one another on an equal footing. Third, a model of political citizenship emphasizes the rights of consumers and recognizes their roles as socio-political actors. Because consumers are not solely economic beings, they ought to be protected from the risks and uncertainties with which only professionals are usually able to cope. To some extent this was adopted in France and the United States and is dependent on the existence of a highly mobilized and vociferous consumer movement to which governments are prepared to respond.[16]

But if these models of citizenship serve as rough categories, they have also been tempered by the existing political and legal structures in which new consumer protection measures have had to be situated. While Trumbull finds consistency across the Scandinavian countries in their pursuit of an associational model of consumer citizenship, other consumer protection regimes have been influenced by existing policies that determine the role of the producer in the economy and the state. Within the economic model Britain has largely sought more market-based solutions, while Germany and Austria have adopted more corporatist consumer-producer mechanisms. In Japan the consumer has also had to fit in with a strong state and the existence of great producer political power at the center. Similarly, while France and the United States have regarded the consumer as a political entity, the latter has sought, as has Britain, market-based solutions to their grievances, while the former, though sporadically and through much experimentation, has mobilized statist mechanisms to protect the consumer. The models of citizenship have just as often served as ideal types for the range of institutions and individuals seeking to speak for the consumer in any one location. This has resulted in much borrowing from one another and the existence of many consumer protection measures that seemingly typify the style of a more general regime identified in another country.

The Scandinavian experience has been most frequently invoked in discussions of consumer protection. The state moved early in its intervention into consumer affairs, incorporating the existing strands of the consumer movement into the official institutions of the state. In Denmark, the government Home Economics Council (Statens Husholdningsråd) was established as early as 1935. In Norway, the Consumer Council (Forbrukerrådet) was created in 1953, drawing on the co-operative, women's and labor movements. And the similarly styled Swedish Consumer Council (Statens Konsumentråd) was created in 1957, promoting consumer research, education, and information. In many ways, these early state interventions have made the need for an independent consumer movement less apparent.

In Sweden especially, the state has taken over many of the roles elsewhere performed by private groups. In 1951, the Institute for Informative Labeling (*Varudeklarationsnämden*, VDN) was established, which has set out product standards that firms have adhered to, guaranteeing consumers information about the commodity and certain minimum levels of quality. In 1957, the Swedish government also created the State Consumer Institute (Statens Institute för Konsumentfrågor, KI), which has undertaken the testing of both goods and their use in the domestic environment.

In contrast, in Denmark, a more successful independent group has developed alongside the state institutions. In 1947 the Danish Housewives Council (Danske Husmødres, Forbrugerråd) was created to draw on the existing strength of women's groups. It expanded into the Consumer Council (Forbrugerrådet) in 1968 when its members included also home economics associations, educational groups, student bodies, the trade unions, pensioners, and disability groups. This has set out consumer views to industry and the state, has encouraged the further representation of consumers on other official bodies, and has promoted standards, quality labeling, and better information for consumers, as well as publishing *Taenk*. It has, however, also relied on government subsidies, thereby complicating the notion of an independent consumer movement in Denmark.[17]

Scandinavian consumer protection has undoubtedly pioneered many forms of state intervention that have acted as benchmarks around the world. First, the Swedish Institute for Informative Labeling proved an inspiration for many consumer activists in the 1960s and 1970s and many attempts, if less successful and comprehensive, were made to replicate it. Second, Sweden also pioneered the use of the consumer ombudsman in 1971 (followed by Norway in 1973, Denmark in 1974, and Finland in 1978), which has mediated disputes between consumers and business, helping to develop binding agreements on trade associations over such matters as advertising standards and standard contract terms. Third, its Market Court has served to manage consumer legal cases brought by the Consumer Ombudsman on behalf of consumers. The availability of this legal tool has strengthened the power of the Consumer Ombudsman to an extent far greater than in similarly conceived systems elsewhere, although the availability of class action suits in countries such as the United States provides an alternative model for seeking redress for many consumers as a collective.[18]

Finally, Scandinavia has also been quick to co-ordinate the different strands of consumer protection policy, placing them within coherent institutional structures. In 1972, the National Board for Consumer Policies (Konsumentverket) was created in Sweden, with a broad policy analysis and recommendation mandate. It was merged with the Consumer Ombudsman in 1976, establishing a super agency with much independence from its government financers.[19] Likewise, the National Consumer Agency was established in Denmark in 1988, which brought together, within the Ministry of Business and Industry, the three strands of state consumer protection: the Home Economics Council, the Consumer Complaints Board, and the consumer ombudsman. Collectively, the Agency is designed to create a balance between organized corporate and consumer interests.[20] The Scandinavian system has not relied on a notion of consumer rights to legitimate state intervention on behalf of consumers. Rather it has regarded consumers as an interest group, which should be provided with the means to communicate with other interests through the state. While this means that consumers from co-operatives, women's groups, and the trade unions have had to work with industry to develop consumer policy, it has also resulted in consumers becoming a powerful, participating constituency in government.

To some extent this associational system is mirrored in the more obviously corporatist systems of Austria and Germany. In the former, the Association for Consumer Information (Verein für Konsumenteninformation) was a direct product of the syndicalist traditions of Austrian politics, since it emerged out of the desire of the Chamber of Labor to represent workers' consumer interests and continues to consist of workers, business and agricultural interests.[21] In Germany, consumer politics has been marked by the absence of activist involvement in consumer groups. Instead, the Alliance of Consumer Associations (Arbeitsgemeinschaft der Verbraucherverbände, AgV) was established in 1953 to act as the umbrella body for all other consumer organizations, including the sixteen consumer councils established at state level (Verbraucherzentralen). Ostensibly, the AgV operates on an equal footing with other economic interest groups, but in reality it has meant that consumer protection in Germany has become geared toward more technical issues, seeking to work with manufacturers to ensure that problems with products are resolved before they enter the market.[22]

Much of this corporatist structure depends on the relative strength and resources of the consumer organizations as compared to other groups incorporated into the state infrastructure. In Japan, for instance, consumer protection has been weakened thanks to the greater entrenchment of producer interests within the central state bureaucracy. The commonly accepted view is that Japanese consumer groups have not been able to challenge the political power of producer groups and, indeed, many have argued for measures that actually support the manufacturers.[23] By arguing for greater food standards and self-sufficiency in agriculture, for instance, Japanese consumers have actually fought against their own immediate economic interests, which could be served by cheaper imports. However, if the opportunities for the expression of consumer interests are limited in government, the Japanese consumer movement has been a diverse entity. Not only has it included the many millions of women attached to the traditional housewives' groups, it has also embraced the 44 million members federated to the Consumer Co-operatives Union, the socialist Consumers Federation of Japan, the communist Japan Women's Association, and two radical groups: the Consumers Union of Japan (established in 1969) and the Seikatsu Consumers' Club Co-operative (established in 1965).[24] When bureaucrats and businessmen have been in alliance consumers have had very little impact. But when there have been divisions and disputes in national politics, this highly mobilized consumer movement has often been able to achieve notable successes (such as the Product Liability Law in 1994) and its relationship with government has been marked less by co-option and more by conflict.[25]

Care must be taken in seeking to classify consumer politics in any one country, especially if a focus on government initiatives, regulations, and institutions masks the history of conflict often bubbling under the surface, conflicts that often go to the heart of the definition of a consumer. In Germany, the producer bias of the corporatist framework has resulted in a system that privileges better information for the individual. Consequently, consumer protection remains largely market-oriented. Similarly, in Japan, the predominance of producer groups resulted in measures such as the 1968 Consumer Protection Basic Law, which subordinated the consumer cause to greater economic growth. Pseudo-independent consumer groups such as the Japan Consumers' Association were also set up by businesses and the state and only rarely joined widespread campaigns of the consumer movement. Instead, they promoted a vision of consumer politics that was individualist, non-confrontational, and in line with the agendas of vested industrial interests.

Yet other consumer institutions have posited very different notions of what it means to be a consumer, and these can explain alternative developments in consumer protection. Japanese consumers stretched the meaning of the consumer in the immediate postwar years to embrace a notion of livelihood in order to show that they were human beings "struggling to survive in a context of economic scarcity."[26] In the United States we cannot categorize consumer protection solely as a market-oriented, individualistic regime. Certainly, the primacy of the market cannot be denied, nor the faith held in it as a solver of consumer problems. But U.S. consumer politics also embrace other forms of protection. Because the individual consumer is also a rights-based citizen, these rights politicize his or her actions in a manner distinct from the associational tendencies of Scandinavian social democracy. In the United States in the 1960s they helped set criteria against which private corporations and the state must not infringe.

Thus, in the late 1960s, there emerged in the United States a regulatory framework often far more rigorous than that achieved in European economies. For President Lyndon B. Johnson consumer protection offered an opportunity for consensus at a time of growing political cleavages and a rediscovery of poverty that threatened to call for expensive government programs. In contrast, consumer protection was cheap and, thanks to the prominence given to Ralph Nader and his attacks on the U.S. automobile industry, extremely popular. Consequently, regulatory agencies were strengthened, including the Federal Trade Commission and the Federal Energy Administration and new agencies were launched, such as the Environmental Protection Agency, the Occupational

Safety and Health Administrations, the Consumer Product Safety Commission. and the National Highway Traffic Safety Administration.[27]

That these highly assertive interventions could be made by the state can also be explained by the pluralistic nature of U.S. politics and society. Whereas corporatist and social democratic models steered the consumer representatives through organized fora, the market-based liberalism of the United States was generally unfavorable to regulation. Yet in defense of individual rights campaigners have found several other points of entry into the U.S. legal and political systems—at state level, through Congress lobbying, through class action suits, or through persuading individual and ambitious politicians to take up a cause in order to make their own name in Washington.

The plurality of points of entry in U.S. consumer politics has been matched by the pluralism of the movement itself. Although older groups such as the National Consumers' League have continued to survive, Consumers Union dominated much of the consumer political environment before the 1960s. In 1968, however, the Consumers Federation of America held its first annual meeting and took up its role as the umbrella organization for U.S. consumerism. It has included within its ranks established bodies such as CU, but also single issue pressure groups dealing with health and housing (e.g., Action on Smoking and Health), state level local groups, specific cohorts of consumers such as student groups and the Gray Panthers, and a whole range of other progressive bodies such as the Association of Community Organizations for Reform Now, the Center for Community Change and Massachusetts Fair Share, which deals with access to public utilities.[28] Also included have been the radical public interest groups associated with the "Nader network": Public Interest Research Group, Public Citizen, Congress Watch, and the Center for the Study of Responsive Law.[29] In the United States, then, while there are many consumer organizations that would have embraced the social democratic opportunities found in European representative systems, others have taken advantage of a pluralistic system. This can admittedly weaken diverse groups of consumers, but it can also reward those that adopt a confrontational stance and have the resources to sustain a highly mobilized campaign.

The existence of, on the one hand, strong state regulations dealing with specific sectors of the economy and, on the other hand, a diverse and committed consumer movement, has existed in other states such as Australia and Belgium. In France, for instance, there have been powerful bodies dealing with such matters as consumer safety and massive grassroots mobilizations of consumers have occurred, especially after the 1972 Talc Morhange scandal when a baby product was found to be adulterated. In the same year, the consumer movement was revitalized by a meeting of the Council of Europe in Paris to discuss consumer protection, Ralph Nader visited the country once again, and the outlets of the high street store, FNAC (*Fédération Nationale d'Achats pour Cadres*), held exhibitions of consumer mobilization. By 1976, there were 800 "clubs de consommateurs" associated with the Associations Populaires Familiales, which was able to organize high profile campaigns such as the 3 – 6 – 9 boycott (to stop buying meat for 3 days, fruit for 6, and mineral water for 9). Two years later, 3 percent of the population had become members of a branch of the consumer movement, while a further 27 percent professed their willingness to join.[30]

Yet again, though, care must be taken not to classify too rigorously the consumer protection regime of any one country. States have learnt and copied from one another, resulting in ad hoc measures that collectively betray the ideal types of many different consumer protection systems. Furthermore, over time states have changed their policies and adapted consumerism both to the demands of the consumer movement itself and the more general ideologies of the political party in power. In France, for example, a strong central state has facilitated many experiments in consumer protection. Initially, and following the traditions of political economy that promoted productivity as the means to economic recovery, consumer protection was influenced by the concerns of producers. The National Consumption Committee (Comité National de la Consommation, CNC) was created in 1960 to serve as a consultative body to several government ministries, though its limited resources made it powerless. Following the lead taken by the German Stiftung Warentest and the relative weakness of French comparative testing organizations, the government created the National Consumption Institute (Institut National de la Consommation, INC) in 1967, which soon began publishing results of its own tests as well as advising on a much broader range of issues than the CNC. Still, even with its remit to cater to all consumers rather than just those willing and able to pay for a consumer testing magazine, the INC largely followed the individualist model found in many British and German consumer policy measures that aimed to provide more information to make the consumer a more efficient and rational shopper.

However, in the 1970s a model of consumer protection based on representation and corporatist negotiation began to appear following pressure from a highly motivated and better resourced grassroots consumer movement. A secretariat of state for consumption was established in 1976 and a flood of consumer protection acts began to appear. The Socialist government quadrupled funding to consumer protection and attempted to place consumers on an equal footing with producers, ultimately culminating with the establishment of a Ministry of Consumption in 1981. Although these initiatives were eventually scaled back, the measures nevertheless added to a strong central consumer politico-legal framework, which also eventually saw the publication of a comprehensive—if not entirely coherent—consumption code (Code de la Consommation) in 1993. While the U.S. political system is known for its pluralism, the centralized state of France created an alternative framework for the establishment of the consumer as a highly politicized aspect of citizenship.

Much of consumer protection owes as much to the efforts of consumers as it does to government. It is difficult to reduce the characteristics of protection regimes solely to the political economic context of each individual state. In

Britain, for instance, the existence of an extremely impressive private comparative testing magazine has meant the state has been partially excused from taking on an advocacy role for consumers. Although the National Consumer Council (NCC) established in 1975 with a remit to speak for the poor and disadvantaged, may have prevented other consumer groups emerging as powerful spokesbodies, the strength of the Consumers' Association also avoided the need to divert as many funds to the NCC as might have occurred in continental Europe. Likewise, Consumentenbond in the Netherlands has also enjoyed an extremely impressive popularity among Dutch consumers, perhaps ensuring the dominance of an information-based model of consumer protection: had Consumentenbond's magazine *Consumentengids* not penetrated so many Dutch households, then the state may have been forced to step in on behalf of consumers to a far greater extent than it did.[31] And if consumer protection is broken down into its constituent parts—into advertising regulation, trade descriptions, price controls, and so on—then ever greater disparities from national norms emerge. The point is less that rigid differences can be determined from cross-national comparisons, but that consumer protection had become an international phenomenon in which states learnt from one another and adopted measures that took best practices from different contexts. The most important point about consumer protection is not that there were differences throughout the world in the ways in which it was implemented, but that consumer protection existed at all.

II

For all the diversity of consumer protection regimes, then, the most fundamental point is that a whole variety of states sought to offer some form of assistance to their citizens in the marketplace. The nature of this assistance might differ, but consumer protection was clearly an international trend, appearing in liberal capitalist, mixed and social market economies. Because many of these systems were fundamental to the pursuit of the Cold War, consumption also became an aspect of a broader geopolitical framework. In many ways, the Soviet bloc had to be seen to be responding to the U.S. pursuit of the standard of living, but members of communist bureaucracies were also influenced by international developments in consumer protection. In this regard, the consumer movement and consumer protection were global trends that cut across Cold War politics pointing to alternative narratives of globalization within contemporary world history. Posited as a neutral political movement, consumerism avoided a polarization across the ideological divide and instead served to harmonize and globalize consumer protection regimes behind the scenes.

Undoubtedly, consumption did play a role in the Cold War. While both sides pursued the goal of greater standards of living and the provision of necessities for all, ultimately capitalism proved more effective at providing comfort and luxury than the command economies of the Soviet bloc. The communism of the party-state failed to either predict or satisfy consumer wants even after several years and decades of industrialization and economic planning.[32] This is not to argue that there was no consumer culture in Central and Eastern Europe. Much research has been undertaken into everyday life that challenges existing assumptions about consumption under communism. Consequently, much is now known about the importance of goods to people's ordinary lives in these societies. Whether the items were blue jeans in Hungary or women's clothing in Bulgaria, the subjects were hippies in Latvia or youths in the GDR, or the spaces were the kitchen in the Soviet Union or the *chata* in Czechoslovakia, consumption clearly mattered.[33] Indeed, almost twenty years after the collapse of the Berlin Wall, former residents of East Germany are looking back with nostalgia—or *Ostalgie*—for the products of the communist marketplace, nowhere captured better than in the 2003 movie *Good Bye Lenin!*[34]

What is less known is that consumer lobbies and consumer movements were known to exist behind the Iron Curtain. These were not so much the products of the spread of comparative testing from the United States, though this certainly played its part—Colston Warne, for instance, added brief visits to Hungary and Czechoslovakia in his 1969 report on consumer organizing in Europe.[35] Rather, advocates of consumer protection emerged within economic planning departments. In reaction to the disastrous strictures of the Stalinist era, Soviet planners allowed the economy to become more responsive to consumer demand in the 1960s.[36] While ultimately unsuccessful, such changes acknowledge the greater attention sometimes paid to consumers. In East Germany, leaders had to contend with the Soviet emphasis on production goods while acknowledging that many of their citizens looked favorably on the new prosperity being enjoyed in the West. As a result, "an unresolved tension persisted between those voices arguing for ever greater productivity in heavy industry and strict modesty in individual consumption, and those calling for a richer, more-developed set of consumption possibilities."[37] In the GDR, a distinct consumer lobby emerged in the 1950s in the Ministry for Trade and Provisioning, which found expression in specialized journals dealing with domestic trade and which developed "a language and a set of goals aiming toward building a more articulated consumption regime, toward a wider and richer array of consumption offerings."[38]

Within the confines of the GDR, though, the consumer lobby was never able to enjoy a persistent power base or a sustained role in the planning of consumption. But in more open societies a fuller recognition of the consumer could take place. Yugoslavia had, perhaps, the strongest tradition of consumer protection stretching back to 1957 and the state-run Federal Board of Family and Households. In 1969, this was reorganized to become the Association of Consumers, a state-funded but reasonably autonomous body with the remit to encourage better quality and lower priced products. Although it could only afford to pay a staff of four, it relied on the involvement of eighty volunteers and was able to publish its own magazine, *Consumer Informer,* containing consumer journalism and even test reports of common household goods.[39]

Later, other communist countries were known to take advantage of the worldwide consumer movement. In China and Cuba, consumer organizations were created from above as deliberate means to contain the political ill-will of consumers in an economy of shortages. Yet in more liberal or reformist regimes the commitment to the consumer was genuine. In countries such as Hungary experiments were conducted in decentralization and "marketized" socialism, while more foolhardy borrowing from Western governments took place in order to increase imports to satisfy consumer demand. As a wider commitment to liberalization, a more grassroots consumer organization emerged in Hungary in 1982 as an offshoot of the Patriotic People's Front—an umbrella for various civil movements.[40]

In Poland, as in East Germany, the party-state followed the Soviet productivist model, which occasionally paid lip service to the consumer but which ultimately focused on the dictates of production. Indeed, consumers were likewise expected to sacrifice their desires to the needs of production, especially during Poland's cyclical price hikes (1951, 1956, 1970, 1976, and 1980) that led to severe reductions in their economic welfare.[41] However, consumption could nevertheless be an important focus for broader political grievances and many of these concerns were taken up by a consumer lobby within the Institute for Domestic Trade and Services (*Instytut Handlu Wewnętrznego i Usług,* IHWiU) from the late 1950s that also looked to learn from the consumer protection regimes of the West. The publications of the consumer movement in Europe and the United States pointed to the many shortcomings of capitalism and therefore escaped much censorship. European consumer institutions, especially in France and northern Europe, also provided organizational models for the implementation of consumer protection within a state socialist system. The Polish consumer lobby was attracted to the broad definitions of consumer protection in the West, which incorporated not only the direct abuse of the consumer in the market place, but the empowerment of consumers through informed choice. In addition, Western consumer models laid much emphasis on representation that suggested to the Polish consumer lobby a means for independent organization and action. According to the assistant director of IHWiU, only "active, independent consumers" could provide the best means for organizing the trading system.[42]

During the later stages of Polish communism, this consumer lobby was able to transform itself into a more genuine consumer movement. Amid the events—associated with Solidarity—of the early 1980s a more independent form of consumer activism emerged when the experts at the IHWiU, together with economists from the magazine *Economic Life* (Życie Gospodarcze) and other journalists dealing with issues of consumption, launched an appeal to join an "independent and uncompromising" association of consumers.[43]

Federacja Konsumentów (Federation of Consumers, FK), established in

1981, was neither an official arm of the state, nor the product of ordinary forms of consumer interaction with the world of goods. It was an association of experts drawn from the civil service and the professions and bore much in common with the increasingly professionalized non-governmental organizations and new social movements of the West. FK's focus was on creating a more just distribution of goods and eradicating the problems of inappropriate production schedules. It aimed to stop the waste of materials on defective products (*bubel*) and defend the purchasing power of consumers who were forced to buy unsatisfactory goods.[44] It organized a network of consumer clubs around the country, launched high-profile campaigns and boycotts, helped individual consumers deal with complaints and problems, and lobbied the government to develop greater protection mechanisms. In 1988, FK took part in an official meeting with the first secretary of the Polish Communist Party and chairman of the National State Council, Wojciech Jaruzelski, about problems of quality in the Polish production sector and the failure of legal remedies in the area of consumer protection. At the end of this courtesy visit Jaruzelski was awarded the official badge of FK and, in return, FK received a consultative voice in various central state institutions.[45]

Crucially, however, the concerns and interests of the consumers attached to FK were focused solely on improving consumer supply under a command economy. They were adapted also from an emerging global discourse of consumer rights and protection to which they, as educated professionals, had access. Many of these rights had to be adapted to the particularities of Polish consumers. Thus, FK articulated a notion of rights in line with a vision of meeting basic standards of living. It adapted the Western rights and promoted also the rights to "the rational and differentiated fulfillment of needs in every household," the right to a "broad development of personality of each member of society," the right to a "healthy, uncontaminated natural environment," the right to "reliable information and education," the right to "democratic participation in shaping social and consumer policy and democratic control over state legislation," as well as the "social security and protection of handicapped people."[46] This attention to consumer rights, necessities, the basic forms of welfare provision, and better choice mirror the attention to basic needs in developing world consumerism in the 1970s and 1980s (see chapter 3). But it also reflects the extent to which the experts of FK behaved not as Cold War warriors, championing one ideological system over another, but as an intermediary cohort of citizens concerned with the condition of their society and economy from a perspective influenced by the international exchange of consumerist thought. As educated professionals, the FK experts were the one element of society most likely to be open to ideas outside of Poland and the Soviet bloc. Their work points not to differences between Western and Eastern Europe, or between the advocates of capitalism and communism, but to the growing internationalization of consumer protection and organized consumerism, which traverses established divisions of twentieth-century history.

III

Undoubtedly, the experience of Polish consumer activists in the 1980s cannot be made to stand in for a wholesale revision of global historical narratives, but their activities attest to the harmonization of the language of consumer protection and the globalization of social movements. It reflects other processes of convergence that can also be seen around the world and were less the consequence of ideological and geopolitical polarization. For instance, the standardization movement has facilitated trade and commerce while also offering basic protections for consumers. National bodies formed at the beginning of the twentieth century such as the British Standards Institute and the Association Française de Normalisation, both in 1901, came together to create the International Organization for Standardization in 1947.[47] Such bodies have been tied into broader process of westernization and even Americanization. The Organization for Economic Cooperation and Development (OECD), for example, began as a facilitator of the Marshall Plan in 1948 and has subsequently become an important focal point for the communication of consumer protection measures. The OECD's Committee on Consumer Policy has reviewed measures undertaken in member states on an annual basis, also providing ten-year summaries that act as reference guides for those wishing to learn about what has been enacted in other contexts. It has helped bring a convergence in consumer policies by focusing member states' attention on common goals particularly, for the OECD, in developing global markets to increase consumer choice.[48]

But harmonization of consumer policy has also come through the intervention of supranational bodies concerned with the regulation of trade and markets. This has resulted in the reduction of consumer protection goals to certain key, if rather vague, principles; namely, the exercise of choice by individuals in a free market. These are issues that will be explored later—chapter 4 examines the work of the United Nations, while chapter 8 explores the development of consumer protection in relation to global trade and commerce. At this stage, though, it is worth reviewing some of the developments in European consumer protection harmonization to highlight some of the broad global trends in the redefinition of both the consumer and consumer society.

Originally, the European Union, in its initial guise as the Common Market, committed itself to satisfying basic consumer needs in its charter of 1957. But beyond this, there was little concern for the consumer, the Treaty of Rome entirely ignoring consumers as a recognized interest group when it set out potential members of an Economic and Social Committee.[49] Thereafter it was slow to develop a consumer policy, but gradually responded to the lobbying of European consumer groups, particularly through their European federation, the Bureau Européen des Unions de Consommateurs (BEUC), set up in 1962.

Resolution 543 of 17 May 1973 by the Council of Europe established a Consumer Protection Charter—based around the five established consumer movement concerns of protection, redress, information, education, and representation—which allowed for the establishment of the Consumers' Consultative Committee (CCC) in the same year. The CCC worked with consumer groups to develop a consumer policy for Europe and in 1975, the Council of Ministers ratified the first Programme for Consumer Protection. Subsequently, the Programme came to be referred to as the Consumer Charter of the Community, again reiterating the same five rights. The first Programme directed European consumer policy in subsequent decades. The modifications and additions made in the second Programme in 1981 did not detract from the underlying rights-based spirit and no substantial changes were made under the Single European Act of 1987 that led to the consolidation of the internal market. Indeed, the third consumer Programme of 1986, A New Impetus for Consumer Protection Policy, was couched within the broader objective of the internal market and, if anything, the rhetoric of rights was toned down as greater competition and choice were held to offer the main protections to the consumer.[50]

The supranational framework provided by Europe both harmonized consumer protection and narrowed it as a concept. As is demonstrated in later chapters, powerful interests were at play in the steering of consumer issues to less social-welfare style goals. Moreover, internal divisions and disputes within the consumer movement have meant that many of the more radical consumer protection mechanisms have not been pursued with quite the same intensity, especially by more affluent groups. European codification of consumer law amid a process of economic integration has ensured that individual member states have adopted protection mechanisms pioneered in other countries. It has meant that Europe has had a tremendous impact on national consumer protection regimes, ensuring that the differences between countries such as France and Germany have been blurred.[51] It has also meant that in those states where consumer protection was weak or underdeveloped—such as Greece, Spain, Italy and Portugal—a ready-made model for consumer protection has been provided.[52] But increasingly, that model of consumer protection has been dictated by the broader goal of market reform, ensuring that consumerism as a regulatory regime has been diluted if not replaced with a notion of consumerism emphasizing choice, competition, and ever expanding markets. Particularly because such harmonization has occurred since the mid-1970s—that is, after the decades of economic expansion when business groups and governments were more willing to tolerate state intervention in the market—it has taken the form of protecting individual consumers acting as shoppers rather than of recognizing consumers as broad-ranging citizens with many rights, entitlements, and legitimate expectations.

For all the work and lobbying of consumer groups at the European level, then, their impact has been limited and a model of consumer protection has been determined by producer interest organizations. BEUC has ensured that lip service is still paid to consumerism. Article 129a of the 1992 Maastricht Treaty empowered the European Commission to ensure a high level of consumer protection in three of Europe's five fundamental consumer rights: health and safety, protection of economic interests, and information and education. In 2008 institutions exist for the articulation of the consumer interest at a range of different levels. Within the European Parliament there is a Committee on Environment, Public Health and Consumer Affairs. A subcommittee on consumer affairs exists within the Economic and Social Committee, which directly advises the Council of Ministers. Since 1989 there has been a Commissioner for Consumer Affairs, a position first held by the Belgian socialist Karel van Miert, followed by a French Conservative Christiane Scrivener in 1994, and an Italian radical Emma Bonino in 1995. In 1995, the Consumer Policy Service, set up by van Miert, was upgraded to a Directorate General (XXIV), with the responsibility for assessing all aspects of EU policy that affected the consumer, though it has come to have an increasing emphasis on food and health. Finally, the increased status of consumer affairs within Europe was apparent in the upgrading of the CCC into a full Council in 1990 (it became a Committee once again in 1995).

But the direction of all these consumer initiatives has largely been toward greater choice, only one element of consumer protection policy in the 1960s. This is partly explained by the relative weakness of consumer lobbying through BEUC. The Single European Act provided a well-documented boom in EU business lobbying. Whereas previously firms had some direct access to the political process at the national and international level, the single market prevented them using their exit as leverage in political negotiations. Instead, being forced to participate in Europe, businesses have created a whole host of lobby groups, such as the European Round Table, which have sought to shift attention away from the Council of Ministers toward the policy formation stage. It has resulted in an "elite pluralism" in European politics, in which many political lobbyists exist, but not all have equal access to the negotiating table.[53] Consequently, business groups have come to influence consumer policy to a far greater extent than consumers themselves. Maastricht, for instance, offered few new opportunities for advocates of regulation and consumer protection.[54] Similarly, in spite of the heated opposition of consumer groups to the Common Agricultural Policy, this protectionist measure still exists.[55] Consumer policy at European level has been unable to expand into new areas, as many expected it would, for example, into questions of sustainability and the environment.[56] And the most recent developments in European consumer policy in the twenty-first century continue to reiterate well-tried philosophies of protection that offer no challenges to the primacy of the market.[57]

This is not to deny the many benefits core protection legislation brings to consumers, or that many leading European consumer activists have been relatively pleased with the gains they have obtained. But European consumer activism has largely followed an information-based approach, whereby consumers have been protected through the provision of better information, making them more efficient and rational and, in turn, improving the operation of the market.[58] Ultimately, their interests were seen to lie in more choice and expanding markets, rather than the greater supply of public goods, a more equitable distribution of commodities or the ability of all consumers to participate on a more equal footing. Admittedly, as in the United States and in Europe through the OECD, extremely strong regulatory protections were made available on matters of consumer safety and food sovereignty, especially as witnessed in the reactions to BSE.[59] But, generally, harmonization of consumer protection policy was attendant with a reduction to the lowest common denominator. While different traditions of consumer activism and the political-economic structure of an individual state might therefore have created very different consumer policy regimes across America, Europe, and the Asia-Pacific region, the work of supranational bodies such as the European Union served to override these differences. And they did so by positing the most global of consumer interests—choice—as the main target of consumer protection. For reasons to which we will repeatedly return, the Europe of the 1990s therefore reflected only one aspect of the vision of consumer society held by those who sought to reconstruct Europe after 1945. As consumer protection regimes first came into existence, there had been a concern to ensure all were protected, with protection meaning access as well as choice. By the 1990s, Europe had much less to say for those who could not actually afford choice.

IV

The developments in European consumer protection in the 1980s and 1990s suggest that the consumer society being built by states at the end of the twentieth century was very different from that which had driven reconstruction in postwar Europe. In the 1950s, whether in the consumer democracy of the United States, the social market economy of Germany, the advocates of planning in France or in social welfare and mixed economies in general, consumer society was offered as the future for every citizen. Politicizing consumption came to be as much about access to affluence as it was about choice for those already enjoying comfort and luxury. And, because a whole new generation of citizens were to be brought into this uncertain age, states had to be seen to respond to consumer's fears and to implement regulatory structures that provided them with the confidence to act in their assigned roles.

The construction of this society of mass consumption was as much the product of consumers themselves as governments. The comparative testers who spearheaded the new consumer activism of the postwar years were often joined and were certainly preceded by many others who had long spoken in the name of the consumer. At the grassroots level, these included the consumer co-operative movements and trade unions concerned with the cost of living. At the philanthropic level, there existed organizations of women and middle-class consumers who sought to defend workers' rights while setting precedents for what could be achieved through consumer mobilization. At the professional level, economists, advertisers, psychologists, and home economists all offered their own expertise to understand consumer behavior and to predict the nature of its demand. Responding to all of these consumer representatives was an important means by which governments could be seen to cater to the public at large. The consumer was a citizen who cut across existing social divisions of class, gender, region, and ethnicity. For populist politicians, or those seeking the middle ground, consumption provided the opportunity to create a politics of the public that all could embrace.

Governments responded to the mobilization of the consumer and consumption became a state project in the sense that the maintenance of rising living standards was a key legitimation of a regime's authority. Particularly after World War II, consumption offered the basis for a new social contract for populations eager to move forward from the austere environment of deprivation and devastation. Despite the fact that the critiques of commodity capitalism persisted and the liberal left remained uneasy with an amoral acceptance of luxury, the consumer societies created in the 1950s steered their public toward an area between necessity and luxury, hunger and excess: a mass consumption, comfortable affluent middle ground that all could enjoy.

But as states responded to citizens as consumers, consumers themselves were acknowledged to be an incredibly diverse entity. Standing in as substitutes for the public, the consumer became as varied as society itself. Enrolling the representatives of the consumer into the state therefore became a politically charged matter. The pioneers of independent comparative testing liked to think as themselves as the only—or at least the true—representative of the consumer, but family associations, women's groups, trade unions, and co-operatives still laid claim to being at the vanguard of the consumer cause. The relative power given to any of these groups, both with the new bodies of consumer representation created since the 1950s, and in the general political economic traditions of a state, therefore directed and determined the type of consumer protection regime constructed. Very different overall systems came into being in Europe, America, and the rest of the world. These did not all follow the consumer democracy of the United States, nor did they agree on the definition of the citizen supposedly at the heart of consumer society: he or she could be a social democratic participant in civil society; a co-opted interest within a corporatist structure; a utility-maximizing individual eager to improve his or her own well being at the same time as the efficiency of industry; or a highly politicized rights-seeking individual capable of making demands of, and gaining intervention by, successive governments in the marketplace.

For all that the organized consumer movement might like to see in twentieth-century consumer protection a progressive narrative of success built on success, these great differences in the models of the consumer-citizen suggest otherwise. Consumer activists have often liked to argue that their heyday was in the 1960s and 1970s; if they have declined as a political and social force thereafter it is due to their having achieved many of their own goals. To some extent, they have a right to be so contented for a variety of reasons: compared to the fledgling technocratic age of the 1950s, commodities no longer break down as soon as they are taken home; guarantees and standard contracts ensure forms of redress are available to dissatisfied customers; advertisements might well continue to exaggerate but there are restrictions on overtly false claims; other sources of information are available to shoppers than those provided by the manufacturer or retailer; and, most dramatically, the danger of death and injury from negligently assembled products has declined.

Yet in all the measures that have been successfully implemented there has also been a narrowing of the vision of consumer protection. As states have borrowed best practices from one another, or avoided the mistaken experiments conducted by others, consumer protection has become harmonized. However, as the European experience demonstrates, this harmonization has taken place around narrowly defined individual rights to choice and information and to ever expanding markets. These were crucial elements of the demands of so many consumer groups, but they were not all. Consumers and states had imagined a consumer society open to everybody, in which all could participate and in which all could operate fairly. These were the driving factors behind many of the consumer protection measures introduced just as the affluent society was coming to fruition. They were designed to ensure that protection existed so that every citizen could enjoy the good life.

However, in the later focus on choice, protection became unevenly distributed. Those who can afford to choose alternatives can bear the costs of deceptive practices. But for the poor and disadvantaged, access to such protection is less readily available and their participation in consumer society comes at a struggle and a cost. This runs against the internationalist vision of consumption promoted in the postwar years when, at the height of the Cold War, the advocates and practitioners of communism and capitalism argued the relative merits of each system in bringing more goods to more people. Particularly since consumer society has continued to have a global remit, stretching beyond the industrialized nations of the world and toward Southeast Asia, Latin America and ultimately Africa, these aspects of consumption have remained crucial. But if the definition of the consumer was restricted to choice, then the implications for less developed countries could be profound. The difficulties faced by consumers in the developing world could be very different from those faced by the affluent, but the solutions that have come to be proposed have not emphasized the same rights to access, participation, and improved standards of living as those that defined the consumer societies of Europe and North America in the 1950s and 1960s. It is to these developing world consumers, and the consequent dilemmas and politics facing a movement seeking to represent everybody that we shall turn to in the next chapter.

POVERTY AMID PROSPERITY

Consumer Protest beyond the Affluent West

Consumer activism is a global phenomenon. The principal organization representing consumers at the global level is Consumers International (formerly the International Organisation of Consumers Unions, or IOCU). It has over 220 members from 115 different countries and, in 2007, elected its first African President, Samuel Ochieng of the Kenyan consumer movement. Its reach stretches from the richer societies of Europe and North America to developing states across Asia, Latin America, and Africa, as well as the former Soviet bloc. Inevitably, as organized consumerism has spread throughout the world it has come across consumers with very different interests and concerns than those found in its affluent heartland. Especially in the 1960s and 1970s, as consumer groups began to appear in the developing world, the organized movement had to address the needs of the poor as well as the desires of the rich. The consumer interests emerging from affluence can be very different from those emerging from necessity. Yet as a global movement that has sought to represent everybody, it is precisely these two very different constituencies that the consumer movement has sought to address.

Throughout their history consumer activists have had to maintain a delicate balancing act between poverty and comfort, trading off the interests of those in the global North with those in the global South. Just as political economic considerations created one such dilemma for the consumer movement—between choice and access—so too did the movement's growth in the developing world create new geographical frictions. In order to understand how the movement has existed across the North and the South, across East and West, it is first necessary to learn how the consumer movement emerged and spread in countries where standards of living were well below those in Europe and North America. And to do this it is instructive to turn to the experiences of consumer activists in one such country—Malaysia.

This chapter begins with a case study of the Malaysian consumer activist experience in order to reflect in general on the consumer issues emerging across the developing world. As we will see, despite the clear and obvious impact Malaysian activists have had on the global consumer movement, their activities were indicative of a widespread developing world consumerism that emerged concurrently with the global community's—principally through the United Nations—renewed commitment to third world economic development. Organized consumerism in Malaysia spearheaded developing world consumer activism, but as the final section of the chapter demonstrates, the issues it faced and campaigned on were those that came from, initially, Southeast Asia and, later, Latin America and Africa. In doing so, the problems facing the majority of the world's consumers—access to basic needs—became a defining feature of global consumer activism.

I

The issues confronting consumers and consumer activists in Malaysia in the 1960s and 1970s were very different from those tackled by the national consumer organizations in Europe and North America. By the mid-1970s, the fishermen of Kuala Juru—a village (or *kampung*) in Province Wellesley on the Malaysian mainland—were struggling to maintain their traditional way of life. There were approximately sixty families in the village and they had for generations alternated their fishing patterns between the sea and the river itself. Yet in its desire to attract foreign investment, the Malaysian federal government had facilitated the establishment of a free trade zone across the river Juru at the Perai Industrial Estate. Disastrously for the fishermen, the effluence spewed out by the new factories resulted in the pollution of the river and the devastation of the village's fish stocks. To exacerbate matters further, the government's grandiose New Economic Policy (NEP) had also encouraged a number of huge investment projects designed to bring the country into the developed world. One such scheme was the North-South highway, the main route by which urban Malaysians every Hari Raya holiday rush headlong into one another in their frantic desire to escape Kuala Lumpur and return to the *kampungs* of their families.

In order for the highway to cross the river Juru, the Tun Abdul Razak bridge was built further upstream from Kuala Juru. Unfortunately, it also served as a dam that restricted the flow of water, causing the Juru to meander and to silt at its mouth. This meant the fishermen were only able to reach their alternative inshore fish stocks at high tide and were unable to travel upstream beyond the bridge. Other threats to their livelihood were also experienced. Even when their sampans could reach the coastal fishing grounds, illegal inshore trawling across the Straits of Malacca further depleted the resources available to them. In 1968, the average monthly income of a fisherman had been estimated at $320 (Malaysian dollars). By the early months of 1976, in some cases, monthly incomes were as low as $80. Taking into account the rising cost of living, one study estimated that real disposable incomes were just one-fifth of what they had been prior to 1968.[1]

The case of the fishermen of Kuala Juru can, no doubt, be matched by several thousand other such examples across the globe, especially in Southeast Asia where the so-called tiger economies rushed toward industrialization and urbanization in the 1970s. Amid such massive social and economic change the inevitable casualties were the peasants and fishermen left behind in the *kampungs* of rural Malaysia and the villages of neighboring states. The plight of these disenfranchised groups has largely been understood in terms of resistance and struggle by the numerous journalists, academics, and civil society activists who have flocked to their cause. In a study of the proletarianization of South America peasants on the Columbian sugar plantations and in the Bolivian tin mines, one author has written of the invocation of the devil as ordinary people have sought to make sense of their apparent alienation and subjugation.[2] Where organized opposition is not always possible other "weapons of the weak" can be used. In a study of "everyday forms of peasant resistance" in the paddy-growing area of the Malaysian state of Kedah, class struggle was held to come not in the form of outright confrontation but in non-compliance, foot dragging, deception, and grumbling behind a public façade of conformity and co-operation. The peasants of Sedaka (a dreamed up name of a real paddy-growing village) underwent similar social changes and economic hardship as those in Kuala Juru, as the introduction of new technologies and especially of double-cropping in rice cultivation in 1972 had profound consequences for the social fabric of *kampung* life.[3] The response of the anthropologist who investigated their conditions was, as in the study of South America devilry, to understand their political interventions within a broader understanding of the alienation of workers amid the onset of commodity capitalism.

If we were to comprehend the reactions of Kuala Juru's fishermen from a similar perspective, we could investigate how they challenged the polluters of the Perai Industrial Estate, how they reacted to the government policies that compounded their difficulties, and how they understood themselves as economic agents in the state-sponsored promotion of modern industrial capitalism associated with the ruling party's New Economic Policy. We might expect the fishermen to have turned to the established sites of resistance such as the Malaysian Trade Union Congress or the opposition Islamic Party of Malaysia (*Parti Islam SeMalaysia, PAS*). Yet the response of the Kuala Juru fishermen conforms neither to an analysis based on underhand resistance or an opposition grounded in the politics of the left or of aggrieved fundamentalism. All such interpretations might be rooted in, or explained by, Marx's concept of alien-

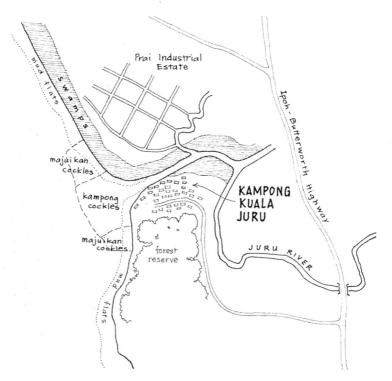

Figure 4. Sketch map of Kuala Juru. From CAP, *Kuala Juru: A People's Co-operative* (Penang: CAP, 1980), 2.

Courtesy of CAP.

ation, in which the identity of the sufferers must primarily be that of workers. Instead, the Kuala Juru fishermen turned not to the trade unions, but to the organized consumer movement. In 1976, they approached the Consumers' Association of Penang (CAP) with a specific request to help them overcome their tragic situation.

Why is it that a struggling community, almost literally bypassed in the process of globalization and economic modernization, should identify itself with an organization committed to a defense of the consumer? Undoubtedly, the fishermen were desperate and, as such, we should not assume they held any great affinity with the consumer cause. But the fact that the Consumers' Association of Penang responded and became their champion suggests a very different notion of consumer activism from what has been witnessed in the West. It demonstrates quite clearly that the response of those left behind in capitalist development cannot always be understood in an overtly ideological manner. Certainly, the fishermen were angry, but this did not translate into a form of political organization or resistance which, on the one hand, a historian of the labor movement might expect or, on the other, a scholar of globalization might assume in the exclusion of the fishermen from the networks of power and capital.

One explanation for the involvement of the consumer movement in such an issue undoubtedly lies in the structures of civil society and the nature of state authority in Malaysia. But the involvement of a consumer group in what was overtly a problem of production—or a problem that affected individuals primarily in their roles as workers—raises questions about both the nature of worker/consumer identities and the meaning of consumer society in states in which the vast majority of citizens were still living in poverty, understood in either relative or in absolute terms. It suggests, as this chapter explores, the meaninglessness of a distinction between how money is earned and how money is spent when there is so very little of it in the first place. Earning and spending become two sides of the same coin, as do poverty and affluence. For by involving itself in an instance of economic and social exclusion, the Consumers' Association of Penang raised the possibility, implicitly acknowledged by Nixon and Khrushchev in their 1959 kitchen debate, that the politics of consumer society was as much about who participated and who did not, as it was about defending the rights of those already within it. In what follows, a case study of Malaysian consumer activism raises more general questions about the place of the developing world in global consumer society. And in the actions of the Consumers' Association of Penang, we can identify a very different form of consumer politics from that emerging in the West and a very different form of consumer activism, both of which would have profound impacts on the global consumer movement and which would ensure that these fundamental questions about participation and exclusion were raised not only in Southeast Asia.

II

The response of the Consumers' Association of Penang (CAP) was to visit Kuala Juru immediately. What it was confronted with was clear evidence that backed up the fishermen's claims. Dead fish floated in the water as the pollution killed those that came near the point at which the factory waste discharged into the river. CAP helped the village to appoint its own leaders, assisting in the establishment of the Kuala Juru Action Committee, which in turn led campaigns for compensation from the factories in the free trade zone, for aid in the form of modern fishing equipment, education and training, and for land on which to cultivate.[4] The Committee met with the Penang Chief Minister, Lim Chong Eu, who had long had links with CAP, and promises were made to provide some form of assistance, particularly in the provision of modern fishing equipment. However, such promises were not acted on and the fishermen were forced to come up with alternative plans for their survival. With the assistance of CAP, and in particular of a young economist Martin Khor (later the Director of Third World Network, an offshoot of CAP) who had recently joined them, the fishermen hit on the idea of cultivating sea-cockles (*kerang*) on the river and sea beds, because the area was highly suitable and demand existed in the local markets.

CAP helped the Action Committee to plan the proposed cockle farm along co-operative principles. Previously, sampan fishing had been a largely individual activity, notwithstanding the collective aspects of *kampung* life, but CAP worked with the fishermen to set out communal work patterns, which reflected the traditions of co-operation within the village community. Detailed plans were set out and then implemented as to the sharing of work and profits, the siphoning off of a certain proportion of dividends to a religious fund (apart from three Chinese families, the entire village was Muslim), a welfare fund, an education project, and the contribution of the village to the Fishermen's Association of Seberang Perai and CAP itself "as a gesture of appreciation."[5] The spirit of co-operation was then taken further, with the leader of the co-operative, Pak Salleh, explaining and extolling the virtues of the experiment to other villages along the coast.

In the short term, the intervention of CAP in Kula Juru was an undoubted success. Instead of encouraging political opposition along traditional party political or ideological lines (as much ethnic as class-based in Malaysia), CAP sought out a practical solution to a specific problem. Pak Salleh and others spoke of the dignity to be found in running the project for themselves, the improvement in their incomes and standard of living, and the community-building aspects of the Village Fund that saw the establishment of a co-operative store and the maintenance of various public and private buildings around the *kampung*. And for CAP the experience of Kuala Juru was no less profound. It marked a transition in its attitudes to consumerism, development, and social justice. In 1980 CAP concluded that "the success of the Juru Co-operative is a symbol of the self-reliance and organizing potential of the fishermen. It has also proven the superiority of collective ventures over individualized efforts."[6] The Kuala Juru case forced CAP to take note of similar stories of pollution and of those left behind by modern development, as well as the absence of controls or—where they existed on paper such as the 1974 Environmental Quality Act—their ineffective enforcement by the state. Along with the villagers CAP realized that effective action can come through taking powerful positions on clear injustices and doing so not according to party political ideology or a predetermined notion as to where an organization's limits lay. For one observer, "the act of standing up against the state" and the chief minister "was as revolutionary an act as could be expected": "poor people realize that they cannot eat militancy."[7] For CAP, as it was faced with so many clear injustices in the 1970s, consumerism would come to mean a principled opposition to many specific abuses within the overall framework of a New Economic Policy that left so many ordinary workers, citizens, and consumers behind.

Kuala Juru acted as a catalyst and a provocation to CAP to think in broader and more critical terms about the politics of consumer society from a developing world perspective. It shifted the analysis to a focus on those excluded from rather than included within the world of goods. CAP's work serves to help us reflect in general on the problems of poor consumers. In one of the earliest studies of developing world consumers, commissioned by the Swedish Consumer Council (Statens Konsumentråd) in the early 1960s, it was found that international aid and economic assistance could be entirely inappropriate if the needs of consumers with weak purchasing power were not considered. For example, advice literature distributed in Tanganyika on household management proved to be ineffective as it was based on the use of goods unobtainable for all but a tiny minority of the population. Instead, it was argued that improving the lot of the consumer required as much attention to their roles as producers as it did to their roles as consumers, especially in the promotion of vegetable cultivation and poultry keeping, activities on which traditional practices of African households are built. Similarly, attention to the poor quality cloth worn by consumers, such as the flimsy cotton wraps or "kangas" favored by many women, drew attention not to information asymetries, unwise purchasing, or the lack of advice literature, but to the absence of indigenous cotton spinning mills, which meant the market relied on cheap imports rather than better quality home-produced goods.

Development initiatives, the report claimed, should take into account traditional skills and local knowledge, as well as customs and habits. Accordingly, the distinction between a producer and a consumer perspective was broken down. The same study of Tanganyikan consumers discussed not the individual purchasing preferences of potential urban consumers, but the communal nature of family and social life, where washing, cleaning, and cooking duties were often shared by families based around a particular block of dwellings. Such collectivist social traditions gave rise to the economic and social philosophy of *ujamaa* (derived from the word for "extended family" or "familyhood" in Swahili) promoted by Julius Nyerere after Tanzania obtained independence in 1964, but they have appeared little in discussions of the consumer in the development literature.[8] Indeed, Nyerere himself was attuned to a consumer perspective. In his 1970 New Year broadcast to the nation, he urged his citizens "to realize that we do not have to live miserably in hovels, or cultivate with bad jembes [hoes], or suffer from many diseases; . . . we ourselves have the ability to obtain better houses, better tools, and better health."[9]

According to the consumer movement, poor people in the developing world do experience problems as consumers. Unsafe products, poor nutrition, adulteration, the absence of locally produced goods, high prices relative to low wages, and the lack of regulations on the market have left the developing world consumer far more alone and atomized than the Western.[10] Women as consumers in particular have experienced greater problems, from the dangers involved in cooking on poorly constructed stoves to the harm caused to their families after the purchase of fraudulently manufactured foods.[11] As the 1985 Filipino Women's Manifesto stated, "We are the housewives who can barely make ends meet because of the dwindling value of the peso and spiralling prices; We are the consumers, victims of monopolies, price fixing, hoarding and false advertising."[12] According to a study conducted in Thailand in 1974, many developing countries existed in a state of "cryptocapitalism" marked by government corruption and the entrenchment of industrial interest groups resulting in a sellers' market. Under these circumstances, Thai consumers were often well aware of the existence of consumer fraud, counterfeit brands, and low-quality products, but were reluctant to take action, given the seemingly insurmountable odds stacked against them.[13]

The consumer movement has urged that attention must be paid to these concerns as well as those of the affluent. It has sought to apply the principles of Article 25 of the Universal Declaration of Human Rights: "Everyone has the right to a standard of living adequate for health and well-being of himself and of his family, including food, clothing, housing and medical care."[14] It is precisely these concerns that motivated organizations such as the Consumers Association of Penang. Notwithstanding the incredible social, cultural, and political differences across the developing world, the similar set of economic and market-based problems allows us to focus in on one national consumer movement to draw attention to more general questions that have faced developing world consumers. Just a decade after the formation of a consumer movement across North America and Western Europe in the 1950s, a clear trend could be seen in the extension of organized consumerism into the developing world, united more around questions of access to basic needs than the freedom of choice enjoyed in the selection of comforts and luxuries.

Perhaps the earliest consumer organization to emerge outside of Europe and North America was the Kenya Consumers' Organization. Although it did not officially adopt this name until 1974, it had been in existence since 1951 when self-styled "housewives" had come together in Nairobi to boycott stores known to overcharge customers.[15] Yet consumerism as a basic needs movement developed more readily in Asia, perhaps building on the traditions and tactics of the *swadeshi* movement spearheaded by Ghandi. In 1956, the Indian Association of Consumers emerged, and similar initiatives were begun in Pakistan around the same time. In Southeast Asia, organized consumerism proved particularly popular. In 1963, the Consumers Federated Groups of the Philippines was launched, followed by the Consumer Association of Singapore (CASE) in 1971, the Philippine Consumers Movement (*Kilusan ng mga Mamimili ng Philipinas, Ink., KMPI*) also in 1971, and the Indonesian Consumers Organisation (*Yayasan Lembaga Konsumen Indonesia, YLKI*) in 1973.[16]

In Malaysia, the first move to create a consumer movement began in December 1964. The Penang Consumers' Association was established to campaign against high prices and was set up by the Member of Parliament (MP) Dr. Lim Chong Eu. Lim was a former president of the Malaysian Chinese Association and later a member of the opposition party, *Gerakan:* in 1976, he would prove incapable of responding adequately to the Kuala Juru fishermen.[17] In 1964, though, his new consumer organization was unable to keep members interested and the Association never progressed beyond its first meeting, though it inspired a number of professionals, teachers, and civil servants to create an equivalent body, the Selangor Consumers' Association (SCA) in Kuala Lumpur just one month later.[18] Initially prompted by the concern of middle-class Malaysians with the cost of newspaper delivery charges, the SCA soon went on to adopt many of the classic concerns associated with the consumer movements of Western Europe and North America. By the end of the 1960s, the SCA had begun a complaints service, was publishing its own magazine *Berita Pengguna* (*Consumer News*), and was giving talks to schools, rotary clubs, and other bodies typical of metropolitan associational life. It had also begun to engage in some rudimentary forms of product testing and its membership base consisted of around 2,000 white-collar workers, two-thirds of whom were male. Furthermore, many members held prominent positions around the city and had links to the Selangor *Menteri Besar* (Chief Minister) as well as federal government departments that looked favorably on this fledgling consumer movement as a means to educate consumers to support Malaysian industry and to assist in the efficient running of the market.[19]

The focus of this chapter, though, are those consumer organizations that have persisted in directing their attention to the poor and the disadvantaged rather than the minority municipal elites that have had more in common with their consumer equivalents in the West. The Consumers' Association of Penang constitutes the ideal case study to examine in more detail the consumer politics of the developing world. CAP was not only one of the strongest consumer movements outside of Europe and North America, but ultimately one of the principal agenda setters for the consumer movement as a whole. Its staff and ideas had an impact not only within Malaysia but on the whole dynamic of global civil society and the operations of many other international non-governmental organizations as well. And the issues it has had to deal with in a country undergoing rapid industrialization has meant its activities have often reached into the heart of the tensions operating within consumer society globally.

III

The Malaysian consumer movement cannot be understood without reference to the landmark events in Kuala Lumpur of 1969. On 13 May, three days after the federal elections that had seen the ruling Alliance fail to secure a two-thirds majority, racial riots broke out in the capital. The Malay vote had been split between the government and the opposition in many states enabling the Chinese candidates of the Democratic Action Party (DAP) and Gerakan (Malaysian's

People's Movement, or *Gerakan Rakyat Malaysia*) to secure notable victories. Supporters of the latter two parties took to the streets in celebration, only waiting for ethnic Malays to respond, and a series of racial riots ensued. By 14 May the government had declared a state of emergency and, according to official figures, 196 people had died and 409 had been injured.[20]

Most commentators agree that the government response to the riots led to a further repression of civil society and the consolidation of race as the dominant form of political rhetoric in Malaysia (the population is roughly one-tenth Indian, one-third Chinese, and just over one-half Malay). Most famously, Malaysia's fourth prime minister and exponent of "Asian values," Mahathir Mohamad, then regarded as a firebrand politician, argued along eugenicist lines that centuries of feudalism and colonialism, together with the favorable conditions of the Malaysian climate, had rendered rural Malays a weak, inbred, and passive race. Only through affirmative action could the poor Malay peasant be brought into the modern world so that he could assume his true position—economically, socially, culturally, and politically—within independent Malaysia; otherwise, he was likely to become frustrated and resort to running *amok* as in the 1969 riots.[21] For his reaffirmation of "the myth of the lazy native" and his inflammation of existing racial tensions, Mahathir was temporarily expelled from the United Malays National Organization (UMNO, the principal party of the ruling Alliance). However, his arguments were subsequently enshrined in the New Economic Policy of the 1970s promoted by the new ruling, again UMNO-dominated, coalition of the *Barisan Nasional* (BN, National Front).[22] The NEP aimed to eradicate poverty among ethnic Muslim Malays by providing special privileges in education and capital ownership for the so-called *bumiputera* ("sons of the soil"). In response to the 1969 riots an ascendant Malay nationalism was placed at the heart of Malaysian economic development, which ensured the perpetuation of a communalist politics and its reach into all areas of life, given the attendant restrictions on other forms of social and political organizing.[23]

It is this context that explains the rise of the Consumers' Association of Penang.[24] According to Anwar Fazal, a principal founder of CAP, the riots were very much in the minds of the organization's creators as they sought to find "a new type of public commentary" not inflected by communal politics and which could sidestep the prohibitions on political activity after 1969.[25] To the authorities, consumer organizing was "neutral" and "respectable," all the more so since the first President of CAP, S. M. Mohamed Idris, had himself stood unsuccessfully in the Penang state elections on an UMNO ticket.[26]

This is not to say that consumerism in Malaysia did not emerge out of the classic concerns of consumers the world over. Anwar Fazal, inspired by such works as Ralph Nader's *Unsafe at Any Speed,* working as a government official in Penang's capital, Georgetown, organized numerous talks, displays, and meetings on consumer protection in the late 1960s, particularly in collaboration with the City Council's Food and Drug Department; and Idris himself had long been associated with "progressive causes that transcended politics."[27] Independent Malaysia's emerging middle class, insecure about the changes taking place in a modernizing market place, began to see the benefits of consumer organizing—just as the Western middle class did. The riots merely acted as a catalyst to these developments, but they did so with an added potency because they provided consumerism with a symbolic opportunity to unite Malaysians from all backgrounds around common causes.[28]

Organizational support for the foundation of CAP came from the University of Malaya Graduates' Society, with its appropriately named post-riot newsletter, *The Phoenix,* and CAP was launched at the end of 1969.[29] It entered Malaysian civil society at a time when few other voluntary organizations were tolerated. While its primary focus was ostensibly to be on practical day-to-day consumer concerns such as product quality, under-weight and fraudulent selling, and the fixing of prices, it was ideally placed to tackle a wider set of socio-economic issues addressed by few other groups operating beyond the communalist confines of the party political system. As Idris would later claim, consumer problems affect everybody regardless of race and, as such, organized consumerism is vital to the achievement of racial unity and avoiding the "inter-racial back-biting" elsewhere so frequently observed in Malaysia.[30]

CAP's immediate focus was on core consumer issues—consumer education, complaints handling, exposing market abuses, pressing for protective legislation—but its officers soon realized "the potential power of this movement."[31] CAP could fight for a basic consumer injustice, such as the use of a prawn-paste Blachan, adulterated with the toxin Rhodomine-B, and then appeal to all consumers, rich and poor alike, because the flavoring was a staple of Malaysian cooking.[32] CAP realized—to a far greater extent than in the West—that there were two types of consumer in Malaysia: the poor and the rich—and that different interests arose accordingly and had to be dealt with in different ways. It meant that CAP's operating activities expanded incrementally in the 1970s, moving from one specific issue to the next, while at the same time extrapolating from the particular to comment on the general issues facing all consumers and the structural causes that prevented the poor from having the same access to consumer rights and opportunities as the rich. For Anwar Fazal, the dynamic of CAP lay in its gradual shifts in consumer policy: "Our language changed as CAP broadened out to cover bigger issues. We took care to take individual complaints seriously; and that rootedness connected us to the wider lifestyle. This link, from the particular to the general, was the basis of CAP's mandate. Each complaint was the embodiment of a whole structure behind it."[33]

Shortly after its formation CAP was addressing a range of issues that questioned the model of development then being pursued by the Malaysian government. It began to turn its attention to the activities of multinational corporations and it asked questions about the effects of modernization on the environment.[34] It questioned the "colossal waste of public funds" diverted to prestige projects such as the construction of Penang Bridge.[35] And it identified problems that would become not only the celebrated issues of Malaysian consumerism, but the rallying points for an expanding global civil society in the 1970s and 1980s, including the marketing of inappropriate breast milk substitutes and the inadequate regulation of pesticides (as set out in the Pesticides Act of 1974).[36]

The case of the Kuala Juru fishermen came at a crucial moment in CAP's history. Just as CAP leaders had begun to focus on wider developmental issues, here was a specific problem that seemed to touch on the broadest questions about pollution, international trade agreements, consumer welfare, and the power of the nation-state to protect its citizens. At this point, Idris claimed that it was time to "get tough" with private enterprise and government.[37] By the mid-1970s CAP had transformed itself from defending individual consumers to using consumption as the entry point to criticize the whole society supposedly being built in their name. Kuala Juru symbolically represented a transition in CAP's work when it came to question the entire process of development, but it also demonstrated the incremental expansion of its activities: CAP had identified a specific problem and responded to it as it saw fit. This typifies what one commentator claims has been the "organic" growth of CAP: "it has listened to and responded to the needs of the people . . . as these have arisen; it has facilitated and supported popular resistance as and when it has been asked to do so. This is how the critique of development has evolved—not according to theory or any preconceived idea of what development is or is not, but by weighing the effects of this or that project on the people who are supposed to be the beneficiaries or who turn out to be disadvantaged by it."[38]

Here was a model of consumerism that took account of not only the interests of individual shoppers but the concerns of those seemingly excluded from consumer society. And here was a model of social and economic engagement of tremendous attraction to a rising generation of Malaysian activists. When interviewed, CAP staff have attested to the appeal of an organization that presented an alternative form of development based on a different value framework than one found in the "money-driven" consumer society.[39] CAP's activities, as expressed in its newspaper, *Utusan Konsumer,* were attractive to a wider population concerned with both the strengths and weaknesses of development; that is, they appreciated CAP's concerns with basic consumer issues and also admired its focus on people who were not able to share in the rising consumption patterns.[40] Sales of *Utusan Konsumer* had reached 6,500 in the 1970s and in May of 1979 a *Bahasa Malaysia* edition was launched. This helped take sales to 25,000 by 1981 and 40,000 just four years later, a figure all the more remarkable if one compares it to the figure of 200,000 that represented the largest circulation for a daily newspaper in Malaysia in the mid-1980s.[41]

By this time, CAP's work was being directed to a whole series of cases similar to Kuala Juru. It examined the plight of Malaysian fishermen in general, as well as those of other communities, be they rural market gardeners deprived of their traditional farming patterns, padi farmers whose crops were destroyed by industrial pollution or the indigenous (*Orang Asli*) populations pushed aside to make way for commercial logging.[42] Though issues of value-for-money to self-interested shoppers remained core concerns,[43] CAP's approach to the whole notion of consumer society meant it also critiqued advertising and marketing practices, the portrayal of women in the media, and the inequities of a global trading system that enabled multinationals to engage in practices (such as the selling of dangerous pharmaceuticals), which had been banned elsewhere. The environment remained such a persistent problem that Idris established CAP's first sister organization Friends of the Earth Malaysia (SAM, *Sahabat Alam Malaysia*) in 1977, with himself as president.[44]

Idris argued that there needed "to be a radical rethinking of development concepts, economic strategies, even the concepts of law and justice, if the people are going to survive."[45] In 1987, he prophesized the apocalyptic nature of Malaysian development under the slogan, "stop the train, we're going to crash." Moreover, CAP's Research Director, Martin Khor, launched a broad-ranging assessment of Malaysia thirty years after independence, highlighting the restrictions on democracy, equality and civil liberties, the absence of social justice measures within development programs, and the diversion of resources away from the poor to self-glorifying and wasteful luxury projects.[46] To blame was the "businessman's government" whose politicians continued to divert the people with arguments about race, while engaging in corrupt practices themselves and adorning one another with state and federal honors awarded by the sultans.[47] While the government promoted prestige projects such as the North-South Highway, Penang Bridge, the Petronas Twin Towers, and the Kuala Lumpur International Airport, CAP emphasized the traditional Malaysian customs and values associated with *kampung* life and the indigenous forms of technology as found in the traditional Malay house.[48]

For all the respectability of consumer activism as compared to the seemingly more radical enterprises of human rights activism and ecological protest, it is of little surprise that CAP's activities by the 1980s had begun to attract the attention of the federal authorities. In 1987, Mahathir, then prime minister of an increasingly authoritarian government, decided to clamp down on an expanding civil society by drawing up a list of those to be detained under the Internal Security Act. In *Operasi Lallang*, Mahathir launched a crackdown on his political opponents and members of civil society groups, which led to the arrest of over 100 members of the opposition parties, the Chinese education movement and prominent NGO activists. Also included was CAP's legal officer Meena Rahman, and SAM's activist in Sarawak, Harrison Ngau, while Martin Khor (who at the time was in Europe) and Idris himself were rumored to have been on the original list.[49] Mahathir's intention had been to send out a warning to what he perceived to be an irritating NGO community and to nip in the bud an increasingly vociferous anti-development agenda.[50]

CAP's Meena Raman was included on the list because she had defended the land rights of a group of small market gardeners on the Thean Teik estate in

Penang and had been involved in the Asian Rare Earth radioactive waste case where she had defended the residents of Bukit Merah in the state of Perak in their campaign to prevent the dumping of dangerous wastes in their area.[51] Raman found herself detained with other members of the Perak Anti-Radioactivity Committee, as well as allies in the Environmental Protection Society of Malaysia. Her arrest with Harrison Ngau reflected government anger at CAP and SAM's support for the indigenous Penan people of Sarawak in their struggles against commercial loggers. Placed in solitary confinement for forty-seven days and given no access to ordinary legal procedures, she has never been formally charged or given an official explanation for her supposed crime.[52]

Arrest and imprisonment are certainly not the experiences we associate with the consumer movements of Western Europe and North America, yet the intimidation and harassment of consumer activists is not specific to Malaysia. In Greece, following the refusal of the Consumers Protection Institute to accept any financial funding from the governing military junta and its boycott of high-priced products and polluting manufacturers, seven members of its Council were arrested in March 1974 while its founder, Haralambos Kouris, fled to Germany. Despite protests from the international community, they were held in a prison presided over by a security officer well known as a torturer and were not released until after the collapse of the Regime of the Colonels in July of the same year.[53] In the Philippines, at the end of 1980, the government attempted to arrest the consumer and labor activist, Nicky Morales, using an Arrest, Search and Seizure order. He went into hiding from where he wrote to the Labor Committee of the Philippine Consumers Movement explaining his politics of consumption. He had come under the scrutiny of the military authorities because he believed the protection of poor consumers to be a movement for "liberation," whereby the laboring classes would be united "under the banner of consumerism." Eventually, his friends and supporters were able to smuggle him to Hong Kong, from where he then escaped to the United States, supported by a grant from the international consumer movement (the "Colstone Warne prize"), which provided him with an income for one year.[54]

It is not difficult to understand why CAP had attracted Mahathir's attention in 1987. By 1987 CAP appeared to have an economic agenda, a set of ideas that could form the basis of a social welfare program, a populist cultural celebration of traditional "Malaysian" values, a range of charges against the ruling government, and a Third World perspective that had the potential to direct foreign and international trade policy. Consequently, it had come to the attention of the international community. S. M. Mohamed Idris was a winner of a Right Livelihood Award (the "alternative Nobel Prize") in 1988 (along with Harrison Ngau) and CAP's work attracted a number of foreign volunteers and interest by international campaigning journalists.[55] This was simply incompatible with the restrictions placed on Malaysian civil society by a state variously described as semi-authoritarian, quasi-democratic or, for those who have had greater experience of its restrictive interventions, authoritarian.[56]

Throughout the 1970s, the Internal Security Act was frequently used to detain political insurgents, preventing the flourishing of NGOs. Despite the existence of older philanthropic bodies, ratepayer groups, Rotary Clubs, educational clubs, and religious associations, the NGO community of the 1970s was largely confined to the women's movement, the human rights movement, environmental protectionism, and the growth of Islamic organizations.[57] For instance, CAP was joined in Penang by the human rights NGO and reform think tank Aliran (*Aliran Kesedran Negara,* or National Consciousness Movement), established in 1977, led by Chandra Muzaffar, another detainee under *Operasi Lallang.*[58] The other particularly prominent NGO in this period was the Malaysian Islamic Youth Movement (*Angkatan Belia Islam Malaysia, ABIM*), founded and presided over by the future deputy prime minister, Anwar Ibrahim, from 1974 to 1982.

This did not constitute an independent civil society equivalent to—or comparable to—that which has been said to exist in the West. Many of the main civil society groups really only flourished and expanded in the 1980s and the state's persistent interference in the activities of the press and social activists severely restricted oppositional politics. In many ways, then, CAP's rise to prominence in the 1970s was largely due to the absence of alternative NGOs, other than a moderate women's movement and a Malaysian Trades Union Congress closely monitored by the state authorities.[59] This led CAP into tackling issues which, elsewhere, might have been dealt with by other organizations and so the advantages of organizing as consumers rather than as citizens, workers, or human rights activists were apparent. Yet this should not lead us into arguing that CAP was simply a front for other progressive causes. CAP's consumer activism emphasized the satisfaction of the needs of the majority of the population rather than the desires of an affluent minority. It had developed an "ideology" or practice of consumerism, which succeeded rather than preceded its approach to specific market abuses and which became radically different from that of the consumer testing organizations of the West from which it had originally taken its cue. In this model of consumer politics, the distinction between citizen and consumer was indistinguishable and consumer issues were synonymous with environmentalism and the post-colonial struggle against economic development in general. Where the majority of consumers are poor, access to goods and services becomes the primary consumer demand, and the systems of providing such goods and services the primary focus of consumer advocacy. Indeed, after creating SAM as an offshoot of CAP, Idris went on to establish Third World Network (TWN), with CAP's economist Martin Khor as director. To this day, Idris remains President of all three organizations with TWN in particular now assuming a prominent role among global NGO activists, while Khor is a frequent speaker at meetings such as the European and World Social Forums and is regarded as one of the leaders of the so-called anti-globalization movement.[60]

CAP persisted in these broader consumerist politics after the 1987 arrests. It continued to campaign on a similar range of issues and has attacked the government on its policies in relation to, for instance, indigenous land rights, rural poverty, the education system, and the environment.[61] A subtle change can be detected in CAP's rhetoric however. Although Idris's own political formation had begun in the 1940s amid the anti-colonialist concerns of Indian nationalism and his own commitment to Jinnah's vision of an independent Pakistan, by the 1970s his focus had turned away from the West and toward the Malaysian state. But after the detentions of *Operasi Lallang,* criticism and blame of the government were pronounced less vociferously. Instead, the new system of global economic governance emerging from the Uruguay Round of trade negotiations (especially the creation of the World Trade Organization) meant that Idris and CAP renewed their anti-colonial attack on the West. This has occurred at the same time that Mahathir has wished to present himself as a potential leader of the Third World, and thus the former opponents have found much common ground—especially during the Asian financial crisis of the late 1990s when both CAP and Mahathir shunned the advice of the International Monetary Fund and thus avoided many of the worst effects of the recession that shook Malaysia's neighboring states.[62] As we will see in chapter 8, while Western consumer organizations have remained committed to the principle of free trade, Third World Network has advocated certain protectionist measures that some would argue reduce the benefits to consumers.

IV

The history of CAP is not the history of consumerism in its entirety in Malaysia. There have been other consumer organizations that reflect the tensions of activism within a more authoritarian state and which demonstrate the differences in developing world consumer perspectives, which are by no means uniform. Indeed, CAP had been preceded in Malaysia by the Selangor Consumers' Association (SCA). In 1969, SCA officials assisted in the creation of CAP, as well as in other Malaysian states as the SCA Vice-President Syed Adam Al-Ja'fri, traveled around the country on a mission to create a movement.[63] The next logical stage was to develop a national federation of consumer groups. CAP publicized the developments in consumer organizing in *Utusan Konsumer* and pushed for a National Consumer Council.[64] Its staff met with representatives of the SCA for such a purpose in 1970 and again in 1971.[65] A National Consumer Council was in fact proposed, with Syed Adam as the first secretary-general, but at this time government scrutiny of the SCA's activities had led to a formal protest and the resignation of the entire SCA committee. As a means of highlighting the abusive powers of the police and the state, the SCA plan backfired, because it enabled a new committee to be elected far more amenable to the interests of business and much more willing to work with the government, including the seeking of financial support and the consequent loss of independence. CAP, emphasizing the importance of complete consumer independence, refused to negotiate any further with the SCA in the formation of a consumer federation and the impetus shifted to the federal state.[66]

The Malaysian Ministry of Commerce and Industry believed it would be useful to have a movement with which to link up, particularly in the areas of prices and inflation.[67] In June 1973, the Federation of Malaysian Consumers' Associations (FOMCA) was formed under the leadership of Mohamed Sopiee, Malaysia's director of information. FOMCA was formed through the direct initiative of the government, helped on a practical level by the new secretary of the SCA who had close links with that government.[68] For CAP, the links between FOMCA and the government have remained too close and to this day CAP has remained independent of the Federation.[69]

FOMCA has nevertheless expanded as consumer organizations have appeared in every Malaysian state, culminating with the Consumers' Association of Sabah (CASH) in Borneo in 1980. Most of these associations have suffered from a limited membership base but this has not put consumer leaders off from trying to become a mass-based organization, nor have their funding from government sources deterred many from following CAP's lead. According to Mohd Hamdan Adnan, president of FOMCA from 1991 to 2004, "consumerism in Malaysia is a social movement that is crusading for a just society."[70] Rokia Talib, a chair of the National Advisory Council for Consumer Protection and an Honorary Secretary of the SCA, argued that consumerism "is basically a social movement concerned with the value for people and their lifestyle, and the value for money spent by consumers in the marketplace."[71] Several consumer leaders have attempted to develop consumerism into a grassroots movement: Bishan Singh of the Pahang Consumers' Association set up a network of district associations across the federal state of Pahang in the 1970s while the SCA established a number of district committees in the early 1980s, which attempted to mobilize consumers around such CAP-inspired projects as deforestation as well as encouraging school children to protest against junk food.[72]

If CAP chose to resist hegemonic understandings of development in the 1970s and 1980s, FOMCA has nevertheless had to adopt a "consensual and collaborative" role. For many, this relationship has been too close. It has smacked of co-option and has lain behind CAP's continued decision not to join FOMCA. Yet the activities of—and the relationship between—CAP and FOMCA attest to the problems of consumer organizing in general in developing countries. On the one hand, closer relationships have had to be developed with states that have secured the financial viability of the enterprise but that have risked a consequent lack of independence. On the other hand, where consumer groups have been able to connect with the concerns of the majority poor, radically different forms of consumer politics have emerged, which offer important challenges to the meanings of both consumer society and consumer activism. These contradictions have undoubtedly prevented consumerism emerging as strong a social force as its leaders would perhaps have liked or imagined. In Malaysia, one can only speculate as to how powerful the consumer movement might have been had the intellectual influence and radicalism of CAP been combined with the potential practical influence of FOMCA through its representative role in the government.

However, these institutional dilemmas have merely provided a further set of difficulties for a global consumer movement already having to cope with the challenge of expanding into the developing world. It meant a politics of basic needs, access, and participation came in direct contact with a politics of choice, freedom, and protection. These competing agendas are explored further in later chapters, but for our purposes here they demonstrate that any organization seeking to represent consumers internationally had to take account of the poor as well as the affluent of both the global South and of the global North.

The growth in consumer organizing in countries such as Malaysia was reflected in the increasing number of consumer groups affiliating themselves to the international federation. In 1970, IOCU could count among its members consumer groups from Pakistan, Puerto Rico, Trinidad, Jamaica, Nigeria, and India.[73] Undoubtedly, many of these consumer organizations were the products of urban, affluent, and often colonial elites, but as they sought to represent the whole variety of consumer concerns in their respective countries, they contributed to a movement that spoke of the concerns of the poor. They were soon joined by consumer organizations from Guyana, Sri Lanka, Indonesia, Korea, Thailand, Vietnam, Hong Kong, and Mexico and by the 1980s, consumerism as a social movement could claim to be truly global. At an international gathering of consumers in Bangkok in 1984, organizations from twelve Asian countries, three states of Latin America, and five African countries were represented.[74]

These figures under-represent the strength of the Latin American and African consumer movements, because of the difficulties of physically getting to Bangkok, but they do at least attest to the diversity and geographic spread of consumerism in the Asia-Pacific region throughout the 1960s and 1970s. Certainly, many of these relied on state funding, as in the case of FOMCA, but by the mid-1970s it was fair to point to a considerable number of organizations acting exclusively on behalf of consumers that were voluntary and democratic in character, as well as being largely independent and uninfluenced by other organized or institutional interests.[75] At the southern end of this region were the affluent Anglophone organizations of Australia and New Zealand. At the very north was the incredible range of consumer groups from Japan. These included women's organizations such as Shufuren and Chifuren and the Consumers Union of Japan, originally founded by men in 1969 as a counter to the existing consumer groups dominated by women. The Consumers Union of Japan took its cue from the muckraking exposé traditions of U.S. consumer activism and developed an all-encompassing consumer politics similar to that of CAP's. It claimed to campaign generally for "the enhancement of human life and health" and provided the means for establishing better links between the previously fragmented civil society groups connected to the anti-pollution movement, the anti-nuclear movement, and the nature preservation cause.[76]

Between these geographic extremes existed other prominent consumer organizations. The Indian consumer movement has certainly been the most diverse. Although many of the consumer groups that have sprung up around the country, and especially in Delhi have proved short-lived, other—such as the Consumer Guidance Society (established in 1966 in Bombay), the Consumer Education and Research Centre (1978, Ahmedabad), the Voluntary Organisation in Interest of Consumer Education (1983, New Delhi), and the Consumer Unity and Trust Society (1983, Rajasthan)—have advocated a consumerism that has focused on basic needs such as food security concerns and the environment, drawing especially on Gandhian philosophical traditions.[77] Indeed, the Indian consumer movement, marked by moralistic and ethical undertones, has focused its attention on the concerns of the poor rather than the rich: activists have spoken of the necessities of "food, clothing and shelter" (*roti, kapda aur makan*), adding over the years other basic consumer needs of water, sanitation, and education.[78] The Indian consumer movement received a huge boost with the passing of the 1986 Consumer Protection Act, which enabled consumer organizations to file legal petitions on behalf of consumers. This spur to public interest group action led to the proliferation of local consumer groups, resulting in an estimated 2,000 consumer organizations operating around the country.[79]

A similar focus on basic needs, or on a consumerism that emphasizes the "fundamental right to survival" can be seen in places such as Pakistan and Bangladesh.[80] Certainly the protection of consumers as an activity of the state is an idea that has spread around the region.[81] Consumer movements have been identified in the remotest of locations from as far afield as Nepal, Fiji, Vietnam, Papua New Guinea, Mongolia, and the Pacific Islands.[82] But the strongest organizations appeared in countries witnessing rapid social and economic change in the 1970s. As well as in Malaysia, the region's most prominent consumer movements have developed in the Philippines, Thailand, and Indonesia.[83] The Filipino consumer movement has witnessed divisions between the radical and the reformist, similar to CAP and FOMCA, and the Indonesian Consumers Organisation (YLK) could claim to have had an equal impact on the international movement, not least because the YLK's Erma Witoelar became the president of the international movement from 1991 to 1997. The YLK's necessary focus on basic needs has led to successful campaigns in the spheres of food additives, the use of condensed milk as a baby food, pesticide sales, and a whole range of environmental problems.[84]

It would be inappropriate to claim that the Malaysian consumer movement, and CAP in particular, was the inspiration for all of these developing world consumer initiatives. The range of organizations was simply too diverse for that, and many were able to arrive at similar conclusions as CAP at the same time. CAP did certainly spearhead the developing world perspective within the global consumer debates, but just as in the West, the consumer interest promoted by such organizations grew out of the ordinary concerns facing consumers in their everyday lives in these countries. It would be fruitless to compare the statistical evidence for patterns of consumption with those of the industrialized, capitalist world so obvious is it that poverty was the primary experience of the majority of consumers in these countries during the difficult moments of economic transition. Such bodies as CAP in Malaysia and KMPI in the Philippines were led and run by a small minority of urban elites; eventually, if they were to configure their activities as a social movement, their concerns would have to shift to the interests, problems, and issues facing all consumers in their countries. As we have seen in the case of CAP, such a shift could create a very different politics of consumption and these organizations could face hostility and repression in authoritarian contexts. But also, it meant the politics of global consumer society had to take into account the activism of these basic needs consumerists. As we will see, developing world consumer activism created dilemmas for a consumer movement that sought to represent everybody, rich and poor alike, but it pointed also to the dilemmas we have all faced in consumer society as to whether we wish to improve choice for the individual or to improve the opportunities for others to enjoy any choice at all.

V

We cannot complete our case study of Malaysia and CAP without finishing the story of the fishermen of Kuala Juru. Here there was an unintended irony, which points to the internal dilemmas of consumerism in the developing world. In the short and the medium term, the cockle co-operative was a success for the village. Rising incomes were ploughed into communal ventures decided on by the Action Committee. It also left sufficient monies for the fishermen to spend on themselves and their families. Indeed, so improved were some incomes that many enjoyed unprecedentedly high standards of living. For some villagers and outside observers this was an ambiguous gain. Commercial, albeit co-operative, enterprise had arguably provoked more materialist lifestyles, which some villagers believed had the potential to "break up our old way of living."[85] In seeking an alternative developmental model, it was as though CAP had encouraged the westernization of consumption patterns, which went against its own faith in traditional Malaysian values.

Despite that CAP eschewed an overtly ideological position, and despite that it sought to respond to specific issues with specific solutions, there was and is an undoubted anti-Western perspective to its politics of consumption. Since the 1980s, CAP has resorted to a defensive attack against the West, which has much sympathy across Malaysia and the developing world in general. But its invocations of traditional ways of life rest uncomfortably with the pursuit of mass consumption enjoyed by a new generation of Malaysians keen to enjoy the fruits of their hard labor.[86] It has resulted in an attack on a whole variety of "western" goods, which CAP believes damages the physical, emotional, and social health of the people, but which goes against the desires of the vast majority of consumers if the statistics of these goods' consumption is anything to go by.[87] In the rising levels of consumption in Kuala Juru, especially of western-style goods, CAP officials could only observe their success with some discomfort.

Consumers in Malaysia have been implicitly criticized by CAP for purchasing non-"Malaysian" goods and Western commodities as a whole have been condemned for the moral and physical degradation they cause. There are three quotations kept on Idris's desk for him to observe every day. There is an extract from Simone de Beauvoir on the value of life;[88] the full version of St. Francis's "A simple prayer"; and Henry Wadsworth Longfellow's "The Village Blacksmith" with its invocation of the "honest sweat" of real work, which allows a man to look "the whole world in its face."[89] These three passages amount to a worldview that fuels CAP's and Idris's anti-westernism and their idealist demands for an alternative way of life, which embraces an assumed communitarianism of the past and rejects an equally assumed individualism of the present. Yet, in the mega-malls and shopping centers of Penang and Kuala Lumpur, it is a message of simplicity unheard by a rising generation keen to enjoy the rewards of their parents' hard work in the struggle to obtain First World status as set out in Mahathir's Vision 2020. If the so-called Asian values were cynically promoted by Mahathir and Lee Kuan Yew of Singapore so that Southeast Asian citizens surrendered political freedoms for economic growth, it was a trade off many were keen to accept.[90] According to one critic, Malaysians have embraced a culture of "developmentalism" in which they have welcomed "not only economic growth, rising living standards, and the resultant consumerist lifestyles, but also the political stability which it necessitated, associated in the minds of most Malaysians with the BN [National Front]."[91] Does CAP's consumerist critique of consumerism therefore find itself consigned to the harshest decades of economic transition?

Another way of putting the question is to ask just how much is enough? It is a central predicament at the heart of the politics of consumption. Clearly, most people are committed to ensuring that those living in abject poverty are able to escape their destitute condition and enjoy the benefits of the world of goods. But at what point does that participation threaten any pre-existing culture, normatively held to be morally superior or, from an environmentalist perspective, ecologically sustainable? The world welcomes China into the society of consumers, but what if every one of its 1.3 billion consumers purchases as much as an average American?

Notwithstanding these important considerations to which we will return, we should not be blind to the appeal of CAP's consumer political vision and its style of activism in the 1970s and 1980s. A cartoonist named Lat enjoys great commercial success in Malaysia. His character, *Kampung Boy,* is portrayed in various scenes taken from his creator's rural childhood. For a generation of middle-age Malayians who now enjoy material success, Kampung Boy's appeal is easy to understand as, amid the rapid economic and social changes witnessed in concrete form in Kuala Lumpur on a weekly basis, his images offer psychological security in the memory of the privations—but also the pleasures—of a rural childhood *kampung* existence.[92] These cultural reifications have bolstered the radical critiques against the West offered by Idris and have formed the backbone of a conservative nationalism embraced by UMNO and Mahathir. In many ways, their popularity mirrors and even explains the high sales of CAP's *Utusan Konsumer*. CAP appealed to a generation of Malaysians enjoying certain benefits of economic growth, who at the same time were ill at ease with such changes as they remembered their own poverty and way of life (just as the rationality of Western product testing appealed to the frugal sentiments of an affluent generation raised amid the deprivations of the 1930s depression). Whether it will continue to appeal to today's young Malaysians is another matter, especially because civil society is increasingly dominated by human rights perspectives, and organizations.

Indeed, this focus on human rights by powerful Malaysian NGOs such as Aliran, *Suara Rakyat Malaysia* (*Suaram*, Voice of the Malaysian People), and *Tenaganita* (Women's Force), alerts us the specificities of CAP's activism. It adopted an explicitly non-ideological and non-partisan consumer politics, which focused on single issues and which resulted in the incremental growth of its campaigns and programs over the decades. For Western consumer groups, independence from business and any political party have been crucial to their operations as they have extrapolated from specific consumer abuses to more general problematizations of market structures. For Malaysian consumer activists, transethnic solidarities were vital means to address social and economic questions otherwise ignored by a communalist party politics. For CAP, practical consumer concerns led to the expansion of its activities, notwithstanding the long-term anti-colonial discourse of figures such as S. M. Mohamed Idris. Ideology—in terms of what constitutes the Left and the Right—did not play a prescriptive role in the determination of issues to be addressed and the solutions proposed. Instead, single issues have been the key to its activities and its appeal both within and beyond Malaysia.

For all the problems of CAP, the restrictions placed on it and its increasingly contradictory attitudes to consumption patterns, it must be re-emphasized that it has been incredibly influential. Its work proved particularly appealing to an international community, long before the establishment of what is now the most well known of Idris's three organizations—Third World Network. Lacking finances from federal authorities in Malaysia, CAP has been able to bolster its income from the sales of *Utusan Konsumer* with international grants from development agencies and other NGOs such as Christian Aid. Its work attracted the attention of the British activist and writer, Jeremy Seabrook, who had long planned a biography of Idris and his work, while the UK Labour MP Jeremy Corbyn even cited *Utusan Konsumer* in the House of Commons in 1994.[93] To take one crude measure of influence, we can count the number of winners from CAP of the Right Livelihood Award. This "alternative Nobel Prize" was awarded to Idris and Harrison Ngau in 1988, and other activists connected with CAP have gone on to win it. In 2005, the founder and director of *Tenaganita*, Irene Ferandez, was awarded the prize for her defense of women and migrant workers. These issues seem a long way from those of the consumer movement, but Fernandez had begun her activist career as a volunteer with CAP, as had her sister Josie, who established Education and Research Association for Consumers in 1987 to provide an organization like CAP for the Malaysian mainland.[94] In 1998, the award went to the organization International Baby Food Action Network—a direct offshoot of the international consumer movement based in Penang. In 1993, a winner was Vandana Shiva, the Indian environmentalist and eco-feminist, who had also worked for CAP in the 1980s on a specific project to save Penang Hill from commercial development.[95]

One of the earliest winners of the award, in 1982, was Anwar Fazal, the co-founder of CAP with Idris. He was presented with the prize not so much for his work with CAP, but for his leadership of the international consumer movement. In Fazal's receipt of the award there is perhaps the most direct evidence of CAP's influence. By becoming president of the International Organisation of Consumers Unions and director of its regional office for Asia and the Pacific, Fazal embodied the transfer of CAP's agenda and the developing world politics of consumption onto the international arena. In doing so, the consumer movement became an international movement in which questions emerging from the global South over access to basic needs came to reside alongside the concerns over choice commonly articulated by consumers from the global North. Greater individual choice versus greater collective access are in many ways contradictory aims but they are a central dilemma of consumer society and for a number of decades were carefully negotiated, not always successfully, by the international consumer movement. It is this global politics of consumption that we shall discuss next.

Consumers of the World Unite

Consumption and the New Global Order

Since 1945, the United Nations has been the focal point for what has tentatively come to be referred to as global civil society. Consumers have not usually been thought of as part of this activist landscape. Instead, trade unions, women's groups, development organizations, faith-based charities, business associations, and advocacy networks have all been seen to have worked with and through UN bodies such as the Economic and Social Council (ECOSOC), the Educational, Scientific and Cultural Organization (UNESCO), the World Health Organization (WHO), the Food and Agriculture Office (FAO), and the General Assembly itself. For several decades the umbrella term used to categorize all these various actors has been "non-governmental organization" (NGO). It is a problematic phrase, but it has gained common currency among the international community and it at least helps us to appreciate the multitude of non-state actors, which, alongside nation-states, have sought to direct the forms and structures of global governance.

The term NGO was first used in the establishment of the United Nations. Although the international organization was the product of the signatures of fifty governments, NGOs had also been invited to attend the San Francisco conference in April 1945, which led to the UN's creation. Forty-two NGOs worked with the official U.S. delegation in advising on the economic and social aspects of international relations, while a total of 1,200 voluntary groups had some form of presence. Their most significant impact was on the opening words of the UN Charter—"We, the peoples of the United Nations . . ."—and on the inclusion of Article 71, which enabled the ECOSOC to communicate with NGOs.

Those initially granted "consultative status" by ECOSOC consisted of

NGOs concerned with social, economic, and humanitarian issues, and those that had large memberships such as Rotary International, the International Conference of Free Trade Unions, and the International Chamber of Commerce.[1] In subsequent years, they have been joined by a whole range of NGO actors, participating in both ECOSOC and UN-sponsored conferences. By 1990, there were more than 90 UN offices handling NGO relations and, to cite just one example, 4,000 NGOs participated in the 1995 Beijing Women's Conference. The number of NGOs with consultative status has increased from 41 in 1948 to 377 in 1968 to 1,350 in 1998 and over 2,500 by 2000. Moreover, the existence of the UN has undoubtedly acted as a spur to a more general growth in international NGOs. Just fifteen years after the UN's formation there were estimated to be 2,000 international NGOs. By 1980, this figure had increased to 4,000 and by 2000 stood at around 13,000, the 1990s in particular witnessing an explosion in international NGO activity. If looser definitions of "international" are taken so that we include any national-based NGO campaigning on global issues, then the figures run into many hundreds of thousands.[2]

The contribution of NGOs to global history is just beginning to be recognized. Usually, the drivers of globalization are held to be anonymous economic forces and the diplomatic initiatives of national governments and their foreign embassies. Some historians have begun to examine the "world culture" of global institutions, which refers to not only the contributions made by representatives of nation-states, but to those made by international organizations and non-state actors such as NGOs. Others have pointed to the "global community" of various transnational actors operating as an "epistemic community" with shared terms of references and using similar conventions of debate. Global civil society itself is said to be made up of "networks of interdependence" as NGOs are tied in with states and intergovernmental organizations in the development and articulation of global politics. To be sure, NGOs are not thought to constitute a coherent community, or to have an equal negotiating role with official delegates of nation-states, but they are beginning to be recognized as influential contributors to the debates we now associate with the rather open-ended concept of globalization.[3]

So far work on NGOs and civil society has tended to focus on the more dramatic forms of campaigning and protest that emerged out of the new social movements associated with the 1960s: women's rights, environmentalism, human rights, peace movements, anti-nuclear campaigns, and the anti-apartheid movement.[4] Many of these NGOs have been particularly effective at capturing the public imagination, especially those able to have impact on the modern media such as Greenpeace, Friends of the Earth, and Amnesty International. But they have not always been the most influential players in global civil society. For instance, a study conducted at the beginning of the 1980s found that the top ten international NGOs most likely to be able to influence intergovernmental organizations were not those we usually associate with global activism. Instead, the list consisted of trade unionists and co-operators, but also those connected with commercial interests, especially the International Organization for Standardization, the International Chamber of Commerce, and the International Federation of Agricultural Producers. Of those we more usually think of as NGOs, only the International Council of Voluntary Agencies, the International Union for Conservation of Nature and Natural Resources, and the League of Red Cross Societies made it to the top ten.[5]

Admittedly, the study was far from being a definitive guide. It was based on the number of consultative relationships the NGO held with international governmental organizations. Formal relationships cannot be said to constitute influence and many NGOs have felt better placed to direct the terms of the debate by operating through other forms of communication, such as the media. But it does alert us to the fact that many NGOs have contributed to that rather amorphous entity—global civil society. It also alerts us to the role of the international consumers' movement, represented by the International Organisation of Consumers Unions (IOCU). IOCU was ranked fourteenth, alongside the International Electrotechnical Commission, the World Federation of Trade Unions, and the World Federation of United Nations Associations. This meant it was ranked well above more well-known organizations associated with human rights and environmentalism, or indeed any type of NGO associated with investigations into global civil society. Yet the academic attention paid to the political campaigning of consumers is negligible when compared to the emerging work on these other spheres.

Indeed, when scholars have examined political consumerism at the global level, the focus has been on the more recent actions of those associated with ethical shopping or the anti-globalization movement. A 1992 investigation into movements for social change, for instance, only considered the consumer when he or she operated as a "progressive" in organizsations such as the radical Japanese Seikatsu Co-operative or through the types of "alternative trading organization," which became the backbone of the present-day fair-trade movement.[6]

The aim of this chapter is to examine the role of the organized consumer movement, as both a phenomenon of the global North and the global South, and to explore its relationship and influence on the institutions of global governance, particularly those associated with the United Nations. It will assess its impact on globalization, particularly because the consumer movement had to balance the very different interests of its varied constituency from around the world. In some ways, the consumer movement contributed to the processes of harmonization explored in chapter 2 at the European level. In this sense, consumer activism could be said to have imposed global norms on international institutions, yet at the same time it brought to such intergovernmental agencies the problems of specific groups of consumers whose interests might elsewhere expect to have been overridden amid the apparently unstoppable force of economic globalization. Above all, this chapter seeks to explain what the ranking of the fourteenth place at the UN meant in practice and how the consumer movement had come to obtain such a prominent position at the global level.

For an organization to be awarded so many consultative relationships is dependent on its ability to demonstrate that it represents a broad global constituency. The consumer movement had, by the early 1980s, to be able to claim that it spoke not only for the middle-income subscribers to comparative testing magazines in North America and Europe, but also for consumers beyond the affluent West. The consumer movement has always been aware of the discrepancy between its own "information seeker" cohort of the population and the mass of consumers in general. The two have not been the same thing and in order for the former to speak for the latter, consumer groups had to find ways of offering themselves as the legitimate spokesbodies for all consumers, especially because older groups such as the International Co-operative Alliance could still seek—and claimed—this function. IOCU has recognized its limitations in appealing to all consumers within affluent societies and has instead sought growth across the world. The first part of this chapter summarizes this growth and development. By the 1970s, IOCU could reasonably claim to be a truly international NGO, its associated groups stretching much further around the globe than many better-known organizations. This provided it with a legitimacy that further fuelled its representative function in the institutions of global governance and civil society.

But expansion and representation are nothing if they are not made effective. The second part of this chapter concentrates on how IOCU positioned itself as the sole speaker on consumer interests at the global level. In many ways this was relatively straightforward. As the number of consultative relationships were increased with workers' organizations, women's groups, agricultural interests and trade associations, it was in some sense natural—according to a corporatist logic followed in many nation-states—to seek the voice of the new consumer movement. While co-operation as a campaigning entity remained wedded to the wider labor movement, IOCU positioned itself as a non-aligned and non-party political entity that could claim a seat at the table alongside other recognized social and economic interests. Moreover, it could trade on its own respectable and moderate image, obtained through its fiercely independent existence in Britain and the United States or conferred on it by governments in countries where public funds were used to support comparative testing.

Again, though, representation can as easily mean co-option as it does influence. Later chapters explore some of the more radical agendas of the consumer movement as the concerns of poor consumers around the world were used to mobilize IOCU at the global level. But for much of its early existence, the consumer movement seemed at ease in simply increasing the number of committees and organizations where it represented the consumer. In this sense, organized consumerism could be accused less of influencing the dynamic of global civil society and more of reinforcing capitalist liberal democracy by participating in the institutions that have promoted and assured its hegemony. A third section presents a case study of the main campaign issue for the consumer movement in the first quarter century of its existence, that of establishing a set of international guidelines for consumer protection measures and regulations. For many consumer activists in Europe and North America, the 1985 UN Guidelines on Consumer Protection were the crowning achievement of the organized consumer movement. But in many ways such a focus merely replicated the reduction of consumer protection to safeguarding individual choice that occurred in Europe and in other developed capitalist economies (see chapter 2).

Certainly, the Guidelines were not the only campaign issue of the consumer movement and in themselves such consumer protection measures were a reflection of the internationalist spirit of consumer activists. They represented the classic liberal concern with citizenship rights, because they were about ensuring that all consumers in the marketplace—and a global marketplace at that— were provided with the same basic protections that were offered, by the 1970s, to those living in Europe and North America. Here was another democratic aspect to the vision of consumer society promoted by the consumer movement and through the institutions of global governance. But in providing a set of lowest common denominators of regulation, the consumer movement unwittingly contributed to a narrowing of the vision of the politics of consumption that would increasingly come to the fore by the 1990s. Access rather than choice would persist as the principal focus for many Southern consumer groups, and the guidelines on consumer protection were the basic building block for establishing more equitable consumer societies around the world. Although the Guidelines were only one aspect of the politics of consumption for much of the first half of the international consumer movement's existence they directed its attention, pointing to many tensions about how the "consumer interest" was to be determined for so varied a constituency. What is also apparent is that, for better or for worse, the consumer movement was able to have an impact and with long-term consequences, whether intended or not. This chapter serves as a case study of one NGO's impact on global governance and of the ambivalent relationship one movement has had with global society's principal institutions. It contributes to a growing debate on the driving forces of globalization and shows the extent to which non-state—as opposed to state—actors have influenced these processes.

I

If the consumer movement that emerged across the developed capitalist world in the 1950s was ever going to be an influential player in global civil society it needed to create an organization that could claim to be a movement of global proportions. It needed to be able to step outside of its North American and Western European core and suggest that organized consumerism was a social phenomenon attractive to a whole range of consumers, rich and poor alike. If the movement could mobilize consumers from around the world then so much the better could it claim to speak as the authentic voice of the consumer interest, and more so than any other self-appointed expert on consumer affairs, be it the labor movement, a professional association, a commercial interest, a women's organization, or the International Co-operative Alliance.

This was certainly not the intention of the original consumer activists who came together in 1960 to establish the International Organisation of Consumers Unions. When Elizabeth Schadee of the Dutch Consumentenbond teamed up with Caspar Brook of the UK Consumers' Association in 1958, the purpose was to explore opportunities for collaboration in product testing. Realizing that other national consumer groups might also be interested in such ventures, they approached and received the enthusiastic support of Colston Warne of the U.S. Consumers Union. The three organizations provided the funding for an international conference on product testing held in The Hague from 30 March to 1 April 1960 and were attended by thirty-seven people from seventeen organizations from fourteen countries. It resulted in the immediate establishment of IOCU by the three sponsoring groups, plus the Belgian Associations des Consommateurs and the Australian Consumers' Association.

With an executive secretary appointed in The Hague, IOCU began publishing a monthly bulletin, listing the product tests members were proposing to carry out so that test information could be shared. In its formative years IOCU's focus was almost entirely on the organizational and technical aspects of product testing. Although some consumerists imbued with the technocratic ethos of scientific rationality and industrial efficiency could optimistically proclaim that testing itself was "a road map to guide consumers to higher standards of living," IOCU's initial raison d'être did not extend beyond the most obvious needs of the subscriber magazines.[7] Representatives of the state-assisted consumer councils of Northern and Central Europe were invited to participate in the IOCU conferences, but the ideal type of consumer organization envisioned by IOCU was the non-profit, independent, private member/subscriber, comparative testing model practiced by Consumers Union, the Consumers' Association, and Consumentenbond.[8]

Just as national consumer groups expanded their political orbit as they realized many of the problems raised by their tests could not be solved by rational individualism and informed choice alone, so too did IOCU's work make it apparent that some degree of consumer lobbying of international organizations would further its cause. IOCU recognized that if it did not put itself forward as the representative of the consumer, then other groups and individuals might step into the void. This was precisely the reason why European consumer groups were quick to mobilize in the Common Market, establishing the Bureau Européen des Unions de Consommateurs (BEUC) in 1962 to lobby for consumers in the European Economic Community.[9] And it also explains why IOCU quickly realized that a focus on testing was inadequate to defend consumer interests in their entirety. Very soon after its inception IOCU leaders discussed how they might increase their representative role.

However, participation in international politics and society was not simply

Figure 5. Logo of the International Organisation of Consumers Unions.

Courtesy of IOCU.

the result of calculated expediency. Idealism too played its part. Many of the consumer leaders who envisioned a wide-ranging social movement in their respective national contexts were equally committed to a democratic internationalism that would serve the interests of all consumers. Throughout the early history of IOCU conferences and meetings were interrupted with impassioned calls for the establishment of a broad-based global movement. Activists argued that it was their responsibility to speak for the poor as well as the affluent consumer. While this had long been the policy within national contexts, at the global level it meant extending organized consumerism into the developing world. In 1964, Jeremy Mitchell of UK Consumers' Association challenged the movement to fill the large gaps on the world map where consumerism had failed to take off: "Firstly, Latin America, there is virtually nothing; in Africa, nothing from Cairo to the Cape, and lastly, in Asia, with the exception of Japan and an embryonic group in Delhi, there is nothing."[10]

His speech resonated with the internationalism of so many other activists who believed the organized consumer movement offered much more than assistance to the individual shopper. Colston Warne, the first President of IOCU, saw the organization as an opportunity to develop a form of socio-political action denied to his own Consumers Union. He spoke of the "international obligation" of IOCU to assist all consumers: "The world consumer movement must not only be attentive to the problems of choosing automobiles, air conditioners and refrigerators, but, if it is to attain its true purpose, it must deal also with the day to day issues of those in countries which have not yet attained an advanced technology."[11]

In an angst-ridden speech, Henry Epstein of the Australian Consumers Association bemoaned the acquisitive materialism of the modern world and the inability of people to appreciate the true worth of goods. His consumerism embraced both the technocratic and the aesthetic imagination and called into question the purpose of comparative testing: IOCU "should be complemented by some plan showing that we don't intend to march around in a circle to a tune played with one finger on a cash register."[12] Michael Young, the founder of the UK Consumers' Association and a keen advocate of social democracy, urged IOCU to pay attention to public as well as private goods, to the standard of living and the quality of life, and to the needs of the poor as well as the needs of the rich. According to Young, consumerism ought to consider not only the freedom of choice, but the absence of choice for the majority of the world's population. It ought to move beyond a focus on products and question the whole purpose of consumer society itself.[13] Several years later, Young returned to this theme. He seemingly embraced many of the arguments of the 1960s countercultural generation and some of the economic theory of Marx. The price of a commodity, he told an audience of consumer leaders, does not consider "the full social costs of producing and consuming goods and services."[14]

For many activists consumerism constituted a social movement comparable to that of organized labor. Eva Preiss, president of the Austrian VKI, believed the consumer movement was at a stage comparable to that of the workers' movement just prior to the formation of trade unions.[15] The true potential of this "sleeping giant" was just about to be realized. For others, consumerism was "part of a deep social change" associated with the 1960s that saw comparable movements of students, the poor and the elderly: "ordinary citizens who must be recognized as human beings and be respected for their identity and needs and who want recognition of their rights."[16]

Unlike many other movements, it was claimed, consumerism offered "a unique blend of idealism and pragmatism."[17] It provided the opportunity to address social issues without recourse to party political ideology, which nevertheless addressed many of the world's greatest problems. Even a one-time British Conservative Party candidate was able to claim that the ultimate goal of consumerism was the eradication of poverty: "The existence in our so-called affluent world of millions upon millions of our fellow men and women who do not command consumer purchasing power adequate enough for them to sustain their dignity, to feed their children, to house their families, to keep themselves in health."[18] These broadest of considerations became the operating rationale for an organization that for all its work to provide independent information to shoppers in the affluent West saw itself as a social movement at the global level. By the 1980s, international consumerism had even found its equivalent anthem to "we shall overcome." In an action that must surely have made some of IOCU's more socially and politically conservative members physically wince, the General Assembly of the organization was interrupted in Bangkok in 1984 by Raj Anand of the Consumer Guidance Society of India. After explaining the Gandhian sentiments in the lines of the Bengali poet Tagore, Anand led the IOCU executive on stage in clasp-handed communal singing of "Walk alone."[19] Three years later, the conference theme was heralded as "solidarity: for a better world."[20]

In addition to being providers of independent information consumer organizations were prepared to borrow from Galbraith and claim a role as "a countervailing power in legislation which will afford protection to *all* consumers." These universalist sympathies lay behind the gathering momentum for an expansion of the consumer movement across the globe. Accordingly, in 1961, the Consumers Union librarian Florence Mason was appointed by IOCU to spread the gospel of consumerism. Over the next two decades she maintained a staggering correspondence with fledgling consumer groups from 140 countries around the world, as well as with many hundreds of other individuals interested in establishing organizations in their own particular city, state, or region. She wrote to related groups that had interests in consumer affairs extolling the benefits of specific consumer organizing. She traveled around Europe, North America, and the Asia-Pacific region offering practical advice and support and she was able to draw on a specially created Loan Fund to provide more concrete assistance to fledgling bodies.[21] She was joined by Colston Warne, whose proselytizing trips to Europe in the late 1950s and early 1960s were followed by tours across Australasia, Asia, and the Middle East.[22]

If the ideal consumer organization remained the "pure" form of the private, independent membership organization, IOCU quickly learnt that to impose this as a rigorous standard would be counterproductive to its own expansion. Not only did many groups require government support, most lacked the resources to undertake their own product tests. Their focus has come to be more on targeted campaigning and lobbying rather than the publication of magazines and buying guides. IOCU therefore immediately revised its attitude toward membership and engaged in exactly the same set of debates as so many other NGOs, which have extended into countries with very different economic, social, and political circumstances. Although independence from all commercial interests has remained a key principle of the global consumer movement, independence from the state has not been policed so inflexibly. The original constitution of IOCU established an Executive Council with permanent seats for the five original founder organizations, though state-assisted consumer groups were allowed to become members of IOCU. But within just a few years it was realized that such a division between the pure and the tarnished had actually created an undemocratic structure. Power was permanently vested in the independent Dutch, Belgian, Australian, British, and U.S. consumer groups, while the rapid expansion of IOCU occurred in countries where privately organized comparative testing was not viable. By 1968, the IOCU constitution was revised to reflect the growth in the number of non-testing organizations principally concerned with consumer education and protection. Following the amendments, the Executive Council retained its functions, but ultimate sovereignty within IOCU was passed to the General Assembly, which consisted of associated member organizations who now only had to demonstrate their exclusive focus on consumer interests rather than their ability to engage in independent comparative testing.[23]

This more liberal definition of consumerism was a direct consequence of the rapid growth of the movement. In the 1960s an average of four or five new national consumer groups appeared every year. In the 1970s, this figure increased to around twelve per year. After the first decade of its existence, the IOCU Council consisted not only of the five founders, but of the state consumer councils of the Scandinavian countries, West Germany, and the United Kingdom. Next elected members came from Austria, New Zealand, Israel, and Canada. Another sixteen organizations qualified as associate members, while twenty-three were corresponding members. Eight years later, in 1978, there were thirty-eight associate members and sixty-seven correspondents and, after another eight years, forty-eight associate and eighty-five corresponding members. Of the total one hundred and thirty-three members in 1986, sixty-one were from Europe and North America, fifty-five from Asia and the Pacific, twelve from Latin America and the Caribbean, and five from Africa. By the early 1990s, there were consumer organizations from over eighty countries, and by the turn of the millennium, there were 253 members from one hundred and fifteen different states. By this time, numbers had been expanded following the collapse of the Soviet bloc and the spread of consumerism into Africa, notably into some of the world's poorest economies. It would be ridiculous to conclude that by the 1990s consumerism as a social movement touched all people all around the world, but it is fair to claim that the organized consumer movement had obtained a global reach that far exceeded that of many more prominent NGOs.[24]

As we saw in the previous chapter, this growth has largely come about through the autonomous actions of urban professionals eager to organize as consumers in their respective localities. IOCU has been keen to assist the initiatives and it has proved adept at building on regional developments by creating infrastructures that have encouraged further growth. It first sought to foster a coherent regional policy in the Caribbean, though focus quickly shifted to Asia following the creation of so many groups across the continent in the 1960s. In 1971, IOCU's Aid Committee planned a seminar in Kuala Lumpur to be hosted by the Selangor Consumers' Association. Due to the internal divisions that split this organization, the location was shifted to Bombay, only to be moved again to Singapore because of the worsening political situation between Pakistan and India. The ultimate outcome of this event was to convince IOCU to establish a regional office in 1974 in Singapore with Anwar Fazal of the Consumers' Association of Penang as Regional Director. The political tension between Malaysia and Singapore was such that Fazal's one year record as a teacher in the Malaysian military led to him being accused of spying (despite protests from IOCU to the Prime Minister Lee Kuan Yew). Consequently, the Regional Office for the Asia-Pacific (ROAP) was relocated to Fazal's home town of Penang, thereby creating a physical connection between IOCU and Asia's most vibrant consumer organization.[25]

ROAP's role was to promote consumer organizing around the region through the provision of technical assistance, the hosting of training seminars, and acting as a clearing house for the exchange of information between various consumer groups. This it certainly did and it has ensured that the Asia-Pacific region remains one of IOCU's strongest spheres of influence. It has set up specific initiatives to promote consumer organizing on the subcontinent and across the Pacific Islands. By the 1990s, apart from certain failed ventures in countries such as Papua New Guinea, consumerism was represented in just about every state, the majority of which was sufficiently strong to exist as formal accredited members of IOCU. Even those nations with weaker ties to international civil society, such as Nepal, Brunei, and Mongolia, have been assisted in their consumer organizing by the Penang office.[26]

But more important than geographical spread was the shift in the center of gravity of the international movement from The Hague to Penang, providing IOCU with a prominent Southern perspective in its policy formulations. From 1974 to Fazal's departure from the movement in 1991, and especially from 1978 to 1984 when he served as both employer and employee during his presidency of IOCU, the consumer movement was being directed in all but name from Malaysia. For instance, in an analysis of IOCU publications conducted in 1989, it was found that most were emanating from Penang. Of the 218 special publications produced by IOCU since 1960, only 94 were from The Hague while 120 were from Penang. Moreover, many of the European publications were on core consumer activities such as conference reports, surveys of legislation, and guidebooks on testing procedures. The vast majority of policy-oriented publications had emerged from Penang, demonstrating an initiative and drive on the part of its staff that was much commented on at the time.[27] According to its director Fazal, this influence was momentous: "we transformed the consumer movement from a fringe group for the middle classes into a movement that was central to the process of Sustainable Human Development. We were able to project it as a movement that meant real things to real people—the billions of poor, oppressed, exploited, disempowered."[28] Such claims are tested in later chapters, but Fazal's own contribution has been repeatedly acknowledged, even by those Western consumer leaders who have sympathized with complaints that he took the politics of consumption far from the concerns of the subscribers to *Consumer Reports* and *Which?*[29]

Part of the transformation that Fazal claimed for Penang could only take place with the expansion of the movement beyond Asia. In the 1970s, IOCU worked to promote consumerism in the Mediterranean region after the collapse of the military regimes in Spain, Portugal, and Greece. In Spain, for instance, consumer rights were written into the new constitution after 1975, relatively strong state consumer protection measures were put in place, and a burgeoning grassroots movement emerged immediately after Franco's death. Within ten years, around half a dozen national consumer organizations had been established, over twenty governmental bodies dealt with consumer affairs, and nearly a hundred local and regional consumer bodies had appeared all over the country.[30]

At the same time, IOCU returned to the Americas. In 1975, Consumers

Union supported the publication of *Hungry for Profits* by Robert Ledogar, which criticized the damage caused by U.S. food and drug corporations to Latin American consumers and economies. The exposé proved a spur to consumer organizing, and IOCU began publishing in Spanish from 1977 to further encourage this trend. In 1981, the Mexican consumers' movement published the quarterly *La Voz del Consumidor,* in collaboration with IOCU and more formal contacts began to be made with Latin American consumer activists following a 1984 meeting at Curitiba, Brazil. In 1986, IOCU organized the first regional conference for Latin America and the Caribbean, with broad support from the Spanish consumer groups and South American governments, as well as representatives attending from twenty-two countries. It was followed one year later with the creation of IOCU's second developing world office, the Regional Office for Latin America and the Caribbean (ROLAC), situated in Montevideo, Uruguay and with Jose Vargas, a Chilean political refugee, appointed regional director.[31]

As with the Asia-Pacific office, ROLAC promoted a version of consumerism more in line with the general issues of social and economic development. In contrast to the developed capitalist West, Latin American consumer problems could not be resolved "at an individual level." Instead, consumer groups had to be political: not in the party political sense but in recognition that they had to intervene in political and economic affairs. Accordingly, Latin American consumerism has proved the second most important plank in IOCU's developing world politics of consumption, with the main issues being not value for money, but access to basic needs, global trade policies, and the regulation of multinational corporations.[32] As in Asia, growth was rapid as soon as IOCU was seen to respond to the needs of poor consumers and by 1991, over twenty Latin American consumer groups had affiliated themselves with the international body. From 2003 to 2007, IOCU was presided over by Marilena Lazzarini of the Brazilian Instituto de Defesa do Consumidor.[33]

At the same time, IOCU conferences also pointed to the failure to develop consumerism as a movement in Africa. Many from the continent believed IOCU had been slow to respond to grassroots activism, despite Mitchell's identification of Africa as a potential growth area as early as 1964. In 1987, the twenty-eight African delegates to the World Consumer Congress called on IOCU to co-ordinate consumer movement development in Africa. After years of relative neglect, IOCU was quick to respond. An African Task Force was immediately created building on existing strengths in African consumerism, principally in Kenya, Zimbabwe, and Mauritius. This was followed with a Consultative Committee that organized regional conferences for Francophone West Africa in Senegal and for Anglophone Africa in Kenya, both in 1988. The resulting Dakar and Nairobi declarations both pointed to the specific problems of African consumers, the vast majority of whom lived in poverty and who suffered from the consequences of trade liberalization and privatization measures, which further hampered their ability to access basic goods and services.

Understandably for a continent laboring under a poor communications infrastructure, much of IOCU's work has been directed toward capacity building, the first stage of any consumer politics being seen to be the creation of a viable and widespread movement. While African consumerism was initially slow to develop, the expansion in the 1990s was reasonably impressive. There had been just five established consumer groups on the continent in the 1980s, but by the mid-1990s IOCU had contacts with around one hundred organizations. With considerable support from the Dutch, Canadian, and Scandinavian governments, as well as already well-established NGOs working in Africa—particularly Environment and Development Action in the Third World (ENDA), based in Dakar—IOCU was able to build a movement across the continent. In 1994, a Regional Office for Africa was created in Harare, Zimbabwe, which relocated to Accra, Ghana, in 2005.[34]

Finally, the last main region that has seen the incursion of the global consumer movement in recent decades is that of the former Soviet bloc. During the later 1980s, consumerism emerged amid wider democracy movements, spearheaded by Poland's Federacja Konsumentów. Federacja Konsumentów has been an IOCU member since 1981 and in 1988 it approached IOCU having organized the First Congress of Consumers' Organizations from the Socialist Countries with delegates from China, Bulgaria, Cuba, Hungary, and the Soviet Union. IOCU began to work with Federacja Konsumentów and following another consumer meeting in November 1989, the Warsaw declaration was launched committing all signatories to the defense of the consumer interest. No one could have predicted the rapidity with which the command economies collapsed and IOCU had to move quickly in creating twinning arrangements so that Western groups could assist individuals and fledgling bodies in Eastern Europe. In late 1989 and early 1990, toward a dozen new consumer groups were founded across the Soviet bloc.[35]

And, just as Warne and Mason had done so elsewhere, consumer missionaries were sent out to develop new organizations. Alastair Macgeorge, the former deputy director of the UK Consumers' Association, made a number of trips around Central and Eastern Europe, meeting representatives of new state consumer councils alongside the most basic voluntary efforts appearing sporadically everywhere. In a series of highly entertaining mission reports, in which he recounted his experiences and frustrations in tracking down the self-styled new leaders of post-Soviet consumerism, Macgeorge helped foster a series of contacts that became the basis for the global movement's growth in the 1990s.[36] Although many of the individuals and initiatives he reported on eventually came to nothing, others were put in contact with one another and consumerism spread rapidly. In 1992, eighty-nine invited participants representing consumer groups from every former Soviet state attended a regional conference in Bled, Slovenia. The conference led to a fully coordinated development program, which worked with the European Community's PHARE (Poland, Hungary Aid for the Reconstruction of the Economy) fund to develop the already established 100 pioneering groups.[37] Admittedly, these groups varied enormously; for example, Polish Federacja Konsumentów could rely on its 20,000 members to pay for a staff of 65, while, only two lawyers volunteering their personal time could claim to be the consumer movement in Tatarstan.[38]

Such a growth in membership provides one part of the explanation as to why IOCU was able to achieve so many consultative relationships with the United Nations by the 1980s and why it continues to hold such a respected status with international bodies such as the World Trade Organization. Yet what is generally not known by the millions of subscribers to testing magazines in the affluent West is that it is their money that has indirectly funded the creation of a global movement. While in the past various national government aid agencies have provided the support for regional conferences and development initiatives, and while IOCU now relies on specific grant and aid donations, for most of its history, the U.S. Consumers Union and the UK Consumers' Association have provided the bulk of the practical and financial assistance to pay for the establishment of regional offices. Throughout the first quarter century of its existence, almost all of IOCU's income came from member subscriptions, the majority of which was always ultimately provided by the subscribers to *Which?* and *Consumer Reports*. In 1975–76, for instance, around a quarter of IOCU's income came from Americans and one-fifth from the British. Another 12 percent came from the Dutch and the Germans while all other consumer groups together only provided one-third of IOCU's funds.[39] Undoubtedly, this was due to the larger financial resources that CU and CA had available to them. But it also attests to the internationalist vision of so many of their leaders who saw in the global consumer movement an opportunity to address the wider range of social and economic issues often denied to them in their own testing magazines.

Before we can begin to criticize and assess the nature of the global movement, it has to be acknowledged just how impressive this international reach was. A cursory glance through the membership profiles of many of today's leading NGOs quickly demonstrates the relative success of IOCU's development program. For instance, Greenpeace can claim a global reach with its thirty to forty offices, but as a federation it remains an essentially Northern organization, as are so many other "international" NGOs; only a few, such as IOCU and Amnesty International, can claim to be truly global. Some of these organizations have an incredibly impressive reach: Friends of the Earth, for example, has over 1 million members and 5,000 local groups attached to it, but this growth has come since the 1990s; prior to this, few other NGOs could compete with IOCU's global membership.[40]

Moreover, IOCU's expansion is all the more remarkable because of the sheer diversity of interests contained within it. The consumer interest in having cheaper import duties on foreign luxury vehicles is very different from that arising from the lack of fuel and water supplies to entire towns and villages. Yet both interests are represented in the movement. Certainly, as national consumer organizations in the affluent West have met with success at home on some of their core safety, redress, and information demands, it has meant that the global movement has been able to focus on the questions of poverty more relevant to poor consumers of the world. It has also meant that the nature of consumer organizing at the global level has been different from that found in the testing magazines—it more obviously resembles a social movement. For Ruth Simmons Vermeer, an early Dutch volunteer at IOCU's Penang office, consumerism's vitality owed as much to its diversity as to any coherence behind the consumer cause. "In the final analysis," she argued in a paper on the need for consumerism in the developing world, "the struggle for consumer rights is part of a large movement for economic justice, for new economic orders . . . The consumer movement is a voluntary movement. It is a movement for and by the people."[41]

II

No matter how much the consumer movement spread around the world, all that development was for nothing if it could not be translated into effectiveness. The ultimate purpose of the growth of consumerism was not only to address local consumer issues in different national contexts but to ensure a powerful presence in the institutions of global governance. What the consumer movement has sought to do, therefore, is increase its representative role in international organizations and to lobby on behalf of the world's consumers on a whole range of social and economic issues.

The one organization that has provided the focus for IOCU's campaigning internationalism has been, above all, the United Nations and its Economic and Social Council (ECOSOC). Indeed, IOCU's own history is intimately bound up with that of the United Nations and the growth of NGO consultancy in general. Consultative status opened up the entire ECOSOC system, including its subsidiaries such as the International Labor Organization (ILO), the Food and Agriculture Office (FAO), the United Nations Educational, Scientific and Cultural Organization (UNESCO), the World Health Organization (WHO), and the World Bank. In 1968, the rules on consultation were tightened and the NGOs were given a status based on three categories. Category I NGOs have a broad economic and social remit, have the broadest access to ECOSOC, and can propose agenda items. Category II NGOs have more specialized interests, can observe all ECOSOC meetings, but only have the right to submit written statements on specific issues. Finally, Category III NGOs (on the "roster") are allowed to make occasional contributions at the request of an ECOSOC official. The figures cited earlier on the growth of NGOs in the UN system refer to all three categories. When these are broken down, they suggest the degree of importance attached to each category. For the period from 1948 to 1991, the number of NGOs granted Category I status increased from 7 to 41. For those with Category II status, the numbers jumped from 32 to 354. Thus, the greatest growth has been among NGOs on the roster, leaving only a relatively small number of large NGOs with all the privileges of Category I status.[42]

Of studies so far conducted into the influence of NGOs at the UN, most have focused on the established social movement concerns of human rights and the women's movement.[43] Generally, it is claimed that in the 1950s and 1960s, the rapid growth of the UN led to a diffusion of economic and social issues so that NGOs found it difficult to aim toward a point of focus. Instead, NGOs became "more concerned with the mechanics and prestige of their status than their role in the issues."[44] Certainly this was the case with IOCU as it sought to establish itself as a recognized presence at the UN. This was achieved in April 1963 when it was granted a position on the roster.[45] In May 1969, following a general ECOSOC review of consultative arrangements, IOCU was reclassified to Category II.[46]

The consumer movement remained uncertain as to what to do with its newfound position. At their 1964 Congress, global consumers leaders committed themselves to increasing their role at the UN, but the precise details of what this role ought to consist of remained unclear. Rather grandiose statements that IOCU should work toward the creation of an International Consumer Organization to mirror the work of the ILO worked very well when uttered by Colston Warne to rally his staff, but it took IOCU many years to find its feet at the UN.[47] Just reviewing the areas where the consumer movement might contribute seemed to take up much of the time of the experienced economist, UN lobbyist, and former Consumer Counsel to the state of New York, Persia Campbell—IOCU's first representative at ECOSOC from 1963. For perhaps the better part of the 1960s IOCU's role at the UN consisted of simply increasing its representative function as an end in itself. With limited resources to develop the expertise required to operate effectively in a diffuse and technical body, IOCU's potential as an influential international NGO was rather limited.[48]

But just as other NGOs began to mobilize by the end of the 1960s so too did IOCU. The impetus again came from the changing role of the UN. Since the late 1950s the UN had become more of a global institution as U.S. hegemony in the General Assembly declined with the burgeoning accession of new member states following de-colonization. In 1961, the Burmese Buddhist and socialist, U Thant, was appointed General Secretary and saw in global politics less of a division between capitalism and communism than between rich and poor. The developing world states refused to become attached to the U.S. and Soviet power blocs, instead creating a "non-aligned movement" that revived the original ethos of the signatories to the UN Charter that the organization should work to establish a more peaceful world through its economic and social policies.[49]

Further impetus came from President Kennedy's announcement of a "decade of development" in 1961 and the creation of the United Nations Conference on Trade and Development (UNCTAD) in 1964. Many of these initiatives faltered but by the turn of the 1970s, with the moral leadership of the United States in decline because of the war in Vietnam and the global economy increasingly beleaguered, the developing world was able to lobby as a more cohesive unit. Assisted by the greater bargaining power of the oil-producing states, the global South was able to press for a New International Economic Order (NIEO), especially during the Second Development Decade announced by the UN for the

1970s. Many NGOs that had formerly focused on purely humanitarian issues—such as Care, set up in 1945 to deal with the relief of survivors of World War II—now broadened their remit to deal with the same issues being raised in the General Assembly by Third World states. By the 1970s, many NGOs extended their immediate aid work on the ground into lobbying organizations dedicated to tackling the root causes of hunger and poverty. They soon found themselves becoming outspoken critics of the relevant systems of international trade, food policy, and economic and social justice.[50]

IOCU was by no means as fast to respond to these changing dynamics of global civil society as NGOs such as Oxfam; nevertheless they began to see new opportunities for themselves. By the beginning of the 1970s, many consumer groups operating at the national level had begun to comment on wider economic and social issues, recognizing that there existed significant structural issues in the marketplace, which went against the consumer interest and which could only be rectified by government intervention. It was also felt that many global consumer problems could only be solved through a more interventionist UN system in the sphere of the society and the economy.

The UN Second Development Decade began with a commitment from the members of the General Assembly to act as "partners in progress" and a comprehensive International Development Strategy was set out to which IOCU broadly aligned itself. In particular, Persia Campbell, in a series of articles and submissions to ECOSOC, sought to outline the areas of concern to consumers and areas where IOCU could be expected to contribute. IOCU believed it should become a frequent commentator on, and contributor to, the development of international trade policy, the technical advice given to developing countries, the impact of multinational corporations, the regulations of retailing, and the provision of legislative consumer protection and education measures. At a more abstract level, IOCU committed itself to ensuring that consumer rights were to be recognized as a key component of the UN's new emphasis on economic and social rights in its Declaration on Social Progress and Development. In the IOCU statements to the UN, the repeated theme was that "economic growth is not an end in itself." The increasing reliance of ever greater numbers of people on money incomes ought to take into account not only how the money was received but how it was translated into goods and services: "the worker's right to income has to be translated into its market value, into the consumer's right to a fair exchange for money earned—into "real income.""[51]

Such abstract principles were made into concrete consumer proposals through an insistence on the need for consumer education clauses in development projects. This was a rather unambitious outcome for a movement that realized—in theory at least—what the Second Development Decade offered for a global and wide-ranging politics of consumption. The limitations of IOCU's approach were reflected in the continuing weakness of its negotiating and campaigning tactics for the first part of the 1970s. IOCU's UN representative Campbell was replaced by Dorothy Willner, an academic sociologist by training and also the representative of the International Council of Women at UNICEF. To some extent she continued the policy of increasing representation as an end in itself. Certainly for a number of consumer leaders of the time, she lacked the determination, experience, and political savvy that would be attributed to later IOCU negotiators.[52] During the Second Development Decade IOCU campaigned on a number of issues. It contributed to the Commission on the Status of Women and the Commission on Transnational Corporations. It enjoyed constant representation at UNICEF, UNESCO, and UNIDO (UN Industrial Development Organization), and it had long been an active discussant on the Codex Alimentarius Commission, which dealt with food standards. At ECOSOC it was asked to provide written statement on a number of issues, from science and technology to disability rights to education programs and the legal aspects of consumer protection.[53]

Yet much of this representation was of a rather passive nature: IOCU attended meetings and briefing sessions for NGOs, but it was clearly taking more information from the UN than it was providing. Even Willner was forced to complain in 1976 that IOCU was not taking seriously its potential influence at the UN. Her own expenses were not paid as part of a salary, she received payments only sporadically, and at times she felt the need to fund her own travel to UN regional conferences, as IOCU took too long to become aware of an event's significance.[54] Something of a turning point came in 1976 when IOCU's consultative status was upgraded from Category II to Category I, enabling it to play a fuller role in all aspects of the ECOSOC's activities by being able to initiate, rather than merely respond to, debate and issues. This had long been the goal of IOCU's UN representatives.[55] It immediately opened up the number of opportunities for effective action and placed it among the top division of international NGOs. Prior to re-classification, IOCU had enjoyed the same status as one hundred and ninety-five other NGOs in Category II, including the well-known pressure groups such as Amnesty International. The promotion placed it with twenty-four of the largest and general-issue NGOs, including manufacturing, distribution, trade union, and agricultural interests, as well as the women's movement, social welfare, and youth-based groups.[56]

The promotion also expanded the amount of work IOCU had the potential to contribute to, should IOCU have chosen to match these opportunities with sufficient resources, mobilization, and will power. By the turn of the next decade, specially focused consumer lobbyists were frequent attenders at meetings of UNICEF, UNESCO, and UNIDO to discuss special education programs for various disadvantaged consumers and to comment on a range of economic development initiatives.[57] Often this took the form of lobbying for basic consumer protection provisions in existing UN initiatives, but in other areas IOCU's role was more sustained and proactive. Food standards had long been a principal concern of consumers. IOCU participated in the technical aspects of the FAO/WHO Codex Alimentarius Commission, advising on principles of hygiene and the use of adulterants in foodstuffs. In 1979 it supported the Commission's recommendation that a Code of Ethics for the International Trade in Food be adopted by national governments. If at first IOCU had felt overwhelmed by the sheer scale of the issues relating to food standards, from the 1980s it has become increasingly professional and vociferous.[58] Food standards have been translated into the broader campaigning concept of food security, which has seen IOCU become more involved in the regulation of the food industry. In 1996, it organized a worldwide campaign to mobilize civil society around food issues ahead of the UN World Food Summit in November of the same year. By this stage, IOCU had developed a more holistic approach to food issues, campaigning not only on hygiene standards, but also on the broader questions of biotechnology and genetic modification, the availability of food to poor consumers, the ability of farmers to make a living from food cultivation, and the entire system of global food distribution.[59]

One area of activity at the UN that marked IOCU's potential leadership of international NGOs was the Consumer Interpol. The sale of, and trade in, dangerous goods—be they chemicals, pharmaceuticals, pesticides, and unsafe commodities—was a classic concern of the Western consumer movement. Although national regulations had dealt with many of these problems in Europe and North America, the absence of equivalent measures elsewhere meant that consumers unfortunate enough to be born in legislative contexts that lacked the necessary safeguards were open to harm from shoddy goods. This was especially true as multinational companies often dumped products on the developing world when the developed world no longer accepted them. There were no easy solutions to such problems, and IOCU recognized that a package of protections would be required, ranging from voluntary codes of conduct, national consumer protection legislation, and the greater intervention of the UN and other international bodies. But one practical initiative it developed on its own was the creation of a Consumer Interpol in 1981, which aimed to create a global hazard alert system covering dangerous goods, foods and toys, pollutants, unsafe pharmaceuticals, pesticides, and hazardous industries and technologies. The Interpol relied on the exchange of information around the world by IOCU's 120 or so members and it required the production of data it could not hope to achieve on its own shoestring budget. Fortunately, IOCU knew that most of the information was already available in UN databanks such as the International Register of Potentially Toxic Chemicals and in information held by the ILO. It was able to issue its first alert in November 1981, which was then relayed around consumer groups in the developing world so that they could place pressure on their governments to intervene.[60]

The Consumer Interpol was not a UN venture but it relied on a close working relationship with the UN, especially concerning the information it held on dangerous goods. IOCU's actions provided momentum to other concerned voices at the UN and at the end of 1982 the General Assembly resolved to create a "Consolidated List of Products Whose Consumption and/or Sale Have

Been Banned, Withdrawn, Severely Restricted or Not Approved by Governments." The resolution was passed almost unanimously, with only one dissenting vote coming from the United States which, as we will see, marked the usual approach of that government to the UN's increasing intervention in trade issues in the 1980s. The first list was published in December 1983 and contained details of 421 products. IOCU has worked to provide the UN with further information, which has since been regularly updated. And Consumer Interpol has been able to step in to overcome any shortcomings in the promotion of the List by ensuring that its alerting system communicated the key problems.[61] Perhaps just as significantly, Consumer Interpol enabled IOCU to assume a global prominence that matched its elevation to Category I status. Managed entirely from the Penang regional office, Consumer Interpol attracted the praise of the international community. So much was this the case that in 1982 Anwar Fazal, as President of IOCU and the guiding force behind the initiative, was awarded the Right Livelihood Award, which he shared with five others who had also focused on developmental issues, including the German environmentalist Petra Kelly.[62]

By the 1980s IOCU was campaigning on a range of issues that brought it into line with the developmental goals of both the UN and an ever expanding number of international NGOs. Through certain initiatives, including Consumer Interpol and the specific campaigns on pesticides, pharmaceuticals, and breast milk substitutes (which are examined in the next chapter), IOCU was able to claim that it had become a world leader of global civil society at this time. However, its role and effectiveness must not be exaggerated. The sheer scale of global governance simply dwarfed the activities of any one NGO. For instance, just after it was granted Category I status at the UN in 1976, IOCU still had to compete as one voice among so many others. To take just one example, at the 63rd session of ECOSOC in Geneva, 19 July 1977, IOCU had only two representatives, who found themselves sitting alongside many hundreds of delegates. Each of the fifty-five member states of the Council arrived with delegations of up to twenty staff. A further thirty-four UN member states and three non-UN members sent observers, and large teams of staff attended from the specialized agencies such as the ILO, FAO, WHO, World Bank, International Monetary Fund, and so on. Intergovernmental agencies such as the Council of Europe, the League of Arab States, and the Organization of African Unity were also represented in large numbers. Any NGO presence would be small in comparison, but even here there were issues of size and scale. All the Category I NGOs sent a handful of representatives, as did thirty-seven bodies with Category II status, plus a further five delegations from those on the roster who had been invited to participate on that particular day. IOCU representatives Dorothy Willner and Hélène Chervet could not hope to dominate proceedings nor even to ensure that IOCU concerns were aired at all.[63]

The consumer movement is also a rather complicated body. It is a general issue organization, which has sought to represent a considerable variety of definitions of the consumer interest. Even at this time it could not simply be categorized as a developmental NGO alongside the likes of Oxfam or Christian Aid. As an organization funded and supported by the respectable affluent classes of Europe and North America it also stood as much inside as outside the dynamics of international capitalism. If the term "anti-globalization movement" had been common parlance in the 1980s, then IOCU's ambivalent position would have been obvious. As a leading campaigner on global civil society issues, it would have been at the forefront of any notion of anti-globalization. But as a campaigner for the consumer interests of the rich and the poor, IOCU must also be recognized as a promoter of globalization, notwithstanding how variedly this has been understood. It has fought for standards and regulations that offer the same protections to all consumers around the world. There is a clear ethic of internationalism and global justice to this, as well as a desire to see all—rather than the favored few living in the West—participate in the consumer society. But it also represents a force for harmonization, which could be argued to have assisted rather than restricted the forward march of the capitalist market. Certainly this could be claimed for IOCU's campaign to extend consumer protection legislation around the world, perhaps the main focus of the consumer movement's work at the UN for much of the 1970s and 1980s.

III

As early as 1964, the international consumer movement was aware of the limitations inherent to promoting consumer protection legislation. For Elizabeth Schadee of Consumentenbond, many consumer protection regulations in Europe and North America had been introduced to serve the interests of the bona fide manufacturer against fraudulent, adulterous, and criminal traders: any benefits accruing to consumers were usually incidental. Harmonization of legislation, then, as encouraged by international organizations and intergovernmental bodies such as ISO and the Common Market, only served to replicate these tendencies. Food and drugs standards could be introduced to facilitate greater commercial exchange between nations, for instance, but the consumer protections they also offered, Schadee claimed, were of a lowest common denominator variety that did not serve the consumer's true interests.[64]

The consumer movement therefore promoted its own protection proposals that would counteract those offered by commercial organizations with their conflicting interests. But a consequence of this tactic was a concentration of political consumerism on the legal protection of shoppers acting as individuals. The proposals put forward by IOCU would come to be based on the best practices observed in different national contexts, but which were still all broadly focused on providing more information, better forms of redress, and legal guarantees for the individual. What protection legislation did not offer was the means to address questions arising from access to basic needs and economic and social justice that were emerging from consumer groups in the global South. It also meant that in IOCU's demand for global consumer protection it campaigned for measures that served to modify the market rather than overhaul it. In this sense, we can see how globalization cannot be simply attributed to rather abstract forces of westernization or, more critically, Americanization. NGOs have also played their role in these processes. This is not to identify NGOs themselves as forces of westernization—although this criticism has sometimes been made, particularly in the field of human rights[65]—but to point to the complexity of interactions between state and non-state actors whereby only certain of the demands of an NGO are met or are channeled toward ends that coalesce with the interests of others. For the consumer movement, it meant its most discernible success would be in an arena adaptable to the interests of competing pressure groups. Such success would contrast with the failures of many of its other campaigns.

Establishing a set of Guidelines on Consumer Protection was a logical extension of the sets of consumer rights—the right to safety, the right to be informed, the right to choose, and the right to be heard—which had become the operating philosophy of IOCU during the 1960s. Declarations of principles, codes of practice and charters had also become increasingly fashionable among the international community eager to create benchmarks for the details of development initiatives. In 1970, the International Co-operative Alliance followed the lead taken by IOCU in the new politics of consumption and set about establishing its own charter on consumer rights.[66] But it would be IOCU that ran with the concept of international standards, provided most of the ideas for its content, and pushed it through the committees and organizations of the UN.

In 1975, at its Consumer Congress in Sydney, IOCU resolved to press the UN for a set of guidelines on consumer protection. It wanted the UN to conduct a survey of consumer protection legislation around the world, for ECOSOC to appoint an expert panel to draw up a Model Code of Consumer Protection Practice, and for the General Assembly to recommend that member states adopt such a code while the UN itself would create a Consumer Protection Agency to monitor its effectiveness. Dorothy Willner, who had already sounded out a number of officials at the UN to discuss whether such a set of proposals would be realizable, was charged with taking the resolution to ECOSOC. Her first point of entry was the Commission on Transnational Corporations where she argued in 1976 that the proposed Code of Conduct on Transnational Corporations offered insufficient protection for consumers. She then approach ECOSOC itself and tabled a statement requesting the organization to formulate model guidelines on consumer protection.[67]

IOCU's promotion to Category I status afforded it much greater authority in pressing for the guidelines. It made another bid in 1977 and ECOSOC conceded that the UN's interests in consumer protection had so far been inadequate or, at best, "marginal."[68] ECOSOC accordingly voted to request the Secretary-General to prepare a survey of consumer protection at different national levels, which was duly published the following year.[69] Discussions about consumer protection and further action opened up over the following two years.[70] IOCU lobbied hard at this time. It arranged for national consumer groups to pressurize their own governments.[71] It monitored the motivations and actions of different national governments so it knew best whom to approach.[72] It repeatedly urged ECOSOC itself to advance to the next stage in developing the guidelines.[73] It held its own seminars to better formulate its own ideas on consumer protection legislation.[74] And it worked with the UN Economic and Social Commission for Asia and the Pacific, which held a consultation on consumer protection in Bangkok in 1981.[75] That same year ECOSOC finally issued a request to the Secretary-General to develop a set of guidelines on consumer protection, which he immediately did. What they consisted of at this stage were some general principles, which also took into account the needs of developing world consumers, but which largely borrowed from the best practices of Western capitalist states, and which reaffirmed a model of protection that ultimately sought to protect the consumer mainly as an individual shopper.[76]

However, there was still much detail to be worked out and much opposition to be overcome. A Norwegian civil servant, Lars Broch, was appointed to produce a draft set of guidelines, which first appeared in 1983 and which were accompanied by another statement from the Secretary-General on consumer protection, in which the measures to be taken to regulate transnational corporations had been removed or watered down.[77] The international business community had long objected to the need for any such guidelines. The International Chamber of Commerce (ICC) for instance, preferred a system of voluntary codes of practice. But it had also been receptive to the idea of protection and willing to engage in further discussion with consumer representatives.[78] Perhaps the ICC took comfort in knowing that it would always be able to put forward its case with more force than the consumer movement. During a 1979 consultation at ECOSOC, for instance, Willner fought as a lone voice among an NGO delegatation consisting largely of those manufacturing and employers' organizations that had long enjoyed Category I status.[79]

In the 1980s, however, the mood changed and tremendous hostility to the guidelines was noted in the U.S. government delegation to UN committees. Murray Wiedenbaum, Mallinckrodt Distinguished University Professor and Director of the Center for the Study of American Business at Washington University in St. Louis, Missouri, led the U.S. government opposition, working closely with newly confident business organizations inspired by the more aggressive, anti-regulatory tone of the Reagan administration at home. Later, after the UN passed the Guidelines, he would claim they were a "model of vagueness and overblown phraseology," which nevertheless acted as "a blueprint for a centrally directed society."[80] He argued that consumers much preferred cheapness over either safety, regulation, or any commitment to vague ideals, which only produced "high-mindedness and fuzzy-thinking." He even challenged the legitimacy of the UN in acting on behalf of consumers and saw in the Guidelines yet another example of UN interference in private enterprise.

This opposition eventually resulted in a dilution of some of the key elements of the Guidelines in their slow progress through the UN bureaucracy during the first half of the 1980s. By 1985, IOCU complained that the revised Guidelines had deleted the provisions of advertising controls while specifically encouraging business codes of marketing, which it felt would never be as rigorous or as effective as its own proposals. The Guidelines also further accepted the principle that the business community has a role in the education of the consumer, an activity that the consumer groups believed should be left to independent organizations such as themselves.[81] IOCU, however, was in many ways well prepared for any such battle with business. It formulated close ties with the drafter of the Guidelines, leading to Broch's becoming director-general of IOCU in the mid-1980s. And it replaced Willner as its UN representative with Esther Peterson, a veteran U.S. labor and consumer lobbyist who had worked with several administrations dealing with consumer affairs. She worked with both Broch and several government delegations favorably inclined toward the Guidelines, including Pakistan and Sweden, and in 1985 the UN eventually passed them. This was not without a considerable fight. Many compromises and concessions had to be made before the U.S. government finally gave way, though many felt that the 1984 Bhopal tragedy—when a Union Carbide factory leaked forty tons of toxic gas killing thousands of people—helped create a more pro-regulatory culture for a short while. But the international consumer movement was left bruised from the encounter because the eventual 1985 UN Guidelines on Consumer Protection fell far short of the protections given by the U.S. government to its own citizens at the domestic level.[82]

The passing of the Guidelines reflects more broadly on IOCU's politics of consumption, if not the dilemmas inherent to consumer society in general. On the one hand, they were a clear success for organized consumerism. They demonstrated the ability of an NGO to lobby an organization as large as the UN and to achieve its stated goals. The Guidelines have indeed also served their intended purpose. They have become the basis for consumer protection legislation around the world. Within just one year, the Indian government passed a Consumer Protection Act, which borrowed heavily from the UN model. Other countries have followed suit, with IOCU diverting much of its resources to assisting national governments in drawing up national guidelines. Whereas the UN Consumer Protection Advisory Service proved relatively weak, the willingness of IOCU to act in a similar role has ensured that consumer protection legislation has been adopted all over the world.[83] Furthermore, IOCU has subsequently worked to get the guidelines extended. Although they have not been so successful in clawing back some of the concessions made in the 1980s, they have ensured that today the guidelines have been broadened, particularly in the promotion of sustainable consumption.[84]

On the other hand, the Guidelines have diverted much of IOCU's attention away from questions of access and they have resulted in a model of consumer protection, which has helped define the politics of consumption—at the official level—as being based essentially on these legal statements. As the activities of consumer groups in the developing world have demonstrated, there is much more to consumer society than offering basic protections to individual shoppers in the market. Aspects of economic and social justice are largely excluded from the Guidelines, rendering consumer protection a rather limited concept, one that is divorced from a notion of a social movement that organized consumerism seemed to have become by the 1970s. For the conflicting interests contained within the consumer movement, and perhaps within all of ourselves as we have to trade off the specific protections we want for ourselves with the more general protections we want for citizens as a whole, the Guidelines have come to represent different things. For some socially and politically conservative moderates they are the crowning achievement of IOCU's raison d'être. For others they are a reflection of the blinkered vision of organized consumerism, which directed too much of its energies to the Guidelines at the expense of the interests of the poor and the disadvantaged.

IV

The complexities of the relationship between IOCU and the UN can be teased out by comparing two of the consumer lobbyists at ECOSOC. Dorothy Willner, IOCU's chief campaigner throughout the 1970s, belonged very much to the era of respectable postwar associational life, rather than to the new wave of social protest witnessed since the 1960s.[85] She was tied to the international women's organizations that had played a role in international affairs ever since the establishment of the League of Nations in 1919.[86] She was not connected to the new generation of women's activism associated with second wave feminism. Nor was she a natural ally of the new form of consumer politics being driven by groups such as the Consumers' Association of Penang. Indeed, the acrimony she expressed toward Anwar Fazal following her departure from IOCU in 1983 testifies to the huge social, political, and cultural divide between the two—North and South—strands of the consumer movement.[87] Her objective had been very much to increase the profile of IOCU. This was as much an end in itself, because there was relatively little discussion on how that representation should be put into practice. According to consumer leaders today, this stage of IOCU's involvement with the UN reflected a naivety, albeit one shared by many committed internationalists in the NGO community who attempted to align their organizations with the more progressive and liberal ideals of the UN in the 1960s and 1970s.[88]

At a surface level Esther Peterson was a similar character. She was of the same generation and had also been associated with that spirit of internationalism, which permeated through the women's organizations in the decades following World War II. Peterson came from the labor movement, her debating skills had been sharpened in the New England textile industry's labor disputes of the depression era, and she had accumulated decades of experience as a lobbyist and

Figure 6. Esther Peterson, speaking at the Triangle Shirtwaist Factory fire memorial in 1961.

Courtesy of the UNITE HERE Archives, Kheel Center, Cornell University.

political manipulator along the corridors of power in Washington, DC. She had served as Assistant Secretary of Labor under Kennedy, before becoming Johnson's Special Advisor on Consumer Affairs. After advising industry on consumer issues for a few years, she returned to government in 1977, when Carter brought her in specifically to ease through the passage of the Consumer Protection Agency Bill. Although this Bill was unsuccessful, she obtained widespread praise from the consumer movement and this encouraged IOCU to acquire her services. She knew how to deal with some of the more aggressive factions of the U.S. government and she had firsthand experience of tackling corporate lobbyists head on. In the run up to the passing of the Guidelines in 1985, she used these contacts to engage in behind-the-scenes informal contacts with many individuals who were her enemies in public fora. It was this knowledge of her negotiating enemy that made Peterson a more effective lobbyist than Willner in what she herself described as the "bitter controversy" over the UN Guidelines.[89]

Willner and Peterson therefore embody the two main approaches to the UN adopted by IOCU. Willner's term of office reflected the coming to an end of a complacent period in IOCU's contributions to global affairs when the mere achievement of a representative function was regarded as a sufficient claim to success. But there is a world of difference between having a seat at the table and having something to say, never mind ensuring that others are going to listen and act on one's words. Once IOCU had obtained Category I status, it was opened up to the sheer scale of the organization confronting them. Acting as a solitary amateur voice amid so many seasoned, professional, and even mercenary negotiators and lobbyists was simply not enough. IOCU realized this when the opposition to the Guidelines began to mobilize and it could look back with satisfaction on its decision to appoint Peterson and bring in a new style of consumer activism.

Nevertheless, these changes in style should not detract from an appreciation of another aspect of IOCU's relationship with the UN. For all the differences between Willner and Peterson, they were both campaigning for the same result: the passing of a rather diluted set of guidelines, which did not reflect the full politics of consumption articulated within the movement. In this regard, we can have some sympathy with claims that NGOs such as IOCU have contributed to a process of westernization as they have posited European and North American best practices as the models toward which the rest of the world ought to strive. Because NGOs were there at the creation of the UN and because so many shared its vision, they have been implicated in a process of globalization said to be dominated and directed by the West and, principally, the United States.

This is a view that too readily seeks to map NGOs onto the existing contours of global diplomatic history. What is not captured is the extent to which NGOs have operated as independent agents and the extent to which they have often identified with developing world agendas. Certainly so many NGOs such as IOCU were galvanized by the UN's Second Development Decade of the 1970s. The accusation that NGOs were a key element of westernization and Americanization also ignores the extent to which figures such as Peterson had to tackle a set of opponents who emerged directly from the United States and the West. It is difficult to claim in such an uncomplicated manner that IOCU was transposing U.S. values onto the world stage when the very opponents of its proposals were the officials of the U.S. government.

Instead, the contribution of NGOs to global civil society and to intergovernmental organizations has to be seen as a complex phenomenon. In this case, rather than seeing organized consumerism as the handmaiden of capitalism, it is better to analyze the processes of harmonization and convergence that were inspired from so many different quarters. Globalization is therefore a process encouraged by many competing interests, not just those of Western or U.S. governments. The role of NGOs in these processes has to be acknowledged and their contributions admitted, without forcing them to one side of the divide in a narrative of the Cold War or of the so-called anti-globalization movement. Instead, one can see in the period from the 1960s to the 1980s a varied set of roles undertaken by NGOs that were both, at differing times, running counter to and alongside wider trends in global history. Often this was through a growing unity between a whole range of NGOs inspired by U Thant's vision of the UN and the movement of the non-aligned states to develop a New International Economic Order. The UN Second Development Decade provides a link between the classic Cold War and the era of globalization. Organizations such as IOCU were the forerunners of so many modern NGOs inadequately categorized as for or against globalization.[90]

Indeed, IOCU's work at the UN in the 1970s and 1980s demonstrates the complexity of the relationship between NGOs and global governance. Further chapters will explore the more obviously oppositional politics IOCU adopted during this period, but the detailed case study on consumer protection presented here shows how IOCU could, on the day to day level, be opposing the interests of the U.S. government while, at the more abstract level, be supporting the central pillars of U.S. liberal individualism. IOCU adopted an issues-based approach to consumer problems, a tactic that acknowledged the potentially divisive differences that can exist in an organization that seeks to represent the world's poor and the world's affluent. And the success it had on these issues was influenced by the extent to which their campaigns matched the interests of other actors at the UN. In the example of the Guidelines on Consumer Protection, the U.S. government reluctantly conceded defeat, but only after the Guidelines had become so diluted that any victory claimed by the consumer movement could be called into question, and from within its own ranks.

In some senses IOCU was allowed a victory in this sphere of activity. It channeled consumerism to politically acceptable arenas. Superficially, this positioned IOCU as the promoter of a weak regulatory environment that has done more to bolster rather than fundamentally reform the capitalist marketplace. But elsewhere IOCU's campaigns would meet with more obvious signs of failure. As it embarked on a series of high-profile campaigns, IOCU appeared to be at the forefront of a fledgling anti-globalization movement. But by looking at the whole spectrum of IOCU's activities we can see an NGO that has been both for and against globalization. It has contributed to processes of harmonization and convergence but it has also opposed them. In these apparent contradictions, we have an insight into the operations of NGOs as a whole. It is too simple to examine them as capitalist or communist, conservative or radical. They have adopted a variety of positions to suit a variety of contexts. That some appear more progressive than others, or that the activities of some attract more attention from scholars than others, does not detract from the fact that they have played a significant role in global history since 1945.

THE ALL-CONSUMING NETWORK

The Politics of Protest in an Age of Consumption

According to statistics compiled by the World Health Organization, over 4,000 babies die every day because they are not breast-fed. This amounts to approximately 1.5 million every year or one infant mortality every thirty seconds. The nature of the problem, as argued by a number of campaigning organizations such as Baby Milk Action, La Leche League, and the World Alliance for Breastfeeding Action, is now reasonably familiar. Multinational corporations have promoted infant formulas and alternatives to mother's milk, which are either less nutritious or downright dangerous. Particularly in areas where water is unsafe, it is claimed that babies are up to twenty-five times more likely to die if bottle fed, either because dirty water is added to the milk formula or because bottles and teats are not sterilized. Infections lead to diarrhea and death, while the money spent on the formulas further reduces family incomes encouraging mothers to dilute the product more than recommended ensuring the child—and possibly its siblings—are malnourished. Even where adequate clear water supplies are assured, it is claimed that manufactured products cannot compete with the quality of breast milk. Several NGOs argue that in countries such as the UK bottle-fed babies are ten times more likely to be hospitalized with gastrointestinal illness and that breast-fed babies are less likely to die of cot death or suffer from allergies.[1]

Many of these claims are undoubtedly disputed, but the core problem of the inappropriate use of breast milk alternatives has persisted over the decades. The starting point for the current movement stretches back prior to World War II when the pediatrician Dr. Cicely Williams began campaigning in Malaya against manufacturers of canned and dried milk. In 1939, she addressed the

Singapore Rotary Club with her speech "Milk and Murder," a stirring defense of breast milk over bottled milk that continues to inspire milk activists to this day.[2] What is significant about the defense of breast milk is the more confrontational stance against the milk formula industry taken by activists and the sheer number of NGOs involved in high profile campaigns, particularly the boycott of Nestlé, which has now existed for over thirty years. Opponents of bottled milk have been angered over industry practices such as the dressing of sales staff as nurses and the unsubstantiated claims made of the nutritional benefits of infant formulas. But the promoters of breast milk include not only the critics of multinational capitalist enterprise; they also consist of public health workers, environmentalists, women's groups, consumers, feminists, and conservative reactionaries who have sought to use breast-feeding as a means to extol the virtues of mothering.

It is this combination of a variety of groups and individuals from across the political spectrum that makes the campaign against breast milk substitutes indicative of trends in global civil society. The Nestlé boycott may have involved organizations specifically established to campaign against infant formula, and to some extent it mobilized sufficient sections of the population to suggest it represented a new social movement in the manner of environmentalism and feminism. But it was also marked by the coming together of pre-existing institutions prepared to unite on a specific issue. They did this through the construction of a transnational network administered and co-ordinated by the global consumer movement. Whereas previously global civil society had been characterized by the campaigns of general issue federations—of the labor movement, the women's movement, the consumer movement, and so on—since the late 1970s these groups increasingly worked together in less formal networks and coalitions, which allowed them to pool their resources and respond quickly to perceived specific failings of the market. The networks override any more fundamental and political differences that might exist within different branches of the NGO community and constitute an agreement by diverse entities to set aside their more general agendas in order to focus specifically on one particular problem. The campaigns that have arisen against the use of pesticides or the dumping of pharmaceutical products on unregulated Third World markets have not been regarded as first steps in a wider set of co-ordinated reforms. They have been seen as ends in themselves, the members of the network accepting that the network should disband and that each should go their own separate way once a particular problem has been resolved.

This focus on networking has certainly attracted a tremendous amount of popular attention. For example, the 2005 movie *The Constant Gardener*, based on John le Carré's novel, highlighted the work of Health Action International and other NGOs in protesting the trial of drugs in Africa where the consumer protection mechanisms of Europe and North America are absent. Equally important, Naomi Klein's 2000 anti-globalization "manifesto," *No Logo*, suggested that the "web" of brands, or the network of the global economy, could

Figure 7. "Milk and Murder." Publicity poster for the International Organisation of Consumers Unions, 1981.

Courtesy of IOCU.

be matched by a new wave of social activism. While many dismissed the anti-globalization movement for its sheer diversity and lack of political or ideological coherence, Klein celebrated its anarchic and pluralist spirit. She claimed that street protestors, fair traders, culture "jammers," human rights activists, and ethical shareholders were all connected; if not by their commitment to some utopian alternative to capitalism, then at least by their commitment to work together to limit, restrict, and restore a sense of balance to corporate power.[3] As she has since argued, global civil society consists of up to 30,000 NGOs, all connected to the web of protest, but all "free to dip in and out" as they enter and exit numerous specific campaigns.[4] *No Logo* certainly captured a mood, evidenced by the proliferation of books by journalists, activists, and academics demonstrating disillusionment with the politics of the traditional Left and with the identity politics of the 1960s. Instead, they have advocated a political engagement consistent with the single-issue focus of campaigning networks. Here, no grand narrative is necessarily posed. As one populist account put, there might be one "no" to the anti-globalization movement, but there are many "yeses."[5]

To be sure, a number of writers have tried to impose coherence on this tremendous array of social activists and NGOs. The broad processes of political and economic globalization themselves are held to produce an oppositional coalition, which unites Left and Right on a whole range of issues.[6] Some have attempted to provide a sense of direction to global civil society, setting out a model of global governance and democracy.[7] But just as often as these attempts at intellectual or goal-oriented coherence fail to produce new answers, they also tie themselves in analytical knots that see them advocating traditional solutions behind a veneer of radicalism.[8] And, to some extent, they are rather missing the point in trying to go beyond a politics of networks and single-issue campaigning. It is precisely that pluralist spirit and the refusal to impose an intellectual grand narrative or political vision that has continued to inspire new generations of global campaigners. Whether this is an appropriate political tactic or otherwise, it is nevertheless clear that the exponential growth in NGO organizing since the 1980s has constituted a desire by many involved to seek new forms of political engagement, which allows them to protest against particular abuses without signing up to a broader set of ideological goals. Even when new organizations such as the French-based ATTAC (Association pour la Taxation des Transactions financières pour l'Aide aux Citoyens) emerged out of established leftist circles, there has been an embrace of the sheer range of proposed alternatives to what are generally seen as the problems of neoliberalism. It is this diversity that not only marks the characteristics of many subsequent networks, but the sense of optimism that pervaded the spirit of diversity surrounding the creation of the World and European Social Forums.[9]

No matter how extensive the celebration of networks and coalitions since the 1990s has been, it is the contention of this chapter that they actually came about much earlier than is usually assumed. Their existence further highlights the dynamics and influence of non-state actors in global history as set out in the previous chapter. Moreover, the consumer movement played a crucial role in the establishment of certain key networks relating to baby foods, pesticides, and pharmaceuticals, which proved to be important forerunners of networking as an organizing tactic for so many NGOs in the 1990s. Indeed, in many ways, the consumer movement was ideally placed to develop networks because its own commitment to political neutrality assured it was well disposed to the formation of links between pre-existing organizations which might, in other circumstances, be opposed to one another or be reluctant to become campaigning allies. The consumer movement had long relied on a politics of pragmatism, in both the developing and the developed world, which had enabled it to take stands on certain key issues while attracting support from across the political spectrum. Networks would work in precisely the same manner and it is consequently appropriate that organized consumerism was such a driving force behind their establishment at the global level. The consumer movement presented itself as a neutral entity, to which other NGOs could attach themselves without invoking wider divisions based on broader value frameworks. As such, networks would enable socialists and Christians, conservatives and radicals to come together on specific subjects, just as the global consumer movement contained elements from across the political spectrum within its own national organizations.

This chapter begins with an overview of the politics and tactics of networking, before moving on to consider the three principal networks associated with the consumer movement: the International Baby Food Action Network (IBFAN), the Pesticide Action Network (PAN), and Health Action International (HAI). The chapter argues that the consumer movement's promotion of networks enabled it to assume an importance within the global NGO community in the 1980s that it has subsequently never been able to surpass. In particular, the networks facilitated a whole range of lesser and Southern NGO voices to be filtered through the consumer movement as the International Organisation of Consumers Unions took advantage of its consultative status at the UN to promote the causes advocated by IBFAN, PAN, and HAI. Moreover, it suggests that networking itself is a form of political campaigning intrinsic to consumer society. By focusing on the specific issue, the consumer movement does not require the consumer to oppose the whole system of the market economy. It enables an abuse to be identified and potentially rectified without calling on its opponents to sign up to a wider alternative or utopian project. It enables activists to participate in society as citizens, while accepting that they will still want to behave as consumers in other spheres of their life. Citizenship and consumption are therefore not understood as alternatives in the politics of networking. They allow both participation in consumer society and an enjoyment of its benefits while remaining alert to the potential problems faced by individuals and the difficulties that other consumers might experience. At this stage, we can suspend judgment as to whether networks are the most effective form of global civil society action, but the integral nature of networks to consumer activism—and to socio-political action in general—should be acknowledged.

I

At the end of the 1970s, the international consumer movement made the deliberate decision to adopt a greater leadership role on global affairs. This meant it addressed a whole range of questions that went beyond the uncontroversial topics of consumer information and education. By this time, the activities of IOCU's Regional Office for the Asia-Pacific had come to dominate the work of the organization as a whole. It meant that the issues affecting developing world consumers came to dominate the work of IOCU as a whole. This was particularly the case during Anwar Fazal's presidency from 1978 to 1984. As a representative of the Consumers' Association of Penang and as leader of the global movement, Fazal became the figurehead of an ascendant developing world consumerism that would have made itself heard at some point. Yet for those involved in the consumer movement no doubts exist as to the impact Fazal had on consumerism during his term of office. Speaking long after Fazal had left IOCU, and under acrimonious circumstances (see chapter 7), subsequent director-generals and presidents of IOCU have attested to his influence not only

Figure 8. Anwar Fazal, Asia's Ralph Nader?

Courtesy of Anwar Fazal.

in promoting developing world agendas but in ensuring these were heard within the international community of NGOs and intergovernmental organizations.[10] Julian Edwards, the Director of IOCU from the mid-1990s admitted that "through to the mid-1980s, for ten years, the centre of gravity and most of the work of the organization was being done by Anwar and the office he set up in Malaysia."[11] For Rhoda Karpatkin, Director of the U.S. Consumers Union and the President of IOCU after Fazal, "he was a brilliant man and the best thinker by far of all of us at any time in the whole consumer movement"; "his energy, his visionary qualities, the networks: he made it a very dynamic organization from what had been a sleeping one."[12]

Fazal's position as President and Director frustrated many other Executive Committee members who disliked the speed at which new agendas were adopted and seen through with little consultation. Particularly angered were representatives of Western consumer movements who felt it inappropriate that the concerns of poor consumers were coming to dominate IOCU's work. Undoubtedly this was actually the case. Fazal provided the direct mechanism through which the issues affecting consumers in Malaysia were brought to bear on the global campaigns. In 1975 he reflected on the kind of society Malaysia might become in 2001 and warned of the dangers of becoming "prisoners" to technology and rampant materialism. Criticizing the capital, Kuala Lumpur, as the symbol of inappropriate economic development he proposed instead an alternative, responsible lifestyle based on environmentalism, fighting injustices in the marketplace, and regulating the worst effects of capitalist industry. The consumer movement, he claimed, ought to act as the umbrella organization for civil society and a revived active citizenship, enabling older bodies such as the women's institutes, the trade unions, youth groups, and civic associations such as Rotary to embrace new concerns, including environmentalism, public health, and consumer safety.[13] It was precisely these concerns that became the basis for Fazal's international work. Although he drew on the experience of consumers everywhere, he returned again and again to his experiences in Penang. At one international consumer conference, consumer leaders from the Asia-Pacific region actually met some of the fishermen that CAP had helped in Kuala Juru (see chapter 3).[14]

Yet in addition to his dynamism and energy what was ultimately more significant were the mechanisms Fazal proposed to bring these problems affecting local communities to the international arena. In the early 1970s, he had been well aware of the limited resources of the Malaysian consumer movement. In initiatives such as consumer education programs, cost of living seminars, and testing projects, he recognized the advantages of creating partnerships with other organizations where there existed a "coincidence of interest": "the value of such partnerships is that while you are sharing costs and manpower you are also obtaining *entré* into other elite and important groups in the community and enlarging their consumer consciousness."[15] As President of IOCU, he was aware of the mutual benefits to consumer and non-consumer groups alike in coming together in networks. Following the establishment of the International Baby Food Action Network in 1979 Fazal realized he had created a model for other international campaigns. IBFAN had "brought together a variety of social and development action groups, each independent and yet acting in complete empathy and concert."[16] It connected the consumer movement to a number of NGOs, while these in turn were able to unite beneath the outwardly respectable umbrella of organized consumerism.

The consumer movement's attention to the power of networks from the 1970s actually predated by a number of years the popular advocacy of networking by many NGOs and activists in the 1990s. The debate on networks took off following various claims about the modern—or late modern and sometimes postmodern—nature of commodity capitalism. As various cultural critics proclaimed "the end of disorganised capitalism," economists began to speak of a "new economy" based around the globalization of markets, the free and rapid movement of financial capital, and the transference of power and authority from the governments of nation-states to intergovernmental organizations symbolized by the growing ascendancy of the World Trade Organization. Here was a market capitalism with its vehement defenders and critics, characterized by a new dynamism as multinational corporations seemed to become de-linked from any host community within which they operated, its executives forming a "transnational capitalist class" seemingly imbued with a greater influence on the world's affairs than any democratically elected politician.[17]

The interventions in Afghanistan and Iraq subsequent to 9/11 have suggested for many that such claims for a postmodern globalized economy are perhaps premature and some have preferred instead a return to interpretations more reminiscent of Eisenhower's notion of a "military industrial complex." Yet, in the more socio-cultural analyses of globalization there have been perhaps more lasting interpretations of what has been termed "the information age" and "the network society." This is a world in which everything is apparently connected. Capital is no longer simply rooted in traditional sources of power such as the state, but is now highly flexible, adaptable, and moveable. Indeed, capital in its financial form can be transferred rapidly along the systems of communication pioneered by the revolutions in information technology. Electronic information travels in much the same way as electronic capital, and its spread ultimately touches every one of us. Power is therefore rooted not so much in specific geographical locations, although the cities of London, New York, Tokyo, Paris, and so on retain important nodal functions in the network, but in the flows of information, which move so fast and over such distances that it has been claimed time and space themselves have collapsed. To be influential is to be in the network. Where one physically resides is less important: so long as one has the financial, social, and cultural capital to communicate on the main arteries of the network, then one can participate in the information age.[18]

The claims about networks match many of the assertions of de-centralization made by commentators on the new global economy. Where the notion of networks becomes more useful to us, however, is in the changes in civil society. Social movements have become based on who we think we are rather than what we know we do. Thus since the 1960s there has been a decline in social movements based on our identities as workers and instead a rise in "identity" politics shaped by our cultural affinities to certain value systems promoted by, for example, feminism, environmentalism, and the defense of human rights. Participating effectively in civil society comes to be about recreating the networks of markets, capital, and information in order to ensure that one is not excluded from such flows and movements of power. From such a position a social movement can then influence the world, though the nature of the information age is such that forms of defensive identity are promoted by those excluded from the network, the most extreme cases being nationalism and religious fundamentalism. Effective social movements combine several different strands which, in isolation, might find themselves within or excluded from the network. A case in point is environmentalism, which contains groups ranging from highly effective manipulators of modern information sources (such as Greenpeace) to mobilized citizens and socio-political actors (such as *Die Grünen*), to nature lovers and defenders of the wilderness and on to reactionaries often labeled as Nimbys (Not In My Back Yard). Alone, some of these groups might find themselves switched off from the network, but in coalition they can participate and do so by providing alternative perspectives to those more commonly found in the communication of information and capital.[19]

This is by no means all that can be said of the roles of NGOs in the network society and there is an extended and ongoing discussion of all aspects of "global civil society."[20] But for our purposes, the important characteristic is the rise of networks as a campaigning tactic more suited to the dynamics of the world economy and polity in general. It is important to be precise about what we mean by networks. As interesting as they are we are not concerned with the social networks of groups and individuals, which have given rise to social movements ever since the eighteenth century and which began to attract the attention of social movement analysts in the 1980s.[21] Likewise, we are not referring to international federations of earlier social movements such as the labor and women's movements or even to more specifically focused bodies and agendas such as Anti-Slavery International (an NGO that can trace its organizational history all the way back to the early abolitionists of Britain and America).[22] These, for all their specific concerns, were, like the consumer movement, groupings of national organizations based on the same issue. They were not made up of a range of different actors coming together on the same practical issue.[23]

What we are concerned with, then, is something more specific to the period beginning in the latter quarter of the twentieth century and which is tied in to the changing dynamics of economic and political globalization. We are interested in the most rapidly growing sector of transnational politics; that is, "transnational advocacy networks" as they have been termed.[24] They are coalitions exchanging the resources and information of their constituent bodies in order to make more effective a particular campaign on a chosen subject. They consist of a tremendous variety of civil society actors, including international NGOs, local and national-based social movements, foundations and charities, the media, churches, trade unions, consumer groups, intellectuals, journalists, and even parts of intergovernmental organizations and branches of national governments. They enable communication to take place beyond national boundaries and the development of transnational agendas to emerge, while enabling local, grassroots groups to bypass their own governments, on whom they might have very little influence, in order instead to bring pressure from the international community. They have grown out of social movements willing to combine their resources and knowledge, while provoking new social movements focused on campaigning for a single issue in new national contexts. Indeed, it is claimed that networks create "'imagined commonalities' which provide otherwise isolated activists with the impression that they are part of broader, more cosmopolitan movements."[25]

Transnational advocacy networks have been particularly associated with the environmental, women's, and human rights movements. As channels through which local campaigns can affect global agendas, they have also been particularly prominent in the championing of indigenous rights. They include such prominent coalitions as El Taller, formed in 1992 to bring together NGOs concerned with "the dispossession of peoples, the destruction of cultures and the deepening of poverty"; Climate Action Network formed in 1989 to limit global warming and which draws on 365 existing NGOs; and Social Watch, a Southern-based network of human rights, labor, and women's groups that came together at the World Summit on Social Development in Copenhagen in 1995 to act as a citizens' watchdog on social development policies.[26] They have culminated in the massive network-based campaigns of Jubilee 2000, Trade Justice, and the Stop the War Coalition. Jubilee 2000's campaign for debt relief began in 1988 when NGOs such as Christian Aid, Tearfund, Friends of the Earth, Oxfam, and the World Development Movement established the Debt Crisis Network. By 2000 the network consisted of twenty-seven Coalitions in Europe and North America, seventeen in Central and Latin America, fifteen in Africa, and ten in Asia. An indication of the size of the network can be seen by the fact that there were one hundred and ten NGOs connected to the UK Coalition alone and that, collectively, Jubilee 2000 was able to produce a petition of 24 million signatures from over sixty different countries.[27] If such networks have gained the most prominence, the logic of networking has been most permanently embedded in the World Social Forum, itself the collaboration of the Brazilian Association of Entrepreneurs for Citizenship (CIVES) and the French-based ATTAC and which, at just its second meeting in 2002, had already attracted the registration of just under 5,000 NGOs.[28]

What binds a network together is not only the commitment to share information and ideas and the use of a particular political rhetoric, but also a set of "shared values."[29] NGOs operating in networks, it is assumed, are united by a liberal/progressive framework, especially in those committed to the alleviation of poverty and the protection of the environment. Yet this is not necessarily the case: beyond a commitment to the removal of the debt of Third World states, for instance, the number of shared values of economists, pop stars, Christians, socialists, and street protestors was potentially very few. Rather, what unites the members of the formally instituted network is a commitment to the particular subject being discussed. To speak of shared values is reminiscent of the more informal social networks enjoyed by those coming from a similar cultural and political milieu. However, what marks the history of organized networking of the late 1970s on is the willingness of many disparate groups to come together on one—and perhaps only one—issue. If we follow the logic of networks to their conclusion, then we must assume that all who joined a network must also be prepared to go their separate ways after the particular problem is resolved. The commitment to the network can be as much about a hard-nosed assessment of political tactics among NGOs as it is to an optimistic first stage in the creation of an alternative anti-global alliance. There are simply too many thousands of NGOs out there to imagine that vague references to shared values can provide any basis for solidarity beyond the network itself.

What we are referring to are formally instituted global campaigning networks devoted to specific social, political, cultural, and economic problems, based on the alliance of many pre-existing NGOs and civil society groups purposefully committed to working together on the subject in hand. Historically, we can regard the networks that began to emerge in the 1970s as a distinct period that fills an important gap in understandings of social movement organizing between the new social movements associated with the 1960s and the mass mobilizations of NGOs in the present (associated with the likes of Trade Justice and the World Social Forum). During the 1980s there was a number of networks that relied on the resources of their membership and, as such, were only minimal operations in themselves, often consisting of just a few staff armed with powerful communication routes. As a pre-existing organization with a potentially enormous set of concerns, the consumer movement was, in theory at least, ideally placed to begin to make more formal alliances with many other types of international NGO at this time.

This is not to claim that the consumer movement became the sole instigator of global networking. It could be argued that networks began much earlier. Some would claim that anti-slavery itself is a single-issue campaign network, though other examples such as the campaign at the turn of the twentieth century conducted by Western missionaries and Chinese reformers to eradicate foot binding better serve as a forerunner of late twentieth-century networking.[30] In the 1970s, groups organized informally in Latin America to campaign against human rights abuses in Argentina. Yet the number of formally constituted global networks was relatively few. In the same decade, environmental organizations began to network within their own nation-states and, in 1976, at the HABITAT Forum of the UN Conference on Human Settlements, the Transnational Network for Appropriate/Alternative Technologies (TRANET) was established.[31] Yet until the 1980s few environmental organizations had the time or the resources to devote to networking. Of those early networks that did exist were the Asian-Pacific Peoples' Environmental Network (1983), the Third World Network (1984), and the World Rainforest Network (1986). All three were based in Penang and were important forerunners of future coalitions.

The importance of consumer movements to the development of these formalized global networks should not be overlooked. Of the three networks in Penang just cited, all were due to the initiatives of the Consumers' Association of Penang and Sahabat Alam Malaysia (SAM, Friends of the Earth, Malaysia)— a 1977 offshoot of CAP. The original founder of CAP, S. M. Mohamed Idris, still serves as President of all these organizations, and Anwar Fazal was heavily involved in their creation. At the same time Fazal developed a whole host of other networks with the support of the IOCU regional office. Following the success of the International Baby Food Action Network in 1979, IOCU embarked on a near frenzy of network organizing. Consumer Interpol, which acted as a watchdog on the sale of goods banned under the UN Consolidated List (see chapter 4), could itself be seen as a network because it relied on the participation and co-operation of a number of NGOs in different nation-states. But it was followed by a series of other initiatives more obviously identifiable as networks, which together enjoyed varying degrees of success and longevity. In 1984, the World Consumer Congress resolved to campaign against the tobacco industry, leading to the formation of AGHAST (Action Group to Halt Advertising and Sponsorship of Tobacco), which drew on prominent anti-smoking campaigners like Simon Chapman, whose IOCU-published manual for countering the tobacco industry, *The Lung Goodbye,* had been formerly printed by the Australian Consumer Association on behalf of Consumer Interpol.[32] On World Consumer Rights Day, 15 March 1985, the Seeds Action Network was launched in Rome, sparking initiatives that would ultimately go well beyond the consumer movement and adopt a life of its own when prominent global activists such as Vandana Shiva campaigned in India for the collective ownership of seed varieties.[33] Following the tragedy of the Union Carbide gas leak in Bhopal in 1984, IOCU launched a No-More-Bhopals Network two months later and co-ordinated the International Coalition for Justice in Bhopal. Within a couple of years, several other networks could be added to the list: the Coalition Against Dangerous Exports, the International Toxic Waste Action Network, the Consumer Educators Network, Booklink, the Global Greenhouse Network, and the Food Irradiation Network International.[34]

The focus of the rest of this chapter is on the three most prominent and long-lasting networks established and administered by IOCU: International Baby Food Action Network formed in 1979, Health Action International formed in 1981, and Pesticide Action Network formed in 1982. All three campaigns represented specific problems around which a large number of NGOs could express a concern. All three were focused on the use of dangerous or inappropriate goods that had long histories of attracting social reformers, often as far back as the nineteenth-century campaigns over adulteration, food and drugs legislation, and public health. And the market sectors on which they were focused all involved the activities of powerful multinational corporations. For these reasons, not only did the three networks set important precedents for the campaigning tactics of global civil society, but they also directed their anger toward a common obstacle to which many NGOs would increasingly turn their attention starting in the 1980s. During this decade, the existence of IBFAN, PAN, and HAI enabled the consumer movement to enjoy something of a leadership role within global civil society as a whole.

II

IBFAN emerged in 1979 from the long-standing campaign against bottle feeding. For decades after Cicely Williams spoke of the "massacre of the innocent by unsuitable feeding" NGOs maintained the pressure on the infant formula industry, bolstered by Williams's own appointment in 1948 as head of the World Health Organization's Maternal and Child Health Services.[35] By the

1970s, after the term "commerciogenic malnutrition" had been coined to describe the impact of industry marketing practices on infant health and after the UN established the Protein-Calorie Advisory Group (1970), the pressure on companies such as Nestlé and Bristol-Myers (now Bristol-Myers-Squibb) increased. In 1973, an influential *New Internationalist* article was published, "The baby food tragedy," which was followed the following year by *The Baby Killer*—a report on bottle feeding in the Third World published by War on Want. This was translated in Switzerland as *Nestlé Kills Babies* by the Bern Third World Action Group. This led to a libel suit brought by the company that Nestlé eventually won in 1976 though not without bringing about a tremendous amount of bad publicity. At the same time, shareholder actions, led by the Sisters of the Precious Blood, continued to put pressure on Bristol-Myers, while in North America the Infant Formula Action Coalition (INFACT) was formed in 1977 and launched the long-standing consumer boycott of Nestlé. Beginning to feel the heat, the industry responded with the establishment of the International Council of Infant Food Industries, which set out its own voluntary code for the marketing of breast milk substitutes.[36]

The consumer movement played its part in these campaigns. Earlier, in 1972, IOCU had drawn up its own code of practice for the advertising of infant foods and submitted this to the WHO's Codex Alimentarius Commission, only for it to be largely ignored at the time. It nevertheless maintained its interest in the issue and, following concerns about the weaknesses of the industry's voluntary code, it conducted a survey in eight Asian countries on the promotion of sweetened condensed milk, finding that it was widely promoted as a suitable infant food. Most important, in 1979 it contributed to the WHO/UNICEF Meeting on Infant and Young Child Feeding, which reissued the call for a more rigorous code of conduct. And it was at this meeting that IOCU joined with other baby food campaign groups to form IBFAN.[37]

IOCU itself was a crucial instigator of the network, providing both the secretariat and the administrative support. It marked an important precedent for consumerism as it allied itself with other citizen-based movements as represented by the other five founders of IBFAN: Oxfam, War on Want, the Bern Third World Action Group, INFACT, and the Interfaith Center on Corporate Social Responsibility. To these were added another 100 groups from sixty-four different countries in the first five years of its existence. The network was organized around a small staff based at IOCU's regional office in Penang. Further "central offices" were later formed at INFACT's headquarters in Minneapolis and at the Geneva Infant Feeding Association, while twelve regional centers were created elsewhere in the offices of other attached NGOs. The network was therefore the product of its membership. Its own resources were small, but it could constantly and flexibly draw on those of the attached NGOs.[38]

The reasons IBFAN became such "a prime example of the potential of global networking" was due to the immediate success it enjoyed in obtaining a code of conduct on the industry.[39] IOCU and other NGO lobbyists pressured the

World Health Assembly into adopting a Code of Marketing for Breast Milk Substitutes in 1981. This set out a number of conventions, including the prohibition of dressing sales staff as nurses, the direct advertising of breast milk substitutes, and the distribution of free samples, while product labels were expected to attest to the benefits of breast-feeding. Thereafter, the principal activities of IBFAN have included the publicizing of the Code, monitoring its implementation, and lobbying national governments to implement it as law. IBFAN certainly met with some success. Improvements were made in the marketing of baby foods and, beginning with Peru in 1982, national legislation was introduced. The industry resisted these pressures, despite the consumer boycott of Nestlé spreading to an increasing number of countries. In 1982, it established the Nestlé Infant Formula Audit Commission to monitor its marketing practices using its own guidelines rather than those provided in the Code. Mounting international pressure ultimately led the company to give way to its critics and it signed a commitment in 1984 with the leading NGOs to abide by the main principles of the Code, and the boycott was temporarily lifted in October of that year.[40]

IBFAN, however, continued to monitor the Code and push for more stringent regulation at the European and UN level, including the 1986 World Health Assembly's Resolution 39.28 banning free and subsidized supplies. More worrying, evidence began to mount from activists on the ground that the larger companies were violating the Code on a regular basis, especially in the distribution of free samples to health facilities. In 1988, IBFAN relaunched the boycott of Nestlé while other NGOs around the world tackled similar companies with adverse publicity campaigns. Since the 1980s IBFAN has continued its work on issues similar to those that had provoked its creation a decade earlier. The 1990 Innocenti Declaration, signed by thirty-two countries, acted as a further spur to the adoption of the Code as a minimum basis for national legislation, but infringements have continued and organizations such as UNICEF and WHO have persistently bemoaned the continued use of bottled milk in unsafe areas. At the turn of the millennium, all companies claimed compliance with the Code, but IBFAN's investigations found otherwise. Nestlé, as the world market leader, continued to record the highest number of violations, followed by Milupa of Germany and then the U.S. corporations, Wyeth, Abbott Ross, and Mead Johnson which, IBFAN claimed, practiced the most blatant infringements of the Code.[41]

IBFAN today remains a robust organization and its membership has continued to increase. It has been joined by other global coordinating networks such as the World Alliance for Breastfeeding Action, also based in Penang and created by Anwar Fazal after he left the organized consumer movement. The problems it has dealt with are indicative of the broader issues faced by networks. Most ominous, in terms of future attempts at international regulations on the activities of multinational corporations, was the opposition IBFAN faced from the industry and the U.S. government. The Reagan administration cast the sole vote against the Code in 1981, despite several compromises being made by the NGOs to accommodate U.S. concerns. It was a foretaste of future confrontational voting behavior at the UN throughout the 1980s and it attests to the growing influence of big business on U.S. politicians which, for some time, opposed both federal and international government regulation. Indeed, when the Nestlé Infant Formula Audit Commission was created its first chair was Edmund Muskie, U.S. secretary of state under Jimmy Carter. It symbolized the close ties between American governments and large-scale multinational corporations which, as we will see in the next chapter, became a defining feature of the American attack on regulation and organized consumerism in the 1980s. Just as NGOs created a new dynamism to their activities through networking, so too did multinationals respond with the establishment of their own lobby groups, think tanks, and industry associations. For the networks, as IOCU complained in 1989, it seemed these often had greater access to the staff of bodies such as WHO and UNICEF than the NGOs themselves.[42]

But the problems facing networks were caused not only by the opposition they faced from outside. What is remarkable is that they held together despite some of the differences in outlook that are apparent in its membership. While there was—and is—broad agreement over the issue of the inappropriate marketing of breast milk substitutes in the developing world, attitudes to breast-feeding itself continue to vary. For some, the problem is specific to the Third World, because poor water supplies, limited health services, and unregulated markets are the key issues. For others, breast-feeding is a "womanly art" to be promoted in the affluent West as well. In the advice literature produced by the various organizations, there is clearly some unease about the topic among western women who feel sufficiently informed and safe to make up their own minds over breast-feeding versus bottle-feeding. As one reader of a guidance book produced by La Leche League felt, "La Leche almost looks down on mothers who return to work and do not stay home to breastfeed their children."[43]

Nevertheless, the successes that IBFAN did obtain, and specifically the production of the Code in 1981, certainly acted as a spur for civil society action in the 1980s, and especially for the consumer movement.[44] Following on from baby foods, IOCU turned to networking to deal with other issues affecting consumers and which had concerned citizens for decades.

Pesticide use had long attracted the attention of the public, not least because of the spectacular success of Rachel Carson's *Silent Spring*, published in 1962. Ultimately, the book led to the banning of the pesticide DDT in the United States ten years later, although similar regulations were only intermittently and erratically introduced around the rest of the world, and often with poor subsequent enforcement. Pesticides, like baby foods, represented a concern affecting many different types of citizen and which, at its core, consisted of a basic health and safety issue that had the potential to appeal to a vast cross-section of the world's citizens. Not only did it damage consumers in the broadest sense, in the concerns for the destruction of the environment around them, but growing fears over food safety also raised questions about the extent of adulteration in everyday goods. From a developing world consumer perspective, the poor suffered not only as consumers but also as the impoverished workers expected to spray crops and thus risk their own health. As Carson herself originally put it, this was a truly global issue: "For the first time in the history of the world, every human being is now subjected to contact with dangerous chemicals, from the moment of conception until death. In the less than two decades of their use, the synthetic pesticides have been so thoroughly distributed throughout the animate and inanimate world that they occur virtually everywhere."[45] Here was an issue with the potential to unite all consumers, rich and poor alike, while at the same time reaching out to other NGOs concerned with public health, human rights, and the environment.

In the 1970s, IOCU had begun to examine the problem of pesticides just as it monitored the sale of other dangerous goods. It was well aware of the rising power of multinational agro-chemical enterprises such as the Swiss-based Ciba-Geigy and the German-based Bayer. Likewise, it knew of the increasing reliance of farmers on pesticides following the "Green Revolution" of the 1960s, which had resulted in higher yielding crops that required the greater use of chemical fertilizers. Furthermore, it was aware of the dangers posed to farmers who handled the pesticides and the ecological and humanitarian disasters that had occurred as a consequence. An Indian report estimated that 73 percent of workers in the production and distribution of pesticides displayed symptoms of toxicity; while in central Thailand, the unregulated use of the pesticides, paraquat and carbufuran, meant that water drained from the rice fields where they were both heavily used resulted in the contamination of rivers and canals used by other farmers and the destruction of an estimated 5 million kilograms of fish. Ironically, though, it was the Malaysian fishing village, Kuala Juru, that again found itself at the center of attention. Although the fishermen had, by the end of the decade, moved on to co-operative cockle farming, the problem of pollution from the nearby Prai Industrial Estate remained. In 1980, the radical Consumers Union of Japan was taken around the estate by the Consumers Association of Penang, particularly to visit Prai Agricultural Chemicals, a joint venture between Malaysian and Japanese companies. The photographs taken by the Japanese consumer activists became the basis for a media campaign back home, leading to a mass demonstration by Japanese housewives at the headquarters of the Nihon Nohyaku Company. The resulting pressure led to the managing director visiting Penang and some pollution controls were implemented, with CAP invited to witness their effectiveness.[46]

By this time, CAP had developed its sister organization, Sahabat Alam Malaysia (SAM, Friends of the Earth Malaysia), which pushed for the creation of a transnational network to enable such local issues to be heard on the global arena. With Anwar Fazal forming the bridge, SAM organized a conference in Penang with IOCU in 1982 on the global pesticide trade. The organizations of consumers, farmers, women, and environmentalists that attended the meeting agreed to form the Pesticide Action Network which, as with IBFAN, aimed specifically to obtain a code of conduct to maintain greater regulatory controls over the agro-chemical industry. As a network, its organization also mirrored that of IBFAN's. It soon obtained a global reach of over 300 NGOs from forty-nine countries affiliating within the first two years. Contact between such a diverse collection was maintained through the establishment of regional centers and headquarters at IOCU in Penang, as well as the formation of national PAN coalitions in dozens of countries. The regional offices were housed and supported by the constituent organizations; for example, PAN Europe was run by Oxfam in Oxford. Again, then, the network drew on the strength and resources of many types of NGO, but the consumer movement provided the leadership from its now established center of gravity in Penang.[47]

The stated purpose of PAN was to seek greater regulation on the sale of pesticides, to obtain similar controls for all countries when a particular government banned a pesticide in its own country, and to seek out alternatives to reduce their use. As with baby foods, pesticides had long attracted the attention of the UN, but the network was created to lobby and speed up this work. The Food and Agriculture Office had appointed a panel of experts as far back as 1959 to examine the growing use of pesticides and proposals for controls were regularly made throughout the 1970s. To some extent, the UN Consolidated List of Banned Substances dealt with some of the more dangerous pesticides, but the Food and Agriculture Organization (FAO) also recommended a specific code to deal with the control of exports and imports and their subsequent use. The slow rate with which these proposals moved at the UN encouraged the formation of PAN.[48] The problem, as PAN saw it, was not that pesticides were inherently wrong, or that their use should be banned entirely, but too often there was insufficient testing of their potential toxicity, their persistent use had resulted in the creation of "super-pests," and the prices of pesticides did not reflect the wider social and environmental costs that their use provoked. In addition, PAN worried, in anticipation of many later environmental campaigns, that the research activities of agro-chemical companies were geared more toward increasing the reliance on pesticides than on actually improving the yield of the crops. As Anwar Fazal argued in 1987, "pesticides and the pesticide industry have been allowed to run amok and the consequences have been devastating in their toll and impact. . . . The wild pesticide party of quick-fix chemical cocktails and the global addiction to such toxic chemicals must end."[49]

The initial activities of PAN were consequently geared toward lobbying for and publicizing the FAO's draft code of conduct, as well as promoting further research into organic alternatives. At its first international meeting in 1984, sponsored by the Dutch government, PAN publicized the use and misuse of pesticides around the world, bringing into the public arena information usually withheld by interested parties. This resulted in *The Pesticide Handbook*, compiled by both the consumer movement and the pesticide network, which amounted to a profile of forty-four problem pesticides, mirroring IOCU's earlier investigation into forty-four problem drugs.[50] More significant, PAN chose to focus on twelve of the most dangerous—and increasingly notorious—pesticides in its "Dirty Dozen Campaign" launched in June 1985. The pesticides were also chosen to enable the targeting of their twelve producers, including the "gang of five" that consisted of Bayer, Ciba-Geigy, Shell, Monsanto, and ICI. The resultant bad publicity and the greater attention to the problem of pesticides across the NGO community (for instance, in the same year, the International Youth Federation ran a Pesticides Export Project), created the backdrop to the decision by the FAO to adopt unanimously the International Code of Conduct on the Distribution and Use of Pesticides in November 1985.[51]

As with breast milk the pesticide network was able to obtain an immediate success, though problems remained for both IOCU and PAN. The Pesticide Code deliberately excluded the concept of "prior informed consent" that would have prevented the export of banned and restricted pesticides without the specific written consent of the importing country. PAN has focused on attempting to amend the code and, like IBFAN, monitoring its implementation.[52] It continued to update the *Handbook* and, increasingly it has promoted alternatives publicized in its book, *Escape from the Pesticide Treadmill,* which features reports on successful agricultural schemes that have not relied on chemicals. PAN has run training workshops in order to widen knowledge about the dangers of handling pesticides, particularly among vulnerable groups such as women plantation workers, and it has followed the established principles of information-based consumerism in supporting improved labeling schemes to highlight a product's dangers and composition.[53]

The issue of pesticides both expanded the scope of consumer activism and increased the number of NGOs and concerned citizens campaigning under the banner of consumer protection. One of the most important publications of PAN, *Breaking the Pesticide Habit,* was published by IOCU in 1990 from its Penang office, although it was actually written by Terry Gips, an American environmental activist working at the time for the International Alliance for Sustainable Agriculture, an NGO set up in 1983 and based at the Newman Center at the University of Minnesota.[54] This collaboration reflected the entry of the consumer movement into wider questions about the concept and viability of environmental and economic "sustainability" that would increasingly inform IOCU's work in the 1990s.[55] Likewise, the specific problems of pesticides provoked a broader discussion of agricultural issues that lay behind IOCU's questioning of the appropriateness of biotechnology and the use of genetically modified crops. These concerns have been translated into the general attention to "food security," a subject which, like infant formula and pesticides before it, continues to be the focus of Southern groups and which has led to collaborations with a wider network of NGOs such as the Forum for the Protection of the Public Interest and the South Asia Watch on Trade, Economics and Environment.[56]

But the pesticide network also enabled other civil society issues to be framed within the remit of consumer protection and activism. For instance, an early exposé of the pesticide industry, *Circle of Poison,* written by two American investigative journalists, castigated multinational firms for the exposure to toxic chemicals to which they subjected their workers and consumers. This was a book within the longstanding traditions of American muckraking, but more important the journalists also emphasized how the industry violated the core consumer rights to safety and to information.[57] For the 1980s, at least, pesticide use was an issue of global concern but which was often understood through the prism of organized consumerism—a trend deliberately reinforced by the leading role IOCU took in the establishment of the pesticide network.

The last of the triumvirate of major networks organized by the consumer movement was Health Action International. This was concerned with the multinational pharmaceutical industry and arose out of the consumer movement's longstanding interest in patent medicines. Dangerous drugs had often acted as the spur to national consumer organizing. The side effects of the talcum powder, "talc Morhange," which killed thirty-six children in France in 1972 led to a huge increase in the popularity of French consumer activism, though this in itself was relatively minor compared to the devastating effects of the drug Thalidomide, when it was marketed across Western Europe in the late 1950s and early 1960s resulting in thousands of victims.[58] Because many of these drugs were sold across the world, they acted as early points of international collaboration for the consumer movement. In 1970, IOCU became particularly concerned with the absence of regulations on the pharmaceutical industry as it exported drugs to the developing world. A 1973 study conducted by the UK-based Research Institute for Consumer Affairs on behalf of IOCU found that the antibiotic, chloramphenicol, was sold with varying degrees of information across twenty-one countries and as a treatment for a variety of ailments, whereas as in the West, its recommended uses were extremely narrow and its distribution restricted to doctor's prescriptions.

Far more serious was the case of the anti-infectant, clioquinol. In the 1960s, it had been used in large doses in Japan, resulting in the SMON epidemic, a disease of the nervous system that left over 10,000 people paralyzed and/or blind. Its sale was subsequently prohibited in Japan and the United States although used properly, the drug could be an effective treatment against diarrhea. A 1975 study of clioquinol in the developing world found that it was marketed under a whole variety of brand names, few regulations existed on its use, and consumers were provided with only rudimentary, inadequate, and often contradictory information. A campaign led by IOCU for the rest of the decade eventually resulted in the phased withdrawal of the drug by its manufacturers, Ciba-Geigy, but the case only raised the more general issue of the dumping of drugs in the developing world when their use had been banned or restricted in the West.[59] To clioquinol, the consumer movement could add a whole number of other dangerous products, ultimately provoking the establishment of the

Consumer Interpol. But following the success of IBFAN, IOCU turned to networking once again, especially because, and again as with pesticides and infant formula, UN agencies had begun to consider their use: in this case, in 1978, the World Health Assembly had given WHO a mandate to develop a code of practice on the marketing of essential drugs. IOCU monitored these developments and accordingly instigated the creation of HAI in 1981.

HAI followed the model of the other two networks. It was formed following an international conference, organized by IOCU and BUKO (Die Bundeskoordination Internationalismus, or Federal Coordination of Internationalism), a German Third World development NGO, with other major participants including Oxfam, the Interfaith Center on Corporate Responsibility, and the UK's Social Audit—an offshoot of the Consumers' Association set up by Charles Medawar, a consumer activist inspired by the public interest consumerism of Ralph Nader.[60] HAI brought together 50 (rising to 120 in five years) public interest, development action, health, and consumer groups from both developed and developing countries and IOCU provided the secretariat from its offices in The Hague and Penang.[61] HAI set out to promote a drug agenda so that all drugs met real needs, had significant therapeutic value, were safe, and offered value for money. These were hardly radical aims, although the activities of multinationals and international organizations have made them appear so at times. HAI's early work was focused on opposing the influence of the pharmaceutical companies at the World Health Assembly, especially the Code of Marketing Practice proposed by the International Federation of Pharmaceutical Manufacturers' Associations, which the consumer movement believed was designed specifically to forestall the imposition of any external regulation of the industry. Instead, HAI presented its own draft code on pharmaceuticals to the UNCTAD Committee on the Transfer of Technology in 1982.[62]

Immediately, though, the problem of pharmaceuticals broadened into a much greater issue, with far more at stake, than the more focused topics of baby foods and pesticides. There was less agreement within the international community as to what could be considered a safe good and the relative weight given to the potential side effects of a medicine had to be considered alongside the potential benefits to any one society. In this regard, the imposition of tight regulations such as existed in the West might actually be opposed by the developing state's own government, especially when the more expensive, safer versions of the drugs could not be afforded. The pharmaceutical industry also became more entrenched in its opposition to regulation, not least because of the much greater size of the market for drugs: the total output of the industry was estimated to be $100 billion in 1985. The codes of conduct on pesticides and baby foods had been regarded as dangerous precedents whose general applicability was opposed throughout the 1980s, especially by industries with much greater profits to lose.[63]

While the work of IBFAN and PAN had concentrated on the implementation and monitoring of specific codes of conduct in the 1980s, HAI's work was increasingly geared toward developing alternative systems of provision and principles in the distribution of drugs. This did not mean that it did not undertake exposés of the type that marked the work of the other networks: indeed, in 1981 it followed up its critique of clioquinol with a list of Forty-Four Problem Drugs for activists to campaign against.[64] But in general HAI attempted to focus the range of its work by seeking to define "essential" drugs, leaving the problems about the promotion of non-essential and inappropriate drugs as a separate issue. In 1982, HAI supported the Bangladesh Martial Law Administration's move to eliminate 1,700 harmful, useless, or inessential drugs from its market, creating public health systems based around meeting essential needs.[65] This developed into a "rational use of drugs" policy that has become the guiding principal of HAI. By rational, HAI has meant improving the availability of a small number of essential drugs that have the potential to dramatically improve world health, opposing the direction of resources to heavily promoted, marginally useful, and often dangerous drugs, and providing better information to ensure appropriate prescription and even the "informed consent" of well-informed patient-consumers.[66] It has meant it has persistently opposed multinational marketing practices, going so far as to equate the global system of pharmaceutical distribution with colonialism and slavery in terms of its exploitation of ordinary people.[67] It has opposed particularly the granting of patents to multinational corporations for certain natural products and it has attacked them for their pricing policies in the Third World, which have been geared, it is claimed, toward the profits of the firm rather than the needs of the unwell.[68] As Kumariah Balasubramaniam, HAI's director and leading advocate of rational drugs policies has put it, the case of the network is deceptively simple: "No one will ever argue for the irrational use of drugs. If drugs are to be used rationally, all drugs available in the market should be safe, effective, cost-efficient and meet the health needs of the people. However, . . . rational drug use is the exception rather than the rule, for the markets in most countries are flooded with thousands of ineffective and potentially harmful drugs."[69]

HAI's work has undoubtedly had some impact on the marketing of drugs. It has increased public awareness of a whole range of drugs, from ineffective treatments for diarrhea (the only real answer is oral rehydration) to the dangers of anabolic steroids.[70] Its work has led to the removal from the market of certain drugs highlighted in its campaigns, and agreements have been made with companies such as Ciba-Geigy to restrict their sale in certain regions.[71] HAI has helped increase our understanding of the problems faced by particular groups of consumers such as women and AIDS sufferers. It has provoked new initiatives such as Action for Rational Drugs in Asia (1986), which have gone on to enjoy a separate existence.[72] And it has developed a broad-ranging critique of national health policies, which has seen it comment on the goals of global health programs as a whole.[73] Yet for all its recognition within the global community of intergovernmental organizations and civil society actors, HAI has not been able to see the development of a specific, external code of conduct dealing with the sale of pharmaceuticals. HAI is as much a single-issue campaigning network as PAN and IBFAN, but the range of products it covered as soon as it was established was enormous: the difficulties of developing a coherent and workable code for such a huge industry were perhaps insurmountable. The more important factor was the willingness of the pharmaceutical companies to oppose the work of HAI. This continues to the present day, and the consumer movement still finds itself campaigning on exactly the same sorts of issues that HAI initiated at the beginning of the 1980s.[74]

Although HAI was established before PAN, it was unable to achieve an immediate, clear-cut victory and its work to obtain a code in the 1980s was damaged by the precedents set in the baby milk and pesticide industries. Moreover, by this time, as we will see in the following chapter, the consumer movement and global civil society had learned from the experience of dealing with multinational corporations and was attempting to set out a Code of Conduct on Transnational Corporations. That this was defeated in the late 1980s by an anti-regulatory movement far more organized than it had been at the birth of networking in 1979 is perhaps testament to the potential PAN, IBFAN, and HAI were held to have for NGO effectiveness as a whole.

III

The consumer movement was well aware of the advantages of networking to itself and to the effectiveness of global civil society in general. HAI, PAN, and IBFAN shared many similar characteristics. All were directed at causes that had long attracted the attention of progressive organizations, whether based on the consumer interest, public health policy, the environment, or women's rights. All could draw on a well-established literature, often centered on a certain classic such as Carson's *Silent Spring* or Williams's *Milk and Murder*. All could position themselves as defenders of a wider citizenship interest, which could form the basis of an alliance of many types of NGO. And all had a common enemy toward which anger and campaigns could be directed: for the baby food, pesticide, and drug networks this was multinational capitalism, represented by a select number of corporations that often operated in all three sectors. Consequently, IBFAN, PAN, and HAI all adopted similar basic aims: to stop the sale of inappropriate and/or dangerous goods; to encourage local campaigning against transnational business practices; to link this local work to national, regional, and global campaigns; to represent consumers in the broadest sense of the term—at international bodies, mainly connected with Europe and the UN; and "to provide a forceful global response to the power of the multinational corporations."[75]

What the networks did, then, was to enable smaller groups operating at the local or national level to connect to the institutions of global civil society and global governance through the intermediaries of more established, better resourced, and widely recognized NGOs such as IOCU. Local NGOs helped in the formulation of network policy, which was then presented to bodies such as WHO, the FAO, and ECOSOC by IOCU and others that had already been granted consultative status by the UN and thus the right to speak, initiate, and participate in debates. IOCU recognized that networks could amount to little more than a token gesture as groups could form a new organization but only intermittently contribute to it. At their best networks involved "pooling groups' resources (manpower, money, creativity) together to achieve mutually agreed ends in such a way that the total output exceeds the sum of the parts)."[76] Networking enabled IOCU to draw on the strengths of other groups so that they became "a means of enlarging and strengthening the consumer voice on worldwide specific issues."[77]

Admittedly, such collaboration produced tension and unease, particularly for the constituent members from the affluent West who did not see the immediacy of the problems of pesticides, baby foods, and pharmaceutical selling to the interests of North American and West European consumers. Accordingly, as we will see in more detail in chapter 7, they expressed misgivings about the networks that would eventually lead to IOCU's disassociation from PAN and IBFAN at the beginning of the 1990s. The networks were certainly never a product of affluent consumer society and their location in Penang only reinforced the point about their global, transnational, or non-Western character.[78] Their informality, in terms of how agendas were raised, decisions were reached, and actions were taken was a bureaucratic affront to the commercial professionalism of the experienced advocates of Consumers Union and the Consumers' Association who had long enjoyed strong central control within their own organizations. Moreover, as the networks strengthened the consumer movement and it continued to grow in the 1980s, the shift in the center of gravity to Penang was increasingly frowned on by the Western leaders whose organizations had provided the funds for IOCU's expansion. The networks bolstered the power and authority of the regional office, while others in the consumer movement wished to return control to the headquarters in The Hague.[79]

Yet the central point needs to be re-emphasized: networking enabled the consumer movement to become a much broader campaigning force, bringing to the definition of consumerism a meaning that embraced the concerns of the poor as well as the rich. In an assessment of the contribution of its own networks, IOCU argued in 1983 that the networks:

> gave direction and purpose, punch and power, visibility and skills, short-cuts to research and outlets for its [IOCU's] own fact finding. [The networks] brought the word "consumer" into the language of developmental groups and agencies and it invigorated part of IOCU's own constituency. The international business world is increasingly noticing IOCU as an element to reckon with and UN agencies are beginning to take IOCU more seriously.[80]

Anwar Fazal, characteristically, added to this upbeat assessment. Consumerism, he claimed in 1982 at the height of the enthusiasm for networking, is about "people." The difference between "people" and "consumers" was irrelevant: it is "about the food we eat, the drink we take, the medicines we use, the products and services we get or don't get."[81] Networking constituted a form of political "hitchhiking," enabling groups to hook up with particular causes and move faster than they would have been able to do on their own.[82] Cumulatively, it had enabled a new consumer "conscience" to develop, based on global thinking, environmentalism, human rights, cultural diversity, and responsibility for the future.[83] Here was a missionary fervor expressed by the leader of the consumer movement reminiscent of the spirit of Colston Warne as he traveled around Europe and the wider world establishing a global organization in the 1950s and 1960s. And here was a vision of consumer activism that infected even the more sober and business-oriented calculations of his successors. In 1985, Rhoda Karpatkin drew on the achievements of the global movement to urge her fellow American consumer professionals to develop a "social agenda" that focused on poverty and exclusion and that would re-instill her Consumers Union with the concerns for the worker that had so motivated the strikers at Consumers' Research in 1936.[84] Just as the global consumer movement drew on the experiences of both the rich and the poor so it seemed, in 1985 at least, that the consumer movement in the most affluent of all nations should do so as well.

Notwithstanding these more enthusiastic and wishful claims of consumer activists themselves, there are certain conclusions that can be reached about the importance of networking, especially when placed in the light of what others have argued about civil society and globalization in the modern world. The 1960s witnessed an explosion in new social movements which, during the 1970s, continued to grow in size and scale, as well as entered mainstream political debates. Few, however, could claim the global reach enjoyed by IOCU and few could organize as effectively at the global level. Although in the first decade of the twenty-first century the strength of NGOs such as Care, Oxfam, Amnesty International, and Médecins Sans Frontières is well established, as are the highly impressive mobilizations behind networks such as Jubilee 2000, at the turn of the 1980s few institutional structures existed for global campaigning unless they obtained the direct involvement of federations of older civil society actors, such as the trade unions and the established—not necessarily feminist—women's movement. Informal networking certainly took place, as other scholars have attested, but the more formal, institutional networks that brought together pre-existing organizations were an important connection between the social movements of the 1960s and the huge expansion in civil society organizing associated with the 1990s. IBFAN, PAN, and HAI were crucial to the turn to networking in the 1980s, as was the consumer movement itself. That said, it has become apparent that networking took on a life of its own, with global civil society apparently being based around as many networks as it is around specific NGOs.

If we are to follow the claims made by others as to the contribution made by networks to global civil society, then on the positive side, we can argue that HAI, PAN, and IBFAN helped bridge the gap between those existing within and outside "the network society." The organization of the United Nations, and the dominant shadow it has cast over the operations of NGOs, has meant that such a division was always possible, especially between those granted consultative status and those that were not, between those who had access to the communication channels of the information age and those relegated to the local and the national campaigns of their specific problems. What the networks did was create the mechanisms through which the local became the global and through which the smaller NGO could participate in the debates heard throughout the UN-based organizations. As such, the defender of indigenous rights in Borneo, Harrison Ngau, could be connected to the global community through his membership of Sahabat Alam Malaysia. This was tied to the consumer movement at the national level through CAP, and at the global level through its work with IOCU in developing PAN.

But on the negative side, networks have to be judged alongside other forms of political campaigning. It has been claimed that for all the informality and fluidity of networks and NGOs and for all the media attention they have attracted at the global level from the 1990s onward, their deliberate disassociation from formal channels of party political power has meant they can never achieve the same level of sustained influence as obtained by many groups associated with the labor movement and the Left for much of the twentieth century. This is an issue about core and periphery. Despite the fact that NGOs might have access to the UN, they are often forced to operate as lone lobbyists amid an incredibly complex and monumental structure, while their participation often rests on the invitation of the UN agency involved. NGOs and networks do not have an automatic right of entry into global debates, they lack the accountability common to national democratic organizations, and they cannot assume that formal channels exist in principle and in practice to ensure that their voices are heard. They remain on the periphery of power with no guaranteed route to the political core. In contrast, it has been argued that despite all the fragmentation and splintering of organizations associated with the Left, especially during the 1960s and 1970s, most remained affiliated with more established political organizations, which in turn were often affiliated with mainstream political parties. Formally, if not always in practice, there existed opportunities for agendas raised on the margins to reach their way to the center, ensuring a necessary channel of communication not dependent on a local organization's ability to manipulate the media to ensure that the flow of information takes place.[85]

Likewise, it cannot be assumed, as so many writers have of present-day "anti-globalization," that there exists a coherence within NGO politics; that the myriad networks and civil society groups collectively constitute the basis for an alternative structuring of the world economy and polity. Again, comparison with the traditional Left of the labor movement is useful because of all the diversity in left-wing thought and practice the potential for division was by no means as great as it is within the NGO community today. Networks have been celebrated for their effectiveness in making alliances out of seemingly regionally and ideologically disparate groups. It would be a mistake to claim that longstanding unities can be developed between trade unions, humanitarian relief agencies, Northern and Southern-based NGOs, never mind the increasing number of civil society actors sponsored by corporate funds: the differences in attitudes to global trade—from free trade to protection—bear testimony to this, as we will see in the final chapter. So, while accepting that political division within the Left has existed, and often with devastatingly tragic results, the sense of purpose shared has been generally more consistent than one can assume exists within a global civil society of non-state actors. The opportunities for fragmentation are much greater.

One minor example pertinent to the issues discussed above is that there has been a remarkable sense of agreement about the overwhelming power of multinational pharmaceutical companies which, for many networks and NGOs, has led to a broader critique of multinational capitalism as a whole. Yet many of the people who would support a citizen initiative to obtain cheaper drugs in the developing world have also done so in the developed world. But while the struggle in the developing world has resulted in an alliance against "big pharma," the struggle in the developed world has often resulted in a struggle allied with "big pharma," especially in patient groups' attempts to bypass the financial strictures of impoverished health systems unwilling to provide their patients with the more expensive patented medicines. Both issues might attract our sympathy and our support. But one has resulted in an attack on global capitalism, the other in its defense. If we adopt a politics of pragmatism, as so many NGOs and consumer groups have, then the two campaigns can be supported. But if we wish to assume that in global civil society there exists an anti-globalization movement with potential revolutionary consequences, then we are likely to be disappointed. There are simply too many contradictions for that.

All of this leads to the conclusion that in the politics of networking there is perhaps a reflection of the politics of protest in an age of consumption. The logic of consumer activism has been to take one issue at a time, a pragmatism that admits to the potential for contradiction but places greater significance on rectifying a perceived abuse within the marketplace as currently constituted. The networks, as pioneered by the consumer movement at the global level, represent a coming together of political identities—be they based on human rights, environmental values, gender identities, and so on—but not in ways that are ideologically or practically binding. Despite the postmodern critics' claims that identities are in flux, it is the network itself that provides the flux, the informality, and the flexibility to which we can bring our identities as workers, producers, consumers, and citizens. This can be very enriching, but it is not an ideology or a coherent political movement. It is a form of politics that perhaps reflects our attitudes toward consumption in general. That is, networks provide a means by which we can exercise our political principles, but we are free to pick and choose, to enter and retreat, from any number of campaigns. As in our consumption decisions, these affinities might not always be ideologically consistent, but why should such a rigid form of political responsibility be placed on the individual?

In the aftermath of Naomi Klein's *No Logo* and in response to the rise of ethical consumerism, a reaction took place against the expectation that every individual shopper should bring to bear the weight of the whole world's problems in each and every consumption decision he or she makes. Klein's response was not to advocate such moral purity: it was simply impossible in a world in which Western activists have grown up enjoying the benefits of consumer society and would like to continue doing so in the future. Instead, she urged consumers to think of other ways in which to exercise their citizenship: to continue to shop but to protest through letter writing, demonstration, education, and participation.[86] Networks are the institutional expression of this dual-edged sentiment. They enable the supporters of the constituent members to continue enjoying living in consumer society, while offering an effective mechanism through which to campaign against specific abuses without imposing a moral, political, or intellectual obligation on its participants. To some, this is political cowardice; to others, political pragmatism. To the consumer movement, and to hundreds of other international NGOs operating in global civil society since the 1970s, it has been the reality of political action in an era of globalization.

Backlash

The Corporate Critique of Consumerism

One of the more peculiar characters associated with consumer activism in the twentieth century was that of Dr. J. B. Matthews. Originally a Methodist missionary and self-proclaimed "religious fundamentalist," an ongoing intellectual journey of self-discovery led him first to pacifism and then to the socialism associated in the United States with Norman Thomas—six-time presidential candidate for the Socialist Party of America. A further radicalization of his views took Matthews to the Communist Party in 1932 and he became a fervent advocate of Marxism. At the same time, he also maintained a prominent position at Consumers' Research, where he became a close confidant and adviser to the founder, F. J. Schlink. The creation of Consumers Union, following the strike of 1936, however, provoked a remarkable political U-turn that would see Matthews turn on his former comrades. Along with Schlink, he became a profound detester of union organizing and moved toward a political ideology that aggressively promoted the virtues of the free market and opposed all forms of government regulation. Moreover, Matthews left Consumers' Research in 1938 to become the first research director of the House Un-American Activities Committee (HUAC), at that time chaired by Martin Dies. From his office in Washington, DC, Matthews persisted in baiting the union supporters of Consumers Union while as a writer for the magazines of the infamous newspaper magnate William Randolph Hearst, he maintained the charges that Colston Warne, Arthur Kallet, and their associates were running a Communist-controlled front organization.[1]

The range of attitudes to organized consumerism represented by the idiosyncratic career of J. B. Matthews covers the whole spectrum of opinions that have been voiced against the movement over the last three quarters of a century. From radical Right to radical Left, consumer organizations have attracted a whole range of political sympathies. For many critics comparative testing consumerism has been a handmaiden to capitalist industry, but for others an interference which, through its promotion of regulations and protection mechanisms, has attacked the very principles of the free running of the economy. On the one hand, it can be argued that in theory at least, consumerism is good for business. It takes on many of the marketing activities of a firm, determining which goods are most suited to consumers' needs and promoting only those manufactured by the most efficient companies. On the other hand, certain businessmen and business groups have opposed the organized consumer movement, claiming it represents an unnecessary interference in the running of an economy. Unrestrained capitalism, they argue, will ultimately ensure that the sovereign, rational, and informed consumer will get what he or she wants or deserves. In the attacks on the consumer co-operative movement, in the defense of big business amid the clamor of anti-trust reform, and in the opposition to specific regulations dealing with food and drug safety, business associations have often led the charge against consumer groups for perverting the normal course of the market economy.

Does the consumer movement promote or oppose the free market? Is it the friend or the foe of business? Who are its natural political allies? Certainly, if we compare, as we have done in previous chapters, the consumer movement to other forms of new social movement and other types of political activism, then it is not an immediate associate of the 1960s countercultural radicalism or New Left political experimentalism. It would be very difficult to firmly identify consumerism as a product of the political Left, even acknowledging the liberal tendencies of much of its leadership. Consumer organizations have opposed certain business practices, but they have also repeatedly attested their faith in choice and the free market. They have opposed the lack of concern for the individual shopper and citizen inherent to many large-scale organizations, whether privately or publicly owned. They have been largely reformist organizations, which have nevertheless constituted a social movement that has deliberately sought to sidestep the complications arising from a political identity associated with either the Right or the Left. To whatever extent radical socialists and communists may once have counted among its membership, consumer groups have also courted the support of pro-business interests. Throughout the political life of J. B. Matthews, then, it is unlikely that the consumer movement ever asked for his support as a socialist nor deserved his hostility as a reawakened scourge of communism.

Nevertheless, what has marked the history of consumer organizing is the almost seemingly persistent opposition groups have faced from the organized business community. Notwithstanding the very real repression of consumer activists by authoritarian regimes in the developing world, Western consumerists have had to withstand charges of communist subversion, its leaders have been subjected to invasive investigations of their private lives, and its chief representatives have had to defend themselves against accusations of being foreign and enemy agents seeking to undermine national economic and political interests. This is not to assume that business interests are in any way unified or coherent. Important economic and political differences can exist between firms operating in different states and regions. Divisions and disputes can occur between structurally similar enterprises that operate under very different market conditions and in very different sectors. And huge divergences of opinion exist between businesses operating at different stages along the chain of production and distribution, or between those working as either large- or small-scale enterprises. But in the history of consumer activism what becomes undeniable is the existence of a determined set of voices opposing consumer reforms. These are voices often associated with large manufacturers who have had the funds to promote industrial lobby groups and to foster close ties with individuals and parties close to governments and the seats of political power. It is these voices that have most consistently attacked the consumer movement and it is these voices that have sought most persistently to undermine the regulatory frameworks promoted in the politics of consumption.

To understand both the ongoing pressures acting against consumer groups necessitates a return to a focus on the United States. In chapter 8, we will turn to the confrontation between organized consumers and organized business in the international arena, making it apparent that certain business interests the world over have opposed consumer protection regulations and multinational corporations in particular have sought to recast the institutions of global governance in line with their own interests. But it is in the United States that we find the most persistent critique by business of consumer initiatives and, moreover, the direct translation of these interests into a political movement. Here, "big business" became allied to a revitalized political Right, which had long opposed government intervention at both the federal and international level. By the 1980s this anti-regulatory agenda was being strongly promoted by the U.S. government, and the anti-consumer protection voices in the United States were also being heard at the United Nations.

The themes and issues covered in this chapter can be identified in other national contexts. But to truly understand the nature of the opposition to consumer initiatives a global perspective must be put to one side and the narrative must focus directly on events in the United States. In the United States, there has long existed a corporate critique of consumerism, which has built on Matthews's accusations and pursued them over several decades of consumer activism. Accordingly, this chapter begins by examining the political context of the charges made against comparative testing consumerism from the 1930s on. We will see that organized business interests have continually sought to hold the consumer movement in check, by positing the capitalist corporation as the true defender of the consumer interest. To some extent, this has occurred across the Western world, but in the United States a more adversarial political culture enabled, by the 1970s, a particularly well-organized and well-orchestrated backlash against the consumer movement. This was led by a number of national producer organizations and intellectual think tanks that would later be identified, if not entirely consistently, as "neoconservative".

It is the contention of this chapter that this political movement, associated with the administrations of Ronald Reagan and George W. Bush, arose out of a context of an ascendant consumer protection movement. Particularly in response to the public interest politics of Ralph Nader, "big business" responded by first attacking Nader himself and then the whole range of reforms he advocated in the 1970s. Symbolically, organized business defeated both Nader and the wider consumer movement in the campaign to introduce a federal Consumer Protection Agency. This brought to an end the growing momentum for consumer protection, which seemed to the neoconservatives to have been dragging the United States toward a level of state interference more usually associated with the social democratic states of Western Europe.

The rise of Ralph Nader and the battle over the Consumer Protection Agency throughout the administrations of Richard Nixon, Gerald Ford, and Jimmy Carter has not been properly acknowledged in existing accounts of consumer politics in the twentieth century. Too many scholars have rushed to dismiss the efforts made by a Nader-inspired consumer movement and have criticized instead its seemingly apolitical nature and even the acquisitive individualist tendencies of comparative testing shopping. This book focuses on the contradictions and dilemmas inherent to consumer activism and to the politics of consumer society in general. But in the context of consumer organization and business group relations, defeat rather than acquiescence perhaps better describes the history of the consumer movement since the 1970s, an interpretation that is confirmed once we step beyond American politics and look to the wider global governance of the market economy. For having opposed the advocates of state consumerism in the United States, the U.S. anti-regulatory movement turned its attention to the United Nations. As new alliances were forged between business and government during Reagan's two terms of office, U.S. diplomats attacked the regulatory impulse of the United Nations Economic and Social Council. And, once again, they turned their attention to the consumer movement, pursuing the leaders of the international organization in much the same manner as Martin Dies and Joseph McCarthy had earlier pursued consumer activists in Washington. Moreover, U.S. political and trade negotiators undermined the codes of conduct promoted by the consumer movement and global civil society, which ultimately created a very different basis for global economic governance. By the end of the 1980s, the International Organisation of Consumers Unions suffered some of the same setbacks that had befallen Nader and Consumers Union a decade earlier. Its implications for the politics of consumption would be deep and long lasting.

I

When J. B. Matthews turned on his former colleagues at Consumers' Research, he was merely spearheading a more concerted anti-consumer movement, which had emerged simultaneously with the consumer movement itself and which would continue for the next half century. From the beginnings of the New Deal to the period of Ralph Nader's greatest popularity in the early 1970s, there existed a persistent attack on the consumer movement. This ebbed and flowed with the general prominence and influence afforded to organized business in U.S. public life, but throughout Franklin D. Roosevelt's promotion of "freedom from want," the postwar celebration of the "consumer's republic," John F. Kennedy's articulation of a set of consumer rights, Lyndon B. Johnson's vision of the "Great society," and Richard Nixon's flurry of consumer protection legislation, the consumer movement itself came under the scrutiny of anti-communists and defenders of the free market.

To be sure, much of this opposition was defensive in character. The opponents of consumer activism were often directly responding to new consumer initiatives either promoted by the consumer movement or implemented by the government. During the New Deal, the tighter regulations proposed on trading activities by the National Recovery Administration and the Agricultural Adjustment Administration resulted in Consumers' Research being seen as the natural enemy of companies affected by the new measures. The critique of advertising inherent to the consumerist ideologies of Chase and Schlink provoked many a response from advertising executives aggrieved at what they felt was the ungrateful response of consumers to the gains brought about by industry. The consumer activists of Consumers' Research, the Home Economics Association, the General Federation of Women's Clubs, the American Association of University Women, the League of Women Voters, and the Women's Trade Union League were all held to constitute an alliance of "pink-cheeked professors" and government bureaucrats who were dragging ordinary Americans along the road to Russian-style collectivism.[2]

However, the consumer movement's opponents were more than capable of taking to the offensive as well. From the time of the strike at Consumers' Research in 1936 until the end of the 1960s, Consumers Union (CU) found itself repeatedly fending off accusations of communist infiltration. When J. B. Matthews left the consumer movement to assist Martin Dies at HUAC he was able to provide a more relentless harrying of the leaders of CU. Building on the close ties CU initially sought with the labor movement and the trade unions and its desire to report on the conditions under which products were manufactured, Matthews was able to continually point to the communist sympathies of Colston Warne and his associates. Specifically, Matthews charged in his 1938 autobiography, *Odyssey of a Fellow Traveler,* that after 1935 Arthur Kallet had become one of the leading agents acting on behalf of Moscow whose role was to subvert the consumer movement to the communist cause.[3]

The accusations were not entirely without foundation. Kallet, Warne, and others had advocated a radical consumer philosophy in the 1930s and socialist views were routinely articulated in a number of consumer organizations. But there also existed a commitment to a non-partisan course that made Matthews's claims simply absurd.[4] Nevertheless, Matthews repeated the claims in his formal submission to the Dies Committee, which was taken by a stenographer at a secret Sunday evening session in December 1939 when Dies did not even notify his Committee's own members. Kallet, Matthews claimed, had never been convinced of the potential for consumer organizing until a 1935 Communist Party directive instructed the formation of a whole series of front organizations that included not only Kallet's own organization, but the League of Women Shoppers, the Milk Consumers' Protective Committee, the Consumer-Farmer Cooperative, the New York Consumers' Council, the United Conference against the High Cost of Living (Chicago), and the Consumers' National Federation. Moreover, Matthews took the consumer activists' disdain for commercial puffery as an attempt to destroy the entire economic system.[5]

The accusations were largely ludicrous. Even fellow Dies Committee members were angered over the way in which Matthews's evidence was taken and then presented as the view of the Committee, and Roosevelt himself was said to have disapproved at the way in which Matthews's statement was received and treated.[6] Yet Matthews's accusations were picked up by the media across the United States and CU found itself constantly having to defend itself against charges of Communist infiltration.[7] Indeed, Matthews's evidence was distributed to major advertisers by *Good Housekeeping* magazine (published by Hearst) before it was even received by many newspapers. And George Sokolsky, a publicist for the National Association of Manufacturers who had recently befriended F. J. Schlink, was commissioned by the journal *Liberty* to write a series of articles denouncing the consumer movement associated with CU.[8] During the 1940s many publications continued to refuse to accept CU advertising, including all those associated with the *New York Times* and the publishers Hearst, Scribner's, and Crowell.[9]

For many years CU struggled against these accusations and the open hostility of sections of the business, advertising, and publishing community. It meant that prominent intellectuals such as the sociologist Robert Lynd, who had previously been well disposed toward organized consumerism, shunned offers of board membership issued by CU.[10] And, during the war years, CU's publishing of *Bread and Butter*—a journal designed to reach low income consumers, which discussed the broader aspects of economic theory in relation to the cost of living—did little to put off those who believed CU had a radical hidden agenda.[11] From Matthews's evidence until the end of the war CU did not escape the continued attention of HUAC. Following the principle of "mud sticks," state institutions such as the California Committee on Un-American Activities and the New York City Council repeated Matthews's accusations, as did a 1944 report of the Special Committee of HUAC.[12]

The most obvious impact of the charges was a desire by CU to assert its re-spectable non-party political credentials. Over the first two decades of its exis-tence it gradually de-linked the associations it had attempted to make between the worker and the consumer and it emerged from the war years as an organi-zation primarily devoted to obtaining better value for money for its subscribers. It modified its prior commitment to a Veblenesque critique of consumption and fell into line with the U.S. government's brand of Keynesianism, which pro-moted mass consumption as the key to economic growth and a healthy democ-racy.[13] For CU this meant a reorientation of its product appraisal techniques, away from the ascetic considerations of simplicity and economy, and more to-ward the politically safe factors of convenience and safety. At the same time Kallet, ever eager to avoid further charges of being subversive to free enterprise, constructed a more conservative board membership that perhaps better re-flected CU's middle-class subscriber base.[14] This was a move not without its provocations and many of Kallet's long-term colleagues disliked the increas-ingly apolitical nature of the organization. By 1957 *Consumer Reports* was no longer a radical journal of political economy but a magazine that simply pro-claimed that "the quality of life itself would be better as the quality of goods improved."[15]

Not that these political compromises did anything to deter those who be-lieved CU to be a communist front. In 1951, just after Joseph McCarthy had instigated a new bout of anti-communism, CU again found itself under inves-tigation. Matthews's accusations against Kallet were reiterated and CU was placed on the list of subversive organizations by HUAC in 1951. There followed an almost concerted attack by a number of publications committed to oppos-ing organized consumerism. In 1952, *The Freeman* repeated the claim that CU was a "Red Front" and the Hearst newspapers reprinted as an editorial an ac-cusatory syndicated column by the journalist E. P. Tompkins.[16] Again Kallet had to defend himself and again CU was forced into issuing a public state-ment.[17] Following a tense discussion among CU board members a statement was printed in the April 1953 edition of *Consumer Reports,* which reaffirmed CU's "faith in a democratic society in which the production of goods and ser-vices is guided by the free choice of consumers."[18] CU further confirmed its commitment to the new ruling political economy of U.S. society in a passage that might well have been written by a propagandist of the Marshall Plan, in-cluding its commitment to "freedom of choice," "democratic society," and "helping business."[19]

It was not until 1954 that CU was removed from the list and not until 1957, when McCarthy's witch hunts came to an end, that the matter could be put to rest.[20] Of course, CU was hardly unique in its position as a reasonably pro-gressive, broadly liberal organization that had to deal with accusations of com-munism at this time. Moreover, the accusations were not so serious that it was placed on the more important list drawn up by the Attorney General nor was it the only consumer organization to be pursued. Mary Dublin Keyserling, a veteran feminist, labor, and consumer activist associated with the League of Women Shoppers, the National Consumers' League, and the Consumers' National Federation, took nearly a year to clear her name before HUAC.[21] Yet we should not be too dismissive of the harassment of CU either. There was a persistent baiting of CU that resurfaced throughout the postwar period. In 1970, the HUAC charges reappeared in the prestigious business periodical *Barron's*, and once again CU board members were required to dispute the allegations.[22]

The opponents of the consumer movement remained vigilant in their monitoring of consumer protection programs. After World War II federal consumer protection initiatives were largely non-existent and the anti-consumer lobbyists had little to worry about. However, once President Kennedy's domestic agenda got under way, there was a renewed attention to consumer affairs. On 15 March 1962 Kennedy outlined a federal consumer protection program. A Consumer Advisory Council was created to advise the President's Council of Economic Advisors made up of academics and consumer representatives, including Colston Warne. Although it was largely toothless because it held no effective powers and was limited to setting out general principles, it nevertheless attracted the attention of government officials concerned with the apparent threat represented by consumer protectionism.[23] In an anonymous document of 1962, possibly compiled by Matthews (died in 1966), the communist red-baiting tactics of Dies and McCarthy were resurrected once again. The individuals appointed to the Advisory Council were castigated for their communist links, the previous accusations against Kallet and Warne were repeated, and the Advisory Council was particularly chastised for appointing five members with strong connections to CU, for which "incontrovertible proof" had already been established that it was "the creation of the Communist apparatus."[24]

Perhaps as a consequence, though the members were also well aware of the thankless nature of their irrelevant role, the Advisory Council's first report of October 1963 turned out to be its last and the Council never met again. In its place, Lyndon B. Johnson established the President's Committee on Consumer Interests (PCCI) in January 1964. Although this too lacked effective powers, there was the potential for a more powerful voice since the PCCI was bolstered by the appointment of Esther Peterson as the Special Assistant to the President for Consumer Affairs.[25] Peterson made her voice heard, and in her calls for truth-in-packaging regulations and other similar core consumer demands, she began to make a nuisance of herself. She particularly raised eyebrows when she seemingly offered her support to a protest against bread prices in Phoenix, Arizona. Johnson came under pressure to remove her as she was seen as too effective a spokesperson for consumer affairs. In 1967 Johnson replaced her with a TV personality and former film actor Betty Furness, an appointment that many in the consumer movement derided as a sham particularly because her opening consumer speech expressed her commitment to a more cautious approach than that of her predecessor.[26]

As it turned out, Furness would eventually win the respect of many in the consumer movement, even if it were widely accepted that her appointment had been made to appease the advertising industry upset by Peterson's high profile.[27] But the more enduring point about Peterson's dismissal was the authority given to industry lobbyists who were frequently able to overturn any initiatives begun by the consumer movement within government. It is perhaps too much to talk of a coherent and organized anti-consumer movement in the period from CU's foundation until the end of the 1960s, but there was undoubtedly a persistent niggling tension that constantly undermined the causes espoused by consumer groups. This vigilant surveillance of the activities of consumer groups provided the foundation for the development of a more powerful and assertive anti-regulatory movement later. For at the end of the 1960s, the consumer movement was being rejuvenated, this time from a more aggressive form of investigative muckraking, spearheaded by Ralph Nader and the various individuals and groups who swarmed around his nascent public interest movement. This latest wave of consumer activism would inspire an equally effective campaign of resistance.

II

Ralph Nader famously burst onto the American public scene in 1965 with his indictment of the U.S. automobile industry, *Unsafe at Any Speed*.[28] The story of Nader's rise to prominence is well known. As a lawyer practicing in Connecticut in the early 1960s, Nader had increasingly become interested in automobile accidents for which drivers were blamed but which he believed were the fault of the automobiles themselves. After working as a traffic safety consultant in the Department of Labor in Washington, DC, Nader published *Unsafe at Any Speed* to coincide with the hearings of a Senate subcommittee on automobile safety for which he had undertaken much of the preparatory research. Initially, the book attracted little attention, but thanks to the General Motors' response, Nader soon became a household name and regarded as a David taking on the giant of the automobile industry.[29]

In January 1966, Nader learnt that General Motors had hired a private detective to uncover dirt on his personal life. The espionage was particularly ham-fisted and included a crass attempt to lure Nader into a sexually compromising situation. The plan spectacularly backfired. The Senate subcommittee changed the focus of its questions on to General Motors' illegal actions, Nader became a hero to the little guy, and in March 1966, less than a year after the Senate hearings had begun, Congress passed the National Traffic and Vehicle Safety Act. Furthermore, Nader took out an action against General Motors for invasion of his privacy and in an out-of-court settlement in 1970 the car company paid over $425,000. The money was immediately channeled back into Nader's expanding empire of public interest organizations and served to consolidate his reputation as the nation's foremost "consumer crusader," as *Newsweek* dubbed him in 1968 when it featured him on its cover dressed in a suit of armor.[30]

The popular support enjoyed by Nader at this time was truly phenomenal. One commentator went so far as to champion Nader as "an American Pied Piper, a male Jeanne d'Arc. A Lenin, some would say, or—others—a Luther."[31] There was clearly great fascination in the man and what made him tick. His support rested on his image as that of the patriotic "average man" fighting back against the corrupt power elite.[32] But the level of interest with the intricate details of Nader's personality and lifestyle reflected a wider sense of self-absorption about the extent of affluence and the success of consumer society. Nader's infamous asceticism—cheap lodging house accommodation, identical utilitarian suits, refusal to drive a car, disregard for all forms of ostentatious display, apparent lack of vices of any kind, and the few hours of sleep he restricted himself to each night so that he could commit to public, selfless causes—all spoke of an innocent, pre-modern America uncorrupted by money and excess, which invoked notions of patriotic public participatory citizenship on which the country was held to be based. If ordinary consumers could not deny themselves the morally dubious and ephemeral pleasures of commodity capitalism, they could at least admire in others a man who seemed to embody their competing desires for a more rational, a more authentic, and a more democratic lifestyle.

This is not to deny the legions of detractors of Nader's lifestyle who detected in his simplicity a priggish puritanism and an alien refusal to share in a world of mass consumption, on which America's economic growth was supposedly based. But in the late 1960s and early 1970s Nader was a social phenomenon. Extensive interviews were conducted with him in leading serious publications such as *Time* and the *New Yorker,* hagiographies of his life kept being churned out and an interview was conducted by *Playboy.*[33] By 1971 he appeared to be everywhere. He was constantly ranked in lists of every ten-most-admired people, the *New York Times* ran 148 articles on him in 1971 alone, and he was the subject of 38 feature stories in major magazines in the same year.[34] There was even room for Nader to mock his own public persona: in 1977 he hosted an episode of *Saturday Night Live,* dressed in a powder blue cowboy suit and delivering a series of one-liners and set-pieces poking fun at the more intricate details of his consumer protection campaigns.[35]

Nader's ascendency came on the back of an expanding middle-class activism and a more general social consciousness associated with the 1960s. If Nader rarely attached himself to the more celebrated social movements of civil rights and peace protest, he did clearly build on the broader questioning of society, which ranged from countercultural experimentation to the anger felt by many ordinary Americans over the injustices publicized in works such as Rachel Carson's *Silent Spring.*[36] Distinguishable from new social movements by its less utopian or radical agenda, Nader's brand of public interest activism mushroomed after his success with automobile safety. It has been argued that the

Figure 9. Ralph Nader spearheaded a rejuvenated consumer movement in the late 1960s, marked by a more aggressive form of investigative muckraking. Here Nader is photographed speaking to the staff of Lawrence Berkeley Laboratory in June 1971.

Courtesy of Lawrence Berkeley National Laboratory.

public interest movement has been based on a "mistrust of both business and government." It was believed that government has been unable to control the prerogatives of business and that "instead of regulating business, the government has more often been regulated by it."[37] Public interest activists have consisted of concerned citizens fighting for issues that offer no immediate benefits to those involved. Because public interest activism fights in the interests of all affected by government and business, it equates "public" with other broad-ranging terms and has occasionally been referred to as a "people's movement," a "citizen's movement," and, because of its overlap with some of the classic concerns of CU, a "consumer's movement." It is, in the words of one contemporary, a movement not of subversives, dropouts, or idealistic dreamers, but of "middle American radicals".[38]

In the late 1960s and 1970s the public interest movement was roughly equitable with the organizations linked to the activism of Ralph Nader, which came to be known by many as the "Nader network".[39] It included the young lawyers and students who were quickly dubbed "Nader's Raiders" for their work in 1968 assessing the effectiveness of the Federal Trade Commission.[40] But it also included a whole series of long-lasting organizations such as the Center for the Study of Responsive Law, created in 1969, which investigated other government regulatory agencies, including the Food and Drug Administration and the Interstate Commerce Commission. In 1970 Nader ploughed the money obtained from his settlement with General Motors into a new legal firm, Public Interest Research Group, which drew on the voluntary spirit of students eager to address public issues during their vacations while obtaining valuable work experience.[41] One year later, Public Citizen was established to lobby on topics such as consumer rights, public health, and trade policy. There are a myriad of other organizations connected to Nader, including state and local level citizen action groups, as well as other groups not linked to his network such as Common Cause (a group set up in 1970 to lobby for good government measures), which clearly emerged amid this tide of public interest activism.[42]

Through all of these organizations Nader espoused a politics based on a critique of corporate power in modern U.S. life. The one underlying motive of his work has been to campaign against the irresponsibility of corporations, which have grown so large he felt they no longer responded to the needs of their customers nor contributed to the virtues of competition and free enterprise so central to U.S. national ideals. Instead, they have consolidated their privileged status in both the economy and in Washington, so that their operating rationale has become one of self-serving profiteering rather than responding to the needs of the people. From his examination of General Motors automobile safety policies through his presidential campaigns at the end of the century, Nader consistently turned his attention to the "big boys" of U.S. capitalism, arguing that so enthralled have all politicians become to their interests that neither the Republican nor the Democratic Party offers any real hope for a future healthy democracy. Throughout the administrations of Carter, Reagan, Clinton, and Bush senior and junior, Nader has continued to monitor what he regards as the obeisance of presidents to multinational firms. This is why, in his own mind, his political interventions have been entirely justifiable and he does at least demonstrate an impressive tenacity in his pursuit of corruption.[43]

More problematic is whether "Naderism" could be said to constitute a political philosophy as a whole. Certainly he is prone to making patriotic nods to the founding fathers espousing a form of Jeffersonian republicanism that privileges the rights of the little man against big government.[44] He has attempted to marry the rights-based approach of his legalistic inclinations with a more sweeping concern for an abstract value of justice: "justice for consumers, labourers, taxpayers, injured persons, and others who are all too often denied their rights."[45] Without such justice being available, Nader argues that individuals are unable to exercise their citizenship or participate in modern society. Active citizenship, for which his own self-denying lifestyle serves as an exemplar, is the key to his notion of political philosophy.[46]

Yet very rarely has Nader dealt with such conceptual abstractions. Really, his political vision has been entirely in accord with the best traditions of muckraking journalism. Nader's self-confessed heroes have been the likes of Upton Sinclair and his novel on the Chicago meat-packing industry, *The Jungle*.[47] If Nader developed his thinking about such exposés, it was only to locate them within a liberal framework espoused by the likes of J. K. Galbraith. According to one early study of the public interest movement, Nader and his supporters demonstrated a new populism in U.S. politics, a cynical approach to both business and government that owed more to the campaigns of the Progressive Era at the turn of the twentieth century than it did to the statism of the New Deal. It offered little in the way of an "apocalyptic transformation of the infrastructures of power" and therefore had little in common with the utopian dreaming of the '68 generation.[48] From this perspective it is easy to understand why radical proponents of the 1960s New Left could regard Nader as "not one of us" despite the obvious affinities in their opinions as to the nature of the perceived malaise in U.S. politics and society. The differences between Nader's reformism and the New Left's radicalism resulted in a consequent "mutual lack of interest".[49] New social movements were inspired by the critiques of consumer society found in the texts of Herbert Marcuse or Guy Debord. From Nader's perspective, his political acts were "an attempt to preserve the enterprise economy by making the market work better."[50]

If Nader's vision of the alternative society was limited in scope, his public interest liberalism certainly opened up the opportunities for reform and action. Moreover, it provided the possibility for a much broader view of the politicized consumer. Consumer organizing, he would later claim, had the potential "to help create a consumer culture that places value on quality, good value, and ecological and social considerations in production processes . . . [It] contributes to a shift in the buyer paradigm from conspicuous to conscious and conscientious consumption."[51] Despite all the weaknesses of Nader's ideology, his entry into public life helped revive the consumer movement. In the United States in the late 1960s, organized consumer activism began to grow not only in terms of subscription rates to CU but also in the number of institutions focussng on the consumer: the Consumer Federation of America was created in 1967 to act as an umbrella organization for a burgeoning movement and CU itself opened up a Washington office in 1969 to focus on political lobbying.[52] Although not all those involved in the consumer movement at the time would go so far as to claim that Nader alone was responsible for its success, most agree that his ideas and actions provided the direction for the best part of two decades.[53]

Nader worked with the consumer movement in the 1960s and 1970s. He joined the Board of CU for a time and spoke regularly at consumer conferences and meetings.[54] And in overturning the accusation made against consumer activists—that they subscribed to "consumerism"—a "disruptive ideology concocted by self-appointing bleeding hearts and politicians who find that it pays off to attack the corporations"—he provided the movement with a positive identity.[55] It enabled organizations such as CU to break out of their restricted role and embrace once again the wider social issues of consumer poverty, especially following the lead taken by David Caplowitz in his study of the "disadvantaged consumer."[56] Nader addressed the big questions raised by multinational corporations that would provide the leadership for many developing world consumer activists in the 1970s. He directed his attention to pharmaceutical companies, to problems of international trade and to the power of multinational corporations generally—all issues that inspired the international consumer movement at this time.[57]

In the United States, Nader's rise helped provoke one of the most successful periods in the consumer movement's history, in terms of making an impact on the regulatory framework of the federal government. In just a few years after the publication of *Unsafe at Any Speed,* a flurry of legislation was introduced on behalf of consumers, including the Fair Packaging and Labeling Act (1966), the National Traffic and Motor Vehicle Safety Act (1966), the Child Protection Act (1966), the Cigarette Labeling Act (1966), the Flammable Fabrics Amendment Act (1967), the Wholesome Meat Act (1967), the Consumer Credit Protection Act (1968), the Wholesome Poultry Products Act (1968), and the Child Protection and Toy Safety Act (1969). If these measures could be regarded as the sympathetic response of a Democratic president (Johnson) attune to the demands of citizen-consumers, then the bolstering of the regulatory apparatus by his Republican successor, President Richard Nixon, attests to the more general vote-winning potential of consumer protection that we discussed in chapter 2. During Nixon's administration, the Federal Trade Commission, the Food and Drug Administration, and the Federal Energy Administration were strengthened and new agencies such as the Environmental Protection Agency, the Occupational Safety and Health Administrations, and the National Highway Traffic Safety Administration were launched. Thanks to Nader and the groundswell of opinion in favor of consumerism, Nixon became perhaps the foremost pro-consumer U.S. president in the twentieth century.[58]

III

It was precisely because of these successes that public interest activism, organized consumerism, and Naderism were soon matched by an anti-regulatory backlash that would seek to rein in the perceived encroachment of the state on the free market. By the early 1970s, the downturn in the global economy meant far fewer U.S. corporations were prepared to tolerate the perceived luxury of government regulation. Beginning with attacks on Nader himself, business groups, journalists, politicians, and intellectuals began to react against the consumer protection measures introduced by Johnson and Nixon. By the early 1970s, a growing number of voices came to be heard questioning Nader's methods, politics, and personality. On a number of occasions, the criticisms came from former staff and volunteers, disgruntled by their experience of a man with whom it was allegedly difficult to get along.[59] But more often the criticisms were clearly conceived and aimed carefully at their target. Since his rise to national prominence, there had always been questioning of Nader's self-appointed role.[60] In the 1970s, more general questions were directed toward his advocacy of increased government intervention, claiming it would considerably increase commercial costs, making American enterprises unprofitable and uncompetitive in the global economy.[61]

In addition, the Nader network of public interest groups came to be understood in almost conspiratorial undertones, the suggestion being that Nader had built up an interlocking and highly complex set of institutions with shared personnel, resources, and ideologies all targeted at reducing the power and influence of U.S. corporations.[62] Over the years, these attacks became increasingly malicious, suggesting that Nader operated in secret in a "citadel of silence" unaccountable to the public and employing methods that had "very little in common with any of the public interest principles they seemingly avow to represent or protect."[63]

But putting aside the fascination with Nader's asceticism and personal life, his early critics arose out of a distaste for all of the consumer protection measures introduced by Nixon. Officials connected to the government Better Business Bureau accused consumer activists of harassing U.S. business and pushing it into a "deepening decline."[64] Consumer protection, it was claimed by anti-regulatory journalists, was "anti-business" and only served to increase the prices paid by consumers for ordinary commodities. Collectively, the public interest activists were said to constitute a "disaster lobby" whose emotional, unscientific, and irrational "prophecies of doom" led to a wholesale "denigration of the entire free enterprise system," especially because the model of private ownership and government control they appeared to be advocating most closely resembled the corporatism of European-style fascism.[65] Others, such as the Freedom Committee—an organization set up in the early 1960s to publish the works of free marketeers and consisting of such thinkers as Milton Friedman and F. A. Hayek—conceded that consumer activists were "well meaning" but that their naïveté resulted in the promotion of counterproductive regulations.[66] Increasingly, the public criticisms of regulation and consumer activism took on a much more hostile tone. Consumers Union was dismissed as a "fraud" by one pundit and, almost inevitably, the old charges of communist infiltration were resurrected once again.[67]

U.S. business began to reorganize and to mobilize. Significantly, it learned not only from the tactics of organized labor, but from the public interest and consumer movements as well. In the early 1970s, the number of corporate and trade association officials in Washington, DC, increased dramatically, CEOs began to address the public directly, new coalitions and ad hoc alliances were formed, and allies were sought across the campuses and in the media. The sheer scale of this mobilization has to be appreciated. By 1977, an average of one trade association per week was relocating its headquarters to Washington. From 1972 to 1978 the number of lawyers in the Washington Bar Association nearly doubled in size due to the greater recourse to the law taken by companies. CEOs were appointed for their knowledge of government rather than of business and companies attempted to create grassroots social movements of their employees and stockholders. By the late 1970s one study estimated that between $850 and $900 million per year was being spent by corporations on stockholder mobilizations. Furthermore, individual corporations channeled millions of dollars into advertising campaigns geared solely to advocating their position on a particular political issue.[68]

Most ironic was the use made of political action committees (PACs). The public interest and labor movements had long opposed the ability of wealthy individuals to influence politics through substantial donations. Campaign finance reforms therefore restricted individual donations to $500 and the labor unions in particular made use of their memberships to raise funds through PACs, which were then channelld to parties and candidates. Corporations also turned to PACs, calling on their stockholders and supporters to make individual donations that, collectively, produced immense funds and actually served to consolidate corporate influence in Washington. It has been estimated that there were 201 labor PACs and 89 corporate ones at the beginning of the 1970s. By 1980, though, while the number of labor PACs had increased to 297, there were 1,206 corporate PACs. By 1978, the amount of funds raised by corporate PACs was more than double that raised by the labor unions.[69]

Several commentators have written of a growing class consciousness among U.S. business elites. This was symbolized most clearly with the creation of the Business Roundtable in 1972, an organization consisting of the "inner circle" of the capitalist class—the CEOs of the major U.S. corporations—which helped them to see their interests as lying not with their individual company but with all large-scale enterprises.[70] Moreover, although these business leaders were clearly reacting against the regulatory measures introduced in recent years, they also came to be associated with a particular ideology that consolidated their identity and provided them with a positive agenda for political change. Since the early 1960s, political conservatives had drawn on a number of texts that celebrated individualism and opportunities afforded by the free market. Taking their cue from Hayek's *The Road to Serfdom*, U.S. thinkers produced what would become the classic works of conservatism, such as Russell Kirk's *The Conservative Mind* (1953) and William F. Buckley's *God and Man* (1951). They also founded their own journals such as Buckley's *National Review* and launched institutes such as the Center for Strategic and International Studies

(1962) at Georgetown University, the staff of which would go on to provide many of the foreign policy and national security personnel for Ronald Reagan.[71]

In the 1970s, many liberals famously became attracted to such thinking and became known as the "neoconservatives." Although the term has subsequently come to be applied so variously as to lose its meaning, initially it was understood to refer to a loose collection of intellectuals and politicians who placed far greater attention on the reforming potential of voluntary action, the market, and individual character than on government intervention. They included intellectuals Michael Novak and the husband and wife team of Irving Kristol and Gertrude Himmelfarb, the Democratic Senator Daniel Patrick Moynihan and disillusioned former Democrats like Jeane Kirkpatrick. They were reacting to the Great Society and the counterculture of the 1960s, believing they were defending liberalism from the radicals, and proposing a retreat from the regulatory impulse of the previous few years. Their outlets were in journals such as *Commentary,* published by the American Jewish Committee, which attacked the cultural revolution of the 1960s, and *The Public Interest,* which targeted public policy initiatives. While disagreement exists as to their precise beliefs it is generally held that their radical, aggressive faith in the liberalism of the market is tempered by a countervailing faith in the stability provided by the family and intermediate institutions, including churches and neighborhood groups.[72]

For our purposes the most relevant aspect of the neoconservatives at this time was that their ideology became increasingly linked to the interests of big business and the more established sections of the American Right. As an investigation into their beliefs argued in 1979, despite that their faith in the market denied any necessary support for one particular commercial institution over another, the unity of interests between corporations, intellectuals, and politicians opposed to government regulation has meant they have remained closely allied and have operated in similar social, academic, and political networks.[73] Most obviously this has taken place through the number of think tanks either founded or rejuvenated in the early 1970s as a deliberate attempt to counter the power of a perceived liberal intelligentsia located in such bodies as the Ford Foundation. The American Enterprise Institute was formed in 1943 to promote U.S. freedom and capitalist democracy. For the first few decades of its existence, its importance was eclipsed by the presence of more influential liberal think tanks but in the early 1970s funds were channeled toward it from business donors. Over the course of the decade, American Enterprise Institute expenditures increased tenfold and other conservative think tanks such as the Hoover Institution and the American Institute for Public Policy Research experienced similar growth. The American Enterprise Institute forged links with leading neoconservatives and published what would become influential journals such as *Public Opinion* and *Regulation,* the latter having as its logo, "Competition of ideas is fundamental to a free society."[74]

More spectacular, however, was the creation of new think tanks with explicitly conservative agendas to counter the perceived hegemony of the liberal intelligentsia: the Cato Institute was created in 1971 by activists connected to the Libertarian Party; the Institute for Contemporary Studies was founded in 1972 by Reagan's supporters in California; and the Manhattan Institute for Policy Research was set up in 1978 by William J. Casey, who would go on to co-ordinate Reagan's first presidential campaign.[75] Most impressive was the Heritage Foundation, that "feisty new kid on the conservative block" as Reagan described it, which was set up in 1973 following a grant of $250,000 from the Colorado brewer Joseph Coors. The publisher of *Policy Review*, Heritage enjoyed spectacular success and attracted donations from several business leaders as well as an impressive subscriber base. By 1985, its annual budget exceeded $10 million, it employed a staff of over 105, and it could count 36 individuals who had gone on to join the Reagan administration. It is proud of its record in influencing government policy and claims to have advised and shaped policies as diverse as those relating to welfare, taxation, social security, the "culture war," health care, international trad, and the Strategic Defense Initiative. Not only has Heritage courted leading neoconservative thinkers such as Hayek and Kirk, but it has been linked to foreign leaders, including the UK's Margaret Thatcher, Israel's Benjamin Netanyahu, and Singapore's Lee Kuan Yew (the proponent of "Asian values"). In the United States, it has been associated with politicians such as Barry Goldwater, Newt Gingrich, Jeb Bush, and especially Ronald Reagan.[76]

In the 1970s, this neoconservative "counter Reformation" was principally targeted at government regulation. It identified the reforms of the late 1960s and early 1970s as the "regulatory revolution," which it committed itself to reversing.[77] It opposed the "liberal elite" of "coercive utopians," claiming meddlers such as Nader would "accelerate the decline in our standard of living, erode our democratic system, and may well result in the loss of genuine national independence."[78] The public interest that Nader and others professed to represent was actually only their own special interest because the proposals they put forward were usually self-serving measures to increase the authority and standing of public interest lawyers, professors, and bureaucrats. The consumer movement was also clearly in the sights of this revitaliszd Right. In 1972 an American Enterprise Institute pamphlet argued forcefully that organized consumerism actually went against the real consumer interest, which only business could ultimately support: consumer advocates instead were actually opposed to the perfectly legitimate "quest for profit."[79] A Cato Institute publication later concluded that consumer protection "destabilizes the free enterprise system through regulation, the attempted nationalization of industry, and plain harassment. Ultimately, it is the consumers who must pay the bill for this effort."[80] Instead, neoconservatives such as Russell Kirk were drafted to present an alternative "popular conservatism" to counter the perceived thrust of regulatory consumerism.[81]

The opposition to the U.S. consumer movement gathered momentum in the mid-1970s, particularly when it came to the campaign to create a federal Consumer Protection Agency. Along with the Labor Law Reform Bill and the Economic Recovery Tax Act, the Consumer Protection Agency (CPA) Bill assumed a symbolic importance for both the consumer and the anti-regulatory movements. For consumer activists it would have instituted a government protective framework similar to—if admittedly less effective than—many existing in Western Europe. For big business and conservative intellectuals its defeat was crucial to bringing to a halt—and starting the reversal of—the regulatory reforms begun in the 1960s. According to Ronald Reagan, the proposed Agency would only please "professional consumerists who thrive on finding more ways to tighten the federal vise."[82] It amounted to an "Orwellian" surveillance of corporate activities by consumerists "obsessed with the idea of controlling the economy."[83] In the words of the conservative former segregationist and grammarian James J. Kirkpatrick, the proposed agency was a bureaucratic "monster" inspired by "costly, needless and autocratic legislation."[84]

The CPA Bill had a long history in Congress. It was first introduced by Estes Kefauver in 1959 and was conceived as a corporatist body to speak for the consumer in government in much the same way that the Departments of Agriculture, Commerce, and Labor spoke for their specific interest groups. The Bill achieved little success but was revived at the end of the 1960s when Ralph Nader urged the establishment of an independent consumer advocacy body rather than a government department. Nader, along with CU, Esther Peterson, and the Consumer Federation of America believed a government department would merely transfer existing state consumer officials to one organization, making it easier for business groups to target and ultimately "capture." In 1969 a revised CPA Bill was introduced, beginning a nine-year legislative history that would see many further revisions, although in general terms the proposed Agency was to consist of an independent body able to represent consumers in federal agencies and courts, act as a watchdog on government consumer protection regulations, and serve as a clearing house for individual complaints against business enterprises. In the 91st Congress (1969–70), the Senate passed a CPA Bill but it did not reach a vote in the House. The following year another Bill was passed by the House, but blocked by a filibuster in the Senate. In the 93rd Congress (1973–74), the House again passed a weakened Bill and another filibuster blocked it in the Senate. In 1975 there was sufficient momentum behind the Bill for it to be passed by both chambers, but the majority in the House was felt to be too small to override President Gerald Ford's expected veto and so it was abandoned. With the arrival of Carter's administration, renewed efforts were made as the White House made it clear it would support the Bill. But following extensive campaigns launched by both supporters and opponents, in 1978 the House actually defeated the Bill for the first time (by 227 votes to 189) and it was never picked up again.[85]

The supporters of the Bill in Congress were backed up by an impressive mobilization of the consumer movement outside Washington. Nader joined with

CU and 120 other national and local citizen and community groups and devoted much more time in the 1970s to the CPA Bill than to any other project.[86] In 1977 he estimated that the actual cost of the proposed agency would amount to little more than five cents per year for every citizen. He, therefore, launched a "nickel campaign" urging members of the public to send a nickel to every member of Congress known to oppose the Bill: an estimated 400,000 nickels arrived in Washington within the first two months.[87] The consumer coalition lobbied Senators, especially Bob Dole and the like, who stopped their support for the Bill when the struggle became a major political issue under Ford.[88] And they felt rejuvenated once Jimmy Carter came into office and announced his support for the CPA.[89]

In addition, Carter recalled Esther Peterson to government as the Special Assistant to the President on Consumer Affairs, appointing her specifically to steer the Bill through Congress and to ensure it was passed. She guided the Bill through its committee stages and then lobbied hard, coordinating efforts from the White House through an informal CPA Group. She met and sought to appease business groups opposed to the Bill and she targeted key politicians. Most important, she complemented Nader's grassroots efforts outside Washington with the establishment of the Coalition for a Consumer Protection Agency, which was funded by commercial organizations in favor of the Bill and staffed by volunteers connected to the consumer movement. Within its ranks it included 126 businesses supporting the Bill, as well as a number of high-profile national labor organizations and a range of civil society bodies from the American Association of Retired Persons to Friends of the Earth to the National Association for the Advancement of Colored People.[90]

However, all this mobilization and co-ordination by an experienced consumer lobbyist was insufficient to force the passing of the Bill. Its failure has been attributed to a variety of factors. Nader himself has been blamed as he was held to work ineffectively with others in the Coalition while his belligerent stance with the Bill's opponents meant he was unable to make the sort of political compromises that more experienced negotiators in Washington thought necessary. Certainly Peterson felt that too much of her work was spent re-building the bridges burnt by a confrontational Nader and the evidence of his own letters to Presidents and Congressmen reflects a level of aggression unlikely to have persuaded those already disinclined to vote for the Bill.[91] Yet more general studies of public interest activism have pointed to the inability of reform movements to obtain legislative change, especially when the issue has become a hot political topic. The real reason for the defeat of the CPA Bill therefore lies not so much with the weakness of the public interest and consumer campaigns, but in the strength of the defensive counterefforts made by the organized business community.

By far the most important reason why the CPA Bill did not succeed was due to the greater mobilization of the special interests associated with an organized business lobby backed up with a set of free market, anti-regulatory arguments propounded in the public sphere by an increasingly influential set of right-wing think tanks. As countless commentators noted at the time, the defeat of the CPA signaled the presence of a resurgent business community. Mark Green, the director of Public Citizen's Congress Watch—one of the major supporters of the CPA Bill—commented in *The Nation* on the combination of interest and ideology in the opposition to the Bill as the National Association of Manufacturers, the Business Roundtable, and the Chamber of Commerce managed to tie their cause to party politics, making "the bill a litmus-test issue of a Representative's fidelity to their creed."[92] The opponents of the Bill made the issue not one so much about the minor details of consumer protection but a symbolic campaign against those who wished to expand the role of the state. The Bill came to be about "big government" and the defense of special interests was wedded to a wider agenda, which was attracting adherents not only from the Republican right, but from among political moderates and those Democrats who would experience their neoconservative anti-regulatory epiphanies at this time. In 1978 a total of 101 Democrats voted against the Bill, many believing the proposed $15 million non-regulatory advocacy office was something akin to the great bureaucracies of the New Deal.

The scale of business lobbying on Capitol Hill was unprecedented. Thomas "Tip" O'Neill, Speaker of the House of Representatives (1977–87), claimed that in twenty-five years he had "never seen such extensive lobbying."[93] Beginning in 1969, the Consumer Issues Working Group united and co-ordinated a huge coalition of over 400 separate business and trade associations, dominated by the Business Roundtable, the National Association of Manufacturers, the Grocery Manufacturers' Association, and the U.S. Chamber of Commerce, as well as key corporations such as Ford, General Motors, Procter and Gamble, and Pepsi.[94] It started as an informal attempt to co-ordinate lobbying in Washington but became a powerful steering group for a many-sided assault on the CPA supporters' coalition. Its effectiveness is perhaps measured by the fact that it became the model for corporate lobbying on many similar issues.[95]

The tactics of the Consumer Issues Working Group were certainly impressive. They fought a high-profile campaign in the media especially after the Business Roundtable hired the well-regarded and highly credible Watergate Special Prosecutor, Leon Jaworski, to head the lobbying effort. In addition, the North American Press Syndicate was employed to send around editorials and cartoons to just under 4,000 newspapers and weeklies.[96] These prepared statements appeared approximately 2,000 times and only rarely was their special interest source acknowledged. The Business Roundtable also commissioned an opinion poll, which claimed that 75 percent of Americans were opposed to the Bill, although several organizations questioned the validity of the research and the claims.[97] Further grassroots activism was encouraged through stockholder mobilizations: Procter and Gamble and General Foods wrote to all their stockholders asking them to contact legislators and express their opposition to the Bill while the Chamber of Commerce published a "Business Responsiveness

Kit" to advise individual firms on how to respond to the "Nader Enabling Act."[98] At the same time, more intimidating tactics were also employed: General Motors and Procter and Gamble threatened to withdraw their business from Blue Cross, the medical-insurance providers, if it continued to offer its support for the Bill.[99] And politicians were approached directly with the financial advantages made apparent. At the height of the battle over the CPA, corporate contributions through political action committees began to exceed those made by the trade unions, and legislators with marginal seats were said to have been made very aware of the money, which could be subsequently raised or withdrawn from their campaign funds.[100]

From an early stage, consumer leaders such as Nader were well aware of the strength of the business opposition, but were simply unable to compete with the level of influence business lobbyists enjoyed in Washington.[101] Consumer lobbyists frequently believed that both Nixon and Ford worked behind the scenes to defeat earlier versions of the Bill, an accusation not without foundation given the level of access the business community had to these Presidents.[102] As soon as Carter was elected, consumerists were referring to the "secret war" being fought by an "inner circle" of CPA opponents. It was claimed in conspiratorial tones that they attempted to persuade Carter to insert extra clauses they knew Congress would never accept.[103] Whether this was the case or not, the strength of the anti-regulatory lobby certainly increased throughout the decade of the 1970s. In the weeks and months leading up to the final rounds of the voting in 1977 and 1978, Carter admitted that the business lobbyists "have come out of the woodwork," putting Nader and his allies on the defensive.[104] Despite that the new Democrat President seemed committed to consumer protection: perhaps he knew which way the wind was blowing. Certainly, both Nader and Peterson were angry at Carter's non-committal attitude toward the end of the Bill's life. By late 1977, Peterson was complaining of the "half-hearted" enthusiasm shown by the White House and in the final round of telephone calls necessary to persuade swing voters in the House, Nader was angry that Carter had only bothered to get halfway through his list.[105]

Peterson was well aware of the significance of the defeat of the CPA Bill. As she told Carter at the end of the campaign, "this is precedent setting. If we lose this bill, we lose them all."[106] To this extent, she was in agreement with those who have subsequently claimed that the conservatives did not enter into power with Reagan in 1980; they had largely obtained their hold on American politics by 1978.[107] In a series of memos between Peterson and White House staffers discussing the fallout of the defeat, the symbolism of the CPA Bill was not lost on the principal actors at the time. They warned of a "de facto takeover of Congress by Right-Wing Corporate Interests," an analysis that, if a little apocalyptic in tone, broadly conveys the sense of importance political scientists have attributed to the CPA Bill and the Labor Law Reform Bill—both of which have been held to have broken up any nominal effort at consensus building the corporate lobby might formally have attempted with other interest groups.[108]

It left the consumer movement defeated and placed on the defensive for some time thereafter.

The eventual outcome of a decade of campaigning for a federal consumer protection system was a Presidential Executive Order of September 1979 that forced federal agencies to develop consumer programs. It was a long way short of the CPA but in the new political climate it was the best the consumer movement could hope for.[109] While the success of the consumer and public interest movements in the late 1960s and early 1970s had led many to celebrate the pluralist nature of U.S. politics, studies conducted later pointed to the entrenched power of U.S. business interests. The consumer movement did not bother pushing again for a federal agency and instead chose in the 1980s to focus on specific industries and government institutions.[110] It became enmeshed in wider networks of public interest activism and its role in Washington did not decline, although it would not develop again a similar holistic model of state-consumer relations.[111]

The 1978 defeat was even more bitter for Ralph Nader than it was for Peterson. The first ten years of Nader's career as a public activist had been marked by a sense of the possible and his presence symbolized an optimism about what could be obtained from government in the consumer interest. During the 1976 presidential campaign, Nader had actually umpired a Carter softball game, implying a level of judgment Nader might exercise over the candidate. But early into Carter's administration Nader was furious at what he saw as the increasing number of government appointments led by corporate interests when he had fully expected that official appointments might even be run past him for approval.[112] By the end of the 1970s, so disillusioned was Nader with the absence of reforms that he even took to attacking and criticizing the work of his former colleagues who had managed to be appointed to positions within the Carter administration.[113] Once Ronald Reagan came into office, Nader retreated from national life and focused on building state and local organizations to counter business influence.[114] In the 1980s for him, consumerism came to be about creating private, small-scale, and even co-operative initiatives that could negotiate better conditions of buying for consumers.[115] He would re-emerge as a prominent public spokesperson on consumer and public issues, but the first two decades of his national career had witnessed a meteoric rise and a gradual descent that related inversely to the power of the business community, which he had spent so long opposing.

IV

The implications of the "corporatization" of U.S. politics did not end in Washington. It constituted a more general victory of free market principles that would result in the export of an anti-regulatory and pro-big business agenda on to the world stage. It has long been argued that regulatory agencies are prone to capture by the very industries they have been set up to regulate.[116] But in the 1980s, the influence of business on government was far more general than that resulting from the targeting of key institutions. Reagan came into power on the back of a resurgent Right and was supported by a number of key neoconservative think tanks that capitalized on the anti-regulatory mood they had helped foster among the U.S. public. By the end of the 1970s, advocates of consumer protection could no longer count on the mass support of the public for their measures. According to one expert on consumer protection, the subject was no longer a "motherhood and applie pie" issue that had once been "so entrenched that even President Nixon paid obeisance to it."[117] Instead, consumer leaders were increasingly presented, with some evidence, as being out of step with the majority of actual consumers and greater attention in the public media was being given to the arguments of the American Enterprise Institute, the Heritage Foundation, and the Cato Institute as well as to figures such as Milton Friedman.[118] In 1980, Friedman broadcast a ten-part documentary series titled, *Free to Choose*, which distilled the free market arguments he first set out in 1962 in *Capitalism and Freedom*. In the accompanying book, Friedman attacked the consumer movement and reveled in the "growing recognition of the dangers of big government."[119]

The most spectacular sign of the ascendancy of the Right was with the influence of the Heritage Foundation on the first Reagan administration. At the beginning of 1980 it published its *Mandate for Leadership: Policy Management in a Conservative Administration*—a thousand-page compendium of conservative policy proposals, 60 percent of which the Foundation would later claim were implemented. Reagan was a Heritage Foundation man. He personally endorsed the *Mandate* and distributed copies of it at the very first meeting of his cabinet—he would subsequently appoint many of the book's contributors to government positions.[120] Heritage has been rightly proud of its achievements in influencing policy and certainly Reagan's anti-regulatory rhetoric was entirely in line with its own. It built on Reagan's longstanding links with groups such as the Business Roundtable and influenced especially his Task Force on Regulatory Relief, which resulted in budget cuts for the Federal Trade Commission and the Occupational Health and Safety Administration.[121] Moreover, it established new relations between think tanks and government, which would provoke some commentators into speaking of a new "corporate elite as a ruling class."[122] Admittedly, fractures were soon evident in this new alliance of business, government, and conservative ideology, not least because of the high spending programs that Reagan could not avoid and that served to limit the influence of corporations.[123] But the consumer movement was certainly well aware of the implications for its own agendas, arguing that Reagan's policies in his first year marked a "clear break from the 95 year history of progress" in consumer protection.[124]

In terms of global history what was even more significant about U.S. politics in the 1980s was the transference of this anti-regulatory impulse to the international stage. The politics of consumption espoused by IOCU became intricately bound up with the politics of regulation emanating from the United States. Whereas in other countries, especially Japan and those of Western Europe, multinational corporations urged their home governments to oppose international regulation, the links between business, ideology, and international diplomacy were never as direct as in the United States. The Heritage Foundation deliberately courted international links, channeling funds to Britain and Western European countries in order to develop a "common international agenda" among what amounted to a "co-operative relationship" between 200 political parties, individuals, think tanks, and media organizations.[125] Similarly, the American Enterprise Institute turned its attention to the perceived problems of regulation at the international level. In its journal *Regulation* it attacked the "global straightjacket" imposed on business by bodies such as UNCTAD while it accused WHO and the NGOs who lobbied it of "biting the hand that cures them."[126]

In the attempts to impose codes of conduct on the marketing of pharmaceuticals and baby foods, the American Enterprise Institute accused bodies supporting the consumer movement's campaigns of an implicit "colonialism" because they assumed that indigenous peoples—now operating as independent states—were "incapable of governing themselves."[127] In 1983, Jeane Kirkpatrick, U.S. Ambassador to the UN in the early 1980s who at the time was taking an American Enterprise Institute-sponsored sabbatical at Georgetown University, launched an attack on the "new class" of activists signed up to the New International Economic Order that was directing the UN to a system of "global paternalism."[128]

The Heritage Foundation likewise launched a comprehensive critique against the institutions of global governance. Since 1982 it systematically monitored the work of the UN, seemingly seeking to undermine the entire infrastructure.[129] Disappointed with the diplomatic attitude of the Reagan foreign policy advisers, the Heritage Foundation called for a more "fundamental rethinking of the US role in the UN."[130] In a 1984 publication written with a foreword by Kirkpatrick's Deputy Charles Lichenstein it argued that the UN had become "exceedingly anti-US, anti-West and anti-free enterprise."[131] Burton Yales Pines, a Heritage vice president, wrote:

> Most dangerous, perhaps, is the U.N.'s crusade against the free enterprise system. In many respects, the UN has become the headquarters and strategic planning center of an anti-free enterprise campaign. In almost every UN body and almost always in the General Assembly, seldom is an opportunity lost to attack the free enterprise system . . . And the UN crusade attacks the very essence and philosophical base of the free enterprise system. It is an assault which condemns . . . the notion that the dynamo of growth and economic expansion is individual initiative, creativity and the incentive provided by the opportunity of making a profit. This kind of attack even repudiates the notion of economic growth, substituting for it the naïve and economically self-defeating concepts of wealth redistribution and central planning.[132]

To Pines's general critique were added a whole series of specialist studies condemning specific branches of the UN. Much of this harked back to well-established anti-UN positions in U.S. politics. And much was tied in with a revitalized Cold War, but the direction of the Heritage Foundation's concerns suggest the equal importance of concerns more common to narratives of economic globalization than to US-Soviet diplomacy. The World Bank was critiqued for subsidizing what the American Enterprise Institute had earlier referred to as the new colonialism of developing world assistance.[133] UNESCO was charged with having deliberately "promoted the New International Economic Order, trumpeting the socialist policies that have proved so disastrous to Third World economies."[134] Bodies such as WHO and the United Nations Environment Programme were said to have over-reached themselves in their work on pharmaceutical marketing and pesticide regulation, although this was systematic of the entire UN structure since the General Assembly was held to have encroached on the power originally given to it by the Security Council.[135] Many of these attitudes toward the UN are familiar and do not need reworking here. They formed the basis for a U.S. foreign policy that sought to downplay the power of the UN agencies, develop free market solutions to the problems of economic development, and establish a foreign policy more assertively defending U.S. interests.[136] They amounted to a general rethinking of the Bretton Woods Institutions that anti-globalization protestors have charged has dominated neoconservative American policy agendas since the 1990s.[137] But before a positive framework was developed, the basic starting position of the Heritage Foundation and other think tanks was that the regulatory impulse of international governance must be opposed, just as it had been in the U.S. domestic arena a decade earlier.

It was perhaps inevitable that the Heritage Foundation would turn its sights on global consumer activists, their proposed codes of conduct mirroring the symbolic importance the Right had attached to the CPA Bill in the 1970s. Here, the Right's anti-UN and anti-consumer attitudes coalesced though the latter undoubtedly bolstered the former at this time. In a November 1982 pamphlet, the Heritage Foundation claimed multinational corporations were becoming "the first victim of the UN war on free enterprise." This was being directed behind the scenes by "an assault from a growing and potentially dangerous, internationally based, and self-styled 'consumerist' movement that already is helping set the agenda at various UN agencies." Specifically, IOCU was identified as the source of an "anti-capitalist and anti-free enterprise bias, which in the past decade has grown to alarming proportions within UN documents and literature."[138] IOCU had developed a campaigning style based around networks that placed consumers in alliance with trade unions, church-based groups, and less developed countries in order to promote codes of conduct that attacked specific industries.

The pamphlet amounted to a broad-ranging swipe against the UN, the New International Economic Order, and the Commission on Transnational Corporations but which eventually homed in on "the extremist wing of the international consumerist movement," especially IOCU.[139] Heritage identified Anwar Fazal as the main cause of the problem, due to his spawning of a new wave of consumer organizations such as IBFAN, PAN, HAI, and Consumer Interpol. As the only named individual in the document, it rejected his claims about the "violence" of multinational corporations (MNCs) and his "distortions designed to undermine the MNCs and private sector approach to development."[140] It concluded by urging the Reagan Administration to "become more aware of the dangers posed to US-based multinational firms by the internationalist consumerist movement" and to oppose all efforts to implement codes of conduct.[141] This should be achieved, it was argued, by increasing industry participation in UN negotiations and within the U.S. Mission, by proposing weak counterproposals and by forging international alliances with other states even if this meant making it "abundantly clear to those countries that the US does not look favorably upon their support for the anti-free enterprise, restrictive initiatives."[142]

Fazal had become the anti-regulatory movement's Nader at the global level. This identification of the international consumer movement as the main enemy of American conservatism marked the beginning of an escalating hostility by U.S. negotiators at the UN toward any measures that restricted the activities of U.S. corporations. Although IOCU, through its baby food network, had been able to obtain the Code of Marketing for Breast Milk Substitutes in 1981, the heightened attention to the UN by the Heritage Foundation and the American Enterprise Institute meant such successes would be difficult to achieve again. It provides the context that helps explain, as we saw in the last chapter, the failure to obtain an equivalent code for the pharmaceutical industry, and the tremendous difficulties the consumer movement faced in obtaining the UN Guidelines on Consumer Protection in 1985.

Indeed, the experience of IOCU representatives in the 1980s mirrors many of the attacks made on the U.S. consumer movement since the 1930s. Esther Peterson, employed by IOCU to lobby the UN after she left her role as Carter's Special Assistant, faced much of the hostility directly. It was she who experienced the reluctance of the U.S. delegation at the UN to comply with requests for information during the negotiations for the Guidelines. And it was she who stood accused of being a "foreign agent" when she was due to meet Reagan's consumer adviser, Virginia Knauer, to discuss the measures. Because she worked for IOCU, then based at The Hague, it was argued that she should be registered under the 1938 Foreign Agents Registration Act, an action that would have implications for other U.S. citizens working for international NGOs.[143] The accusation never stuck and was, most likely, a delaying tactic to prevent Peterson speaking to Knauer. But later she was forced to exit the room at the UN where negotiations were taking place over the Guidelines. As a representative of an NGO with consultative status she had a right to attend the meeting, but a U.S. Chamber of Commerce delegate and Alan Keyes, then a U.S. ambassador to the

UN and Kirkpatrick's protégé, persuaded the chair that she had to leave.[144] This marked just one of a number of confrontations between Peterson and Keyes, which consumer leaders like to recall: the diminutive and elderly Peterson going "nose to nose" with the physically intimidating Keyes.[145] But at the time such hostile actions merely added to the sense of grievance felt by the U.S. consumer movement that they had never been asked to contribute to U.S. policy in this area, despite this being one form of consultation with the organized consumer movement that Carter's 1979 Executive Order had laid down as necessary and automatic.[146]

Ultimately, as we have seen, the global consumer movement did succeed in getting a version of the Guidelines ratified by the UN General Assembly. However, the hostilities over them signified the startling differences between consumers and business over a measure which, because of its non-enforceability, was unlikely to damage U.S. corporate interests in any significant way. In response to their publication, IOCU invited Peterson and an opponent to put the two sides for and against the Guidelines. Peterson's position was that the Guidelines offered a practical and realizable vision. She claimed that no "divergence of interest" existed between "legitimate business practices and conscientious consumer protection." Indeed, consumer protection created both better consumers and better businesses. She claimed that to disparage their lofty ideals would be to criticize the same high-mindedness of the original U.S. Constitution. But, in point of fact, she argued, such critiques were irrelevant, because the Guidelines were voluntary and could not be construed as a fundamental defense of state socialism—the guidelines were a legitimate area of UN activity that fell well within the operations of the free enterprise system.[147]

Against the Guidelines stood Murray Weidenbaum, Mallinckrodt Distinguished University Professor at Washington University since 1964 and Director of the Center for the Study of American Business since 1975 (subsequently named after him in 2000). Weidenbaum has long been closely associated with such neoconservative organizations as the American Enterprise Institute, the Heritage Foundation, the Center for Strategic Tax Reform, the American Council for Capital Formation, and the Foreign Policy Research Institute, helping to edit their publications and enjoying the patronage of their scholarly fellowships. He played an important role in U.S. economic policy, initially as first Assistant Secretary of the Treasury for Economic Policy in the Nixon administration and later, more important, as Reagan's first chairman of the Council of Economic Advisers from 1981 to 1982. After this he helped in the lobbying of the United Nations in the early 1980s against a series of regulatory initiatives, including those promoted by the consumer movement. For Weidenbaum, the problem was that regulation had become an end in itself, had exceeded its purpose, and had become dominated by "waste, bias, stupidity, concentration on trivia, conflicts among the regulators and, worst of all, arbitrary and uncontrolled power."[148] Moreover, the whole thrust of regulation had turned from controlling capitalism to becoming an attack on the very principles and foundations

Figure 10. Murray Weidenbaum, here shown around the time when he served as chairman of President Ronald Reagan's Council of Economic Advisers (1981–1982).

Courtesy of Weidenbaum Center, Washington University in St. Louis.

of capitalism.[149] He believed the Guidelines themselves to be a "model of vagueness and overblown phraseology," which nevertheless acted as "a blue-print for a centrally directed society."[150] He argued that consumers much pre-ferred cheapness over either safety, regulation, or any commitment to vague ideals that only produced "high-mindedness and fuzzy-thinking." He chal-lenged the legitimacy of the UN in acting on behalf of consumers and saw in the Guidelines yet another example of UN interference in private enterprise.

The battle being fought out between Peterson and Wiedenbaum, both in print and along the corridors of the UN, came down to the differences in the perceived consumer and business interests that had exercised the attention of the protagonists of U.S. consumer politics since the 1930s.

Despite that others have claimed a mutual affinity between consumers and corporations—"what's good for the consumer is good for business"—the his-tory of the groups that have chosen to represent consumers and corporations is one marked more by discord than harmony. Indeed, whenever the consumer movement has been in the ascendant the organized business community has been quick to respond. Using similar arguments and, in some instances, similar personnel, IOCU was attacked at the UN in the 1980s just as Nader and his allies were disparaged in the United States in the 1970s. In the debate between Peterson and Weidenbaum, Peterson may have had the last word because the Guidelines were actually published. However, this was only one concession given by the U.S. Mission to the UN, which it had no intention of repeating.

As we will see in chapter 8, the next campaign Peterson undertook was the drafting of a UN Code of Conduct on Transnational Corporations. As with the CPA Bill, this would be defeated, leading to a reversal in fortunes for the consumer movement that substantially limited its ability to influence governance at either the national or the international level. In the seemingly perpetual conflict between organized business and organized consumers, symbolic victories were twice won by the corporate class, resulting in the ascendancy of the free market and the dominant promotion of consumer protection as synonymous with greater choice for the individual. The notion that choice should be restricted, or subsumed under the alternative needs of the interests of the collective mass of consumers would be downplayed.

V

This history of a U.S. corporate backlash against regulation is by no means specific to the sphere of consumer protection. Although the consumer movement has rarely, if at all, been included in this narrative, it is clearly one that relates to a variety of areas covered by U.S. politics. The neoconservative movement has been most obviously studied as a factor explaining the attempts to roll back the state since the 1980s, the rise of U.S. militarism, the post-1989 foreign policies of several administrations, and the reconstituting of the global economy after the Uruguay round of trade negotiations.[151] These areas have profound and immediate relevance to our lives and there has been justifiable interest in the complex and ever-changing phenomenon of neoconservatism.

Although some are arguing that fractures are beginning to appear in this movement of the Right, especially as it is claimed the U.S. government has pursued a post-9/11 foreign policy based on the promotion of special interests rather than an ideological commitment to the free market, neoconservatism is remarkable in the degree of coherence it demonstrated and the coalescing of its principles with the interests of American business and American government from the mid-1970s.[152] Crucial to this agenda were the defensive, negative aspects behind its rise—opposing the bureaucratic logic of regulation it perceived during the presidencies of Lyndon B. Johnson and Richard Nixon. And crucial too, as many on the Right were well aware of at the time, was the consumer movement, especially after it was revitalized by the confrontational stance adopted by Ralph Nader. The defeat of the CPA Bill had to consist not only of a lobbying action by the organized business community against state interference, but an ideological opposition to the whole nature of government regulation. The very success of the consumer movement, then, helped bring about a truly giant opposition that ultimately overwhelmed the presence of consumer activists on Capitol Hill.

If historians of U.S. business and of the rise of the political Right have paid insufficient attention to the consumer movement and to the symbolic importance of the CPA Bill, then historians of consumer activism have been much more complacent in their assessment of the organized consumer movement since the 1960s. Many of the works on twentieth-century U.S. consumer politics like to end their stories with upbeat references to new forms of consumer activism taking place since the 1990s, be this green and ethical consumerism, fair trade initiatives, the "slow" food movement, "voluntary simplicity," or the "culture jamming" of the Canadian-based anti-advertising organization Adbusters. But behind this fingers-crossed hopefulness lies a deep-seated cultural pessimism of a liberal-left historical scholarship. This is because, on the whole, it has argued that consumer politics and the consumer movement have had little to offer since the 1960s. The American republic has become "consumerized," the culture of commercialism has won, and few now express any "anxieties over affluence."[153] Instead, while they have celebrated the actions of earlier generations of consumer activists in much smaller and less influential organizations such as the League of Women Shoppers and the National Consumers' League, it has been left to market populists to marvel in the triumph of mass marketing, the advantages of advertising, and the wonder of ever more stuff in the de-regulatory reforms since the 1980s.[154] Despite the explicit rejection of the theories of manipulation expounded by the Frankfurt School and a consequent celebration of consumer agency, what is apparent in this historical literature is actually a similar interpretation of consumer politics. It does not claim that consumers have been duped, but it does assume a degree of passivity in consumers, which has seen them become largely accepting of the culture of shopping and increasingly unconcerned with the range of citizen concerns that had so distinguished consumer activism in the past.

What this chapter has sought to do is to show another side to the story. It has not argued that consumer activists have rolled over, embraced a model of market individualism propounded by orthodox economics, and had nothing of interest to say since the 1960s. Instead it has told a story of defeat. The organized consumer movement has had many points to make and many causes to champion during this time. Since the 1980s, it has accepted the changing dynamics of U.S. politics and focused not so much on grand political visions but on isolated issues and on specific questions of reform. While to some extent this does lend itself to a story of inaction, and we will explore the limitations of the politics of the consumer movement in the next chapter, what it does do is acknowledge that consumer activists have "succeeded in keeping their issues before Congress and the media and shaping public opinion";[155] that they have not been able to translate these issues into legislative action or new regulations

has not been their fault. Rather, it has been due to the greater forces and interests against which they have been up. Ralph Nader and the consumer movement's failure with the CPA Bill was a symbolic moment because it stopped the
momentum of federal consumer protection and made consumer activists the ultimate losers in a battle fought with organized business from the 1930s onward.
After the failure of the CPA Bill, the consumer movement has continued to grow
in size and in the scale of its operations. It has had much to contribute and it
has had much to say. However, it is no longer heard to quite the same extent
and it is competing against much better resourced voices and interests. In this
sense, organized consumerism has become one of history's losers, but this
should not mean we write it out of the historical record.

The implications of the CPA Bill need to be reiterated one last time, for they
went far beyond the parochial concerns of U.S. domestic politics. The rise of
the radical Right and the creation of a corporate policy elite in Washington were
taken to the global level. If these groups were not always able to succeed in their
objectives in the 1980s, they demonstrated a remarkably consistent agenda at
both the U.S. and the global political level (a phenomenon explored further in
chapter 8). Just as U.S. political commentators noted the new elites connected
to Reagan, so too have scholars of globalization noted the existence of a
"transnational capitalist class."[156] In the 1980s the unity between U.S. corporate interests, think tank ideologies, and government officials was transferred
to the United Nations where an anti-regulatory agenda was pursued in the same
way as it had been in Washington. As we will see, after the success of the Guidelines on Consumer Protection, the global consumer movement would enjoy few
other notable victories. Just like the U.S. consumer movement, it found itself
operating in a very different political climate that made it increasingly difficult
for its campaigns to become policy. It too suffered a series of setbacks on the
issue of global trade regulation, which would see its basic needs, developmental politics of consumption eclipsed by a free market ideology that proclaimed
that consumer interests lay in greater choice for the individual. At both the U.S.
and the global level defeat rather than passivity better characterizes the history
of consumer activism.

CHOOSE LIFE

Consumer Rights versus Human Rights

The publicity poster in figure 11 lists the eight consumer rights, which together constitute the operating principles of the global consumer movement. They are based on a speech made by President John F. Kennedy to the U.S. Congress on 15 March 1962 when he pledged his support to some of the key demands of consumer activists: "If consumers are offered inferior products, if prices are exorbitant, if drugs are unsafe or worthless, if the consumer is unable to choose on an informed basis, then his dollar is wasted, his health and safety may be threatened, and the national interest suffers." In Kennedy's vision of the marketplace, social and economic justice was to be bolstered as much by the defense of the domestic purse as the wage earner's pay packet: "On the other hand, increased efforts to make the best possible use of their incomes can contribute more to the well-being of most families than equivalent efforts to raise their incomes."[1] The means to achieve the consumer democracy was through the articulation, promotion, and defense of four consumer rights:

1. The right to safety
2. The right to be informed
3. The right to choose
4. The right to be heard

Kennedy's four consumer rights were adopted as the central pillars of IOCU policy and the date chosen for the World Consumer Rights Day was the anniversary of Kennedy's coming out into the consumerist fold. As the consumer movement has spread around the globe, it has supplemented these four rights, first by expanding on the essentially individualist rights to protection outlined

Figure 11. "This is Your World!" Publicity poster for International Organisation of Consumers Unions, 1981.

Courtesy of IOCU.

by Kennedy and then by taking on the more socially oriented interests of developing world consumers. By the end of the 1970s, following the influence of Asian consumerism, IOCU had added four more rights to its list:

5. The right to redress
6. The right to consumer education
7. The right to a healthy environment
8. The right to basic goods and services

These eight rights still continue to direct IOCU operations. They reflect not only the concerns of affluent shoppers seeking a fair deal for themselves in the marketplace, but also the wider goals of organized consumerism that inspired its growth from the 1960s and that tied the consumer cause to broader questions of global economic and social justice. But if we look closely again at figure 11, we will note that something is missing. In this publicity poster there are, in fact, only seven rights listed. The right that is missing is the right to choose. In this global vision of consumerism the consumer movement seemingly excluded the right to the freedom of choice.

The image is that of a poster commissioned by IOCU in 1981 from a graphic designer Chaz Maviyane-Davies. A recent graduate of the Central School of Art and Design in London, Maviyane-Davies worked, studied, and traveled in Asia, spending ten months in Malaysia working with organizations such as IOCU. Specifically, he collaborated with Anwar Fazal in the design of a series of posters that emphasized IOCU's role as a campaigning activist body focused on global issues typically spearheaded by the new transnational advocacy networks.[2]

The absence of choice from the poster was not the innocent mistake of an inexperienced artist unaware and unconcerned with the principles of his client. Nor was it the error of Fazal, too busy with his campaigns on pesticides, baby foods, and pharmaceuticals to be able to properly proof the copy of the list of rights to which consumer leaders perhaps too complacently referred. The omission was deliberate. The decision to exclude choice was the premeditated policy of the world's leading consumer advocate. He was able to produce and distribute an image containing a "mistake," which many consumer activists in the West failed to notice and which contained a cryptic message in what was omitted. For Fazal and other consumer advocates in the developing world, this message was that choice was the privilege of the affluent. They did not deny that choice in itself was a good thing and that it was intimately bound up with notions of freedom, it was simply not a priority for them. Fazal and others believed that the rights to basic needs were far more important concerns for the majority of the world's consumers; by excluding choice, he was sending out a non-too-subtle, if not immediately obvious, message to his Western counterparts.

These graphic disputes over the primacy of particular rights reflect many of the tensions not only within the consumer movement but within consumer society as a whole. They point to the central dilemmas of economic and political planners, as well as citizens in general and to the central concerns that have run throughout this book: obtaining more choice for the individual or promoting greater standards of living for all. By choosing to overlook one particular right, Fazal demonstrated the extent to which a rights-based framework often masked these underlying strains. This is because such a rights-based operating philosophy as adopted by the consumer movement actually served to hide the very real differences that can exist between rich and poor consumers and between consumer movements of the developed and developing worlds. The interests of the consumer in sub-Saharan Africa are very different from those in the industrialized West, as the consumer movements of the different regions have been keen to demonstrate. Which rights and which duties of the consumer are spoken of and fought for become crucial in maintaining a balance between the competing consumer demands of the North and the South.

This chapter is about the rights to choice and the choice of rights. It is about the consumer movement's adoption of a rights-based policy and the politics of the development of these rights. It argues that in many ways what the consumer movement did was to create its own shopping list of rights, selecting a series of causes it has chosen to buy into. Over the years this list has grown alongside the consumer movement's own expansion into a greater number of campaigning initiatives. Yet there are very real, if subtle differences, between maintaining a list of rights and developing a more abstract ideology that consistently incorporates all such rights into one political vision. As we have seen, the consumer movement's pragmatism was a source of its strength as it avoided the intellectual strait-jackets that have arguably restricted the growth of other social movements, but it was also a source of its potential weakness. Just as consumer activists were free to add to the list of rights, they were also free to select from it the rights it sought to prioritize and defend. Choosing the right to choice leads to a very different politics of consumption from choosing the right to basic needs: the former can result in a limited defense of individual economic rights; the latter has potentially no end as it affects so many instances of global justice.

This chapter begins with a discussion of the nature of a rights-based campaigning framework while also briefly describing IOCU's accumulation of rights. The underlying tensions of a rights-based model are then explored by examining particular moments in the history of the consumer movement when such issues came to a head. Perhaps inevitably, these clashes over the prioritization of one right over another manifested themselves in personality disputes between leaders of the consumer movement. The chapter then focuses on Ralph Nader's troubled relationship with the U.S. Consumers Union, together with Anwar Fazal's acrimonious departure from the international organization at the end of the 1980s. Almost as soon as Fazal left the consumer movement, IOCU quickly disassociated itself from the networks that had oriented consumerism toward environmental and human rights and moved it back to the rights to choice and redress, which had so concerned Kennedy and the CU in the 1960s.

The next part of this chapter describes a very different consumer movement in the 1990s from what had developed in Penang in the 1970s. As human rights NGOs have flourished in the last quarter century, they have to some extent eclipsed a consumer movement that has increasingly fallen behind the pace in its advocacy of rights. As the previous chapter showed, the vision and the potential of the consumer movement was restricted by its opponents. But it also played a role in its own partial marginalization as it focused on a narrower concept of rights, which meant it forged fewer alliances with other campaigning organizations. To many more radical consumer activists this has been a development noted with regret. For many moderates, however, it represented the logical tactic for a movement, which in some ways had reached a plateau: in various domestic environments many of the key consumer movement goals had been satisfied through the introduction of consumer protection mechanisms. The role for the consumer movement was now to be restricted to an ongoing monitoring of abuses within the marketplace.

For many consumer activists in the global South such a limited role has been unsatisfactory. Moreover, as the consumer movement has chosen to become less prominent globally, it has done so at a time when other factors have meant it has also been overshadowed at the local level. The final part of this chapter will return to Malaysia, the center of one of the foremost critiques of Western liberal rights-based models: the "Asian values" debate promoted by Singapore and Malaysia's vociferous prime ministers in the 1980s and 1990s, Lee Kuan Yew and Mahathir Mohamad, respectively. Within this context, developing world consumer groups, eager to promote a wider rights-based model as advocated in the politics of consumer necessity, have also struggled to negotiate with an anti-Western critique of rights. It has left them in a rather awkward situation as they both defend consumer rights and criticize their supposedly inherent individualism—a schizophrenia that has seen their rhetoric eclipsed by a new generation of human rights NGOs perhaps better able to deal with the issues that now confront civil society.

I

For all the differences in consumer protection regimes around the world, rights have remained crucial bargaining points for further regulatory mechanisms demanded by the consumer movement. Much of the explanation for the popularity of the rights-based approaches among consumer and civil society campaigners lies in their apparently politically neutral nature. As many political scientists have pointed out, rights-based policies do not necessarily challenge the fundamentals of existing political and economic structures. They are largely, or can be made to be, non-controversial and are much more likely to be implemented than measures that constitute one part of a package of a broader, ideologically driven set of reforms.

According to many exponents of liberal rights frameworks, everybody has a right to an extensive system of equal liberties and that opportunities within the institutions attached to such liberties are open to all. The free market can provide such opportunities, though rational actors will be likely to conclude that any inequities that emerge must be corrected in order to ensure that the least advantaged are not maintained in their relative destitution and that fairness is maintained in principles of justice.[3] Such a system of liberal rights appeals to those who wish to critique rather than overhaul the existing system.[4] Certainly this could serve as a description of the motivation of many consumer activists, from *Consumer Reports* readers to fair traders and ethical shoppers. We must also acknowledge the great differences that can exist between specific rights, as well as in our attitudes toward how they are enforced. For many rights theorists, rights are based on basic human needs, an observation that demands we commit ourselves to ensuring that society does not "disrespect" these rights either in all of us or in sections of the population. This is essentially the negative duty of rights: that we refrain from violating the rights of others. What such a position does not demand is the more positive duty whereby we accept our responsibility for protecting the rights of others and work to ensure the establishment of a social system within which "all its participants have secure access to the objects of their human rights."[5] It is these positive duties that are more obviously apparent not in, say, statements about the right to freedom of choice, but in the proclamations to the right to social security, work, leisure and culture, education, and an adequate standard of living—all of which can be found in Articles 22–27 of the Universal Declaration of Human Rights.[6]

There is a cumulative dimension to the history of rights as ever increasing numbers are found to constitute the human condition. Particularly within nation-states, citizenship has developed through the accumulation of political, economic, and social rights.[7] In histories of rights there is almost a positivist dimension to the narrative as rights first set out in core texts—such as the Magna Carta in England, the Bill of Rights in the United States, the Declaration of the Rights of Man in France, and even the statement on the Fundamental Rights and Duties of Citizens in the Soviet Union in 1936—have been added to ultimately culminate in the international initiatives of the twentieth century associated with the League of Nations and then the United Nations.[8]

Notwithstanding the very real need for a notion of universal human dignity that stood beyond the atrocities committed against "non-citizens" within any nation-state during World War II, we can also detect a pragmatic element to the development of a rights-based language of political campaigning. Especially within the international community of NGOs, rights represent claims on the institutions of governance that can be localized around specific issues. For instance, the women's movement, representing as diverse a constituency as that of consumers, has overridden any potential splits along economic, racial or geographical lines by seeking statements of fundamental rights with universal applicability.[9] For international organizations with little power beyond the consent of their state memberships, rights have become a useful means of issuing statements, protocols, and codes of practice. In the absence of obtaining effective executive remedies, NGOs have encouraged the utterance of global declarations, which they can then use as benchmarks in the monitoring of activities of nation-states. This is why NGOs such as Amnesty International, recognizing that states are unlikely to voluntarily abdicate their powers, have looked to international organizations that can issue high-sounding rights conventions which, it is hoped, may someday permeate and infiltrate nation-state legislative frameworks.[10]

What could be argued is that not only are rights intimately bound up with liberal market societies, but that these have been institutionalized within the UN and promoted by capitalist governments and Western-based NGOs. Indeed, this point lies behind the critique of rights as the imposition of liberal, Western value frameworks, particularly from the perspective of "Asian values" arguments. To some "Asian values" have been cynically promoted by authoritarian leaders to deny their citizens the same political and civil rights as enjoyed by those living under democratic governments. For its adherents Asian values represent a genuine attempt to find unities within non-Western states, blending together principles of Confucianism, Hinduism, and Islam. Asian values are said to consist of a preference for strong government and social harmony rather than democracy and dissent, a willingness to forego certain civil liberties and human rights in order to achieve economic growth and an acceptance that the good of the community and the family ought to come above that of the individual. These are not the arguments solely of authoritarian leaders keen to legitimate their own regimes. They have also been embraced by less cynically motivated civil society actors eager to construct alternatives to perceived processes of westernization and Americanization.[11]

The point to be made about rights-based activism for our purposes is that the relationship of NGOs to human rights has been a mixture of the pragmatic and the ideological. Pragmatic, because rights have been a convenient mechanism to impose regulations and obtain concessions from nation-states; and ideological, because there is nevertheless a genuine commitment to the universal values of what it is to be human. The politics of rights advocacy can be better explored through case histories of NGO sectors that have promoted certain rights. The important questions to be addressed are not ontological ones about the nature of human rights, but practical political ones about whose rights have been defended and which rights have been advocated more than others. It is this choice of rights that must reside behind any history of rights, especially for those of the consumer movement, and be used to explain why, for example, some models might appear Western or why some Southern perspectives might not have been granted primacy in a global campaign. As NGOs have eschewed a coherent and consistent philosophy that lies behind their entire rights-based approach, and adopt instead a more general commitment to rights-based campaigning, the issues to be addressed relate to the articulation of certain rights over others rather than the ideology of rights in general.

This is exactly how we must tackle the history of consumer rights. Originally the "consumer interest" was conceived as purely an economic interest. As we have seen in earlier chapters, it was only through the gradual intervention of governments in consumer affairs that the defense of the consumer became a state and a political project. Attention to fair shares during two world wars, the protection of the innocent through food and drug laws, and the prosecution of the overtly criminal under adulteration and weights and measures legislation gradually incorporated the consumer as a legitimate concern of the state. In post-World War II planning initiatives consumers were positioned at the heart of reviving democracies. It is for this reason that the rights set out in Kennedy's speech were crucial to the consumer movement: they confirmed the transference of the consumer from being an economic interest to being a political citizen. Rights placed the consumer alongside other identities—worker, voter, taxpayer—especially during a period of economic expansion and the promotion of affluence.

From such a base, rights were understandingly taken up by the international consumer movement and used to lobby various governments. We have already seen in chapter 2 how rights provided the platform for European consumer policy. During the 1960s and 1970s, much of the work of IOCU was geared toward getting consumer rights recognized by the wider international community.

The 1968 World Consumer Congress was devoted to further elaborating on these rights and thereafter its work at the UN was focused on establishing consumer rights as human rights.[12] Particularly as the UN's ECOSOC focused on development initiatives, the consumer movement campaigned successfully so that by the late 1970s its rights were recognized as core elements of economic and social rights by the UN.[13] Indeed, as we saw in chapter 4, much of the IOCU's work in obtaining the UN Guidelines on Consumer Protection was about the articulation of the rights first set out by Kennedy two decades earlier.[14]

The cumulative and declaratory approach to rights was not without its critics in the consumer movement. Rights were held to be intrinsically individualistic and did not address all the wider problems facing the world's poor. According to a paper written by a consumer activist in the early 1980s, "The freedom of individual choice is widely taken in the developed world, and among some of the elite in the Third World, as a right to a well nigh limitless acquisition of goods and services without thought to the consequences and without thought to the obligations that such action entails."[15] Choice, as the principal consumer right, could not deal adequately with the social choices facing consumers about the provision of education, health, and policing, as well as public utilities. Indeed, the British activist, Michael Dunne, inspired by the cultural critiques against commodity culture set out by the cultural Marxist and literary critic, Raymond Williams, the right to choose was "illogical, selfish and dangerous as a basis for a consumer philosophy."[16] He was not alone. At almost every world consumer congress, apocalyptic assessments of the consumer movement's contribution to acquisitive affluence have been made by guilt-ridden Western progressives. Likewise, developing world consumer activists have challenged the rights set out by Kennedy. To the supposedly individualistic rights of consumers were added the more positive statements such as the rights to a healthy environment and to basic needs. As we have seen these pushed the consumer movement into issues of poverty reduction and global justice and Fazal, in particular, articulated a corresponding set of consumer obligations. Five consumer duties were selected that the Penang office attempted to push as equivalent and equally important declarations of intent. They consisted of commitments to "critical awareness," "active involvement," "social responsibility," "ecological responsibility," and "solidarity."[17]

Overall these duties or responsibilities have not inspired global consumer activists, especially those emerging from Western organizations. Instead, it is the list of rights that has remained the core consumer ideology of IOCU. And for much of its history, it has preferred to accumulate rather than reflect on the nature of these rights. These might, at times, be said to constitute the basis for the creation of "a just and fair society," but just as often they can remain vague declarations with little to contribute to the program required to create such a society.[18] With such a list of rights, the question becomes one of emphasis. If we return to the distinctions made in rights-based theory, it is clear that some consumer rights inspire negative and positive duties. If choice is selected as the

Figure 12. "The Enlightened Consumer." Publicity poster for International Organisation of Consumers Unions, 1981.

Courtesy of IOCU.

primary right to defend, then the duties it imposes on consumers are largely negative because it can consist solely of a vague commitment to ensuring that others also have choices: little is demanded from the state and the individual retains primacy over the collective. If, however, the right to basic needs is selected, then a more positive response is required. Basic needs raise so many issues of social and economic justice that they automatically involve its advocates in a whole range of institutional settings with relevance to the provision of basic needs. A basic needs approach aligns the consumer movement to all those who have sought to create systems that better ensure the defense of those human rights set out in Articles 22–27 of the Universal Declaration. This is the real choice that has faced the consumer movement: defending the privileged choices of the individual or the impoverished needs of the collective.

The history of consumer organizing is about the selection and prioritization of certain rights over others. As we will see below, the intellectual tensions between a choice-based and a basic-needs approach have manifested themselves in key battles between activists, each fighting for the supposed soul of the consumer movement.

II

It is of no surprise that in a movement that seeks to represent everybody, tensions and splits might well occur. Like the labor movement before it, and the women's movement alongside it, organized consumerism has seen fractures throughout its history. Often these tensions manifested themselves in personality clashes among consumer groups' board members, the most prominent of which was between Ralph Nader and the rest of the CU Board that he had joined in 1967. The relationship between Nader and CU had got off to a good start. He had been welcomed by the consumer movement as a leading figure who could take the movement in new directions and provide it with a broader significance, which would increase the attention given to the consumer in all aspects of public life. Indeed, two years after he joined, CU opened a Washington office to put consumer pressure on Congress. In his speech at the CU Annual Meeting in Chicago in 1970, Nader stated that "the consumer movement deals with the most fundamental values confronting any society."[19] Earlier the consumer movement had even considered publishing *Unsafe at Any Speed,* though in a foretaste of things to come, the CU Board did not embrace Colston Warne's enthusiasm for the book, worrying that it might appear responsible for "Ralph's somewhat overdrawn sallies."[20]

However, during his time on the Board, Nader became increasingly critical of what he thought was the timidity and reluctance of CU to become a forceful consumer advocate. For many on the Board, Nader was too quick to conclude and to condemn, often using only partial research, while his intermittent attendance and forceful manner irritated many established members. The joint ventures—CU subsidized Nader's Center for Auto Safety, for instance—created links with other Nader Raiders that CU felt were unproductive, especially when less experienced advocates put forward less thoroughly researched findings in a confrontational manner, which were confused with CU's own statements in the popular media. For Nader's part, he was frustrated that CU did not share his enthusiasms, speed of action, and sense of wider purpose: even Warne admitted that Nader "mourned over our interminable debates."[21] The tensions ultimately became insurmountable and Nader acrimoniously left the Board in October 1975 stating, "I can better use the ten days a year which would be spent on Consumers Union matters in other pursuits within the consumer movement."[22]

In his resignation letter, Nader touched on the troubling issue at the heart of the U.S. consumer movement: "There is a division of philosophy on the Board as to how much energy and resources are to be directed toward changing major consumer injustices through consumer action instead of just informing some consumers about them."[23] This division came down to one of the selection of rights to focus on, though at the time the debate was understood in terms of the representation of CU member interests. Those opposed to Nader invoked the investigations periodically undertaken into reader attitudes. As was stated at the time of Nader's resignation, even though less than one percent of CU's budget was devoted to its legal advocacy work, this was too much for many of the readers of *Consumer Reports.* But the trouble with these appeals to the demands of the readership was that this readership was a diverse body. Other readers actually wanted CU to increase its political presence. As such, one could argue that the divisions of opinion within the CU readership were reflective of the diversity of opinions held by consumers as a whole. The real issue came down to which sections of consumer opinion CU wished to respond. Indeed, individual consumer leaders on the Board could always point to trends within general consumer attitudes that would support their particular vision of the direction of CU. There undoubtedly existed a rather conservative element to CU's membership in the mid-1970s, but also undoubtedly there existed much support and admiration for the work of figures such as Nader.

It is this relationship between the CU Board and the CU members that needs to be acknowledged if we are to better understand the selection of particular rights to direct the work of the consumer movement. And what is clear is that invocations of the conservative nature of CU's membership have been used to keep the more ambitious and Naderite voices in check. Although CU would continue to work with Nader after 1975 on issues such as the defense of the Consumer Protection Agency Bill, timidity rather than aggression has perhaps marked its interventions in the domestic political sphere.[24] By the 1980s, when the anti-regulatory agenda of the organized business community was beginning to win over ever greater numbers of people, this unwillingness to associate consumerism with radical activism only became more pronounced. So much was the free market agenda in the ascendancy in the early 1980s that the consumer movement was unwilling to criticize the existing state of federal consumer protection measures, lest their opinions be used to dismantle the particular agencies of consumer protection. It resulted in a situation in which while the consumer movement was booming in the developing world and within global civil society, in the domestic arena of U.S. politics it was largely dormant, despite the evidence of numerous surveys suggesting there still existed a considerable degree of public support for consumer action.[25]

This is not to say that there were not those who did not wish to see CU tackle wider social and economic questions. Rhoda Karpatkin, a New York lawyer with a background in civil rights, presided over CU for nearly three decades from 1974 and was an ardent admirer of consumer leaders such as Nader in the United States and Anwar Fazal in Asia.[26] Throughout the 1970s, in her "Memo to Members" column in *Consumer Reports* she kept subscribers up to date with such initiatives as the "nickel campaign" and the moves to create a Consumer Protection Agency. Once Reagan embarked on his intended policy of sweeping cuts across several federal programs, Karpatkin urged a broad-ranging debate on "the economic, social and ethical implications of spending cuts that affect the poor and helpless."[27] She commented on a number of "consumer" issues from fiscal policy to welfare reform and urged a "social agenda for consumerists" that took account of the needs of the poor not only globally but in the United States as well.[28] This agenda coincided with CU's fiftieth anniversary in 1986, an occasion that Karpatkin used to remind her readers of the labor concerns of the CU founders.[29] At the same time, she held a commemorative conference on "Ending Poverty" that coincided with CU's fascinating collaboration with the documentary photographer Eugene Richards. In *Below the Line: Living Poor in America,* published in 1987, CU and Richards explored the problems of poverty facing many contemporary Americans in a manner not dissimilar to the great realist photographers of the New Deal era.[30]

Karpatkin knew she had to be careful in steering her less radical membership toward such issues. On occasion she would actually downplay CU's work on social affairs and most of the topics tentatively raised in her "Memo to Members" column were not repeated elsewhere in *Consumer Reports.* Certainly CU's financing of the sort of work being conducted by the Asia-Pacific and Latin American regional officers of IOCU were being advertised to its members strictly on a need-to-know basis. When CU did embark on new political initiatives, it usually resulted in rapid and angry letters being sent from the organization's more assertively conservative members. Health-care policy in particular came to be regarded as a mistake. Long concerned with the structural problems facing America's patient-consumer, CU's frustrations with the inadequacies of private provision eventually resulted in it advocating the establishment of a universalist system of health insurance, a policy it believed to be in line with national popular opinion, especially given the statements leading up to and during the 1992 Clinton presidential campaign.[31] However, CU received over 3,000 letters of complaint, a reaction that sufficiently burnt CU's fingers to warn it off adopting such controversial campaigns again.

CU's reaction to its more conservative members was perhaps too hasty and a certain self-serving myth has developed within CU as an institution as to the moderate tendencies of its membership. To be sure poverty and health policies that smacked of socialism or European welfarism could provoke angry responses and so many purchasers of CU publications were only concerned to help themselves.[32] These campaigns also provoked letters of support or even criticisms from members who felt CU's basic needs proposals did not go far enough. The assumptions about the readership have often been used as an excuse for inactivity and institutional inertia. Decisions in Board meetings have often been influenced by the myth of the cowardly consumer, yet when investigations have been conducted into reader preferences there has usually been a demand for both more information for individuals and more legislation for all.[33]

By the 1980s both CU and the UK Consumers' Association were operating in very different environments. At the political level, the climate had swung against regulation. And at the membership level, a decline in subscriptions provoked a commercially driven reaction by consumer leaders to focus on the supposedly core areas of testing and publishing. The irony of the world economic recession of the 1970s was that it had a twofold and contradictory impact on the consumer movement. At the global level, a more assertive Third World campaigned to make good the international community's commitment to the "development decade." Yet at the national level, the recession forced many of the private testing organizations—the main funders of IOCU's activities—to tighten their belts and adopt a more business-like attitude. CU and CA professionalized their management structures to ensure the long-term viability of their organizations. However, business survival could only come through a greater emphasis on their commercial activities rather than their political advocacy work. As the Western organizations gradually recovered—in terms of membership and/or subscriber rates—they drew on their faint-hearted assumptions about the political sensibilities of their readership to reassess the organization, direction, and philosophy of the global consumer movement.

Early indications of the clashes of management style came at the beginning of the 1980s when members of IOCU's Executive visited the Penang office. What they found was a ramshackle outfit, with such cramped conditions that Fazal's desk was only the size of an ironing board. Yet the project officers and volunteers demonstrated "a missionary zeal," were prepared to work 60-hour weeks, and preferred to discuss the work that they stated to love rather than their salaries.[34] When reminiscing, former IOCU staff speak of the fun, friendliness, vibrancy, and excitement of the Penang office, recalling fond memories of what they believed then to be very much a progressive social movement dealing with "real issues, real people," which was headed by a "charismatic leader."[35] IOCU executives were forced to concede that the center of gravity had clearly swung from Europe to Asia, though this was not always to their liking. Christopher Zealley, chair of the UK Consumers' Association Council, adopted a rather patrician tone when describing a "driven" and "ambitious" Fazal, whom he thought "able without being clever" and for whom he believed some "mechanism for controlling and influencing" will be needed.[36] For figures in the consumer movement such as Zealley, Southern dynamism was far less important than Northern control.

At this time the initiative was clearly with Fazal and the Penang office. Penang's dynamism was further bolstered by the attitude of the Australian Consumers' Association—an organization that had mirrored the growth of U.S. and European private testing organizations but which by the early 1980s had come to be dominated by the "Militant Tendency." It was said that an internal revolution had taken place, which had reduced the Council of the Australian Consumers' Association "to the decorative role of a modern monarchy and its management to a workers' co-operative reminiscent of Animal Farm."[37] The Australians had become strong supporters of the Penang office and the developing world agenda. According to one critic, warming to this Orwellian theme, they proposed to the IOCU Council

> another palace revolution, tabling a short, sharp paper proposing (*inter alia*): that the Executive Secretary be dismissed; that the office in the Hague be closed down; that the headquarters of IOCU be moved to Penang; that the President [Fazal] be made the Chief Executive; and that the Constitution be changed on the principle that all members of IOCU are equal but non-European members are more equal

than others . . . They are likely to be a dominant distraction from now until the eleventh World Congress in Canada in—what other year could fit so well?—1984.[38]

European consumer leaders could not hide from the reality that the organization they had created and funded had now become a developing world organization. Internal investigations repeatedly acknowledged what Fazal claimed, that Penang had "become a kind of Mecca for consumer and public interest groups."[39] Moreover, he operated according to a very different management culture than that prevailing in Western Europe and North America. The IOCU Executive preferred a business-like organization, with clear channels of communication across recognized hierarchical tiers. According to its model, power was firmly located at the center, with the work of the regional offices being closely supervised. In contrast, Fazal chose to develop a management structure that emphasized balance and movement (see figure 13). In his own personal vision of the IOCU structure, he stressed the global nature of the consumer movement and extolled the virtues of decentralization that gave African, Asian, and Latin American consumer activists an equal say with their North American and European counterparts. The networks as pioneered by Fazal were at the heart of the conflicting systems. For Fazal and the Penang staff, the networks were "a means of enlarging and strengthening the consumer voice worldwide."[40] If controlled too tightly they would be likely to lose their flexibility, a situation that the staff in Penang felt was not appreciated by the IOCU Executive.[41]

For their part, certain European consumer leaders acknowledged that the networks had provided the global consumer movement with "direction and purpose, punch and power." But they felt the overwhelming focus on basic needs was difficult to justify to the subscribers of testing magazines: if the networks continued to operate with an independence that took them to issues far from the immediate concerns of Western consumers, then it was worried that the long-term support for these organizations might be jeopardized.[42] Moreover, more worrying was the increasingly obvious fact that the very success of the networks was attracting attention to a set of issues that Western consumer groups had been happy to support but less willing to advertise too widely. Pesticides, infant formula, pharmaceuticals, dangerous exports, climate change, food irradiation, biotechnology, seeds, and the Bhopal tragedy were clearly the issues exercising the minds of global civil society activists. And all were topics on which IOCU had instigated and participated in networks, although they were admittedly rather distant from the narrowly conceived interests of consumers in the affluent West.

With the appointment of a new director-general in the late 1980s, the pressure increased to control the activities of Fazal, the networks, and the regional office. Perhaps inevitably the clash of management styles, consumer philosophies, and operating policies descended into personality disputes. While Fazal clearly resented the greater attention to his activities, accusations to his com-

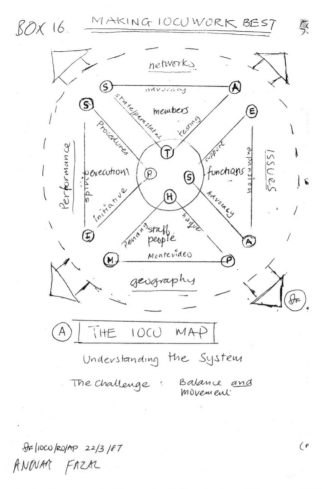

BOX 16. MAKING IOCU WORK BEST

Figure 13. Organizational structure for International Organisation of Consumers Unions as set out by Anwar Fazal in 1987.

Courtesy of IOCU.

petence and ability to control his own staff began to circulate as Europe came to regard him as a loose cannon. Fazal had by this time resolved to leave the consumer movement, and the IOCU Executive was keen for this to happen, although the arrangements took over a year to complete. Certainly there were managerial problems and personality clashes at the Penang office, but the dispute with Fazal was of far greater significance than a simple personnel issue, as many Western consumer leaders have persisted in arguing. The relationship be-

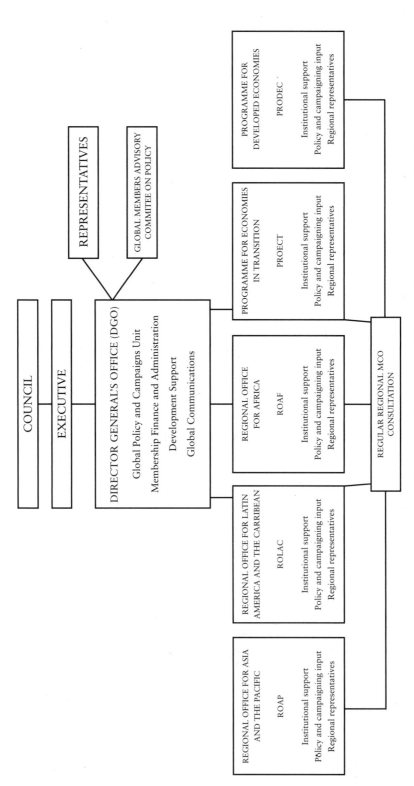

Figure 14. Organizational structure for International Organisation of Consumers Unions as implemented in 1993.

Courtesy of IOCU.

tween Fazal and the Western consumer organizations came down to the very principles of the movement. The Western groups disliked the lack of control they could exercise over the networks, they did not like the authority Fazal held over developing world consumer organizations, and they disliked his attention to duties and responsibilities rather than the core concerns of the rights to choice and information. According to one director-general of IOCU, the Western organizations "could not work with and could not accept the kind of radicalism that Anwar [Fazal] was promoting."[43]

Evidence to support the view that Fazal's departure in 1991 from the consumer movement represented a wider reassertion of Western values over the global organization comes in the rapidity with which his policies and management structure were dismantled after he left. The concern upon his departure was not to construct a legacy of his work and ideas but rather to ensure that he would play no further role in the regional office.[44] IOCU deliberately avoided appointing Fazal's own nominee to succeed him and instead chose another candidate far more willing to execute headquarters policy at the regional level. Even before he had officially left, IOCU moved to re-establish closer links between its campaigns and the interests of its Western membership and they urged the adoption of a more "business-like approach."[45] To this end, they appointed the Manitoba Institute of Management to undertake a thoroughgoing assessment of IOCU's work and organization. The assessment found that the consumer movement was too diverse an entity; lacked a shared, common vision; maintained poor communication channels across its constituent parts; and relied too much on a de-centralized organizational structure that did not encourage the growth of resources, which could sustain IOCU in the future. Moreover, it found that many of the member organizations were insufficiently robust to promise much optimism for the future. In line with the feelings of many on the Executive, the consumer movement needed to reconnect with its members and develop policies that were centrally co-ordinated and consistently promoted across the entire world.[46]

These were certainly serious issues to be addressed, particularly concerning the viability of member organizations and the lack of a clear identity for the consumer movement. But whereas Fazal's supporters liked to celebrate this diversity, arguing that it better reflected the diversity of consumers themselves and enabled them to connect with a variety of other civil society groups, the IOCU Executive preferred to use the Manitoba Institute's findings to bolster its desire to increase central control. Accordingly, following Fazal's departure policy was formulated at the headquarters rather than in Penang, making sure that consumer campaigns would reflect the interests of the affluent as much as the poor. Instead of reassessing its working relationship with the networks, the Executive chose to go it alone, and although Health Action International remained a part of IOCU, Pesticide Action Network and the International Baby Food Action almost immediately disassociated from the consumer movement.

In addition, IOCU symbolically relocated its headquarters from The Hague to London, a hugely expensive move that further directed resources away from the global South. Similarly, the loss of experienced staff at the regional office was deemed acceptable as it created the opportunity to replace them with more amenable workers. Finally, IOCU turned to reviewing its name in 1994, again employing an expensive outside organization to conduct the review. While such practices seemed decadent to struggling consumer groups around the world, the review also highlighted the great discrepancies in attitude toward the role of the consumer movement. While some wanted a value-neutral phrase such as the International Consumers Organization, others preferred a title that reflected its activist role—that is, Consumer Action International. The resulting compromise, Consumers International, reflected the need to take into account the polarized opinions as to the role of the global consumer movement, although by this time control was firmly back in the hands of those organizations who had been the original supporters of IOCU back in 1960.[47]

Consumers International, as IOCU came to be called from January 1995, was clearly a much more professional outfit than it had been ten years earlier. But this more business-like approach and financial stability came at a price. For those consumer activists across Asia who had looked to Penang for inspiration and leadership, Fazal's departure in 1991 was a bitter blow. Nearly two decades after the event it is incredible to witness the anger many still have about the exit of an individual who in many ways recognized that he had done as much as he could do in the consumer organization. But in discussing the matter with those who oversaw the disassociation of the networks, it is evidently still a highly sensitive and emotional subject, and one about which many remain embittered.[48] Indeed, even those seemingly distant from the consumer movement and operating in countries far from Penang and Malaysia, still bemoan the loss to the consumer movement of Anwar Fazal and the institutional ruptures it brought about. For them, Fazal's departure marked a retreat of the consumer movement not only to the concerns of the affluent West, but away from the civil society links that had enabled the consumer movement to obtain such a prominent position in the 1980s.

III

The work of the consumer movement in the 1990s has been strongly geared toward building a more sustainable global organization with robust memberships across Asia, Latin America, and Africa. This growth has continued to be impressive and the consumer movement could reasonably claim to have grown from strength to strength. But it occurred at a time when global civil society was seemingly expanding exponentially. As we have seen in previous chapters, the number of NGOs around the world increased steadily in the postwar period, though the real take off came in the 1980s and grew enormously in the 1990s. If we take a broad definition of an international NGO that includes national NGOs dealing with international issues, then there were approximately 13,000 in 1981 and 47,000 by 2001.[49] The international consumer movement had been able to influence and direct global civil society during a period when it remained relatively small; as civil society expanded in size many times over it was perhaps inevitable that IOCU would be overshadowed, especially as it reigned in on the number of issues it chose to address. By the end of the century a new NGO environment existed, which suggested IOCU could only play a small part. Its own resources had declined relative to the many hundreds of thousands of full time staff—and many millions more volunteers—employed by the NGO sector as a whole; and its own funds were tiny in the context of statistics, which estimated that international NGOs were at this time dispersing more money than the UN, the World Bank, and the IMF together.[50]

The consumer movement was well aware of the role it had played in this non-profit sector. Irna Witoelar of the Indonesian consumer movement and president of IOCU in the early 1990s argued that "the NGO movement should look to IOCU for leadership," based on the assumption that because the consumer was a potential universal identity the consumer movement was uniquely placed to tap into most spheres of civil society activity.[51] And it was not as though the consumer movement simply gave up on some of its previous priorities. The right to a healthy environment and the right to basic needs remained two of its eight core rights, and continue to do so.[52] It was more the case that these two rights were not prioritized to the same extent as they had been in the 1980s. On green issues, for instance, the consumer movement participated in key events such as the Earth Summit in Rio in 1992. It organized and chaired a panel in which consumer advocates such as Martin Khor of Third World Network sat alongside prominent environmental campaigners such as the writer and ecological activist Jonathon Porritt and Richard Sandbrook, co-founder of Friends of the Earth.[53] It has continued to explore the links between environmental and consumer action, focusing on assisting individual consumers to be "green," either through environmental labeling schemes, promoting recycling initiatives, scrutinizing the spurious green credentials of certain manufacturers and, particularly in the Netherlands, incorporating environmental issues such as air miles into product testing.[54]

But just as the consumer co-operative movement lost the initiative to the modern comparative testing consumer movement in the 1950s, so too has the global consumer movement followed rather than provided the lead for environmentalism. Moreover, it has been an uneasy ally of the green movement, sheepishly retreating from what it has perceived to be less mainstream initiatives. For instance, one proposal to the Executive in 1992 recommended allowing ethical, co-operative, and green consumer groups to become members of IOCU.[55] Instead, the consumer movement distanced itself from such "alternative" organizations, delaying the membership of the radical Japanese Seikatsu Club and prevaricating nervously over the issue of allying themselves with new, "less credible" consumer groups.[56] As ethical consumerism and the fair-trade movement began to take off in the 1990s, the consumer movement played little, if any, role.

Basic needs have also continued to be significant in IOCU campaigns and policy, though the right to them has perhaps been championed less vociferously. Following the number of food scares since the 1980s, particularly over BSE (mad cow disease) in Britain, food standards have remained a core concern.[57] IOCU has been a leading NGO in the debate over genetically modified (GM) foods. It has not taken an overtly hostile line, but it has drawn on its established strengths in research and testing. Its position on the issue has enabled it to become more closely aligned to a leading campaign associated with anti-globalization protest, especially in the grassroots protests of national consumer groups in India and Latin America against corporations such as Monsanto.[58] However, the policy of the consumer movement is entirely in accord with its established consumer rights to choice and information: "The consumer position is straightforward: we want labeling of all genetically modified food because the consumer has the right to make an informed choice about the food they buy."[59] These campaigns have existed alongside demands for access to utilities, especially during the years of structural adjustment programs, which have resulted in the privatization of water and energy supply in Africa, Asia, and Latin America.[60] Indeed attention to the whole host of issues affecting disadvantaged consumers has remained a relevant priority for so many consumer groups around the world.[61]

Only rarely, though, have attempts been made to produce more general consumer platforms or philosophies. IOCU's strategy at the turn of the millennium was to commit to "social justice" and its statements in the 1990s seemed to recognize the limitations of a narrowly conceived rights-based model.[62] But it is doubtful whether its high-sounding statements on poverty, fair trade, human rights, and the environment have translated into obvious global campaigns. Indeed, the reality of the consumer movement's work points to a much more conservative agenda, which suggests—as many developing world consumer critics would agree—that too often only lip service had been paid to the social justice agenda. In an examination of IOCU spending patterns from 1991 to 1997, the most remarkable feature was the disproportionate increase in the administrative costs at the London headquarters, ensuring its greater authority over the regional offices and the development of policy from the core rather than the periphery.[63]

One area IOCU has paid attention to the developing world consumer has been in capacity building, creating more enduring organizations that will maintain the long-term viability of the global organization. A new director-general was appointed more for his management, administrative, and fund-raising skills than for the inspiring leadership provided by the likes of a Ralph Nader or an Anwar Fazal.[64] Capacity building has not been achieved through an embrace of new agendas arising from such hotbeds of consumer activism as Penang or Bombay. Instead, growth has been closely controlled, so that the spread of the consumer movement has been tied to the legalistic concern of ensuring the implementation of the UN Guidelines on Consumer Protection in new national regulatory contexts. The established rights-based approach which, legally, has tended to veer more toward the individual rights to choice, information, and redress than the collective rights to basic needs, has come to predominate.[65] Where new initiatives have emerged central control has been reasserted. African consumer activists, for instance, have attempted to raise developmental policies similar to those that had previously concerned S. M. Mohamed Idris at the Consumers' Association of Penang. For instance, in 2000, the Cameroonian consumer group bemoaned the dumping of dangerous goods in Africa—"the rubbish bin of the world"—and called instead for a "Marshall Plan" for Africa, especially the elimination of debt.[66] Others have attempted to add other rights—such as the right to boycott and the right to opportunity— to the list of IOCU's consumer rights.[67] These and many similar proposals have all been vetoed by the Executive, despite becoming mainstream demands and tactics of global civil society; instead, the legislative remedies of the UN Guidelines have been preferred as the most appropriate means of developing consumer policy in Africa.

In terms of numbers the development of the consumer movement has continued, but growth has not occurred in Africa and Latin America with anywhere near the degree of autonomy enjoyed by the Asians in the 1970s and 1980s. The broader questions raised by the rights to basic needs have been channeled into the issue of sustainability—not only of the environment, but of food production, technology, and livelihood. Here again, rather than reaching out, the consumer movement has closed ranks. "Sustainable consumption" has certainly been promoted by the consumer movement, but it has been tied into the narrowly conceived consumer rights of the UN Guidelines.

Since the 1980s, IOCU has worked with the United Nations Environment Programme, ECOSOC, and the UN Commission on Sustainable Development to link sustainability initiatives to a revised version of the Guidelines on Consumer Protection, published in 1999.[68] The problem, as a number of critics have quickly pointed out, is that by tying sustainability initiatives to existing consumer protection programs, an assumption is made by legislators that the environmental and social issues are intrinsically individualistic economic matters. By providing better information to willing shoppers, it is hoped that better consumption decisions are reached and thus individual action in the private sphere—as opposed to collective action in the public sphere—can resolve the world's sustainability issues.[69]

Moreover, it has tied the consumer movement into a set of solutions, which have increasingly distanced its work from other initiatives taking place within global civil society. The rights-based framework—and the mindset that maintains it—traps the consumer movement into modes of thinking that do not let it reach out to the sorts of development initiatives being advocated by other NGOs. Whereas the consumer movement had pioneered global campaigns in the 1970s and 1980s, especially through the networks, the initiative has been seized by many thousands of other NGOs, some of which were only founded in the 1980s but, a decade later, had become more robust organizations with as many resources and occasionally with as global a reach as that of the consumer movement's. On the one hand, these NGOs have been better able to articulate a human rights agenda, especially concerning social, economic, and cultural rights. On the other hand, they have promoted forms of communication and action that we once might have expected the consumer movement to have advocated. The umbrella to civil society organization could no longer be argued to have been provided by the consumer movement at the end of the 1990s. Instead, more radical anti-globalization protestors, coalescing around such meetings as that of the World Social Forum, have provided the initiative while international aid organizations, alongside faith-based groups and development charities, have provided the leadership to such global campaigns as Jubilee 2000, Drop the Debt, and the trade justice movement.

IV

Within the developing world, local consumer groups have felt frustrated at the greater centralization of IOCU's activities and the respectable distance it has kept from other NGOs. Its leaders have been more willing to attend global civil society meetings and fora and to participate in new campaigning networks. Yet the rights-based perspective they have chosen to persist with and to develop has also not been without its problems. This is because they have challenged the rights-based approach in their alternative economic development strategies, while at the same time drawing on a series of economic, social, and cultural rights, which newer NGOs have been much better placed to articulate. This is seen best in the narrative of Malaysia, where the espousal of an "Asian values" framework by Prime Minister Mahathir has highlighted the difficulties and contradictions of a rights-based political perspective. For consumer groups, the issue here is not only one of prioritizing certain rights over others, but it is one of the relevance of rights-based campaigning in general.

In countries such as Malaysia, where the consumer movement flourished in the 1970s, there has been a shift in the dominant discourses used by both the state and NGOs, which has seen the substitution of consumer concerns with those of a human rights agenda. In the 1970s the developmental policies of the Malaysian ruling coalition's New Economic Policy provided the hegemonic language through which civil society operated and against which the Consumers' Association of Penang (CAP) found itself resisting. NGOs such as CAP were reacting against a particular model of economic development but, since then, the ruling coalition—and Mahathir in particular—have rooted these economic policies within a framework of "Asian values," which, it might be argued, have forced civil society to focus attention on the discussion of human rights as a bulwark against the perceived injustices, which Asian values could confer on the general citizenry. Mahathir and Lee Kuan Yew of Singapore have stressed the inappropriateness of individualistic Western liberal models of political rights. These two leaders have contended that Asians are communalist rather than individualist, have demonstrated a "cultural predisposition towards stable leadership rather than political pluralism," and have showed "a proclivity to consensus as opposed to a tendency towards dissent or confrontation." According to them, "Asians, therefore, preferred a strong, even harsh, government, so long as the government's policies and actions continued to deliver economic prosperity."[70] In contrast, NGOs have sought to defend such rights, not least because of the clear abuses of power contained within the Internal Security Act, which have continued to motivate human rights activists in organizations such as Suaram and Tenaganita.

In Malaysia the Asian values position, even if promoted by an authoritarian state, has also found its supporters within civil society. Certainly, Islamic-based organizations have shared in this critique of Western liberalism and have promoted instead the communal nature of Asian values. Chandra Muzaffar—formerly of Penang's other leading NGO, the think tank Aliran, and now leader of the International Movement for a Just World (originally created with Anwar Fazal and S. M. Mohamed Idris—has called for a human rights model, which encompasses not only civil and political rights but also social, cultural, and economic rights, at the same focusing on the meaning of "human dignity" in which human rights are rooted in a spiritual and moral vision of the human being derived from religion.[71]

CAP also has articulated a concern for consumer rights, which both challenges and affirms the basic assumptions of the Asian values protagonists, while problematizing its relationship to a human rights discourse advocated by the broader NGO community. For instance, in 1988 CAP criticized the positive portrayal of homosexuality in advertising for the offence it might cause to the majority of Malaysians.[72] Unlike other rights-based NGOs that have embraced a whole series of rights to sexual identity, CAP has remained deliberately quiet on the issue. The institutions of the global economic order have also been condemned, not only for their effects on people's livelihoods, but for the onslaught mass consumption is said to have launched on traditional Malaysian values. But whereas CAP used to criticize the government for its assistance to such economic forces, by the late 1990s it could "feel confident that this Government's concern for the people will generate a will to initiate a review of its policies and laws which reflect these critical values and concerns."[73] Both Mahathir and Idris adopted an anti-Western set of arguments in defense of a notion of Malaysian—or Asian—ways of life, though the motivation behind the two men's positions might not have been equally sincere. For Idris, the opening of Malaysia's doors to drugs, Hollywood, pop music, magazines, and all the other symbols of consumer society, have destroyed the old communal way of life giving way to a meaningless individualism. Somewhat misty-eyed, he celebrates what he believes were the ways of life and values of his own, or his parents', generation.[74] CAP's rapprochement with Mahathir arose from the mutual desire to defend the East against the West, or the South against the North. It led to a desire by both to invoke a notion of Asian values (despite the complexity and marked differences within Malaysia's ethnic groups and cultures), with CAP's defense of human rights no longer being the absolute standard with which to measure the government's economic and social planning.[75]

Since the 1990s CAP has remained somewhat distant from the rest of the Malaysian consumer movement and, in its moralistic critique, it maintains a distinction from much of the rights-based rhetoric that has elsewhere pervaded Malaysian civil society. Other consumer groups have been much less concerned with values (Asian or otherwise) and have rooted themselves firmly within a defense of human rights articulated by a whole variety of Malaysian NGOs. For instance, the Education and Research Association for Consumers (ERA) was founded in 1987 by Josie Fernandez, a future regional director of IOCU and sister of the women's and minority rights activist, Irene Fernandez. Similar to CAP, ERA has examined core consumer issues such as the problems of direct selling techniques, pyramid schemes, and the costs of pharmaceuticals, while it has also sought foreign funding for larger scale projects on the environment, sustainable development, and food security.[76] But it is human rights that have generated the most excitement within the organization since the turn of the millennium.

Human rights have become one of its most prominent education programs for youths and adults in short courses and workshops all around the country, and it is the human rights desk that has been the most active.[77] ERA has also tried to position itself as a leading spokesbody on human rights, organizing workshops with NGOs such as Hakam (National Human Rights Society), Suaram (Voice of the Malaysian People) and Irene Fernandez's Tenaganita (Women's Force), which have assessed and criticized the performance of the National Human Rights Commission Suhakam.[78]

In a sense, the focus on rights is a recognition that the political identity of the consumer is no longer quite as radical or as all-encompassing as it had been in the 1980s. ERA has used the language of human rights—especially economic, social, and cultural rights—to justify its extension into a whole range of activities. It has argued that consumer rights are a fundamental part of the United Nations' definition of economic, social, and cultural rights and that if these rights are not realized in the lives of ordinary Malaysians then it follows that they have little chance of exercising their rights as consumers. But so do consumer protections, it is claimed, offer some of the most basic safeguards against the abuse of economic and social rights. Consumer rights and human rights thus become indistinguishable, in the minds of a new generation of consumer activist at least, legitimating ERA's involvement in a whole range of activities.

In the twenty-first century, ERA has positioned itself, if not as an expert investigator into a whole range of social justice issues, then at least as a principal educator of everybody as consumers in awareness of these issues. It has published handbooks on domestic violence to help women know their rights and on the role of Islam within an international human rights framework.[79] It has pushed for the government to recognize the International Criminal Court and, as part of its large-scale project to empower poor Indian women, it has set up ten community centers around the country.[80] The location of consumerism within the human rights framework has enabled it to achieve a national prominence quite spectacular for an organization that remains very small and limited to just a handful of full-time staff. However, it has also pointed to certain limits as better resourced and well-established human rights NGOs such as Suaram still maintain a higher public profile on these topics.

This shift to a human rights perspective has not been without consequence, particularly on the role of consumerism in Malaysia and in its relations to other social movements. While human rights have clearly worked as a mobilizing agenda for civil society in general, it is less clear that it has worked for the consumer movement. First, for CAP it has meant the organization has sought to promote alternative value frameworks in opposition to what it sees as the westernization inherent to rights-based rhetoric. Unfortunately, such a position has the potential to alienate it from other NGOs focused on the defense of rights, and while the defense of overtly politically rights is not very controversial, the defense of consumer rights is more problematic. CAP has resorted to a defensive attack against the West, which has had much sympathy across Malaysia and the developing world in general. But its invocations of traditional ways of life rest uncomfortably with the pursuit of mass consumption enjoyed by a new generation of Malaysians keen to enjoy the fruits of their hard labor.[81] It has resulted in an attack on a whole variety of "Western" goods, which CAP believes damages the physical, emotional, and social health of the people, but which goes against the desires of the vast majority of consumers if the statistics of these goods' consumption is anything to go by.[82] Although Asian values have their appeal in the attacks they can lead to on the perceived power of Western nations and the imposition of rights-based frameworks, their relevancy is called into question once consumers have been urged to adopt them in their ordinary life patterns. CAP could thus well find itself fighting the trends of consumer behavior while missing out on a defense of human rights, which has made organizations such as Suaram and Aliran so prominent.

Second, for ERA and to a lesser extent for the state-recognized consumer movement—the Federation of the Malaysia Consumer Associations (FOMCA) —which have attempted to concentrate on consumer rights as human rights, similar problems of irrelevancy are apparent. ERA and FOMCA have emphasized the human rights element of their work in order to remain players in the game of civil society, although in doing so they very much follow the lead provided by other NGOs, which have greater skills and resources focused on dealing with human rights. To root consumerism in a human rights framework is, in a sense, to acknowledge that the consumer movement can no longer enjoy the prominence once attributed to CAP and that the discourse of human rights is far more suited to dealing with the problems facing contemporary Malaysians than the alternative consumerist model of development propounded in the 1970s and 1980s.

Indeed, Malaysian consumer activists are doubtful as to whether they would restart their careers as consumer activists. CAP's Anwar Fazal has gone on to establish or involve himself in a whole range of activities, from the Sustainable Penang Initiative, the World Alliance on Breastfeeding Action, the Taiping Peace Initiative and, with S. M. Mohamed Idris, Citizens International.[83] Similarly, Josie Fernandez has questioned the wider significance of contemporary organized consumerism, implying it has become less a movement in the sense of the success enjoyed by the more prominent human rights, gender equity, workers' rights, and environmental campaigns and perhaps "merely a pressure group specifically to address market place concerns."[84] M. Nadarajah, education officer for the Selangor Consumers' Association in the 1980s, has claimed the consumer movement cannot adequately deal with the problems of over-consumption.[85] Before his death at the end of 2006, Bishan Singh drifted away from the consumer movement believing it to be a means only to "fine tune" rather than overhaul the existing social and economic system.[86] He instead focused his attention on sustainability questions through his Management Institute for Social Change and the Sustainable Development Network.[87] And, interviewed just prior to becoming the President of FOMCA while he still headed ERA, Marimuthu Nadason admitted that were he to start his civil society career all over again, it is likely he would join another type of campaign NGO than that of a consumers' association.[88]

At both the local and the global level human rights have been both a strength and a weakness for the consumer movement. It originally adopted a rather narrowly conceived set of four consumer rights following Kennedy's key consumer address of 1962. The willingness of the international consumer movement to take on board the concerns of poor consumers around the world led both to an expansion of these rights and to a more prominent role for organized consumers in global civil society. But since the 1990s, it has curtailed the further expansion of these rights, leading many consumer activists to question the relevancy of a rights-based approach, while forcing others to tap into rights-based agendas more imaginatively, assertively, and effectively articulated by other NGOs, especially those operating in countries such as Malaysia where the authoritarian tendencies of governments have been diluted with the opening up of civil societies in the 1980s. IOCU's contraction of its sphere of activity was not only the timid response to the myth of the conservative predilections of the *Consumers Reports* and *Which?* reader but an unfortunate tactical decision that secured its long term financial viability at the expense of its leadership role. Even the man who oversaw these policies at IOCU admitted that "something was lost" in the 1990s as its role in global civil society was overshadowed by other

NGOs and, as we shall see in the next chapter, its effectiveness in protecting consumers in the global market was undermined.

V

The choice for the consumer movement has been which rights to emphasize. From the end of the 1980s, the consumer movement deliberately chose not to prioritize basic needs over choice. As it pulled back its operations from the global South and relocated its headquarters to London, it also disassociated from the networks and the broader political vision of consumerism that had been spearheaded by the Penang office over the previous two decades. In doing so, it chose to re-emphasize those individualistic rights that had constituted the founding principles of the global movement at the beginning of the 1960s. Politically and intellectually, it retreated into its established operating principles, steadfastly refusing to engage with alternative ideas as to how a global NGO might address questions of economic and social justice.

Whereas IOCU had earlier tied its operations to a developmental agenda espoused by UN officials, intellectuals, and emerging states, in the 1990s it simply ignored the main theoretical developments in globalization thinking. The headquarters took no account of those books and ideas that continued to inspire their members in the global South, be these the academic writings of figures such as Amartya Sen, the manifestos of the new stars of the inappropriately termed "anti-globalization" movement such as Susan George and David Korten, or even the home-grown musings on international trade as set out by consumer leaders such as Martin Khor of CAP and Third World Network.[89] Instead, IOCU remained committed to its list of rights, seemingly adopting a relativist approach to the comparative importance of each. Thus, choice enjoyed parity with basic needs, opening up space for others to advocate such rights. But as politicians and business groups drew on the consumer movement's agendas, they too were confronted with the shopping list of rights; more awkward and troubling rights to such things as basic needs could be pushed aside in the welcoming embrace of choice, information, and education.

For the consumer movement, the whole approach to consumer rights in the 1980s was very different from what it became in the 1990s. As one political philosopher of human rights wrote, the reason we have arguably chosen to do so little about world poverty is because we have distanced ourselves from it: "Our world is arranged to keep us far away from massive and severe poverty and surrounds us with affluent, civilised people for whom the poor abroad are a remote good cause alongside the spotted owl."[90] Institutionally, the retreat from Penang by IOCU represented such a choice to create distance. In contrast, the networks, as pioneered by the consumer movement had reduced the distance between the North and the South. They gave voice to the subaltern and provided direct contacts between the affluent and the poor. They created exactly the sorts of links that ensured questions of poverty were not remote, impelling the consumer to take action. By disassociating with the networks, it broke down the connection to poverty, which provides the moral imperative to act.

In many ways, rights have provided an operational and intellectual straight-jacket for the consumer movement. Rights to basic needs have appeared at times as mere manifesto rights—bland statements to eradicate poverty for instance rather than detailed demands to reduce insecurity of access to basic goods and services. And in the explosion of rights-based organizations since the 1980s, consumer groups at both the global and the local level have found that these rights have been more effectively articulated by other NGOs. Other rights have been adopted across civil society, which the consumer movement has been reluctant—and has refused—to embrace. To this extent, IOCU has even divorced itself from the concerns of a new generation of ethical and green consumers, as well as the fair trade movement as a whole. These new consumers have been positioned as "alternative," in contrast to IOCU's "mainstream" consumers. But this was and is a false division that has made the consumer movement incredibly slow to recognize the entry of fair trade into the mainstream.

Instead, the consumer movement's narrower version of rights has mirrored the changes in rights as set out in international protocols. The basic needs approach reflected the focus on standards of living as set out in the Universal Declaration of Human Rights. By contrast, the focus on choice reflected the movement away from equality to individual liberty found at the heart of the 1975 Helsinki Declaration on Security and Co-operation in Europe. In the negotiations leading up to the signing of the treaty, "official America backed away from asserting any universal right to a standard of living" and promoted instead "the individual rights to freedom over collective rights to subsistence."[91] Accordingly, the final draft of the Helsinki Declaration avoided any references to a right to a certain standard of living and committed its signatories instead to the promotion of international trade to "contribute to widening the possibilities of choice of products."[92]

For all the problems and contradictions that remain for Southern consumer groups, which both oppose and promote the notion of rights, one final historical irony is that the consumer movement has advocated a set of rights that are not necessarily what even Western consumers want. It is often quality not choice that consumers need and desire. On the subject of health care, elderly Americans have not wanted more choices in the provision of services to them: they have wanted more stability, security, and assurances that health care will be provided.[93] Likewise, surveys of British consumers have found that for them choice is only one element of what they consider their rights and interests to be: quality provision of public services is far more relevant to their lives than any choice—or, really, preference—between equally poor systems of health care, public transport, and local government service provision. As one patient-consumer put it, "I know 'consumer' and 'customer' imply choice and that is what we are supposed to want. I would consider it an acceptable achievement if everyone could have what was best in the matter of treatment as of right."[94]

It is doubtful whether a narrow rights-based perspective can adequately deal with these issues: consumer rights that focus on the individual do not raise the wider system of provision that a basic needs agenda addresses. Yet this is precisely the position that was adopted by the consumer movement during the 1990s. And it did so, as we shall see in the next chapter, during a time when the contours of the world economy were changing rapidly. It is on the subject of world trade that the consumer movement's contradictions, defeats, and divisions become most apparent.

Shopping for Justice

The Freedom of Free Trade

In the early 1970s, the role and activities of transnational—or multinational—corporations came to be seriously scrutinized by the international community. In 1972, President Salvador Allende of Chile complained to the UN General Assembly that two U.S.-based businesses, the Kennecott Copper Corporation and the International Telegraph and Telephone Company, had unduly intervened in Chilean political life and had even conspired to overthrow his government. Over thirty years later, we are more aware of the extent of the U.S. government's direct involvement in Chilean politics. The CIA worked to block Allende's election in 1970 and was associated with the powers backing General Augusto Pinochet's coup of 1973. At the time, though, the international community focused its concerns on the business sector. Allende's charges against private enterprise were the first to be made by a head of state in an international forum and they led not only to a U.S. Senate subcommittee investigation, but to an inquiry by the UN. In July 1972, the Economic and Social Council, acting on the initiative of the Chilean government, requested the Secretary-General to appoint a Group of Eminent Persons to investigate the role of transnational corporations in the economic development of Third World countries as well as the implications of their actions for international relations.

The Group of Eminent Persons consisted of government officials, academics, and a number of selected businessmen. It met throughout 1973 and finally submitted its report in May 1974. It found that "fundamental new problems have arisen as a direct result of the growing internationalization of production as carried out by multinational corporations."[1] Specifically, it accepted that, while uncommon, transnational firms had on occasion promoted political intervention in domestic affairs and that home country governments such as the United

States had used these firms as instruments of their foreign policy and intelligence gathering. In an era of globalization (though the term was hardly used at the time), corporations had to be increasingly monitored in order to ensure that the benefits of global trade and their legitimate commercial activities would be fully realized. The Group of Eminent Persons recommended the establishment of a permanent UN intergovernmental Commission on Transnational Corporations to serve as an advisory body to ECOSOC. It was eventually established in 1975, backed up by an autonomous United Nations Centre on Transnational Corporations (UNCTC), and was charged with researching the technical aspects of transnational corporate activity such as transfer pricing and the transactions between affiliated organizations working across different countries. In addition, it was expected to draft codes of conduct that might eventually govern the operation of transnational corporations, especially in areas such as accountancy and reporting, corrupt practices and illicit payments, and restrictive business practices, which had exercised the concerns of civil society activists and national leaders such as Allende.[2]

The direct consumer interest in the underhand tactics of global corporations is not immediately apparent. Yet the Group of Eminent Persons—and later the UNCTC—cast their net widely. They listed the various interests in the operation of the globalized marketplace from the economies of states affected by multinational trading to the welfare of workers employed by transnational corporations, as well as the firms concerned about their investments in unfamiliar legal and political environments. Added to this list were consumers, whose interests were held to lie in the appropriateness, quality, and price of goods produced by multinational firms. Accordingly, in the testimonies heard by the Group of Eminent Persons, the list included not only CEOs and labor movement figures, but consumer activists such as Ralph Nader and Peter Goldman—director of the UK Consumers' Association and at the time president of the International Organisation of Consumers Unions.[3]

Defined most broadly, consumers, along with all other citizens, share a general interest in the overtly corrupt practices of transnational corporations. Yet it is not so obvious what the precise relationship between the consumer and legitimate global trade should be. On the one hand, consumers want more choice, cheaper products and, simply put, more stuff. On the other hand, they want fairness for other consumers and, as good liberal citizens, they want these other consumers to enjoy the same freedoms that they do. To what extent, then, should consumer activists concern themselves with the wider structural issues about the market as examined by the Commission on Transnational Corporations? The events in Chile in the early 1970s represent an extreme example, and certainly the consumer movement itself never openly commented on the political aspects of either Allende's or Pinochet's governments. But in the criticisms made of corporations such as the International Telegraph and Telephone Company, structural issues about the organization and governance of world trade were raised that could not escape the attention of IOCU.

In the 1950s and 1960s, in various national contexts, value for money testing had raised general questions about the political economy of market societies. This was especially the case when structural inequalities were seen to render choice and information irrelevant to the obtaining of good quality products at fair prices. As the volume of international trade and foreign investment increased, it was perhaps inevitable that consumer protection should become relevant to global issues. It was increasingly apparent that the unregulated legal gray areas of appropriate marketing, dangerous goods distribution, and product dumping were obvious areas of consumer concern. So while the world's attention might periodically focus on the spectacular exposés of global corporate interference in national politics, the consumer movement found itself uncovering abuses in markets dominated by huge corporations. In the light of such problems, broader questions about the structure of the global economy were raised. Most pertinent, the consumer movement had to ask itself the extent to which it could intervene in "free trade," seeking to regulate not only the activities of transnational corporations, but ultimately the quality and quantity of goods available to consumers as individuals

This, perhaps, has been the central dilemma for the consumer movement, if not to the meaning and politics of consumer society in general. The relationship between consumers and trade is explored in this chapter because it represents not only the key divisive issue within the consumer movement but the principal problem we all have to face as consumers. We might welcome protection mechanisms for our own freedom as individual shoppers, but when these protections are provided for whole classes, nations, and regions of consumers, certain restrictions are placed on the market that interfere with the freedom of free trade. Trade in itself promises more stuff for more people, but the control of that trade means some people get more stuff more of the time: restricting the activities of multinational corporations in the global marketplace has profound consequences for who gets what, when, and how. Inevitably, any regulation that might protect the safety or well-being of an individual also limits the choice available to him or her. There is no easy answer to the question about the relationship between the consumer and trade.

This chapter traces the history of the consumer movement's approach to multinational capitalism and the regulation of the global marketplace. It first takes up the story of the Group of Eminent Persons at the UN and traces the consumer movement's involvement in pushing for a Code of Conduct on Transnational Corporations. The failure to obtain such a measure merely added to the defeats outlined in the discussion of the corporate critique of consumerism in chapter 6. Second, this chapter focuses on the consumer movement's approach to trade following its change in orientation at the end of the 1990s as the older generation of liberal internationalists gave way to a new, more commercially minded consumer leadership. In the Uruguay Round of trade negotiations and in the reconstitution of the rules of the global economy, the consumer movement saw an opportunity to increase its power and influence, particularly at the new World Trade Organization. The consumer movement adopted a broadly free trade agenda that ensured it drifted away from many of the other organizations, which emerged within global civil society during the 1990s. Its moderate line ensured it obtained a seat at the negotiating table while other NGOs were left to protest on the other side of the barricades at a WTO ministerial. By the end of the decade it became increasingly obvious that the consumer movement had been mistaken, if not naive. Compared to the opportunities ECOSOC had provided for NGOs such as IOCU to develop regulatory codes of conduct in the 1980s, the WTO provided very few chances for consumer activists to make their voices heard, never mind to have any impact on the regulation of the world market.

By the turn of the millennium the consumer movement encapsulated the entire spectrum of attitudes to trade and the regulation of big business. Increasingly, and this is an oversimplification, this has come to be institutionalized through broadly Northern and Southern approaches to consumer politics. Northern support for free trade has been countered by the emphasis of developing world consumer activists on the need for national government control over international law and they have promoted consumer policies that advocate protection for fledgling home industries operating in struggling economies. The potential for a major split within the consumer movement along the new geopolitical boundaries of North and South is therefore apparent. Unfortunately, if we compare the consumer movement's leadership of global civil society in the 1980s, this division may be of little consequence because IOCU has increasingly marginalized itself from other NGOs. Indeed, IOCU's espousal of a "free trade" position has served to reinforce a false dichotomy between free trade and fair trade. For many other NGOs free trade has seemingly made the consumer movement an advocate of unchecked globalization, while IOCU's moderate policy position has meant it has not gotten its regulatory message across to a wider audience nor won over other NGOs too inadequately represented as "anti-global."

Accordingly, as Southern consumer leaders continue to court alliances with other NGOs and contribute to global meetings such as the World Social Forum, Northern NGOs have only reluctantly embraced the politics of a new generation of activism inspired more by ethical, environmental, and fair trade concerns. But in this institutional dilemma over campaigning for more choice and more stuff, as well as more restrictions on trade, these divisions within the consumer movement perhaps encapsulate many of the contradictions involved in attitudes toward globalization by consumers as a whole.

I

The work of the international consumer movement throughout the 1960s had made it very aware of the problems posed by multinational capitalism. As Peter Goldman stated in his submission to the Group of Eminent Persons, the inappropriate marketing of pharmaceuticals in countries with weaker consumer protection regimes represented merely "the tip of a massive and very threatening iceberg."[4] Transfer pricing, tax avoidance, the movement of funds between subsidiaries, and the sudden shift of production locales all represented fundamental challenges to global development initiatives because each issue had the potential to wreak havoc with any economic policy introduced by a national government in a developing country. As sound pragmatists, the consumer advocates were prepared to work with industrial sectors on the development of voluntary codes of practice. Indeed, many of these were already in place, the International Code of Advertising Practice having been first adopted by the International Chamber of Commerce as early as 1937.[5] But the response of the UN to the situation in Chile in 1972 meant that IOCU became more ambitious in its policies. To the Group of Eminent Persons, Goldman proposed a "supranational organisation, with investigative and punitive powers, to promote effective competition and enforce high standards of corporate behaviour." He further called for a "General Agreement on Multinational Companies," patterned after General Agreement on Trade and Tariffs (GATT), which was "really the least that the world community ought to try to offer by way of moral and practical influence."[6]

These key consumer concerns were incorporated into the UN's work on transnational corporations, though they were also advocated by a range of other NGOs, labor organizations, and civil society spokespersons. Too often, the Group of Eminent Persons held, multinationals did not cater to the "real needs" of developing world consumers.[7] In passages that seemed to paraphrase Goldman's own submission to the Group, their report advocated prior informed consent (that is, from the host government for goods it might deem "socially undesirable") and the homogenization of regulatory mechanisms.

Although consumer protection was but one element of the desire to curb the freedom of multinationals, it was nevertheless included as part of the package of workers' welfare, political autonomy, and financial reforms being pushed by the international labor movement and the developing world states. Once the work of the Group of Eminent Persons was succeeded by the Commission on Transnational Corporations and the UNCTC, the consumer protection clauses continued to be included.[8] Moreover, the impetus for regulation increased throughout the 1970s as the world's attention was further drawn to the activities of multinational firms in particular countries. South Africa was obviously the most infamous example as the bolstering of the white minority regime and the continued exploitation of black labor by transnational corporations provoked not only a series of investigations and resolutions by the UNCTC but a worldwide consumer boycott.[9] But the power of multinationals was also coming to be regarded as a more general phenomenon to which the UN had to respond. The UNCTC was well aware that in 1973–74 the big Swiss corporations (Nestlé, Ciba-Geigy, Sandoz, Hoffman-La Roche, Brown Boveri, and Sulzer) had co-ordinated a campaign to unduly influence the Group of Eminent Persons and to subvert its conclusions.[10]

The activities of the UNCTC and those labor and civil society groups that supported its work increasingly focused on the development of a Code of Conduct on Transnational Corporations. As originally envisaged by the Group of Eminent Persons this would ultimately result in the establishment of a general agreement on transnational corporations with the authority of an international treaty and with provisions for sanctions. The work of the UNCTC was to develop the complicated specific codes for technical areas relating to technology transfer, restrictive business practices, labor relations, and so on. Over time, they would be overseen by a more general Code of Conduct, which would form the basis of the originally intended international agreement.

Attitudes to the Code were predictably influenced by the established divisions of Cold War geopolitics. The socialist countries wanted the Code to only cover privately owned transnational corporations while the developed capitalist nations wanted only a voluntary code addressed to both governments and corporations.[11] However, the main impetus for a compulsory Code, applicable to transnational corporations and not host governments, came from the developing world. The Code of Conduct was a deliberate tool of the UN's Second Development Decade. The need for its provision was acknowledged in the General Assembly's resolution 3202 (S-VI) of May 1974 that adopted a Programme of Action on the Establishment of a New International Economic Order.[12] This accepted the positive role transnational corporations could play in bringing much needed investment and employment to struggling Third World economies, but wished to ensure that these same economies would benefit from the activities of the firm. The New International Economic Order therefore not only sought to prevent the collaboration of multinational enterprises with "racist regimes and colonial administrations" but to ensure that the profits accruing from multinationals' activities were shared with all parties concerned and were reinvested back into their host communities. The protection of citizens as both workers and consumers became tied into a new international agenda that would ultimately call for a reappraisal of the entire Bretton Woods infrastructure, especially the power of veto that could be exercised by World War II victors any time a fundamental problem of the Third World was raised.[13]

The UNCTC took evidence not only from developing world governments but from non-governmental organizations as well. Initially, the majority that submitted evidence were business and employee organizations with strong links to the multinational corporations based in Switzerland and the United States. But labor organizations also gave evidence and shortly afterward IOCU itself was called to set out its own draft guidelines on consumer protection.[14] In 1976, it drew up a Code of Consumer Ethics that it hoped would constitute a separate and complementary document, though the UNCTC chose to incorporate consumer concerns directly into the Code of Conduct.[15] Thereafter, the work of IOCU in relation to the Code was to lobby to ensure that it retained its consumer protection clauses—a campaign it fought successfully for the rest of the 1970s.[16]

A Code of Conduct was first put before the General Assembly in 1981. While this set out broad social and political principles (such as the respect for local values and traditions) and economic and financial considerations (transfer pricing, ownership, and control, etc.), it also controversially attempted to regulate state-industry relations.[17] It immediately ran into trouble. Its mandatory elements were strongly opposed by the U.S. government and by the international business community, as were the proposals that it should not apply to state-owned enterprises. For the International Chamber of Commerce, the Code was to be welcomed, but only as a voluntary measure and only as something that imposed the same rules of disclosure and expectation of conduct on domestic organizations as well. Clearly, transnational corporations wanted to be treated fairly with other firms, but they were well aware that as large-scale organizations they would be better placed than their local rivals to meet the requirements of international trading standards.[18] However, for the developing nations working closely together as the Group of 77 and for the communist states of the Soviet bloc, a voluntary Code would be meaningless if it was not backed up with the full force of international law. It was on these insurmountable differences that the Code faltered in the early 1980s despite the continued work of the UNCTC and the numerous special conventions of the Commission.[19]

As the stalemate beckoned, NGOs increasingly lent their authority to the Code, in the hope that the demonstration of widespread support would persuade its opponents to give way. IOCU responded to the challenge first by replacing their part-time UN lobbyist Dorothy Willner with the more experienced and politically astute Esther Peterson and, second, by urging all its constituent members to engage in secondary level lobbying of their respective national governments.[20] Following its success in campaigning for the UN Guidelines on Consumer Protection in 1985, it focused its resources on the Code of Conduct. A Transnational Action Group was established and experienced consumer advocates were brought in to improve thinking and tactics on transnational corporations.[21] IOCU commissioned studies of corporate activities around the world, from the tobacco industry to the pharmaceutical trade, collaborating with the left-wing Australian political economist Ted Wheelwright, who had long been associated with the critique of global capitalism.[22] In 1986 and 1987, it lobbied hard for the adoption of the Code, especially after various revisions made it appear far less opposed to legitimate commercial activity.[23] Even though it continued to maintain its pro-business and pro-trade message, the politics of lobbying at the UN encouraged the impression that IOCU had moved far to the left. Certainly, it seemed well distant from its self-styled "moderate" position of a previous decade when one UN lobbyist had placed IOCU alongside "the educationalists, the journalists, television and radio experts and . . . family planners and conservationists."[24]

Part of the explanation for this perceived radicalization of IOCU's stance was the spirited defense mounted against the Code by the international business community and the U.S. government. The anti-regulatory agenda that had come to prominence in U.S. domestic politics in the 1970s and was exported to the UN in the 1980s was increasingly vociferous. Moreover, as with the Consumer Protection Agency Bill in 1978, the Code of Conduct on Transnational Corporations began to assume symbolic importance. Concessions had already been made over the marketing of breast milk substitutes and the development of consumer protection guidelines in general: similar victories were not about to be granted to the consumer movement on an issue that had potentially profound implications for the entire global economic system. Indeed, for those involved in the consumer movement's campaign for the Code, it was becoming apparent just how extensive and impressive were the forces arraigned against it. Just as she had in the negotiations over the Guidelines, Peterson found herself once more nose to nose with U.S. ambassador Alan Keyes, both at the UN and in meetings of the House of Representative's Committee on Foreign Affairs.[25] Her experience told her that there was an apparent lack of political will to push through the Code, even after many compromises and concessions had been made. Peterson went all out to develop such a political will, mobilizing the consumer movement to spearhead a campaign at both the international and the national level, while she herself focused on persuading key members of George H. W. Bush's administration to lend their support.[26]

All of this was to little effect. The mobilization against the Code and the consumer movement was already well in place. Following the UN's own investigation, which resulted in a 1978 booklet titled "The Infiltration of the UN System by Multinational Corporations," several other studies attested to the strategies adopted by the major corporations against their critics. A three-day symposium of public relations representatives in Geneva in 1975 had allegedly concluded with the aim to discredit all critics as ignorant, inexperienced, stupid, or ideologically driven.

In the 1980s, the criticisms made of the consumer movement by the Heritage Foundation were complemented by claims about the undue influence of IOCU at the World Health Organization and the United Nations Children's Fund, especially the "stridently anti-western Anwar Fazal." Threats made—and sometimes carried out—by the U.S. government to withdraw aid to such UN bodies as UNESCO further created an atmosphere of intimidation. These diplomatic initiatives were reinforced by direct attacks on the NGOs by transnational corporations. Ciba-Geigy claimed that IOCU aimed to "overturn the social structure of Europe" while the U.S. National Council of Churches was described in *Fortune* magazine as "Marxists marching under the banner of Christ." Instead, faith-based organizations such as Christian Aid and the Catholic Agency for Overseas Development were bypassed by Nestlé executives who worked with the Swiss churches to establish its own Interfaith Association for Ethical Studies in Economics. Transnational corporations worked to separate IOCU activism from the world's consumers, arguing that IOCU's demands were not in line with the majority consumer interest. *Business International* began to monitor the work of IOCU, to the extent that it showed an appreciation of NGO tactics actually in line with the more celebratory accounts of global activism in the 1990s. Consumer groups, the journal claimed, acted "like guerrillas in a war, working to an overall concept but flexibly and independently."[27]

Despite the increasing likelihood of defeat, Peterson and IOCU continued to spearhead the campaign to regulate global business. In 1990, a further diluted Code was drafted and IOCU again stepped up its lobbying.[28] The final date for a decision on the Code was set as July 1992. In the months and weeks leading up to the debate intense meetings were held and briefings were sent to delegates from over fifty countries, but a stalemate was again reached as the United States and other "home countries to the largest and the most powerful global corporations refused to even discuss the Code."[29]

The opposition to the consumer campaign was simply too unified and overpowering. By the 1990s, the U.S. State Department was acting in accord with the interests of big business. It mounted a disinformation campaign about the Code, telexing every one of its embassies around the world to give them the go ahead to mount propaganda campaigns against the Code with their host governments. The U.S. administration uttered seemingly positive public statements in support of a Code, at the same time urging all other countries to denounce it as a waste of time. The consumer movement was askance at such tactics, and found it difficult to comprehend how the United States had drawn on the support of UN members to justify its activities in the Gulf War while in other forums it seemingly worked to deny the legitimacy of the UN in international economic affairs. For Rhoda Karpatkin of Consumers Union, it seemed that the U.S. government was saying, "Yes, we believe in market-driven economies but we don't believe in the UN promulgating any standards of decency and fairness for industrial and commercial enterprises operating across national boundaries."[30]

Following the final collapse of the Code talks in 1992, the consumer movement, backed by the Australian government, doggedly launched a new initiative, a set of Guidelines for Global Business, which consisted of statements of general principles to ethical commerce largely drawn from existing protocols. Despite offering little that was new, and despite drawing on industry's own codes of conduct, such as the International Chamber of Commerce's "Environmental Guidelines for World Industry," this initiative also failed to gain international acceptance.[31] At the same time the UNCTC and the Commission on Transnational Corporations were pushed to an uninfluential corner of the United Nations Conference on Trade and Development bureaucracy, bringing to almost nothing two decades of negotiations.[32] In 1995, all that remained of the Code of Conduct was the consumer movement's own "Charter for Global Business"—a statement of principles that multinational capitalism could simply ignore.[33]

In many ways the sphere of global trade regulation had simply passed the

Code negotiations by. The consumer movement was aware of this. It recognized that the desire to regulate multinational capitalism was "a product of that particular period, the period of the late '70s when there was a commitment by both north and south to carve out a new equitable international economic order. This order is now long since dead and buried."[34] This was a message both transnational corporations and the U.S. government were only too keen to promote. Ominously in their telex to the embassies in 1992, the State Department insisted that the Code was "a relic of another era," supported only by those countries that held to outmoded notions of foreign investment.[35] Indeed, the rules for global trade were being decided in arenas other than that of ECOSOC. As Jane E. Becker, Deputy Assistant Secretary for International Development at the U.S. State Department, testified at the Senate Subcommittee on International Economic Policy, the negotiations on the Code were increasingly irrelevant throughout the Uruguay Round of trade negotiations.[36] Among other matters, these were suggesting stricter rules for investment under a more liberalized financial market that would render the voluntary Code irrelevant. Indeed, while the Uruguay Round of trade negotiations was taking place, developing and transitional economies such as those of Mexico, Chile, Poland, Argentina, and Hungary were unilaterally opting to liberalize their investment regimes, opening up new markets for foreign multinationals and suggesting the Code belonged to a previous period when nation-states held much greater sovereignty in economic affairs.

If we are to insist that the consumer movement was defeated by big business in negotiations over a Code of Conduct, then this was not simply a defeat on a level playing field. But neither was it a defeat because the goal posts had been moved, as they repeatedly were, during the various stages of the Code's progress. Rather it was a defeat in which the consumer movement looked to be playing alone on the field provided by the UN, unaware that there was no longer an opposition. Multinational enterprise, meanwhile, had joined a game being played in another stadium. For them and for governments supporting the system of trade liberalization being promoted by the United States, the real action was taking place at the World Trade Organization and not the UN. Here was a new arena for governing world trade in which the consumer movement would have some considerable difficulty in both understanding the rules and finding either a role to play or a seat from which to spectate.

II

The experience of IOCU over the Code of Conduct on Transnational Corporations brings to a conclusion the narrative of consumer-business relations begun in chapter 6. Yet the failure to regulate multinational capitalism also came at a time when the global movement undertook a retreat from its largely radical South to its more conservative North. Nothing better encapsulates these alternating and equally important tendencies—between defeat and retreat—than the reorientation of IOCU's policy to global trade during the 1990s, a period that saw the massive growth in world trade and the exponential increase in the number of organizations concerned with globalization.

It is worth reminding ourselves of the nature of global economic governance. As is well known to many of today's protestors, the architecture of commerce emerged out of the United Nations Monetary and Financial Conference held in Bretton Woods in New Hampshire in 1944. Motivated by the desire to avoid future world wars, the politicians who listened to the economist John Maynard Keynes created the World Bank to provide loans for reconstruction and infrastructure development and the International Monetary Fund to provide a stable system for international payments and exchange by making funds available for countries to ride out the inevitable swings of the business cycle. Here was a recognition that markets did not always work and intervention was sometimes necessary, a fact that Keynes further chose to build on in his proposal for an International Trade Organization. This governing body was designed to set standards for world trade, including labor regulations, restrictive trade practices, competition, and international investment. Although its charter was approved by the vast majority of delegates at the 1948 UN Conference on Trade and Employment, opposition led by the United States meant it was never ratified. Instead, the international community settled on the more narrowly focused GATT, a multilateral codification of tariff reductions that had been signed in 1947 while deliberations still took place over the precise role and function of the International Trade Organization.[37]

The relatively clear and distinct roles given to the World Bank and the IMF to promote development and stability broke down in the 1970s following sustained pressure on the dollar, the de facto monetary standard, and the consequent collapse of the fixed exchange rate mechanisms first established at Bretton Woods. Thereafter, floating exchange rates arguably provided automatic corrective mechanisms for over and undervalued currencies, but in reality it meant the IMF and World Bank extended their loans to troubled economies, countries sought out non-tariff barriers to trade, and the developed nations moved toward outright protectionism in the 1980s, following a sustained world economic recession. As debts escalated, so did pressures on developing world states to liberalize their trade regimes, especially those seeking rapid economic growth through exports, especially in Southeast Asia. Earlier rounds of trade negotiations had prevented some of the more obvious barriers to trade, though agriculture as a whole remained outside the remit of most multilateral agreements and the United States and Europe continued to subsidize their exports, especially through the increasingly notorious Common Agricultural Policy of the European Union. By the mid-1980s not only were the existing financial institutions struggling to cope with increasing Third World debts, but world trade was marked in complicated ways by regional trade blocs, the use of non-tariff barriers and subsidies, and the often related exclusion of developing countries from world markets.[38]

The Uruguay Round of trade negotiations began in 1986 amid this context of economic recession and regional trade dispute. They originally began with the intention that developing countries would not be asked to open their markets to the same degree as the developed countries. Yet the slow, rigid structure of the Uruguay trade negotiations meant that it was extremely difficult for the smaller delegations of developing countries to have an input into the fifteen areas of global trade being discussed. In the end, it has been claimed, the trade talks effectively consisted of private negotiations between Europe and the United States, with the rest of the world being reduced to bystanders. The final agreement was presented as non-negotiable, meaning that poorer countries were faced with a take it or leave it document. The vast majority were forced to take it, meaning they signed up to trade agreements on reduced tariffs, the inclusion of services, agriculture and textiles in the agreement, the establishment of Trade-Related Intellectual Property Rights (TRIPs) that protected multinational's copyrights and patents, Trade Related Investment Measures that ensured foreign firms operated with the same freedom as domestic firms, and the creation of the World Trade Organization (WTO). The WTO has been the governing body of the Uruguay Round, to which all 141 signatories have joined and which has ensured the trade agreements have been enforced. In itself, it has consisted of just a few hundred staff in Geneva, but it has come to symbolize the new era of global trade and has provoked the most anger among anti-globalization protestors and more moderate and reformist-minded civil society actors.

The other crucial context for these developments in global trade rules was the emergence of a growing consensus among politicians and bureaucrats to the efficacy of the free market. Several commentators have written of a growing "Washington consensus," dictating U.S. trade and foreign policy, which maintains that countries should open up their economies to foreign trade and capital, privatize and deregulate government services, float their exchange rates, and adopt a macroeconomic policy based on low inflation and balancing public budgets. In the absence of strong institutional structures, it has effectively opened up the world economy to those already well-placed to exploit the new opportunities, namely the multinationals corporations. These have been referred to as the new "leviathans," so large are their profits and turnovers in comparison to the GDPs of existing nation-states, and their CEOs have been said to constitute a new "transnational capitalist class" closely tied to the free market consensus being implemented from its base in Washington.[39] Indeed the agenda of the consensus has arguably been pushed through the World Bank, the IMF, and the WTO, especially as the conditionality aspects of global credit provision and structural adjustment programs have forced countries to implement the principal ideas of the elite.

It has been this imposition of a one-size-fits-all approach to economic development that has so infuriated critics of globalization. The phenomenon has been referred to as "thin simplification," whereby narrow-minded policy makers ignore the complexities of reality in order to reduce it to fit a simple model.[40] Success has been achieved, in terms of increasing foreign direct investment and economic growth, but at the cost of ignoring the original goals of the Bretton Woods institutions: that is, economic and social development. Instead, inequalities of wealth are said to have increased.[41] For Joseph Stiglitz, the former chief economist of the World Bank, the economic policies of the IMF have been geared toward protecting the private investments of the multinational corporations. He argues that IMF funds have been used to maintain exchange rates in the short term, enabling the rich to get their money out of a country, and to pay off foreign creditors, effectively funneling funds from the international public purse into private hands.[42] Long-term capital flows—that is, those investments that have the greatest potential to benefit a host nation—have, by contrast, tended to avoid the riskier countries where poor infrastructures offer lower returns. Even the World Bank has come to admit that financial market liberalization, along with a reliance on the private sector and deregulation, has added to economic instability, experienced in extreme form in such instances as the Asian financial crisis of 1997.

As alternatives, the critics of global trade governance have insisted on the continued need for aid over and above private investment, especially because so much of the world still remains outside the networks and beyond the flows of financial capital. In order to reduce the dangers of speculation, many critics have adhered to a system of disincentives, such as a proposed Tobin Tax on capital flows that charges higher rates on short-term flows in order to steer money toward long-term investments that bring greater benefits to the real economy.[43] On the subject of investment, global civil society activists can claim to have had some success, putting to an end the discussions for a Multinational Agreement on Investment, which sought to regulate and standardize international investment but which arguably threatened the sovereign powers of nation-states to deal with foreign investments in their economies.[44] For those activists who have emerged as the stars of the anti-globalization movement, pressure has been placed on them to outline an alternative system of global economic and political governance. Many have been reluctant to do so, while others have adopted varying degrees of a world federalist approach.[45] More often, however, discussions never get much beyond a demand for a "great transformation" similar to that which Keynes demanded of the international community in 1944, and too often other writers are merely derivative or else idiosyncratically utopian.[46]

It is important that such a summary of globalization and its critics is provided because it helps to explain the position adopted by the consumer movement on free trade and its disassociation from many other activists within global civil society in the 1990s. What is most apparent is that whereas the consumer movement could claim some leadership of global civil society in the

1980s, in the 1990s this was no longer the case. Like classic liberals of the nineteenth century, the consumer movement's Western leadership adopted a moderate position that extolled the benefits of free trade, not only because it was believed to increase choice but ultimately because it had the potential to reduce the price paid by the consumer.

What the consumer movement shared with many of the negotiators of the trade treaties of the 1980s was a strong dislike of protectionism. There might well be strong political motives for defending industries through tariffs, export subsidies and the like, but protectionism also maintained artificially high prices and uncompetitive market structures, which had so long been the target of the consumer movement's domestic initiatives. For those Western consumer leaders who eschewed the radicalism emanating from the Penang office in the 1980s, consumerism was essentially an "economics rights movement" that saw in genuine free trade the best opportunity to promote for the individual shopper better access to goods and services, greater choice, improved safety, and more information.[47]

At the turn of the 1990s, while the consumer movement remained very much concerned with the more exploitative dimensions of multinational corporations, it saw in the conclusion of GATT and the creation of the WTO an opportunity for a co-operative working relationship. The consumer movement did not go so far as to be an unreflecting cheerleader for the new organization. It worried, along with so many other critics, that the lion's share of the Uruguay Round agreements would go to industrialized countries.[48] But what it did take note of was the promise made by GATT in the first paragraph of the preamble to the Marrakesh Agreement, which established the WTO in 1995, that the new structure would be aiming to raise "standards of living."[49] This seemingly placed the objectives of the WTO in accord with the aims of the original architects of the Bretton Woods institutions when consumer democracy and improved standards of living were seen as the best guarantors of world peace and stability. In this sense the politics of consumption being espoused by the new institutions governing global trade seemed to be a continuation of the politics articulated by consumer and world leaders since the World War II, which tied consumption to more general plans for greater social welfare.

Accordingly, while it was not in favor of all the policies, IOCU "was positive about the agreement as a whole" and it chose to work with rather than against the new WTO.[50] IOCU's Charter for Global Business was an important symbol of a potentially new working relationship: unlike the Code of Conduct, it was not seeking an externally imposed set of regulations on multinational enterprises but was instead a wish list of what it would like to see businesses do.[51] At the same time, IOCU began to distance itself from other consumer leaders such as Ralph Nader who, at the beginning of the 1990s, was adopting a more protectionist line to defend American workers' jobs.[52] And, entering the spirit of the rhetoric of the WTO, IOCU in 1994 published "The Task Ahead"—a policy paper that set out the consumer agenda for the WTO covering topics such as competition policy, environmental policy, transparency, dispute settlement, labor standards, and the special provisions to protect least developed countries.[53] However, in its new moderation, IOCU chose to go it alone in its relationship with the WTO. It made few overtures to other citizen groups as it had done with the networks. The plight of farmers, for instance, remained a key concern for the consumer movement, especially for developing world groups that cared less for the distinctions between producers and consumers. Yet at the level of global civil society, IOCU did little to reach out to other NGOs concerned with such groups. Indeed, a U.S. farmers' representative worried that if the consumer movement persisted in its free trade line it would become associated with those groups and governments that opposed all interventions on issues of food safety.[54] The concern was not alleviated by the consumer movement's unwillingness in the early 1990s to enter into dialogue with other NGOs concerned with similar issues and the acceptance by many consumer leaders that they had entered into a stage of "splendid isolation."[55]

In the new environment of world trade regulation, the consumer movement faced the difficulty of promoting consumer protection while not adopting protectionism as a whole. It wanted to encourage economic growth, while ensuring that the freedom to trade was not synonymous with the freedom to exploit. In its own logic, for such a situation to arise, it needed to be given a seat at the table of world trade and, for this to happen, it had to posit itself as being based on the assumption that the new trade rules would force nations with limited consumer protection mechanisms and low trading standards to raise them.[56] At worst, IOCU can be regarded as naive as it failed to appreciate the differences that would exist between the rhetoric and the practice of free trade. For consumer leaders, the very freeness of the free market, in a sense, rested on the critical eye of a vigilant consumer movement ever eager to spot abuses and to suggest legislative changes in order to prevent their reoccurrence. As we saw in chapter 2, there might well be many different models of consumer protection and consumer input, but the basic premise remained the same: states were to listen to consumers and intervene in the market on their behalf when necessary. Perhaps such a view could only come from the complacency of a Western leadership satisfied with the gains they had made in their own domestic economies and governments. These did actually provide a reasonable degree of protection for the consumer by the end of the 1980s. At the global level the unforeseen outcome of the Uruguay Round was that the consumer was not to be given an equivalent voice in the architecture of world trade.

This ought to have been obvious to those in the consumer movement. Although IOCU's expertise on world trade during the Uruguay Round was by no means as extensive as it has subsequently become, it was well aware of the complexity of all the issues being discussed.[57] And it was well aware of the relatively little influence it had on the trade negotiations and even the very difficulty of knowing how to get its voice heard.[58] As one lobbyist admitted in 1990, the last session of the Uruguay Round has been "a total disaster for us."[59] The world of international trade rules was a very different place from the comfort zone of NGO influence at the ECOSOC or the representative functions granted to consumer groups by many European governments.

The consumer movement had already had a foretaste of what was to come. It had witnessed the aggressive opposition to the Guidelines on Consumer Protection and the Code of Conduct on Transnational Corporations. It had seen the emergence of new "front" groups, which attempted to capture the initiative from civil society actors. For example, the business-backed Consumers for World Trade emerged in Washington and attempted to co-opt the organized consumer movement into its own version of a free trade agenda that had very little to say about the need for countervailing protection mechanisms.[60] It had witnessed the attempts made by the business lobby to introduce laws that overrode existing consumer protection mechanisms such as the U.S. Hatch Bill of 1985, which sought to enable U.S. companies to export goods banned by their own Food and Drug Administration.[61] It had had to respond to the repeated failure of the international community to implement and police international rules, especially in the field of dangerous exports.[62] And it had seen transnational corporations tire of the criticisms made against them and respond by employing advisers to teach them to "carry the fight to the critics of international capitalism."[63]

With the creation of the WTO, there were ominous signs that the organized consumer movement's input into the new body might be restricted and overshadowed by others seeking to represent the "true" consumer interest. Its own report into the working of GATT had certainly concluded that the stronger members of the WTO would be able to influence it too much in their own interests, and that no provisions whatsoever had been made for NGOs to have any say in its deliberations.[64] Yet despite all this, the consumer movement still chose to work with rather than against the WTO. It inevitably meant that its main area of focus on world trade issues in the mid-1990s was to be initially about getting a voice at the WTO. It campaigned to make the WTO more democratic and to be forced to listen to civil society groups, as well as for greater transparency in its operations.[65] It was able, along with other leading NGOs, to meet leading WTO officials on an informal basis, but it mistakenly believed this access would lead to more formal channels of communication. Instead, IOCU could only express its shock when it became clear in 1996 that the WTO was not going to allow NGO participation and would restrict publication of most of its documents for six months.[66] It would take until May 1997 for the WTO to actually listen to NGOs: a year earlier, at a symposium on trade and the environment, government ministers at the WTO meeting simply failed to turn up. For all the overtures that had been made at the WTO's creation to NGOs and to the key civil society concept of sustainability, leaders of bodies such as IOCU must surely have begun to contrast the admittedly limited gains of the 1980s at the UN with the almost impenetrable wall of the WTO in the 1990s.

For all the barriers to effective influence the policy emphasis on moderation favored by IOCU meant it was unlikely to take a more hostile approach to world trade. Throughout the 1990s, as we have seen, the focus of the international movement was on consolidating its own infrastructure and developing consumer protection laws at the national level.[67] It was, therefore, unlikely that the stronger criticisms being directed against the world trading system by Southern consumer groups were to be aired quite as forcefully as they had been when the center of gravity had been in Malaysia instead of the United Kingdom.

It must be reiterated that IOCU's position was not a complete volte-face; it was more a question of emphasis. Certainly the concerns of the world's poor continued to feed through into the global campaigns on trade. Pharmaceuticals remained a key concern and an important example of the problems of regulating the world economy.[68] At the regional level efforts were made to deal with the frustrations of the WTO and to develop a coherent response. African consumers, for instance, chose to focus on trade as the key issue impacting on ordinary consumers' lives.[69] Moreover, the very real problems faced on a day-to-day basis, especially of access to basic utilities such as water and energy, raised classic consumer concerns about monopolistic provision. These led to campaigns by IOCU headquarters critiquing the structural adjustment programs that had promoted the privatization schemes seen to deprive so many consumers in Africa, Latin America, Asia, and Eastern Europe.[70] In 1996, the consumer movement in Latin America launched the CONSUPAL (Consumer and Public Utilities) project to highlight the problems of utility regulation in different national contexts.[71] And the consumer movement was not entirely divorced from all the concerns preoccupying civil society at this time. IOCU joined the campaign against the Multilateral Agreement on Investment, its membership of the alliance proving an important element in its eventual success.[72]

But for all this the consumer movement did not share in the more radical or aggressive critiques of the WTO and the Bretton Woods institutions that were increasingly popular and vociferous in the 1990s. For some time it persisted in its advocacy of free trade, tempered by a support for specific regulations to cope with market failures. Such a position, it continued to hope, would secure it a respectability and level of access to the seats of power denied to those NGOs that remained on the more media-friendly and spectacular sides of the political barricades. But the sheer level of difficulty the consumer movement had in getting across its pro-capitalist message meant it had to reappraise its position by the turn of the millennium. IOCU was encountering a problem it had faced in the 1970s at the UN: despite its input being requested and sought, this did not necessarily translate into effective influence and representation had become "an end unto itself."[73] It increased the "potential" of its influence but admitted that it had "not had enough direct impact on actual international agreements and decisions."[74]

Moreover, there was an element of co-option involved in its interactions with the WTO, especially when the WTO tried to steer IOCU's work to the comparatively benign arena of consumer education.[75] In 1998, the WTO announced it was to extend its dialogue with NGOs, but this amounted only to a willingness to provide NGOs with briefings of its work.[76] The events at the WTO Ministerial in Seattle in 1999 made the world more aware of civil society activists, but even at the Doha Round of trade negotiations, beginning in 2001, NGOs were there more to listen than to participate, and in any case they continued to be outnumbered by the huge number of corporate delegates.[77] When in 2002 the WTO appointed an NGO consultative group and IOCU was invited to join, only a handful of other NGOs were asked to be involved and the number of full time staff at the WTO dealing with NGOs could still be counted on one hand.[78]

By the end of the 1990s, it was becoming apparent to IOCU that it had been granted only a tiny amount of influence in the new structure governing world trade and that its own profile had suffered as a consequence. It therefore attempted to become not only more vociferous but more proactive in setting out its criticisms of the WTO and what an alternative could look like. While it lost much of the initiative in the 1990s, by the end of the decade it was prepared to use its respectability to advocate positions more in line with other NGOs. While few members of the international consumer movement joined the street protests in Seattle, for instance, the leadership took advantage of its potential to outline its regulated free trade position to the WTO officials on the other side of the police line. It also expressed its frustrations at the failure to implement the recommendations of the Uruguay Round that the developing countries remained on an unequal footing in negotiations. As such, it worked in a manner that complemented the message of the street protestors and it opposed the trade talks leading to an admission by WTO officials that the consumer movement's lukewarm stance significantly contributed to the collapse of the Seattle talks.[79]

IOCU's agenda on world trade by the turn of the millennium had become firmly rooted in a social justice model. At its World Congress in 2000 in Durban, significantly the first to be held in Africa, members acknowledged that free trade alone was insufficient. They declared that "liberalised market economies will not themselves eradicate poverty; indeed, they can worsen it and exacerbate inequalities."[80] Here was an acceptance by IOCU that its tactics at the beginning of the 1990s had been a mistake. What was now required was a more holistic approach to world trade and its associated problems. Consequently, in the same year, IOCU launched a trade and economics program to examine competition policy, agriculture, and services (including utilities). This, along with documents such as "The Way Forward for the WTO," has brought the movement more in line with many of the agendas of global civil society. For instance, on agricultural issues, it has argued that many of the supposed benefits of liberalization are unlikely to be enjoyed in the developing world unless an appropriate infrastructure is put in place. It has argued against TRIPs rules on the basis that they have worked to block consumer access to basic medicines in the developing world. And it has returned to the original principles of the Bretton

Woods institutions, accepting the benefits of free trade, but arguing that this must also be fair, that it must be accompanied by long-term investment, and that it should not be overseen by a rigid dogma that assumes the particularities of any one country can be overridden by the gospel of liberalization. Moreover, it has tied these initiatives into its capacity-building work so that the growth of consumer organizing has gone hand in hand with educating potential consumer leaders about the national impacts of international trade agreements.[81]

At the same time it has worked to become a more effective voice by working again in alliance with other NGOs. At the Doha Round of trade negotiations beginning in 2001, IOCU focused on specific agreements that it believed did not facilitate genuinely free, fair trade.[82] This provided points of focus for consumer activism, which were repeated at the world trade meetings in Cancún in 2003 and Hong Kong in 2005: clear recommendations were made making it easier to pinpoint issues on which it could collaborate with other NGOs. The recommendations included the need to ban export subsidies, the need for special and differential treatment for less developed countries in order to protect small farmers, the need to be able to grant compulsory licenses for the production and distribution of medicines, the need for developing countries to protect the natural world from patenting, and the need to take strong effective action against monopolies and cartels.[83] In recognition of the changed environment of global policy making, members of the consumer movement from North America and Europe eventually formed the Transatlantic Consumer Dialogue (TACD) in 1998 to mirror the work, the effectiveness and, it was hoped, the power of the Transatlantic Business Dialogue—an alliance of U.S. and European CEOs set up in 1995 with the aim of influencing national government legislation and policy formulation.[84]

Nevertheless, the consumer movement's critique of the world trade system has remained largely just that: a critique rather than a rejection of fundamental principles. It has not sought out rationales that could redefine the principles on which the trading system has been based. It has not, for instance, articulated a notion of global public goods that could consist of the line in the sand over which liberalization and privatization ought not to be allowed to cross. Nor has it developed alternative notions of consumer agency inspired, for instance, by the "capabilities" approach that focuses not on the rights of individuals to choose, to participate, and to act, but on their actual capabilities to do so.[85] Instead, it has persisted in its rights-based critique. Its message to the World Bank, the IMF, and the WTO has been that these organizations should adopt the core consumer rights that IOCU has articulated for nearly half a century.[86] Such rights, as we saw in the previous chapter, offer no fundamental challenge to the logic of the market; they serve merely to react to its excesses. And despite the fact that the consumer movement has now come to realize the importance of world trade, the rights-based approach has meant much of IOCU's work is concentrated on the promotion of similarly conceived consumer protection frameworks in different national legislatures. Admittedly, it has achieved considerable success in this field but it has diverted attention from the weaknesses of the consumer protection clauses of the entire global economic architecture.[87]

It is important to re-emphasize just how much the consumer movement's respectable moderation meant it divorced itself from other branches of global civil society. To be sure, it has allied itself with other NGOs on specific issues, but it has been much more wary of doing so, and it has largely preferred to work with the institutions of globalization rather than to oppose them. This has led to much mutual mistrust, the global consumer movement's free trade line in particular seeming to align IOCU with the very forces that many other NGOs have come to oppose. This has been unfortunate, because IOCU's support for free trade has been a pro-regulatory agenda that many NGOs would do well to learn from. Instead, so stymied has the very phrase "free trade" become that many activists attending the World Social Forums have retreated into their own protectionist stances that ignore the very real benefits that expanding trade can bring to poor people's living standards.

From the consumer movement's perspective, it has meant it has been unable to build on the strength of a renewed ethical consumerism that has grown independently of it since the 1980s. IOCU has discussed collaborating on several occasions, but what links there have been with green consumer groups, the consumer co-operatives and the fair-trade organizations have generally occurred at the national rather than the global level. Again, this is unfortunate. Much could be learned from one another, both in terms of mobilizing the concerns of new generations of shoppers and in addressing the bigger questions about the organization of world trade, but the absence of a continuous dialogue has meant both consumer movements have failed to take advantage of one another's strengths. A greater collaboration could have demonstrated to a wider audience, from IOCU's point of view, that free trade could mean fair trade, and, from the ethical consumerist's position, that fair trade could be the starting point for a more provocative engagement with free trade other than the well-meaning actions of the individual shopper.

III

One final consequence of the consumer movement's approach to trade and economics must be explored at greater length. This is in relation to the internal splits that have occurred over trade within the consumer movement itself. Although divisions exist within national consumer movements—witness the attention paid to labor issues by various branches of the consumer movement in the United States—these splits have broadly manifested themselves between the global North and the global South, between the developed and the developing world. This is undoubtedly due to the very different experiences of consumers in the two regions. Although the opening of markets has brought greater choice and cheaper goods to developed world consumers—and unfair subsidies in agriculture and other sectors have ensured their incomes have also been protected so that they can continue to afford such goods—the experience of developing world consumers has been much more problematic.

It is a relatively banal point to state that poverty levels have persisted around the world, so often has this been made by countless development organizations and activists. While overall poverty continues to decline, the annual Human Development reports of the United Nations Development Programme have continued to demonstrate that, for instance, the proportion of people living on less than $1 a day has actually increased in some regions, particularly in sub-Saharan Africa.[88] In these countries the right to basic needs has trumped all other rights in the minds of the poor consumer. One IOCU study into the impact of trade liberalization on Africa (specifically, Chad, Ghana, Mali, Kenya, and Zambia) found that although the GATT rules meant more varied food products had become available on the market this had occurred at the expense of the country's own agricultural sector. This, in turn, meant that the purchasing power of many consumers had been reduced and they could not afford the new products. Similarly, liberalization had actually improved service delivery, but only to those who could afford it. Many consumers continue to have little access to water and health, especially when private firms decide that their services should not extend to poorer districts as it offers too low a return on their investments.[89] Moreover, the consumer movement has for some time joined in the more general international debate over the food crisis in Africa, pointing to ways in which indigenously grown African foods can contribute to relieving hunger and starvation.[90]

What these very real problems faced by ordinary consumers mean in terms of consumer organizing and consumer protest is that the global movement remains incredibly diverse. The problems faced by consumers on the ground have translated into forms of consumer activism that demonstrate the existence of a global movement just as diverse as it was in the 1970s when the center of gravity first shifted from the Netherlands to Malaysia.

In Southeast Asia these traditions of consumer organizing have persisted. Filipino consumer activists, for instance, continue to emphasize that they constitute a movement concerned with lifestyle as much as products, a shift in their work that has seen them move from "value to values."[91] In countries such as Papua New Guinea, the real challenge for activists has been to protect ignorant and illiterate consumers dealing with a new market economy which has transformed their subsistence ways of living.[92] And when consumer groups have moved into rural areas to promote consumer rights, as in Indonesia, they have often found themselves working alongside community workers, rural NGO activists, and Islamic peasant leaders, making the solitary stance of IOCU at the global level irrelevant to grassroots activism.[93]

Likewise, the sheer scale of privatization in Latin America has radicalized a movement far beyond the respectability of the IOCU leadership. In Columbia, for instance, consumers have been known to take to the streets, opposing the privatization of public utilities and promoting a broad defense of consumer citizenship. In 2000, a launch rally for Consumidores Colombia brought together protestors from the Bogota Women's Center, the Center for Business Responsibility, the Colombian Association of Civil Engineers, the United Workers' Central, several universities, and the Corporación Viva la Cuidadanía—a federation of NGOs active in the quest for peace.[94]

In Africa the consumer movement has inevitably become more closely tied to developmental organizations. Much of the support for consumerism in west Africa came from the environmental and human rights NGO ENDA (Organisation internationale pour l'environnement et le développement du Tiers-Monde) and at the local level the division between the consumer and other citizen organizations has been blurred. Consumer issues have been promoted by the African League of People's and Human Rights in Senegal, for example, and by the NGO Democracy, Liberty, Development in Niger.[95] In Mali, consumer workshops have been led by the prominent anti-globalization activist Aminata Dramane Traoré, who worked especially against the unfair subsidies granted to cotton farmers in western nations.[96] Moreover, the overwhelming consumer issues have arisen out of the experience of poverty and consumers have worked with a whole range of organizations to address questions such as gender and development, biotechnology, TRIPs, and privatization. The consumer movement that has emerged in these countries has been much more vociferous in its opposition to the WTO than the leadership based in London.[97]

Care must be taken in assuming a sharp dichotomy between the consumer movement of the North and that of the South. Differences and complications do emerge, not least because of the protectionist support for home agriculture by Japanese and French consumer groups. And in the South, not all have taken a hostile line to the Bretton Woods infrastructure. Perhaps unsurprisingly, given the many hundreds—if not thousands—of consumer groups that have emerged in India since 1986, some groups have sought to work with rather than against the WTO. Pradeep Mehta, leader of the Consumer Unity and Trust Society (CUTS), has argued that globalization is itself inevitable so "we need to make the best of it" rather than adopting a "futile" opposition.[98] But divisions have emerged between the North and the South, with the South less keen to emphasize the virtues of free trade, more eager to defend fledgling industries, and far more willing to publicly criticize the WTO. As new generations of Southern consumer activist have emerged, the potential for division within the consumer movement has become apparent.

The event that best illustrates the two approaches to consumer politics and world trade is the Asian financial crisis of the late 1990s. Following widespread speculation in May 1997 on the Thai currency, the baht, a devaluation was forced, triggering runs on the currencies of several neighboring states and a consequent economic recession across the region. For many, the blame for the crisis lay squarely with the IMF. The IMF had promoted the liberalization of financial markets, enabling such speculations to take place, but it had also encouraged Asian states to maintain high interest rates to promote the inflow of short-term financial capital and it had pegged the local currencies to the dollar in order to reduce the risks faced by investors. In response to the crisis, the IMF's "rescue package" was conditional on a structural adjustment program, which further demanded cuts in government funding and the defense of high interest rates. To many observers the measures only served to further weaken domestic industry and to open up the country to foreign investment and ownership.[99]

The IOCU's response was typically moderate. It shied away from either critiquing the IMF directly or offering statements as to its own proposed solutions to the problems. The crisis was of such enormity, it was felt, that a specific consumer response could only be inadequate or inappropriate. Instead they published a book that attempted to highlight the problems faced by ordinary consumers in coping with the crisis, a publication in which they gave much space to the IMF and the World Bank to justify their measures, while ardent consumer critics in the region were denied an opportunity to express their views.[100] Other options were available to them and the reactions of the Malaysian government suggested that alternative policies could have been pursued. In response to the crisis, Deputy Prime Minister Anwar Ibrahim saw the route out of the financial crisis in an IMF rescue package. Prime Minister Mahathir Mohamed disagreed, leading to a potential division within the government, which Mahathir solved by arresting and imprisoning Ibrahim on the entirely spurious charges of sodomy.

Despite the radicalism and optimism attached to Ibrahim's career in Malaysia, the irony is that Mahathir's authoritarian response proved the more effective. Mahathir fixed the exchange rate and introduced capital controls, defiantly embracing national sovereignty amid the IMF's calls for greater openness. These measures helped stabilize the economy, ensuring that Malaysia avoided some of the worst effects of the crisis experienced by its neighbors. Mahathir's motives were hardly pure. As the principal architect of "crony capitalism," through which lucrative government contracts were distributed to friends, family, and associates, he was extremely unwilling to have Malaysia's private and public monopolies subjected to international trading and capital rules. Yet his capital controls proved a more effective way of dealing with the speculative fallout of the crisis than the measures suggested by the IMF.[101] Moreover, in his direct affront to global hegemony, Mahathir enjoyed the support of the Consumers' Association of Penang and its developmental sister organization Third World Network. This was at first unlikely. As we saw in chapter 3, Mahathir had arrested and imprisoned several NGO activists connected to CAP in 1987 and it had been Anwar Ibrahim who had maintained close links with CAP's President, S. M. Mohamed Idris, in Penang. For Malaysian activists, Ibrahim was the NGO sector's man in the ruling party and for many connected to the Reformasi movement he remains the hope for a democratic future.[102]

CAP, however, strongly disputed Ibrahim's courting of the international financial community. For some time, along with many others in the anti-globalization movement, CAP and Third World Network had taken a strong oppositional line to the policies of the IMF, the WTO, and the World Bank.[103] In 1997 Mahathir and Martin Khor, research director for the two Penang organizations, both believed the IMF's rescue package to be the perfect opportunity for the rich nations "to force open Asian economies" to their own companies.[104] Khor and Idris have insisted on the existence of a distinct Third World consumer movement, meaning they were prepared at the end of the 1990s to throw their weight behind their corrupt one-time potential jail keeper.[105]

Khor has taken a much more hostile consumer approach to the global trade system than that articulated by IOCU. His basic starting point was that there is a lack of tangible benefits to the South, especially in a system that too rigidly proposes one solution to the diverse nature of the world's developmental problems. As with many other anti-globalization protestors, he proposes more flexible liberalization policies that introduce developing countries into the world economy at a rate more appropriate to their stage of development and particular social, political, and cultural situation. As with IOCU, he has questioned the use of TRIPs and the purposes of the Multilateral Agreement on Investment, but unlike his conservative consumer counterparts in the North, he has more assertively expressed his opposition to the conditional aspects of loans and to the undemocratic nature of trade negotiations. He has proposed the greater regulation of financial markets, including the international management of exchange rates and the greater use of national capital controls. And he has urged a return to the principal developmental goals of the Bretton Woods institutions as well as a revival of the authority of the UN over bodies such as the WTO.[106]

Khor's views have been articulated through Third World Network, an organization he has led with Idris to develop more coherent Southern perspectives in global debates.[107] It has focused particularly on the WTO, suggesting reforms that would make its policies more supportive of developing countries.[108] But it has also promoted alternative forms of market organization and control of the economy, either by local governments, nation-states, or civil society involvement, making Khor a frequent and popular speaker at events organized by the World Social Forum and placing him on a level comparable to many other civil society leaders.[109] Similar to IOCU, he has not been opposed to trade, but he has been unwilling to use the prefix "free" and he has promoted a regulated global economy that speaks more directly to the concerns of the consumer movement across the global South. Khor's position perhaps better outlines the general feelings of those new consumer groups emerging in Africa, which have realized that national consumer protection measures are not enough in themselves.[110] They have wanted to focus on the impact of multilateral trading agreements on their economies and they have wanted to express their anger at the WTO in a manner less concerned with the maintenance of a respectable and moderate dialogue that the IOCU leadership has so favored.[111]

What the North-South divide comes down to is a divergence in campaigning and in the emphasis placed on regulatory controls and preferential treatment to developing countries and their fledgling industries. Most commonly these differences have manifested themselves at the World Congresses of the consumer movement. At the 2003 Congress in Lisbon a Bolivian consumer advocate made an impassioned plea to support his comrades in their struggle over the exploitation of his country's gas resources, a protest that led to sixty deaths under martial law. His question was followed by a demand for a fundamental reform of world trade rules by a consumer representative from Benin. Immediately after this, a U.S. consumer spokesperson from the Direct Selling Organization was able to raise the issue of teaching children their consumer rights on the Internet. The contrast between the consumer concerns could not be more stark. They could hardly be said to be of the same weight, yet it is typical for the consumer movement, which seeks to represent the entire world's population, that such diverse issues could be raised consecutively. Which issues are prioritized must have profound effects on the direction of the consumer movement as a whole. For many from the global South, too often since the end of the 1980s, the IOCU headquarters have been concerned with the type of issue raised by the representative from the Direct Selling Organization. This, they feel, has led to insufficient attention being paid to the problems of world trade, to structural adjustment programs, and to the financial liberalization measures being borne by consumers in the South.

IV

The disputes over the accountability and effectiveness of the WTO seem a long way from the international community's original concerns about the operation of multinational corporations in Chile. Yet the opening and concluding discussions of this chapter are essentially about the same subject: the freedom of transnational corporations to go about their business and promote their interests in countries and regions far distant from their home environments. What the consumer movement and other NGOs increasingly categorized under the inadequately phrased "anti-globalization movement" have come to advocate, to varying degrees, is a system of global trade regulation to ensure that ordinary consumers, workers, and citizens share in the benefits of increased trade and that profits are not simply channeled back to the favored few. As such, like so many of the debates over the politics of consumption since the mid-twentieth century, the discussion on trade has been about the standards of living of the community as much as it has been about the standard of living of the individual.

What has been the impact of the consumer movement on these issues? To answer this question, we must return to the complementary narratives of defeat and retreat and to the dilemmas the consumer movement has faced in responding to seemingly contradictory interests. Indeed, the subject of world trade neatly brings to a close the parallel trends in the consumer movement's history. For all the successes enjoyed by consumer organizations in extending national protection institutions and in improving safety standards around the world, its impact on the regulation of either transnational corporations or on world trade as a whole has been minimal. Not only has it failed to see through its key initiatives, be these codes of conducts or specific reform proposals of existing institutions, but it has failed to keep up with the rapidly changing dynamics of global trade rules. Along with so many other NGOs, it has consequently been several steps behind the pace set by those opposed to the regulation of business, industry, and finance.

Moreover, the tactics pursued by the consumer movement have contributed to its problems. It has adopted a conciliatory line in order to obtain a seat at the negotiating table. But the limited access given to IOCU has been relatively worthless, in terms of the concrete measures it could have campaigned for and introduced at the global level. Instead its rhetoric of free trade, although intellectually justifiable, has symbolized its isolation from other civil society actors who have chosen instead to focus on the issue of "fair trade." This has been to the frustration of many consumer groups in the global South which, impatient with the moderate tone and policies emanating from the London headquarters, have adopted a more critical line, especially as their grassroots activists continue to encounter consumers living on the brunt end of trade liberalization policies.

As such, while Martin Khor and consumer leaders of Latin America and Africa have seen in the World Social Forum the most appropriate arena to air their views, the IOCU leadership has concentrated on the World Economic Forum as the site of its lobbying. Obviously, the two approaches could easily complement one another, because NGOs with as diverse a membership as IOCU's could form the link through which the voices of the poor can be expressed to the ears of the powerful. And it should not be assumed that the consumer movement has not attempted to do this: in fact, its continued thriving existence is a testament to its abilities to respond to the problems of both affluence and necessity. Yet it has even been suggested that the IOCU Executive should adopt contradictory policies: the Northern groups should emphasize free trade while the Southern groups should emphasize the need for protection, not only for individuals but for entire economies, sectors, and regions.

It remains to be seen whether IOCU becomes the first international NGO to adopt a mutually incompatible agenda on world trade in order to be seen to respond to the very different demands of the global North and the global South. Yet this potential split takes us to the very nature of contemporary consumer society: more and better stuff for the individual, or more and better stuff for peoples as a whole. This has been the debate at the heart of the politics of consumption since the end of World War II. Sadly for the consumer movement, it is perhaps now a debate only pertinent to its own internal dynamics. For the world has arguably passed it by. New actors have emerged or been strengthened to more effectively take up the cause of the world's poor and new institutions have been created that allow other organizations—political parties, trade associations, and corporations—to speak on behalf of the consumer. The notion of the consumer promoted in the opposition to the Code of Conduct and in the work of the WTO has been that of the individual shopper. For these consumer advocates, the best defense of the consumer interest has been in the market itself, not in its regulation or in the protection provided by state-funded institutions. And for those who govern world trade, the consumer interest has been seen as one of increasing the number and range of products available to those who can afford it. For those who do not have the money, electricity, water, gas, and transport provided by the privatized companies are simply unavailable. For those who do, they get to choose between the vast array of goods and services now available in the market. But in such an economy, the rights to basic needs and to a healthy environment, and all the other concerns of the global consumer movement and the international community, are eclipsed by the rights to information, redress, and, above all, the one overriding logic of the modern market: choice. The real problem for the consumer movement, then, lies in the very redefinition of consumer society that they had so long attempted to direct and define.

CONCLUSION

The Poverty of Choice

Hand in hand with the rise of consumer society has been an attendant critique of it. It is of no surprise to learn that some of the foremost critics of consumer society have emerged from the country that has promoted the pleasures of consumption more than any other—the United States. Notwithstanding the anti-Americanism of European cultural elites or the new advocates of Asian and alternative value frameworks, some of the most prominent denouncers of commodity capitalism have emerged from the United States itself. There exists a rich tradition of liberal browbeating from the writings of John Kenneth Galbraith to the "crisis of confidence" suffered by Jimmy Carter in his anxieties over the acquisitive materialism of his fellow citizens.[1] The present-day equivalents to these ongoing critiques are those downsizers, voluntary simplicity finders, pursuers of a new American dream, and academics who assert "enough is enough!" or ask, "Do Americans shop too much?"[2] They have castigated us for our shopping sins and, like those late nineteenth-century psychologists who identified the new disease of "kleptomania" among female shoppers at metropolitan department stores, they have come up with a new term to describe our diseased approach to the world of goods: "affluenza."[3]

Of course there are many who are happy with the way of life in the consumer society and many books continue to be written that seek to praise the benefits that commercial goods bring to our life.[4] But largely, it seems, we feel the need to express our guilt over our wealth and affluence. One can actually feel jaded by the persistent and instantaneous pleasures of commodity capitalism. But one can also feel jaded by the ongoing and often woefully unoriginal cultural and moralistic critique of it. The jeremiads of consumer culture have been in existence for several centuries and, while they follow the logic of capitalism in chasing ever more novel things to condemn, there is much that is familiar to them. It seems that we have developed not much further than the "embarrassment" felt by many early seventeenth-century Dutch protestants who had just began to enjoy the riches available from the New World.[5]

However, what is perhaps new to the critique of consumer society is the globalization of the same concerns. For now the problem lies not only in our own spiritual malaise, but in the very real decline in the Earth's physical environment. To the various symptoms we can see in the suffering individual shopper we must now add the potentially catastrophic consequences of environmental degradation that will ultimately be borne by all. Sustainability, in terms of one's own lifestyle but also of the lifestyles and resources of the entire planet, has become the key element of the latest consumer critique, linking the thoughts and actions of the individual to the future direction of all.

The cultural discussion of overindulgence has been augmented by an environmental discussion of the consequences of one's actions on the rainforests, water levels, climate change, and the supply of fossil fuels. The politics of consumption has been transferred from the dilemmas over gas-guzzling Americans to the future consequences of China's rapidly expanding market economy. In the first three months of 2007, China's economy grew at an astounding annual rate of 11.1 percent.[6]

The statistics on China are almost beyond belief. But who knows for how long this will continue? Ownership of such basic consumer durables as washing machines has increased from nearly zero to over one half of all households. Big business has been eager to enter the new market; for example, in the years running up to 2006, KFC has been annually adding nearly 200 restaurants and now has a presence in nearly 300 cities. And, since the 1980s, the number of skyscrapers (over fourteen stories) in Shanghai has increased from one to four thousand. In 2006, China was home to six out of the world's top ten shopping malls.[7] These are exciting and probably nerve-racking times for Chinese shoppers, yet discussion in the West tends to focus on the consequences for the environment when 1.3 billion consumers begin to enjoy similar standards of living to those obtained in North America and Europe.

As with the debate on downsizing, these are very real concerns that inevitably have to be addressed. We constantly seek a truer way of life or are alert to the grimmer reality that could be brought about by our unsustainable lifestyles. The practical outcome for many anxious about the worst effects of commodity capitalism has been one of denial, or at least the espousal of it. It is as though opting out is the only means by which consumer alienation can be overcome and a sense of self retrieved. The consumers who have organized through comparative testing magazines, and in numbers often far exceeding their precursors in earlier consumer groups, have remained, at best, relatively neglected and, at worst, condemned as the acquisitive, value-seeking agents of the ills of present-day materialism.

All this is unfortunate, as it masks the ongoing interactions consumers have had with the society being built in their name. Indeed, many today do embrace uncritically the materialist world around them while many (admittedly a lower number) seek to escape from it. But for the vast majority of consumers, we navigate our way through the world of goods acknowledging both the individual and collective dimensions of consumption. We shop to make ourselves happy, but rarely is consumption purely a selfish act: love, regard, and politics all play a role in our everyday purchasing decisions. In the past, consumers, whether as co-operators, citizens, or labor sympathizers, have shared in a more general debate as to the meaning and future of consumer society. And as it has been repeatedly shown in this book, modern consumer activists associated with comparative testing magazines have had much to contribute to the history of consumer society since the mid-twentieth century. The work of the consumer movement covered in the previous chapters suggests types of interactions richer and more varied than doom or denial. This is not to necessarily praise the work of the consumer activists; it is simply to make the negative point that many cultural critics and academics have been wrong to say that the culture of the commodity has triumphed over all before it and that consumers have acquiesced to this irresistible process. Consumers are a diverse body and they cannot be reduced to a homogenous number of self-gratifying mall dwellers awaiting the zombified numbness of their own inevitable consumption.

What this book has tried to show is the full range of issues affecting us as consumers in the modern world. And this is where the experience of a global consumer movement stands in as a case study for the dilemmas and contradictions facing all of us in our attitudes to, and relationship with, consumer society. Although many of the original leaders of the comparative testing movement were in broad sympathy with the liberal critiques of Galbraith and Nader, they recognized that such issues were irrelevant to the majority of the world's consumers. To be sure, overconsumption and excess were always present in the minds of some consumer activists. But what a focus on these apparently politically moderate yet diverse activists allows us to get at is the other side of the coin of consumer society: the persistence of poverty and the existence of those who do not have access to the basic goods and services that constitute the building blocks of a society that enables its citizens to worry about their own comfort. The issue about consumer society is not just about too much; it is also about too little. What the history of the consumer movement does is highlight the understandable struggles many people have made in the developing world to participate in a quality of life enjoyed only by the privileged. In this sense, to focus now on the problems emanating from China is to address only one side of the debate. The other great geographical region that must also be addressed is that of Africa. Here reside many millions far from ever reaching the future problems of overconsumption. Instead they continue to face the problems of the present: hunger, deprivation, and limited opportunity. Any discussion of consumer society must consider both China and Africa and the organized consumer movement becomes a useful case study precisely because it has done just that.

I

If the problems arising from too much and from too little are the key issues facing everybody living inside and outside of consumer society, then the question to ask of consumer activists is the extent to which they have addressed these concerns. To what extent has the movement been representative of wider social, cultural, and political phenomena? Generally speaking, the modern, organized consumer movement, based originally on the comparative testing of different branded commodities, achieved impressive growth and popularity because it tapped into the wider concerns and aspirations of consumers in two key periods. First, as we saw in chapter 1, it offered an opportunity for a whole new generation of Western consumers, experiencing affluence for the first time in the decades following World War II, a means by which they could increase their confidence in the marketplace and participate in the society being built in their name. Not only private testing organizations, but governments, political parties, trade unions, women's groups, journalists, and co-operatives responded to the concerns of these consumers to ensure that the affluent shopper was afforded some protection in this future-oriented economy. As chapter 2 demonstrated, the types of consumer protection regime initiated varied from one country to the next, but so much were the basic aims of the consumer movement—greater choice for good quality, safe products in an expanding marketplace—listened to by competing political systems that traces of it can be identified in the Soviet bloc. Indeed, historians are now beginning to question the interpretations of unqualified neglect and disregard in the attitude of communist states toward consumers.

Second, as educated, professional, urban elites across the world were inspired by the new forms of protest championed by the likes of Ralph Nader, especially in countries where oppositional politics were severely curtailed, consumer activism took off across the global South. As we saw in chapter 3, organized consumerism here not only responded to the familiar problems faced by minority affluent shoppers, but the concerns over access to the basic necessities of life faced by the poor. Accordingly, Third World consumer politics soon tied itself into an emerging developmental agenda promoted by governments attached to what would become the core principles of the New International Economic Order. The consumer movement, financed by a Western liberal elite committed to the internationalist principles of postwar reconstruction, became an important channel for the concerns of ordinary poor citizens to be fed through into the agendas of the international community. As chapters 4 and 5 demonstrated, this enabled the consumer movement to become a leading spokesbody for civil society organizations all over the world, especially as its campaigning tactics (most crucially, networks) enabled specific issues to be addressed by the UN and its constituent bodies, particularly the Economic and Social Council and the World Health Organization.

Although this consumer movement has subsequently continued to expand, in terms of the numbers of national groups attached to the international federation, and in terms of subscribers to the various private testing bodies and the resources available to it, it can be argued that its relevance to the concerns of the world's consumers as a whole is no longer so apparent or so obvious. In the West, there is something to the claim made by consumer leaders that they have actually achieved much of what they set out to do. Goods are no longer quite so unreliable, dangerous, or erroneously advertised as they were fifty years ago. Basic protections are provided to consumers in the marketplace and the defense of the consumer interest is a perennial claim made by the mainstream political parties of Western governments. The original private testing bodies also operate in their own market of consumer information, in which they now compete with other organizations and across several media in the provision of independent information about goods and services: newspapers, magazines, television, and the Internet are all alternative sources of relatively unbiased advice. Furthermore, the level of state interference provided by the consumer protection reforms of, say, the French government in the early 1980s or the U.S. federal administration in the early 1970s were, perhaps, as far as most consumers wanted to go. Beyond these basic provisions, many consumers, operating on decent incomes and enjoying high standards of living, have been content to be left alone to fend for themselves. The consumer movement has fought for and obtained sufficient levels of security for the average consumer-citizen, and sufficient control and regulatory mechanisms are arguably in place to provide the ordered marketplace in which the risks and consequences of ignorance and naïveté are no longer stacked so high.

In the developing world, the continued relevance of the consumer movement can also be called into question. As in the affluent West, the early consumer groups appealed to, and were staffed by, those educated and informed shoppers who were experiencing decent incomes for the first time. They had been brought up with poverty all around them, were keen to embrace the world of goods, but did not wish to be left alone to fend their way through it, nor allow it to create a society from which whole sections of the community would be excluded. The children of this generation have grown up in countries across Asia having enjoyed the fruits of their parent's labor and in ignorance of the sense of massive social dislocation caused by rapid economic growth. Commentary on these consumers, in the megamalls of Mumbai, Kuala Lumpur, and Seoul, is focused not so much on the consumer associations but on the moral consequences of youth's overconsumption and apparent westernization. Here the argument calls into question the extent to which groups such as the Consumers' Association of Penang can reach out to the young. Some have suggested that across Southeast Asia, people have willingly traded off their rights as democratic citizens and their participation in the political process for ever higher standards of living and seemingly perpetual economic growth. In the embrace of consumer culture in the region's cities, the attention to the poor and the marginal is no longer quite so pertinent to the next generation of liberal middle classes whose parents formed the backbone of developing world consumer activism.[8]

Amid the growth of new civil society concerns in an era of heightened globalization, the relevance of the established consumer movement has also been challenged. There is, again, a generational aspect to this shift. The consumers who led the movement in the global North in the 1950s and 1960s, and in the South in the 1970s and 1980s, owed their intellectual heritage to the classic concerns of liberal internationalism embodied in the economic and social institutions of the United Nations. Within the consumer movement many were replaced during the 1980s as more commercially minded managers were brought in to cope with a tougher marketplace for the provision of consumer information. In turn, these management structures were imposed on the global movement, forcing a reorientation of the movement's policy base back to Western Europe. These original "pioneers" have arguably not been replaced with similar-thinking activists and, in the West, new generations of consumer have emerged outside the comparative testing movement concerned more with ethical, environmental, and fair-trade issues than with market reforms based on value for money and fair dealing. More so than the older consumer movement, their agendas have been driven by climate change and the rights of workers in the developing world. They have not articulated a politics that combines consumer and producer concerns, other than in the philanthropic sense of breaking down barriers between Western consumption and developing world production. But instead of bringing similar types of citizens of North and South together in one organization, fair trade has instead relied on the willingness of the rich to pay a premium on their products to provide better conditions for workers or more sustainable forms of consumption.

New consumer concerns are incredibly diverse, as were those incorporated within IOCU. They include overtly radical left-wing agendas, but also a good deal of faith-based activism that builds on the missionary work of previous generations of religious organizations.[9] In the anti-Americanism of certain anti-globalization protests there is much that is potentially reactionary as it is revolutionary: is the sabotaging of a McDonald's restaurant by the French farmer José Bové the positive action of a committed anti-imperialist, or the defensive measure taken by a provincial malcontent eager to maintain a traditional and insular mode of living?[10] Is the espousal of "slow food" in Italy a radical response to the junk food industry and global big business, or a reactionary measure led by those who wish to defend the vested interests of rural and small-town politics?[11] And, to what extent is the rapidly expanding fair trade movement a politically charged activity or a mechanism by which larger supermarkets can satisfy vague demands for ethical responsibility by channeling consumer demand to a few select grocery items? The answer to all these questions is both. However, the point for us is that no matter how we might answer them, or how they will be answered in the course of the next few years, they are questions that have not been tackled head on by the comparative testing consumer movement. It means, as we saw in the discussion of rights in chapter 7, that the consumer movement has not fully embraced the concerns of a new generation of consumer activist.

What we have in the consumer movement, then, is an organization that achieved many successes up until the 1980s but reached something of a plateau at this point. The reasons for this are due not only to the moderate nature of the rights-based agenda but to the tactical defeats it suffered against a new anti-regulatory agenda eager to prevent consumer protection making any further inroads into the running of the global economy. Nevertheless, for all these pointers to the partial marginalization of the consumer movement, there is evidence that it will continue to maintain its presence in the economy and in politics, especially as markets expand and develop in countries such as China and across continents such as Africa. Indeed, there is something intrinsically banal and ordinary about consumption and the politics that develop around it.

Certainly consumption lends itself to spectacular interventions by consumers, especially by resistors to the perceived excesses of capitalism, by those who join forces in high profile boycott movements, and by any of those who use consumption as the point of focus of wider ideological battles. They include those Nazi sympathizers who chose not to shop at Jewish-owned stores, those Gandhian-inspired Indian nationalists who purchased only home-spun cloth, and those civil rights campaigners who bought only from firms that did not adopt segregationist employment policies. But the everyday stuff of consumption—bread, milk, water, and rice—remain intrinsically banal, as do the politics of everyday life that emerge from it. In the modern consumer movement there has been precisely such an ordinary form of politics. The consumer movement has deliberately sought to transcend the party political divide to focus on issues, which might appear trivial to other social activists but which have nevertheless had important consequences for being a consumer in the market and a citizen in the public sector. These issues are unlikely to go away and will ensure that consumer organizing is still required over adulteration, weights and measures legislation, unfair contract terms, trade descriptions, and the right to receive compensation for being unfairly treated.[12]

All these are subjects unlikely to provoke revolutionary movements of millions of people that will lead the world to a new, utopian future. But they are likely to keep concerning consumers, especially whenever there is a food crisis, be it the concerns about mad cow disease, avian flu, or the consequences of biotechnology. Evidence for such a claim can be seen in the relative financial health of consumer movements around the world. Although most have now established good working relationships with their respective governments, the private testers continue to adapt to new market conditions. The total number of subscriptions to all the publications of the U.S. Consumers Union, for instance, tops 7 million, while the campaigning wing of the same organization can draw on the voluntarism of 400,000 activists registered online. The number of subscribers to its website, www.consumerreports.org, is now over 2 million, making it the largest publications-based website in the United States.[13]

In China, where a consumer society is being constructed so quickly and to the concern of so many other consumers around the world, citizens are being increasingly drawn to the political aspects of the problems they face in a changing marketplace. The consumer movement in China was begun as a state initiative and it continues to remain so. It has been viewed cynically as an organization to funnel and contain consumer complaints, yet it has become an important actor in China's embrace of the market. The first consumer association was founded in 1983, followed one year later by the China Consumer Association, based in Beijing. By the mid-1990s, there were over 3,000 connected consumer groups at the provincial and county level, as well as a further reported 45,000 local organizations. The Association claims that the number of all types of consumer organization, supervision, and contact points from the village upward amounts to over 150,000. Notwithstanding the close links the consumer organizations have been forced to maintain with the government, such figures point to a genuine grassroots demand for some form of consumer protection and assistance. By 2000, the number of complaints the China Consumer Association was receiving was approaching one million a year (by the end of 2001, it had dealt with a total of over 6 million). Because of such discontent, the State Administration for Industry and Commerce set up the "12135" consumer complaints hotline. Within five years, this had managed to intervene on behalf of two and a quarter million complaints and is now, after the emergency services, one of the most popular phone numbers in the country.[14]

The politics of the everyday is, by definition, a permanent and perennial concern. So long as citizens live in societies structured around consumption, it simply will be the case that their everyday experiences as consumers will provoke their own thoughts about the market. These, in turn, will inform their political beliefs. Consumer movements are therefore likely to be an important intermediary between the citizen and the state in channeling these complaints, demands, and desires. It means the banality of our myriad interactions with goods, from purchase to use to gift, will continue to inform an everyday politics; that is, the unglamorous world of intricate market regulation that offers little in the way of an idealized vision of the future or emancipatory politics. What is certain is that, especially in economies undergoing rapid change, there will always be a role for either grassroots consumer movements or state institutions created to intervene on the consumer's behalf. Whether these consumer organizations will exist independently of, or merge with, new organizations of consumer concern in the spheres of fair trade, ethics, and the environment, is a matter for the organizations themselves. The consumer groups studied in this book can either rest on their laurels and continue to focus on value-for-money or embrace wholeheartedly these new sets of concerns. To maintain their widest relevance, they may be forced along the latter path, though there are likely to be differences from one country to the next and we will only know as these decisions are made and played out in the near future.

II

What we are really discussing, then, is not so much the relative rise or decline of the organized consumer movement, but the ongoing dilemmas facing all of us in consumer society. In this book, the consumer movement has served as both proxy and causal factor for the exploration of these tensions, contradictions, and competing agendas: between the interests of the global North and the global South; between the interests of the rich and the poor; and the extent to which consumption is to be regarded as an individual activity or a collective aspect of life tied in to broader debates about social welfare and the standard of living. What has been traced is the relative prominence given to either side of these dilemmas by not only the consumer movement but by politicians, bureaucrats, national governments, organized business, and civil society actors.

Here it is important to emphasize two interrelated themes. First, the consumer movement's own operating rationale has tied it to an agenda that has made it difficult to address some of the bigger structural issues facing consumers in global markets. Rights—especially economic, social, and cultural—can only take a movement so far. They can easily be made to support the current organization of the world, so central are they to the main tenets of liberal democratic thought. But, more pertinently to our case study, they can often be contradictory, so the relative weighting given to some rights over others becomes crucial. For various reasons, as we saw in chapter 7, the consumer movement chose to emphasize the right to basic needs in the 1970s and 1980s, and the more individualistic rights to choice and information thereafter. This is not to deny that basic needs agendas might not again become more prominent, especially as the consumer movement continues to expand in Africa, but it is to make the point that in dealing with the dilemmas of consumption the global movement has reoriented its vision of consumer society around choice rather than access.

Second, and running in parallel to these developments, is a narrative of defeat, as outlined in chapter 6. In the backlash against regulation and protection since the late 1970s, the consumer movement has been outgunned in its various battles with organized business. The outcome of these struggles has been the containment of the consumer movement into legislative remedies concerning safety, information, representation, and redress for the individual, about which it has been allowed to obtain many advances. But in the sphere of its other campaigns—basic needs, the environment, the alleviation from suffering for the world's poor consumers, the establishment of a principle that global trade ought to be accountable to citizens, either as workers or consumers—the consumer movement has suffered repeated setbacks. It has resulted in a redefinition of both the consumer and consumer society. Long gone are the efforts to raise the standards of living of everybody who so pervaded Cold War rhetoric. Gone too are any meaningful mechanisms for the regulation of trade as originally envisioned by those UN observers of the activities of multinational corporations in Chile and South Africa back in the 1970s. Instead the dominant definition of consumer society promoted by the institutions of global governance has been the impoverished notion of choice. Choice has been important, not only to all consumers but to the consumer movement especially, but when it is heralded above all other consumer considerations, then it offers a particular view of consumer society that fails to respond to what have been the key demands of the consumer movement since the 1950s.

Protection, information, redress, and safety all remain important considerations for the consumer movement, for ordinary consumers, and for governments at the national and international level. But the one underlying lowest common denominator, promoted by consumers and business alike (if with varying emphasis), is that of choice. The logic of choice as the guiding principle for the citizens of consumer society is that whole areas of policy are excluded from the politics of consumption. Basic needs and poverty result in not only a discussion of value for money, but of the systems of provision that enable the consumer to have access to key goods and services. If we are to couch such issues in the language of choice, then ultimately the choices are between, for instance, a privatized or a nationalized form of provision of basic utilities, or a regulated or unregulated market for dangerous chemicals and pharmaceuticals. But this is not a choice that has been made available to consumers. Instead choice has been posited as something that occurs at the end of the economic process and, in this sense, choice is solely about preference. The consumer is expected to make a decision about goods or services supplied to him or her by manufacturers and retailers. He or she is not expected to have much say in how these goods are made, how they are distributed, the environmental consequences of their production, the equality of provisioning, or the absence of choice for those who cannot afford them. If choice had been the only guiding principle of the consumer movement, they would have found it very difficult to move beyond comparative testing to those issues, which inspired consumer activists across the developing world. It is for this reason that Anwar Fazal and the Penang office of IOCU was so keen to exclude the right to choice in the list of the movement's eight consumer rights.

Furthermore, the logic of choice creates barriers between those who can and those who cannot participate in consumer society. Choice is the privilege of the rich, of those who can afford to choose: it is a luxury available only to those who exist inside the consumer society. Choice is not so relevant to those who do not have the income to participate: for the poor, access, participation, and provision are far more important consumer requirements. At the global level, what choice does is create a division between those inside and those outside consumer society, mirroring the polarized divisions that current sociologists and geographers claim exist between those inside and outside the network society of our globalized world. In this regard, this is where the consumer society of the twenty-first century can be seen as fundamentally different from that being constructed after World War II. For all the inequities of the capitalist consumer democracy, it remained, in potential, a truly mass phenomenon. Whether through trickle down effects, social democratic redistributive justice, or communist collectivism, all were ultimately to participate. Some of these concerns are today still relevant to policy makers and planners around the world. But what an emphasis on choice does is make one blind to the issues of those who are not able to make choices, those who are unable to participate in consumer society at all.

To return to our familiar themes: choice becomes most relevant to the debates about too much; it is less relevant to the debates about too little. As consumer society took hold in China, choice has become a key concern of those millions of citizens who complain to the consumer hotline. And for those liberals guiltily surveying all their possessions, choice becomes their personal nightmare and they advocate their freedom not to choose. But for those living in poverty across the developing world, and especially in Africa, choice is commodity capitalism's cruel joke. While underclasses undoubtedly exist across both the developed and the developing world, entire regions now consist of consumer society's underclass: those citizens disenfranchised from the defining term of consumer society, choice.

In contrast to the debates about too much stuff, the statistics on too little are equally compelling. Annual reports published by the World Bank and the United Nations Development Programme (UNDP) demonstrate that while developing world countries as a whole have experienced higher rates of economic growth than those of the developed nations, the gap between the extremes—the poorest twenty countries and the richest twenty countries—has grown. Polarization, as much as convergence, is a key feature of contemporary global society. Whole areas of the world are simply being left behind amid a general trend of increasing rates of growth. From 1987 to 1998 the number of people living on less than a dollar a day stayed pretty much at the same figure of 1.2 billion. Population growth has meant there has been an overall proportionate decline but not in sub-Saharan Africa. In the system of world trade, liberalization has clearly been a cause: from 1991 to 1996 Africa's share of world agricultural exports decreased from 9 percent to just 3 percent. The gains of the new world order are not being experienced by people living in clearly demarcated regions. Indeed things can be argued to be getting worse. Taking the UNDP's Human Development Index (HDI) as a measure, for instance, the wellbeing of people living in certain countries has declined. Of the eighteen countries whose HDI measure actually worsened from 1990 to 2003, thirteen were in Africa, while the rest were former Soviet republics. Moreover, economic forecasts do not provoke much cause for optimism for these regions. The share of the world's poverty is increasingly likely to be borne by Africans and the gaps in indexes such as child poverty, infant mortality, and education are likely to increase.[15]

For consumers in Africa the primary concerns are not the same as those of Chinese consumers ringing the hotline to complain about the harm they have experienced as individual shoppers. Instead, they are the more collective considerations about the access to basic goods and services, issues that for so long had been at the center of the global consumer movement's campaign agenda. African consumers have therefore organized on the basis of having access to consumer society and their work has been oriented toward understanding the impact of trade agreements on their economies. Moreover, some of their actions provide the perfect allegories for the structure of global consumer culture and the politics of the network society. Privatized utility companies have excluded those who cannot afford to pay their charges, literally by disconnecting them from their supply. Consumer protestors have worked to reconnect ordinary families to such basic consumer services, as in the case of the South African Soweto Electricity Crisis Committee, which has illegally reconnected the electricity supply of people who had been cut off for non-payment of bills. They, and others like them campaigning on water and fuel supply, have worked on very different consumer principles than that of choice. They have opposed the commodification of what they regard as public goods and have argued that the supply of water and electricity, as well as education and transport, are basic human rights that ought to exist beyond the market according to principles of social justice.[16]

Similarly, the organized consumer movement has addressed these issues and it is in Africa that the basic needs agenda of consumer activism has been most relevant and most forcibly articulated. Indeed, the growth of consumerism as a movement since the 1990s has taken place most dramatically in Africa. This has been undertaken in a rather controlled manner, the headquarters in London refusing to grant the same degree of policy independence as enjoyed by the regional office for Asia in Penang in the 1970s and 1980s. Yet as African activists attend global consumer gatherings in ever larger numbers, the challenge for the consumer movement will be to incorporate the concerns of the poor into the primary campaign initiatives emanating from London. For instance, sustainability has become a key agenda, for both the consumer movement and civil society as a whole. To what extent sustainability refers to the problems of too much and to what extent it incorporates the problems arising from too little remains to be seen.

In 2008 these issues appear as questions separate from the debate about consumer society. Unlike in the 1950s, when consumption was so clearly coupled to the social welfare agendas of postwar planners, and unlike in the 1980s when a more radical IOCU brought so many social justice issues under the umbrella of political consumerism, the problems of the poor and the disadvantaged are understood in terms distinct from debates about consumption. As such, while the problems of having too much remain central to the critique of consumer society, the problems of having too little are divorced from it. Certainly this is due to the emphasis on choice and to the direct assault on collective forms of consumption witnessed over the last quarter century. But it is also due to the consumer movement's own unwillingness to engage with other civil society groups. Although it continues to address questions of poverty, other, better-financed, more vociferous, and more well known NGOs have forcibly located debates about poverty within the language of trade justice, international aid, and developmentalism. The consumer movement has taken a backseat on debates about economic and social justice and, as such, it has contributed to the decoupling of poverty and standards of living from debates about the future direction of consumer society.

What is clear is that the consumer movement now finds itself operating within a global consumer society that has made sharp distinctions between those who can afford to exercise choice and those who cannot. Even if the consumer movement were able to coherently bring together the consumer politics of the poor and the affluent, it would find itself operating within a global economy that does not attempt to bridge the differences in quite the same way as it used to. Choice creates insurmountable barriers to the democratic universalism of the world of goods, the consequences of which can be profound. Analysts of the network society have argued that the social and political identities formed in the modern globalized era are those that work as communal sites of resistance by those excluded from the global flows of capital, information, and wealth.[17] They tend to be based on an oppositional logic of little relevance to liberal capitalist democracy and can often be fundamentalist in character: nationalism, religious extremism, and identities based on ethnic and territorial particularities. For those connected to the social movements based on such identities they make perfect sense, so distant are they from the networks of power, finance, and information. In terms of consumer society, they manifest themselves in anti-American and anti-Western sentiments, seen no better than in the battle, as one commentator has put it, of Jihad versus McWorld.[18]

For the post-World War II planners of the consumer democracy, Europe was to escape the retreat into the barbarities of interwar fascism and ideology through the promises of plenty. Consumer society, despite its critics condemning its shallow and ephemeral nature, was understood to be the best means to ensure the West did not return to the destructive chaos of 1939 to 1945.[19] As economies expanded throughout the 1950s and 1960s, and as insecure shoppers asked for guidance in the marketplace, states could afford, but were also willing, to provide basic protections for consumers as consumption was so central to modern forms of citizenship. The world recession of the 1970s meant many governments began to regard regulation as a luxury, which industry could ill afford. The consumer interest came to be stripped of its more political demands for entitlement, leaving choice as the core element of the consumer identity. Especially for those neoconservative defenders of the free market, so long as choice was presented to the public, the market would take care of the rest.

Yet, as growing inequalities have demonstrated, choice has done little to respond to the needs of the poor. Choice remains a privilege of the comfortable: as the defining logic of consumer society it has nothing to say for those who cannot afford choice. The world, therefore, becomes divided between those who can exercise choice and those who cannot. But what is left for the excluded and what promises are made of the future for their present sacrifices remains ever obscured. So long as a route out of poverty and an ability to enjoy the benefits of choice is not provided, the more it is likely that the identities forged in opposition to the fully networked, global consumer society will remain attractive.

The consumer movement finds itself operating within a system of governance, which does not pay heed to all of its demands, and it remains open to questions as to whether the movement will continue in the future to place equal emphasis on all consumers' competing demands. Certainly the consumer movement has not rolled over as the market empire has triumphed over everything put before it. It has continued to have its say, but it is only through the language of choice that its voice is really heard. Instead much of the critique of consumer society now emerges out of the anxieties over too much choice. The problems of excess have come to dominate how many in the West cope with their own angst about their personal levels of consumption. Put in another way, their fears over what will happen when millions of others around the world have as much as they do have come to trouble their environmental consciences. What has been excluded from the discussion of consumer society—and what has been so central to consumer politics as put forward by the comparative testing movement since then 1950s, and the consumer co-operative movement before then—are the problems arising from too little. Both issues must be addressed if consumer society is to be of benefit to all, but so pervasive has the moralistic critique of consumption been that when it comes to discussing poverty, the actions and demands of consumers in Africa, Asia, and Latin America have not been acknowledged. Instead, the basic needs agenda and all that goes with it—redistributive justice, concepts of entitlements and social and economic rights, the alleviation of poverty, and the challenge to international economic development—has been pushed to one side or treated as a poverty issue distinct from the debates about the meaning and future of consumer society. For consumer activists, there remains much more to consumer society than just shopping. But so long as the impoverished language of choice continues to define our consuming identities and societies, then it is unlikely that these other issues will be raised.

NOTES

Introduction: The Wealth of Access

1. Steven C. Clemons, "George Bush: To Beat Terror, Keep Shopping," *The Washington Note*, October 12, 2004, http://www.thewashingtonnote.com/archives/000112.php; Jill Vardy and Chris Wattie, "Shopping Is Patriotic, Leaders Say," *National Post (Canada)*, September 28, 2001, http://www.commondreams.org/headlines01/0929–04.htm.

2. Neil McKendrick, John Brewer, and J. H. Plumb, *The Birth of a Consumer Society: The Commercialisation of Eighteenth-Century England* (London: Europa, 1982).

3. Daniel Roche, *A History of Everyday Things: The Birth of Consumption in France, 1600– 1800* (Cambridge: Cambridge University Press, 2000); T. H. Breen, *The Marketplace of Revolution: How Consumer Politics Shaped American Independence* (Oxford: Oxford University Press, 2004); Evelyn Welch, *Shopping in the Renaissance: Consumer Cultures in Italy 1400–1600* (New Haven, CT: Yale University Press, 2005).

4. Neil McKendrick, John Brewer, and J. H. Plumb, *The Birth of a Consumer Society: The Commercialisation of Eighteenth-Century England* (London: Europa, 1982), 1.

5. Karl Polanyi, *The Great Transformation* (London: Beacon, 2002 [1944]); see also Victoria de Grazia, *Irresistible Empire: America's Advance through Twentieth-Century Europe* (Cambridge, MA: Belknap Press of Harvard University Press, 2005), 18.

6. Erik Langlinay, "Consommation et ravitaillement en France durant la Première Guerre mondiale, 1914–1920" (Consumption and supply in France during the First World War, 1914–1920), in *Au nom du consommateur: consommation et politique en Europe et aux États-Unis au xxe siècle (In the Name of the Consumer: Consumption and Politics in Europe and America in the Twentieth Century)*, ed. Alain Chatriot, Marie-Emmanuelle Chessel, and Matthew Hilton (Paris: La Découverte, 2005), 29–44; Alain Chatriot, Marie-Emmanuelle Chessel, and Matthew Hilton, "Introduction," in *The Expert Consumer: Associations and Professionals in Consumer Society*, ed. Alain Chatriot, Marie-Emmanuelle Chessel, and Matthew Hilton(Aldershot: Ashgate, 2006), 1– 18.

7. Anwar Fazal, "The Citizen As Consumer," (Tun Hussein Onn Memorial Lecture, Kuala Lumpur, Malaysia, October 16, 1993), available at http://anwarfazal.net.

8. Alan Hunt, "The Governance of Consumption: Sumptuary Laws and Shifting Forms of Regulation," *Economy and Society* 25, no. 3 (1996): 410–27; Alan Hunt, *Governance of the Consuming Passions: A History of Sumptuary Regulation* (London: Macmillan, 1996).

9. Martin Daunton, "The Material Politics of Natural Monopoly: Consuming Gas in Victorian Britain," in *The Politics of Consumption: Material Culture and Citizenship in Europe and America,* ed. Martin Daunton and Matthew Hilton (Oxford: Berg, 2001), 69–88; John Burnett, *Liquid Pleasures: A Social History of Drinks in Modern Britain* (London: Routledge, 1999), 13–22; Frank Trentmann and Vanessa Taylor, "From Users to Consumers: Water Politics in Nineteenth-Century London," in *The Making of the Consumer: Knowledge, Power and Identity in the Modern World,* ed. Frank Trentmann (Oxford: Berg, 2006), 53–79.

10. Peter A Koolmees, "Veterinarians, Abattoirs and the Urban Meat Supply in the Netherlands, 1860–1940," in *The Landscape of Food: The Food Relationship of Town and Country in Modern Times,* ed. Marjatta Hietala and Tanja Vahtikari (Helsinki: Finnish Literature Society, 2003), 17–29; Michael French and Jim Phillips, *Cheated Not Poisoned? Food Regulation in the United Kingdom, 1875–1938* (Manchester: Manchester University Press, 2000); J. Burnett, *Plenty and Want: A Social History of Diet in England from 1815 to the Present Day* (London: Nelson, 1966), ch. 5, 72–90; Jim Phillips and Micahel French, "Adulteration and Food Law, 1899–1939," *Twentieth-Century British History* 9, no. 3 (1998): 350–69.

11. Alessandro Stanziani, "Alimentation et santé sous le IIIe RépUblique" (Food and health during the Third Republic), in *Au nom du consommateur,* ed. Chatriot *et al.,* 135–49.

12. Lorine Swainston Goodwin, *The Pure Food, Drink, and Drug Crusaders, 1879–1914* (Jefferson, NC: McFarland, 1999); Mitchell Okun, *Fair Play in the Marketplace: The First Battle for Pure Food and Drugs* (DeKalb: Northern Illinois University Press, 1986).

13. Mark V. Nadel, *The Politics of Consumer Protection* (New York: Bobbs-Merrill, 1971); Upton Sinclair, *The Jungle* (Harmondsworth: Penguin, 1965 [1906]);

14. J. Barzmann, "Entre l'émeute, la manifestation et la concertation: la 'crise de la vie chère' de l'été 1919 au Havre" (Between riot demonstration and consultation: the 'crisis of the cost of living' in the summer of 1919 in Havre), *Le Mouvement Social* 170 (January-March 1995): 61–84; T. Stovall, "Du vieux et du neuf: économie morale et militantisme ouvrier dans les luttes contre la vie chère à Paris en 1919" (The old and the new: moral economny and labour militancy in the battle against the cost of living in Paris in 1919), *Le Mouvement Social* 170 (January-March 1995): 85–113; Langlinay, "Consommation et ravitaillement."

15. Hilton, *Consumerism in Twentieth-Century Britain,* ch. 2, 53–78; Frank Trentmann, "Bread, Milk and Democracy: Consumption and Citizenship in Britain, c. 1903–51," in *The Politics of Consumption,* ed. Daunton and Hilton, 129–63.

16. Joëlle Droux, "The Enemy Within: Food, Nutrition Experts and Consumers in French-Speaking Switzerland, 1900–1946," in *Expert Consumer,* ed. Chatriot *et al.,* 89–104.

17. Daniel Horowitz, *The Anxieties of Affluence: Critiques of American Consumer Culture, 1939–1979* (Boston: University of Massachusetts Press, 2004), ch. 1, 20–47; Lizabeth Cohen, *A Consumers' Republic: The Politics of Mass Consumption in Postwar America* (New York: Alfred A. Knopf, 2003), ch. 2, 62–109; Meg Jacobs, "'How About Some Meat?': The Office of Price Administration, Consumption Politics and State Building from the Bottom Up, 1941–1946," *Journal of American History* 34, no. 3 (1997): 910–41; Lucy Black Creighton, *Pretenders to the Throne: The Consumer Movement in the United States* (Lexington, MA: D. C. Heath, 1976), 30.

18. Zweiniger-Bargielowska, *Austerity in Britain.*

19. P. Miller and N. Rose, "Mobilizing the Consumer: Assembling the Subject of Consumption," *Theory, Culture and Society* 14, no. 1 (1997): 1–36; N. Rose, *Inventing Our Selves: Psychology, Power, and Personhood* (Cambridge: Cambridge University Press, 1996).

20. Donald Winch, "The Problematic Status of the Consumer in Orthodox Economic Thought," in *The Making of the Consumer,* ed. Trentmann, 31–51; Matthew Hilton, "The Legacy of Luxury: Moralities of Consumption Since the Eighteenth Century," *Journal of Consumer Culture* 4, no. 1 (2004): 101–23; Frank Ackerman, "Foundations of Economic Theories of Consumption: Overview Essay," in *The Consumer Society,* ed. Goodwin *et al.,* 149–58; Kathleen G. Donohue, *Freedom from Want: American Liberalism and the Idea of the Consumer* (Baltimore: Johns Hopkins University Press, 2003); Charles F. McGovern, *Sold American: Consumption and Citizenship, 1890–1940* (Chapel Hill: University of North Carolina Press, 2006).

21. Roland Marchand, *Advertising the American Dream: Making Way for Modernity, 1920–1940* (Berkley: University of California Press, 1985); Patricia Johnston, *Real Fantasies: Edward Steichen's Advertising Photography* (Berkeley: University of California Press, 1997) Pamela Walker Laird, *Advertising Progress: American Business and the Rise of Consumer Marketing* (Baltimore: Johns Hopkins University Press, 1998); Christoph Conrad, "Observer les consommateurs. Études

de marché et histoire de la consommation en Allemagne, des années 1930 aux années 1960" (Observing the consumers: Market research and the history of consumption in Germany from the 1930s to the 1960s), *Le Mouvement Social* 206 (2004): 17–39; Stuart Ewen, *Captains of Consciousness: Advertising and the Social Roots of the Consumer Culture* (New York: McGraw-Hill, 1976); Stuart Ewen, *PR! A Social History Spin* (New York: Basic Books, 1997).

22. De Grazia, *Irresistible Empire*, pp. 213, 231.

23. Lizabeth Cohen, "'The New Deal State and the Making of Citizen Consumers," in *Getting and Spending*, ed. Strasser et al., 111–25; Persia Campbell, *Consumer Representation in the New Deal* (New York: Columbia University Press, 1940).

24. Cohen, *A Consumers' Republic;* Creighton, *Pretenders to the Throne,* pp. 25–26; Jacobs, *Pocketbook Politics;* Donohue, *Freedom From Want;* Campbell, *Consumer Representation in the New Deal.*

25. Reagin, "Comparing Apples and Oranges," 254.

26. Hartmut Berghoff, "Enticement and Deprivation: The Regulation of Consumption in Pre-War Nazi Germany," in *Politics of Consumption,* ed. Daunton and Hilton, 165–84.

27. Victoria de Grazia, "Nationalising Women: The Competition Between Fascist and Commercial Cultural Models in Mussolini's Italy", in *The Sex of Things: Gender and Consumption in Historical Perspective,* ed. Victoria de Grazia and Ellen Furlough (Berkeley: University of California Press, 1996), 337–58.

28. Karl Gerth, *China Made: Consumer Culture and the Creation of the Nation* (Cambridge, MA: Harvard University Press, 2003); Michael Edson Robinson, *Cultural Nationalism in Colonial Korea, 1920–1925* (Seattle: University of Washington Press, 1988); Laura C. Nelson, *Status, Gender and Consumer Nationalism in South Korea* (New York: Columbia University Press, 2000); C. A. Bayly, "The Origins of Swadeshi (Home Industry): Cloth and Indian Society, 1700–1930', in *The Social Life of Things: Commodities in Cultural Perspective,* ed. Arjun Appadurai (Cambridge: Cambridge University Press, 1986), 285–322; Lisa N. Trivedi, "Visually Mapping the 'Nation': Swadeshi Politics in Nationalist India, 1920–1930," *Journal of Asian Studies* 62, no. 1 (2003): 11–41; Manu Goswami, "From *Swadeshi* to *Swaraj*: Nation, Economy, Territory in colonial South Asia, 1870 to 1907," *Comparative Studies in Society and History* 40, no. 4 (1998): 609–36.

29. Cohen, *Consumers' Republic,* 113.

30. Régis Boulat, "Jean Fourastié at la naissance de la societé de consummation en France" (Jean Fourastié and the birth of consumer society in France), in *Au nom du consommateur,* edx. Chatriot et al., 98–114; de Grazia, *Irresistible Empire,* 365.

31. Katherine Pence, "Shopping for an 'Economic Miracle': Gendered Politics of Consumer Citizenship in Divided Germany", in *Expert Consumer,* ed. Chatriot et al.,105–20; Mark Landsman, *Dictatorship and Demand: The Politics of Consumerism in East Germany* (Cambridge: Harvard University Press, 2005), 7.

32. De Grazia, *Irresistible Empire,* 344.

33. Greg Castill, "Domesticating the Cold War: Household Consumption as Propaganda in Marshall Plan Germany," *Journal of Contemporary History* 40, no. 2 (2005): 261–88; Susan E. Reid, "The Khrushchev Kitchen: Domesticating the Scientific-Technological Revolution", *Journal of Contemporary History* 40, no. 2 (2005): 289–316; Susan E. Reid, 'Cold War in the Kitchen: Gender and the De-Stalinisation of Consumer Taste in the Soviet Union Under Khrushchev," *Slavic Review* 61, no. 2 (2002): 211–52; Ruth Oldenziel and Karin Zachmann, *Cold War Politics of the Kitchen: Americanisation, Technological Transfer and European Consumer Society in the Twentieth Century* (forthcoming); de Grazia, *Irresistible Empire,* 454–55; Elaine Tyler May, *Homeward Bound: American Families in the Cold War Era* (New York: Basic Books, 1988); Anne Norton, *Republic of Signs: Liberal Theory and American Popular Culture* (Chicago: University of Chicago Press, 1993).

34. Martin Purvis, "Societies of Consumers and Consumer Societies: Co-Operation, Consumption and Politics in Britain and Continental Europe, c. 1850–1920," *Journal of Historical Geography* 24, no. 2 (1998): 147–69; Ellen Furlough and Carl Strikwerda, eds., *Consumers Against Capitalism? Consumer Co-Operation in Europe, North America and Japan, 1840–1990* (Lanham, MD: Rowman and Littlefield, 1999); Ellen Furlough, *Consumer Co-Operation in Modern France: The Politics of Consumption* (Ithaca, NY: Cornell University Press, 1991); Michael Prinz, *Brot und Dividende: Konsumvereine in Deutschland und England vor 1914* (Bread and Divided: Co-operatives in Germany and England before 1914) (Göttingen: Vandenhoeck und Ruprecht, 1996); Peter Gurney, *Co-Operative Culture and the Politics of Consumption in England, c. 1870–1930* (Man-

chester: Manchester University Press, 1996); Johnston Birchall, *The International Co-Operative Movement* (Manchester: Manchester University Press, 1997).

35. Helen Sorenson, *The Consumer Movement: What It Is and What It Means* (New York: Harper and Brothers, 1941); Dana Frank, *Purchasing Power: Consumer Organising, Gender, and the Seattle Labour Movement, 1919–1929* (Cambridge: Cambridge University Press, 1994).

36. Meg Jacobs, *Pocketbook Politics: Economic Citizenship in Twentieth-Century America* (Princeton: Princeton University Press, 2005); Lawrence B. Glickman, *A Living Wage: American Workers and the Making of Consumer Society* (Ithaca, NY: Cornell University Press, 1997); Lawrence Glickman, "Workers of the World, Consume: Ira Steward and the Origins of Labour Consumerism," *International Labour and Working Class History* 52 (1997): 72–86.

37. Julien Vincent, "The Moral Expertise of the British Consumer, c. 1900: A Debate Between the Christian Social Union and the Webbs," in *Expert Consumer,* ed. Chatriot *et al.,* 37–51.

38. Maud Nathan, *The Story of an Epoch-Making Movement* (London: Heinemann, 1926), 23–24; Kathryn Kish Sklar, "The Consumer's White Label Campaign of the National Consumer's League, 1898–1918," in *Getting and Spending: European and American Consumer Societies in the Twentieth Century,* ed. Susan Strasser, Charles McGovern, and Matthias Judt (Cambridge: Cambridge University Press, 1998), 17–35; Warren Breckman, "Disciplining Consumption: The Debate on Luxury in Wilhelmine Germany, 1890–1914," *Journal of Social History* 24, no. 3 (1991): 485–505; Kathryn Kish Sklar, *Florence Kelley and the Nation's Work: The Rise of Women's Political Culture, 1830–1900* (New Haven: Yale University Press, 1995); Louis Lee Athey, "The Consumers' Leagues and Social Reform, 1890–1923," Ph.D. diss., University of Delaware, 1965; Dorothy Rose Blumberg, *Florence Kelley: The Making of a Social Pioneer* (New York: Augustus M. Kelley, 1966); Mary Dublin Keyserling, "The First National Consumers Organisation: The National Consumers' League," in *Consumer Activists: They Made a Difference,* ed. Erma Angevine, (Mount Vernon, NY: Consumers Union, 1982), 343–60; Marie-Emmanuelle Chessel, "Consommation, action sociale et engagement public fin de siècle, des États-Unis à la France" (Consumption, social action, and public engagement in the United States and France at the turn of the twentieth century), in *Au nom du consommateur,* ed. Chatriot *et al.,* 247–61; Marie-Emmanuelle Chessel, "Consommation et réforme sociale à la Belle Époque: la conference internationale des ligues socials d'acheteurs en 1908" (Consumption and social reform during the 'Beautiful Era': the international conference of consumers' leagues), *Sciences de la Societé* 62 (2004) 45–67.

39. Tracey Deutsch, "Des consommatrices américaines très engages, du New Deal à la guerre froide," in *Au nom du consommateur,* ed. Chatriot *et al.,* 361–75; Lawrence B. Glickman, "'Make Lisle the Style": The Politics of Fashion in the Japanese Silk Boycott, 1937–1940," *Journal of Social History* 38, no. 3 (2005) 573–608; Landon R. Y. Storrs, "Red Scare Politics and the Suppression of Popular Front Feminism: The Loyalty Investigation of Mary Dublin Keyserling," *Journal of American History* 90, no. 2 (2003) 491–524; Wendy A. Wiedenhoft, "Consumer Tactics as 'Weapons': Black Lists, Union Labels, and the American Federation of Labor," *Journal of Consumer Culture* 6, no. 2 (2006): 261–85.

40. Monroe Friedman, "American Consumer Boycotts in Response to Rising Food Prices: Housewives' Protests at the Grassroots Level," *Journal of Consumer Policy* 18, no. 1 (1995): 55–72; Monroe Friedman, "Consumer Boycotts in the United States, 1970–1980: Contemporary Events in Historical Perspective", *Journal of Consumer Affairs* 19, no. 1 (1985): 96–117.

41. Belinda J. Davis, *Home Fires Burning: Food, Politics and Everyday Life in World War I Berlin* (Chapel Hill: University Of North Carolina Press, 2000); Dana Frank, "Housewives, Socialists and the Politics of Food: The 1917 New York Cost-of-Living Protests," *Feminist Studies* 11, no. 2 (1985): 255–85; J. Smart, "Feminists, Food and the Fair Price: The Cost of Living Demonstrations in Melbourne, August-September 1917," *Labour History* 50 (1986): 113–31; T. Kaplan, "Female Consciousness and Collective Action: The Case of Barcelona, 1910–1918," *Signs* 7, no. 3 (1982) 545–66; Christoph Nonn, *Verbraucherprotest und Parteiensystem im wilhelminischen Deutschland* (Düsseldorf: Droste, 1996); Jacobs, *Pocketbook Politics,* pp. 53–65; L. T. Lih, *Bread and Authority in Russia, 1914–1921* (Berkeley: University of California Press, 1990).

42. Cheryl Greenberg, "Don't Buy Where You Can't Work," in *Consumer Society in American History: A Reader,* ed. Lawrence B. Glickman (Ithaca, NY: Cornell University Press, 1999), 241–73; David Vogel, "Tracing the American Roots of the Political Consumerism Movement," in *Politics, Products and Markets: Exploring Political Consumerism Past and Present,* ed. Michele Micheletti, Andreas Follesdal, and Dietlind Stolle (London: Transaction, 2004), 83–100.

43. Matthew Anderson, "The History of the Fair Trade Movement in Britain," ongoing PhD research, University of Birmingham.

44. Kenneth Dameron, "The Consumer Movement," *Harvard Business Review* 18 (1939) 271–89 (271).

45. Steven M. Buechler, *Social Movements in Advanced Capitalism: The Political Economy and Cultural Construction of Social Activism* (Oxford: Oxford University Press, 2000); Hanspeter Kriesi, Ruud Koopmans, Ian Willem Dyvendak, and Marco G. Giugni, *New Social Movements in Western Europe: A Comparative Analysis* (Minneapolis: University of Minnesota Press, 1995); Enrique Laraña, Hank Johnston, and Joseph R. Gusfield, eds., *New Social Movements: From Ideology to Identity* (Philadelphia: Temple University Press, 1994); David A. Snow, Sarah A. Soule, and Hanspeter Kriesi, eds., *The Blackwell Companion to Social Movements* (Oxford: Blackwell, 2004); Donatella della Porta and Mario Diani, *Social Movements: An Introduction* (Oxford: Blackwell, 1999); David S. Meyer and Sidney Tarrow, eds., *The Social Movement Society: Contentious Politics for a New Century* (Lanham, MD: Rowman and Littlefield, 1998); Doug McAdam, John D. McCarthy, and Mayer N. Zald, eds., *Comparative Perspective on Social Movements: Political Opportunities, Mobilizing Structures, and Cultural Framings* (Cambridge: Cambridge University Press, 1996); Sidney Tarrow, ed., *Power in Movement: Social Movement and Contentious Politics* (Cambridge: Cambridge University Press, 1998); Nick Thomas, *Protest Movements in 1960s West Germany: A Social History of Dissent and Democracy* (Oxford: Berg, 2003); Paul Byrne, *Social Movements in Britain* (London: Routledge, 1997).

46. Mark Kurlansky, *1968: The Year That Rocked the World* (London: Vintage, 2005); Geoff Eley, *Forging Democracy: The History of the Left in Europe, 1850–2000* (Oxford: Oxford University Press, 2002).

47. Helene Curtis and Mimi Sanderson, *The Unsung Sixties: Memoirs of Social Innovation* (London: Whiting and Birch, 2004).

48. Ronald T. Libby, *Eco-Wars: Political Campaigns and Social Movements* (New York: Columbia University Press, 1998); Kevin Mattson, "Goodbye to All That," *American Prospect,* 28 March 2005, available at http://www.prospect.org/cs/articles?articleId=9389.

49. Thomas Frank, *One Market Under God: Extreme Capitalism, Market Populism and the End of Economic Democracy* (London: Secker and Warburh, 2001); Joseph Heath and Andrew Potter, *Nation of Rebels: Why Counterculture Became Consumer Culture* (New York: HarperCollins, 2004).

50. Alain Touraine, *Beyond Neoliberalism* (Cambridge: Polity, 2001).

51. David Harvey, *Spaces of Capital: Towards a Critical Geography* (Edinburgh: Edinburgh University Press, 2001), 193.

52. Daniel Horowitz, *The Anxieties of Affluence: Critiques of American Consumer Culture, 1939–1979* (Amherst: University of Massachusetts Press, 2004). See also Horowitz's similar analysis for the immediately preceding period, *The Morality of Spending: Attitudes Towards the Consumer Society in America 1875–1940* (Baltimore: Johns Hopkins University Press, 1985) and Gary Cross, *Time and Money: The Making of Consumer Culture* (London: Routledge, 1993). The list of critiques of consumerism is possibly endless, though it is a critique that still finds frequent voice in the works of U.S. liberal intelligentsia; see, for example, Juliet B. Schor, *The Overspent American: Why We Want What We Don't Need* (New York: HarperPerennial, 1999).

53. Avner Offer, *The Challenge of Affluence: Self-Control and Well-Being in the United States and Britain Since 1950* (Oxford: Oxford University Press, 2006).

54. Juliet B. Schor, *Do Americans Shop Too Much?* (Boston: Beacon Press, 2000); Robert Frank, *Luxury Fever: Money and Happiness in an Era of Excess* (Princeton: Princeton University Press, 1999); Daniel Doherty and Amitai Etzioni, eds., *Voluntary Simplicity: Responding to Consumer Culture* (Oxford: Rowman and Littlefield, 2003); Kalle Lasn, *Culture Jam: The Uncooling of America* (New York: Eagle Brook, 1999); John de Graaf, David Wann, and Thomas H. Naylor, *Affluenza: The All-Consuming Epidemic* (San Francisco: Berrett-Koehler, 2001); http://www.newdream.org.

Chapter 1. The Fear of Fortune: The Uneasy Consumer in an Age of Affluence

1. Archives of International Organisation of Consumers Unions (hereafter IOCU Archives), Kuala Lumpur, Malaysia: Box 68: Personalities: File G21.24: "Biographical Sketch of Colston E. Warne," n.d.; Leland J. Gordon, "Colston Estey Warne: Mr. Consumer," *Journal of Consumer Affairs* 4, no. 2 (1970): 89–92; Barbara Warne Newell, "Tribute to Colston E. Warne," *Journal of Consumer Affairs* 14, no. 1 (1980): 1–8.

2. IOCU Archives: Box 68: File G21.8: Colston E. Warne, "Statement on International Orga-

nisation of Consumers Unions," 17 September 1965; Colston E. Warne, "New Initiatives on the International Consumer Front," in *The Consumer Movement: Lectures by Colston E. Warne*, ed. Richard L. D. Morse (Manhattan, KS: Family Economics Trust Press, 1993), 195–221.

3. Consumers Union Archive, Yonkers, New York (hereafter CU Archive): Colston E. Warne Papers: Box 27: Folder 1: IOCU: Letter from André Romieu to Colston E. Warne, 6 January 1956.

4. Colston E. Warne, "The International Growth of Consumer Protective Organisations," memorandum to United Nations, 18 January 1956, in *IOCU on Record: A Documentary History of the International Organization of Consumers Unions, 1960–1990*, ed. Foo Gaik Sim (Yonkers, NY: Consumers Union, 1991), 5; CU Archive: Box 27: Folder 1: Colston E. Warne, "Summary of Discussion with K. M. Wright, United Nations," 15 January 1956.

5. CU Archive: Box 27: Folder 1: Letters from Ray & Dorothy Goodman to Colston E. Warne, 9 November 1955 and 6 February 1956; Matthew Hilton, *Consumerism in Twentieth-Century Britain: The Search for a Historical Movement* (Cambridge: Cambridge University Press, 2003).

6. Victoria de Grazia, *Irresistible Empire: America's Advance Through Twentieth-Century Europe* (Cambridge, MA: Belknap Press for Harvard University Press, 2005); Sheryl Kroen, "La magie des objets, le Plan Marshall et l'instauration d'une démocratie de consommateurs" (The magic of objects, the Marshall Plan and the introduction of consumer democracy), in *Au nom du consommateur: consommation et politique en Europe et aux États-Unis au xxe siècle (In the Name of the Consumer: Consumption and Politics in Europe and America in the Twentieth Century)*, eds. Alain Chatriot, Marie-Emmanuelle Chessel, and Matthew Hilton (Paris: La Découverte, 2005), 80–97; Sheryl Kroen, "Negotiations with the American Way: The Consumer and the Social Contract in Post-War Europe," in *Consuming Cultures, Global Perspective: Historical Trajectories, Transnational Exchanges*, ed. John Brewer and Frank Trentmann (Oxford: Berg, 2006), 251–77; David W. Ellwood, *Rebuilding Europe: Western Europe, America and Postwar Reconstruction* (London: Longman, 1992); Michael J. Hogan, *The Marshall Plan: America, Britain and the Reconstruction of Western Europe, 1947–1952* (Cambridge: Cambridge University Press, 1989); Alan S. Milward, *The Reconstruction of Western Europe, 1945–51* (London: Routledge, 1987).

7. Hans B. Thorelli and Sarah V. Thorelli, *Consumer Information Systems and Consumer Policy* (Cambridge, MA: Ballinger, 1977), 234.

8. Ibid., 340.

9. Hans B. Thorelli and Sarah V. Thorelli, *Consumer Information Handbook: Europe and North America* (New York: Praeger, 1974), xxiv.

10. Tony Judt, *Postwar: A History of Europe Since 1945* (London: Heinemann, 2005), 338.

11. For a case study on the diffusion of products in different national contexts, see Sue Bowden and Avner Offer, "Household Appliances and the Use of Time: The United States and Britain Since the 1920s" *Economic History Review* 47, no. 4 (1994): 725–48.

12. Judt, *Postwar*, 338.

13. De Grazia, *Irresistible Empire*, 361.

14. Sean O'Connell, *The Car in British Society: Class, Gender and Motoring, 1896–1939* (Manchester, UK: Manchester University Press, 1998); Daniel Miller, ed., *Car Cultures* (Oxford: Berg, 2001).

15. Robert O. Hermann, "The Consumer Movement in Historical Perspective," *Paper no. 88, Department of Agricultural Economics and Rural Sociology, Pennsylvania State University* (February 1970); Alvin Wolf, *American Consumers: Is Their Anger Justified?* (Englewood Cliffs, NJ: Prentice-Hall, 1977), 81; Robert N. Mayer, *The Consumer Movement: Guardians of the Marketplace* (Boston: Twayne, 1989), 154. This literature and periodization has largely been set out by writers emerging from within the consumer movement itself. However, later generations of historians have largely followed this model; see, for instance, the periodization found in Lizabeth Cohen, *A Consumers' Republic: The Politics of Mass Consumption in Postwar America* (New York: Alfred A. Knopf, 2003).

16. Stuart Chase, *The Challenge of Waste* (New York: League for Industrial Democracy, 1922); Stuart Chase, *The Tragedy of Waste* (New York: Macmillan, 1925).

17. Stuart Chase and Frederick J. Schlink, *Your Money's Worth: A Study in the Waste of the Consumer's Dollar* (New York, Macmillan, 1927).

18. Arthur Kallet and Frederick J. Schlink, *100,000,000 Guinea Pigs: Dangers in Everyday Foods, Drugs and Cosmetics* (New York: Vanguard Press, 1932); Mayer, *Consumer Movement*, 20–22; Norman Isaac Silber, *Test and Protest: The Influence of Consumers Union* (New York: Holmes & Meier, 1983), 15–19; *A Guide to the Records of Consumers' Research, Inc., Special*

Collections and University Archives, Rutgers University Library, http://www2.scc.rutgers.edu/ead/manuscripts/consumers_introf.html; Helen Sorenson, *The Consumer Movement: What It Is and What It Means* (New York: Harper & Brothers, 1941); Sybil Schwartz, "The Genesis and Growth of the First Consumer Testing Organization," M.A. thesis, Columbia University, 1971; Colston E. Warne, "Ideological Foundations of the Consumer Movement," in *Consumer Movement,* ed. Morse, 1–15; Charles Francis McGovern, "Sold American: Inventing the Consumer, 1890–1940," Ph.D. diss., Harvard University, 1993; Peter L. Spencer, "Consumers' Research," in *Encyclopaedia of the Consumer Movement,* ed. S. Brobeck, R. N. Mayer and R. O. Herrmann (Santa Barbara: ABC-CLIO, 1997), 179–82; Peter Samson, "The Emergence of the Consumer Interest in America, 1870–1930," Ph.D. diss., University of Chicago, 1980.

19. CU Archive: Box 251: "Consumers' Research: Strike Material," Folder: Songs.

20. Lawrence B. Glickman, "The Strike in the Temple of Consumption: Consumer Activism and Twentieth-Century American Political Culture," *Journal of American History* 88, no. 1 (2001): 99–128; Silber, *Test and Protest,* 21–23; "50 Years Ago," *Consumer Reports* 51, no. 1 (January 1986): 8–9 and 51, no. 2 (February 1986): 76–80; Rhoda H. Karpatkin, "Memo to Members," *Consumer Reports* 51, no. 5 (May 1986): 283–84.

21. *Consumer Reports* 1, no. 1 (May 1936): 1.

22. IOCU Archives: Box 68: File G21.3: Colston E. Warne, "The Genesis of the Consumer Movement: The Ideological Roots of Consumerism," 24 January 1976, 11; Cohen, *Consumers' Republic,* 131.

23. Silber, *Test and Protest,* 28; Richard E. Kelley, "Consumers Union of the United States: A Social Evaluation," B.A. thesis, Amherst College, 1943, 67

24. Norman D. Katz, "Consumers Union: The Movement and the Magazine, 1936–1957," Ph.D. diss., Rutgers University, 1977; Sorenson, *The Consumer Movement;* Monte Florman, *Testing: Behind the Scenes at Consumer Reports, 1936–1986* (Mount Vernon, NY: Consumers Union, 1986); Michele Ruffat, *Le Contre-Pouvoir Consommateur aux États Unis* (Paris: Presses Universitaires de France, 1987).

25. CU Archive: Box 240: Alan Goodman, "CU History: The First Twenty Years," unpublished manuscript; Jeanine Gilmartin, "An Historical Analysis of the Growth of the National Consumer Movement in the United States from 1947 to 1967," Ph.D. diss., Georgetown University, 1969.

26. J. Epstein, *The Early Days of Consumers' Association: Interviews with CA's Founders and Those Who Carried on Their Work* (London: Consumers' Association, 1989), 27 (Michael Young); *Which?* 1, no. 2 (1958): 3; Consumers' Association Archive, London: Box 30: "*First Annual Report, 1957–1958,*" 2; Hilton, *Consumerism in Twentieth-Century Britain,* 210

27. CU Archive: Florence Mason Papers (hereafter FM): Box 3: Folder 13: Colston E. Warne, "France," 1959; CU Archive: Persia Campbell Papers (hereafter PC): Box 18: Folder "Reports by Florence Mason, 1961–1973": Report by Florence Mason to Colston Warne on Press Conference of Union Fédérale de la Consommation, 22 December 1961; Box 20: Folder "French Organisations': Notes on Union Fédérale de la Consommation," Union Fédérale de la Consommation, *Les Consommateurs,* publicity pamphlet, no date; Institiut National de la Consommation, "Le consumérisme en France: structures associatives et publiques," *INC HEBDO,* 1135, 19 September 2000; Luc Joossens, "Le mouvement des consommateurs en France: les essays comparatives comme moyen d'information," Mémoire présenté en vue d'obtenir une maîtrise en sociologie," Université de Paris (La Sorbonne), 1972.

28. CU Archive: FM: Box 9: Folder 8: Colston E. Warne, "Netherlands," 1959; Joop Koopman, "Dutch Consumer Movement," in *Encyclopaedia of the Consumer Movement,* ed. Brobeck et al., 227–32.

29. CU Archive: FM: Box 1: Folder 10: Colston E. Warne, "Belgium," October 1959.

30. David Halpin, *Consumers' Choice: Twenty-Five Years of the Australian Consumers' Association* (Marrickville, NSW: Australian Consumers' Association, 1984), 7; IOCU Archive: Box 68: File G21.5: Colston E. Warne, "An Assessment of Consumer Protective Efforts in Israel, Pakistan, India, Japan, Australia and New Zealand," report to the Cultural Exchange Program of the US. Department of State, 23 July 1962, 11.

31. Foo Gaik Sim, *IOCU on Record: A Documentary History of the International Organisation of Consumers Unions, 1960–1990* (Yonkers, NY: Consumers Union, 1991), 27.

32. CU Archive: FM: Box 3: Folder 16: Colston E. Warne, "Germany," 1959; CU Archive: PC: Box 18: Folder "Reports by Florence Mason, 1961–1973": Report by Florence Mason to Colston Warne on Germany, 13 February 1962; Report by Florence Mason to Colston Warne on Arbeits-

gemeinschaft der Verbraucherbände, 18 February 1962; IOCU Archive: Box 68: File G21.4: Colstone E. Warne, "A Cursory Survey of European Consumer Movements," 1959; Gunnar Trumbull, *Consumer Capitalism: Politics, Product Markets and Firm Strategy in France and Germany* (Ithaca, NY: Cornell University Press, 2006).

33. IOCU Archive: Colston Warne Papers (hereafter CW): Box "IOCU Affairs" [not catalogued]: Folder "IOCU, pre-1960": Organisation for European Economic Co-operation, "Meeting of Representatives of Consumers' Associations: Note on the Associations Represented," 10–11 October 1957, 6.

34. CU Archive: FM: Box 24: Folder 2: Consumers Union, *A Digest of the Leading Consumer Movements of the World* (Mount Vernon, NY: Consumers Union, 1962), 17; CU Archive: PC: Box 16: Folder "IOCU Biennial Conference, 1966": Israel Consumers' Association, *Consumers Tribune,* Tel Aviv, 1966.

35. CU Archive: FM: Box 24: Folder 2: Consumers Union, *A Digest,* 17; Thorelli and Thorelli, *Consumer Information Handbook,* 291

36. Iselin Theien, "Shopping for the 'People's Home': Consumer Planning in Norway and Sweden After the Second World War," in *The Expert Consumer: Associations and Professionals in Consumer Society.* ed. Alain Chatriot, Marie-Emmanuelle Chessel, and Matthew Hilton (Aldershot: Ashgate, 2006), 137–50; CU Archive: FM: Box 24: Folder 2: Consumers Union, *A Digest,* 21; Thorelli and Thorelli, *Consumer Information Handbook,* 333–41.

37. CU Archive: FM: Box 24: Folder 2: Consumers Union, *A Digest,* 22; Consumers International, *Balancing the Scales, Part I: Consumer Protection in Sweden and the United Kingdom* (London: Consumers International, 1995); Kai Blomqvist, "Swedish Consumer Movement," in *Encyclopaedia of the Consumer Movement,* ed. Brobeck et al., 544–47.

38. CU Archive: FM: Box 24: Folder 2: Consumers Union, *A Digest,* 7.

39. CU Archive: FM: Box 2: Folder 6: Canadian Association of Consumers, publicity leaflet, c. 1959; Helen J. Morningstar, "The Consumers' Association of Canada: The History of an Effective Organisation," *Canadian Business Review* 4, no. 4 (1977): 30–33.

40. Thorelli and Thorelli, *Consumer Information Systems,* 237.

41. Gary Herrigel and Jonathan Zeitlin, eds. *Americanization and Its Limits: Reworking US Technology and Management in Post-War Europe and Japan* (Oxford: Oxford University Press, 2000); Richard F. Kuisel, *Seducing the French: The Dilemma of Americanization* (Berkeley: University of California Press, 1993); Kipping Matthias and Ove Bjarnar, eds., *The Americanisation of European Business: The Marshall Plan and the Transfer of US Management Models* (London: Routledge, 1998); Richard Pells, *Not Like Us. How Europeans Loved, Hated, and Transformed American Culture Since World War Two* (New York: Basic Books, 1997).

42. De Grazia, *Irresistible Empire.*

43. Charles Maier, "The Politics of Productivity: Foundations of American Economic Policy After World War Two," in *Between Power and Plenty: Foreign Economic Policies of Advanced Industrial Estates,* ed. P. J. Katzenstein (Madison: University of Wisconsin Press, 1978); Bent Boel, *The European Productivity Agency and Transatlantic Relations 1953–1961* (Copenhagen: Museum Tusculanum Press, 2001).

44. IOCU Archive: CW: Box "IOCU Affairs" [not catalogued]: Folder "IOCU, pre-1960": Organisation for European Economic Co-operation, "Meeting of Representatives of Consumers' Associations: Note on the Associations Represented," 10–11 October 1957, 4

45. IOCU Archive: Box 68: File G21.8: Colston E. Warne, "Statement Friday Evening on International Organisation of Consumers Unions," 17 September 1965, 4.

46. CU Archive: CW: Box 27: Folder 1, "IOCU": Colston E. Warne, "Summary of Discussion with K. M. Wright, United Nations," 15 January 1956; Letter from André Romieu to Colston E Warne, 6 January 1956; Colston E Warne, "The International Growth of Consumer Protective Agencies," memo to K. M. Knight, Charles Hogan and Leslie Woodcock, United Nations, 18 January 1956; Letter from Ray and Dorry Goodman to Colston E. Warne, 9 November 1955.

47. CU Archive: CW: Box 39: Folder 6, "England": Letter from Raymond and Dorothy Goodman to Colston E. Warne, 6 February 1956; Letter from Michael Young to Colston E. Warne, 7 January 1957; Letter from Colston E Warne to Michael Young, 15 October 1957; Consumers' Association, *Thirty Years of Which?: Consumers' Association, 1957–1987* (London: Consumers' Association, 1987), 6; S. Franks, "Selling Consumer Protection: Competitive Strategies of the Consumers' Association, 1957–1990," MPhil thesis, University of Oxford, 2000, 26; E. Roberts, *Which? 25: Consumers' Association, 1957–1982* (London: Consumers' Association, 1982), 14; Epstein, *Interviews,* 28 (Michael Young).

48. IOCU Archive: Box 68: File G21.5: Warne, "An Assessment . . . ," 4; CU Archive: CW: Box 27: Folder 1 "IOCU": Letter from Colston E Warne to Barney Rowan, European Productivity Agency, Organisation for European Economic Co-operation, 20 December 1958.

49. Warne, "New Initiatives," 206; IOCU Archive: Box 1: File A2, "Early Years, 1960–1970": A2.7: Letter from J. H. van Veen, Executive Sec, IOCU, to Council Members, 15 October 1964.

50. Thorelli and Thorelli, *Consumer Information System*, 120, 255; CU Archive: FM: Box 9: Folder 8: Letter from Elizabeth A. Schadee, *Consumentenbond*, to W. Masters, Consumers Union, 1 September 1959; Letter from Elizabeth A. Schadee to Colston Warne, January 1960.

51. Colston E. Warne, "Consumer Organisations: An International Conference?" *Cartel: Review of Monopoly Developments and Consumer Protection* 17, vol. 1 (January 1957): 2–5.

52. CU Archive: PC: Box 16: Folder "IOCU": William R. Pabst, "A Summary of Interviews with Leaders of European Consumer Movements," October 1959; CU Archive: CW: Box 27: Folder 1: Letter from Colston E. Warne to European consumer organisations [multiple copies], 15 October 1958.

53. CU Archive: CW: Box 27: Folder 1: International Chamber of Commerce Commission on Distribution, "Existence and Activities of Consumers' Unions in the Various Countries," November 1959.

54. CU Archive: CW: Box 27: Folder 1: Letter from Barney Rowan, European Productivity Agency, Organisation for European Economic Co-operation to Colston E Warne, 22 April 1959.

55. Thorelli and Thorelli, *Consumer Information Handbook,* 252.

56. CU Archive: FM: Box 24: Folder 2: Consumers Union, *A Digest,* 7.

57. CU Archive: FM: Box 1: Folder 10: Colstone E. Warne, "Belgium," October 1959.

58. CU Archive: FM: Box 24: Folder 2: Consumers Union, *A Digest,* 23; Thorelli and Thorelli, Consumer Information Handbook, 37–52.

59. Thorelli and Thorelli, *Consumer Information Handbook,* 74–75.

60. Jonah Goldstein, "Public Interest Groups and Public Policy: The Case of the Consumers' Association of Canada," *Canadian Journal of Political Science* 12, no. 1 (1979): 144.

61. Luc Bihl, *Consommateur: Défends-toi!* (Consumer: Defend Yourself!)(Paris: Denoël, 1976), 102.

62. Trumbull, *Consumer Capitalism,* 109.

63. Helen Curtis and M. Sanderson, *A Review of the National Federation of Consumer Groups* (London: Consumers' Asoociation, 1992); George Smith, *The Consumer Interest* (London: Gollancz, 1982), 291; Hilton, *Consumerism in Twentieth-Century Britain,* 214–15.

64. Trumbull, *Consumer Capitalism,* 53.

65. Gunnar Trumbull, "Contested Ideas of the Consumer: National Strategies of Product Market Regulation in France and Germany," European University Institute Working Papers no. RSC 2000/1, 14, http://www.iue.it/RSCAS/WP-Texts/00_01.pdf.

66. CU Archive: Box 68: File G21.23: Warne, "Genesis of Consumer Movement," 5; Glickman, "The Strike in the Temple of Consumption."

67. Kathleen G. Donohue, *Freedom from Want: American Liberalism and the Idea of the Consumer* (Baltimore: Johns Hopkins University Press, 2003), 175–85; Sorenson, *The Consumer Movement;* Mayer, *The Consumer Movement,* 20–22; Charles McGovern, *Sold American: Consumption and Citizenship, 1890–1945* (Chapel Hill: University of North Carolina Press, 2006); Persia Campbell, *Consumer Protection in the New Deal* (New York: Columbia University Press, 1940); Glickman, "Strike in the Temple of Consumption."

68. Cited in Eugene R. Beem, "Consumer Financed Testing and Rating Agencies in the United States," Ph.D. diss., University of Pennsylvania, 1974, 190.

69. Charles McGovern, "Consumption and Citizenship in the United States, 1900–1940," in *Getting and Spending: European and American Consumer Societies in the Twentieth Century,* ed. Susan Strasser, Charles McGovern, and Matthias Judt (Cambridge: Cambridge University Press, 1998), 51.

70. Pierre Bourdieu, *Distinction: A Social Critique of the Judgement of Taste* (London: Routledge and Kegan Paul, 1986).

71. Edward Steichen has been noted in particular for his reification of the good; see P. Johnston, *Real Fantasies: Edward Steichen's Advertising Photography* (Berkeley: University of California Press, 1997).

72. *Consumer Reports* 1, no. 1 (1936): 8.

73. *Que Choisir* (December 1961), 5; *Que Choisir* (December 1962), 1; *Que Choisir* (October 1963), 1.

74. *Consumentengids* 9, no. 3 (March 1961); *Konsument* 2 (October/November 1961); *Test* (January 1969); *Choice* 1 (April 1960); *Consumer* 1, no. 3 (Winter 1960).

75. *Test Achats* 18 (September 1962): 3.

76. Vance Packard, *The Hidden Persuaders* (Harmondsworth: Penguin, 1960 [1957]); John Kenneth Galbraith, *The Affluent Society* (Harmondsworth: Penguin, 1971 [1958]); Upton Sinclair, *The Jungle* (Harmondsworth: Penguin, 1965 [1906]); Thorstein Veblen, *The Theory of the Leisure Class* (Harmondsworth: Penguin, 1979 [1899]); Thorstein Veblen, *The Engineers and the Price System* (New York: Kelley, 1965 [1921]); Edward Bellamy, *Looking Backward* (Mineola, NY: Dover Publications, 1996 [1888]); CU Archive: Box 68: File G21.23: Warne, "Genesis of Consumer Movement," 3.

77. Emile Zola, *The Ladies Paradise* (Oxford: Oxford University Press, 1998 [1883]).

78. Donohue, *Freedom from Want*, 5, 171–73; Robert B. Westbrook, "Tribune of the technostructure: The Popular Economics of Stuart Chase," *American Quarterly* 32, no. 4, (1980): 387–408.

79. George Orwell, *The Lion and the Unicorn* (Harmondsworth: Penguin, 1982 [1941]), 113.

80. CU Archive: PC; Box 20: Folder "French Organisations: Union Fédérale de la Consommation, "Liste des members actifs de l'association," March 1964.

81. Hilton, *Consumerism in Twentieth-Century Britain;* Lawrence Black, "*Which?*craft in Post-War Britain: The Consumers' Association and the Politics of Affluence," *Albion* 36, no. 1 (2004): 52–82.

82. "Henry Epstein," *International Consumer,* 4 (1968): 8; IOCU Archive: Box 60: Personalities: File G3: Henry Epstein: Roland H. Thorp, "Dr. Henry Epstein," 1968; Halpin, *Consumers' Choice.*

83. Hacob S. Ziegel, "Consumerism in Canada," *Canadian Banker* 78, no. 6 (1971): 4–6; Robert E. Olley, "The Canadian Consumer Movement: Basis and Objectives," *Canadian Business Review* 4, no. 4 (1977): 26–29; James O'Grady, "Protecting Consumers Around the World," *Canadian Business Review* 5, no. 2 (1978): 16–19.

84. Consumentenbond, *Declaration of Consumer Principles* (The Hague: Consumentenbond, 2003), 9, 15.

85. Janet Upton (former secretary of the National Federation of Consumer Groups), interview by the author, 3 April 2002; CU Archive: PC: Box 12: Folder "Correspondence and Memoranda": Letter from Dorothy Goodman to Persia Campbell, 28 January 1962; Box 18: Folder "Reports and Speeches, 1969–1973": André Romieu, "An Assessment of the Relationship of the Consumer Movement to the Government in France," no date.

86. Hans B. Thorelli, Helmut Becker, and Jack Engledow, *The Information Seekers: An International Study of Consumer Information and Advertising Image* (Cambridge, MA: Ballinger, 1975), xxii; Thorelli and Thorelli, *Information Systems,* 21.

87. CU Archive: Board of Directors: Box 94 "Reports to the Board": Folder 1: Benson and Benson, *Survey of Present and Former Subscribers to Consumer Reports* (Princeton, NJ: Benson & Benson, February 1970); Kelley, "Consumers Union," 68.

88. Jacques C. Bourgeois and James G. Barnes, "Viability and Profile of the Consumerist Segment," *Journal of Consumer Research* 5, no. 4 (1979): 217–28; Joy Parr and Gunilla Ekberg, "Mrs. Consumer and Mr. Keynes in Postwar Canada and Sweden," *Gender and History* 8, no. 2 (1996): 212–30.

89. Thorelli and Thorelli, *Consumer Information Systems,* 256.

90. Hans B. Thorelli, "Concentration of Information Power Among Consumers," *Journal of Marketing Research* 8, no. 4 (1971): 427–32; Gallup Poll, *Enquiry into Which?* (London: Social Surveys, 1962); Hans B. Thorelli, Helmut Becker, and Jack Engledow, *The Information Seekers: An International Study of Consumer Information and Advertising Image* (Cambridge, MA: Ballinger, 1975), 95–130, 165–98.

91. Commission of the European Communities, *European Consumers: What Do They Care About? What Do They Want? How Well-Informed Are They?* (Brussels: Commission of the European Communities, 1976).

92. Cohen, *Consumers' Republic,* 359. Gary Cross has similarly written of CU that it has "tended to reinforce both the individualism and the materialism of American consumption" (Gary Cross, *An All-Consuming Century: Why Commercialism Won in Modern America* [New York: Columbia University Press, 2000]), 135.

93. Lucy Black Creighton, *Pretenders to the Throne: The Consumer Movement in the United States* (Lexington, MA: D. C. Heath, 1976).

94. Silber, *Test and Protest,* 126.

95. Adrien Sapiro and Hacques Lendreve, "On the Consumer Front in France, Japan, Sweden, UK and the USA," *European Business* 38 (1973): 43–52.

96. Richard L. D. Morse, "The Consumer Movement: A Middle Class Movement," in *Proceedings of the 27th Annual Conference, The Consumer Movement as Related to Other Social Movements,* American Council on Consumer Interests, Columbia, MO (April, 1981), 160–64.

97. See especially the literature of the Frankfurt school: Max Horkeimer and Theodor W. Adorno, *Dialectic of Enlightenment* (London: Allen Lane, 1973 [1944]); Theodor W. Adorno, *The Culture Industry: Selected Essays on Mass Culture* (London: Routledge, 1991); Herbert Marcuse, *One-Dimensional Man: The Ideology of Industrial Society* (London: Routledge and Kegan Paul, 1994); Jürgen Habermas, *The Structural Transformation of the Public Sphere: An Inquiry into a Category of Bourgeois Society* (Cambridge: Polity, 1989).

98. Guy Debord, *Society of the Spectacle* (London: Black and Red, 1977 [1967]); Roland Barthes, "The Rhetoric of the Image," in *Image-Music Text* (London: Fontana, 1977), 32–51; Jean Baudrillard, *The Consumer Society: Myths and Structures* (London: Sage, 1998); Mike Featherstone, *Consumer Culture and Postmodernism* (London: Sage, 1991); Stuart Ewen, *All Consuming Images: The Politics of Style in Contemporary Culture* (New York: Basic Books, 1988).

99. Dick Hebdige, "Object as Image: The Italian Scooter Cycle," *Block* 5 (1981): 44–64; Dick Hebdige, *Subculture: The Meaning of Style* (London: Routledge, 1979); Stuart Hall and Tony Jefferson, eds., *Resistance Through Rituals: Youth Subcultures in Post-War Britain* (London: Hutchinson, 1976).

100. A. Giddens, *Runaway World: How Globalisation Is Reshaping Our Lives* (London: Profile, 2002); Zygmunt Bauman, *Globalization: The Human Consequences* (Cambridge: Polity, 1998); Manuel Castells, *The Information Age: Economy, Society and Culture. Vol. 1. The Rise of the Network Society* (Oxford: Blackwell, 2000); Manuel Castells, *The Information Age: Economy, Society and Culture, Vol. 3. End of Millenium* (Oxford: Blackwell, 2000); David Harvey, *Spaces of Hope* (Edinburgh: Edinburgh University Press, 2000); Leslie Sklair, *The Transnational Capitalist Class* (Oxford: Blackwell, 2001); Scott Lash and John Urry, *The End of Organised Capitalism* (Cambridge: Polity Press, 1987).

101. Marx, *Capital, Vol. 1,* E. Kamenka, ed., *The Portable Karl Marx* (Harmondsworth: Penguin, 1930), 446–50.

Chapter 2. Cold War Shoppers: Consumerism As State Project

1. Gunnar Trumbull, *Consumer Capitalism: Politics, Product Markets and Firm Strategy in France and Germany* (Ithaca, NY: Cornell University Press, 2006), 8–9.

2. Matthew Hilton, *Consumerism in Twentieth-Century Britain: The Search for a Historical Movement* (Cambridge: Cambridge University Press); Richard Flickinger, "The Comparative Politics of Agenda Setting: The Emergence of Consumer Protection as a Public Policy Issue in Britain and the United States," *Policy Studies Review* 2, no. 3 (1983): 429–44.

3. Robert N. Mayer, *The Consumer Movement: Guardians of the Marketplace* (Boston: Twayne, 1989), 29, 101; James E. Finch, "A History of the Consumer Movement in the United States: Its Literature and Legislation," *Journal of Consumer Studies and Home Economics* 9, no. 1 (1985): 23–33.

4. Iselin Theien, "Shopping for the 'People's Home': Consumer Planning in Norway and Sweden After the Second World War," in *The Expert Consumer: Associations and Professionals in Consumer Society,* ed. Alain Chatriot, Marie-Emmanuelle Chessel, and Matthew Hilton (Aldershot: Ashgate, 2006), 137–50; Victor A Pestoff, "Third Sector and Co-operative Services: an Alternative to Privatisation," *Journal of Consumer Policy,* 15, no. 1 (1992): 21–45.

5. Hilton, *Consumerism in Twentieth-Century Britain;* Peter Gurney, "The Battle of the Consumer in Postwar Britain," *Journal of Modern History,* 77 (December 2005): 956–87; Hans B. Thorelli and Sarah V. Thorelli, *Consumer Information Handbook: Europe and North America* (New York: Praeger, 1974), 89, 235.

6. E. H. Hondius, *Consumer Legislation in the Netherlands: A Study Prepared for the EC Commission* (Wokingham, UK: Van Nostrand Reinhold, 1980), 7; Thorelli and Thorelli, *Consumer Information Handbook,* 67–68, 217, 316.

7. Magda Fahrni, "Counting the Costs of Living: Gender, Citizenship and a Politics of Prices in 1940s Montreal," *Canadian Historical Review* 83, no. 4 (2002): 483–504.

8. Patricia L. Maclachlan, *Consumer Politics in Postwar Japan: The Institutional Boundaries of Citizen Activism* (New York: Columbia University Press, 2002), 62–65; Maki Shōhei, "The Postwar Consumer Movement: Its Emergence from a Movement of Women," *Japan Quarterly* 23, no. 2 (1976): 135–39.

9. M. Fontaine and T. Bourgoignie, *Consumer Legislation in Belgium and Luxemburg: A Study Prepared for the EC Commission* (Wokingham, UK: Van Nostrand Reinhold, 1982), 4; Luc Bihl, *Consommateur: Défends-toi!* (Consumer: Defend Yourself!) (Paris: Denoël, 1976); Hilton, *Consumerism in Twentieth-Century Britain,* ch. 6.

10. Thorelli and Thorelli, *Consumer Information Handbook,* 301, 313, 320.

11. Monroe Friedman, "Local Consumer Organisations: Their Problems, Prospects and a Proposal," *Journal of Consumer Affairs* 2, no. 2 (1968): 205–11; Stephen Brobeck and Nishimura Glenn, *Statistical Report on the Grassroots Consumer Movement* (Washington, DC: Consumer Federation of America, 1983). Simply to record the number of organizations falling within the definition of organized consumerism would require a book in itself: see, for instance, Loree Bykerk and Ardith Maney, *US Consumer Interest Groups: Institutional Profiles* (Westport, CT: Greenwood, 1995).

12. David Vogel, "Consumer Protection and Protectionism in Japan," *Journal of Japanese Studies* 18, no. 1 (1992): 119–154; Shōhei, "The Postwar Consumer Movement"; Maurine A. Kirkpatrick, "Consumerism and Japan's New Citizen Politics," *Asian Survey* 15, no. 3 (1975): 235–49; M. Imai, "Japanese Consumer Movement," in *Encyclopaedia of the Consumer Movement,* ed. S. Brobeck, R. N. Mayer, and R. O. Herrmann (Santa Barbara: ABC-CLIO, 1997), 341–42.

13. Luc Bihl, *Consommateur: Défends-toi!*

14. Trumbull, *Consumer Capitalism,* 52–53.

15. Council of Europe, *The Collective Interests of Consumers: Measures Permitting Agencies or Associations to Ensure the Legal Protection of the Collective Interests of Consumers in Member States of the Council of Europe* (Strasbourg: Council of Europe, 1980); Commission of the European Communities, *Consumer Advice Services in the European Community: A Directory* (London: National Consumer Council, 1992); European Free Trade Association, *Synoptic Table on Consumer Policy in EFTA Countries* (Geneva: EFTA, 1990); Committee on Consumer Policy, *Consumer Policy During the Past Ten Years: Main Developments and Prospects* (Paris: OECD, 1983).

16. Gunnar Trumbull, "National Varieties of Consumerism," *Jahrbuch für Wirtschaftsgeschichte* 1 (2006): 77–93.

17. Theien, "Shopping for the 'People's Home'"; Adrien Sapiro and Hacques Lendreve, "On the Consumer Front in France, Japan, Sweden, UK and the USA," *European Business* 38 (1973): 43–52; P. Söiland, "The Consumers' Council in Norway," *Cartel* 3, no. 6 (October 1953): 210–14; Lawrence E. Rose, "The Role of Interest Groups in Collective Interest Policy-Making: Consumer Protection in Norway and the United States," *European Journal of Political Research* 9, no. 1 (1981): 17–45; Thorelli and Thorelli, *Consumer Information Handbook,* 135–13, 362–83; Hans B. Thorelli and Sarah V. Thorelli, *Consumer Information Systems and Consumer Policy* (Cambridge, MA: Ballinger, 1977), 189–231. The New Zealand experience was also marked by early state intervention, thereby removing the need for a private testing organization: David Russell, "New Zealand Consumer Movement," in *Encyclopaedia of the Consumer Movement,* ed. Brobeck et al., 411–13.

18. Trumbull, "National Varieties of Consumerism," 82–83; Hilton, *Consumerism in Twentieth-Century Britain,* 231.

19. Hans Jeleby, ed., *Facts and Views on Nordic Consumer Policy: An Anthology* (Copenhagen: Nordic Council of Ministers, 1995); Nordic Council of Ministers, *Consumer Policy in the Baltic and Nordic Countries* (Copenhagen: Nordic Council of Ministers, 1995); J. J. Boddewyn, "The Swedish Consumer Ombudsman System and Advertising Self-Regulation," *Journal of Consumer Affairs* 19, no. 1 (1985): 140–62.

20. Børge Dahl, *Consumer Legislation in Denmark* (Wokingham, UK: Van Nostrand Reinhold, 1981).

21. Thorelli and Thorelli, *Consumer Information Handbook,* 67–78; Hans Peter Lehofer, "Austrian Consumer Movement," in *Encyclopaedia of the Consumer Movement,* ed. Brobeck et al., 48–51.

22. Gunnar Trumbull, "Strategies of Consumer Group Mobilisation: France and Germany in the 1970s," in *Politics of Consumption,* ed. Daunton and Hilton, 261–82; Norbert Reich, *Consumer Legislation in the Federal Republic of Germany: A Study Prepared for the EC Commission*

(Wokingham, UK: Van Nostrand Reinhold, 1980); Eberhard Kuhlman, "German Consumer Movement," in *Encyclopaedia of the Consumer Movement*, ed. Brobeck *et al.*, 289–93; Consumers International, *Balancing the Scales, Part 2: Consumer Protection in the Netherlands and Germany* (London: Consumers International, 1995); Karl Kuhne, "Consumer Protection: A German View," *Cartel 5*, no. 3 (July 1955): 89–95.

23. Vogel, "Consumer Protection and Protectionism in Japan," 146.

24. Robin LeBlanc, *Bicycle Citizens: The Political World of the Japanese Housewife* (Berkeley: University of California Press, 1999); J. Gelb and M. Estevez-Abe, "Political Women in Japan: A Case Study of the Seikatsusha Network Movement," *Social Science Japan Journal* 1 (1998): 263–79.

25. Maclachlan, *Consumer Politics in Postwar Japan.*

26. Ibid., p. 80.

27. Simon Lazarus, *The Genteel Populists* (New York: Holt, Rinehart and Winston, 1974); Robert D. Holsworth, *Public Interest Liberalism and the Crisis of Affluence: Reflections on Nader, Environmentalism, and the Politics of a Sustainable Society* (Cambridge, MA: Schenkman, 1980); Richard A. Harris and Sidney M. Milkus, *The Politics of Regulatory Change: A Tale of Two Agencies* (New York: Oxford University Press, 1989); Nadel, *The Politics of Consumer Protection.*

28. Erma Angevina, "The Consumer Federation of America," *Journal of Consumer Affairs* 3, no. 2 (1969): 52–155; Gary J. Logan, "Profile: The Consumer Federation of America," *Everyday Law* (May 1988): 48–52; Goody L. Solomon, *The Radical Consumer's Handbook* (New York: Ballantine Books, 1972).

29. Mayer, *Guardians of the Marketplace*, 45–47.

30. Trumbull, *Consumer Capitalism*, 53; Alain Chatriot, "Qui defend le consommateur? Associations, institutions et politiques publiques en France, 1972–2003" (Who defends the consumer? Aocciations, institutions, and politics in France), in *Au nom du consommateur (In the Name of the Consumer)*, ed. Chatriot *et al.*, 165–81.

31. Hondius, *Consumer Legislation in the Netherlands*, 6. Thorelli and Thorelli, *Consumer Information Systems*, 349–54.

32. Phillip J. Bryson, *The Consumer Under Socialist Planning: The East German Case* (New York: Praeger, 1984); André Steiner, "Dissolution of the 'Dictatorship over Needs'? Consumer Behaviour and Economic Reform in East Germany in the 1960s," in *Getting and Spending*, ed. Strasser *et al.*, 167–85; Philipp Heldmann, "Negotiating Consumption in a Dictatorship: Consumer Politics in the GDR in the 1950s and 1960s," in *The Politics of Consumption*, ed. Daunton and Hilton, 185–202.

33. Ferenc Hammer, "Blue Jeans in Socialist Hungary," paper presented at the Citizenship and Consumption: Agency, Norms, Mediations and Spaces conference, 30 March—1 April 2006, Cambridge University; Mary Neuberger, "Veils, Shalvari and Matters of Dress: Unravelling the Fabric of Women's Lives in Communist Bulgaria" and Mark Allen Svede, "All You Need Is Love Beads: Latvia's Hippies Undress for Success," both in *Style and Socialism: Modernity and Material Culture in Post-War Eastern Europe*, ed. Susan E. Reid and David Crowley (Oxford: Berg, 2000), 169–87, 189–208; Susan E. Reid, "The Khrushchev Kitchen: Domesticating the Scientific-Technological Revolution," *Journal of Contemporary History* 40, no. 2 (2005): 289–316; Paulina Bren, "Weekend Getaways: The *Chata*, the Tramp and the Politics of Private Life in Post-1968 Czechoslovakia," in *Socialist Spaces: Sites of Everyday Life in the Eastern Bloc*, ed. David Crowley and Susan E. Reid (Oxford: Berg, 2002).

34. Ina Merkel, "From Stigma to Cult: Changing Meanings in East German Consumer Culture," in *The Making of the Consumer: Knowledge, Power and Identity in the Modern World*, ed. Frank Trentmann (Oxford: Berg, 2006), 249–70.

35. Archives of International Organisation of Consumers Unions (hereafter IOCU Archives), Kuala Lumpur, Malaysia: Box 68: Personalities: File G21.24: Colston E. Warne, "Report on Trip to Europe, 11–30 June 1969."

36. Philip Hanson, *The Consumer in the Soviet Economy* (London: Macmillan, 1968).

37. Landsman, *Dictatorship and Demand*, 11

38. Ibid., 91.

39. Alastair Macgeorge, "Yugoslavian Consumer Movement," in *Encyclopaedia of the Consumer Movement*, ed. Brobeck *et al.*, 629; Thorelli and Thorelli, *Consumer Information Handbook*, 472–78.

40. IOCU Archive, Box 151: I45.16: "Warsaw declaration," 16 November 1989; Andrzej K.

Kominski, "Consumers in Transition from the Centrally Planned Economy to the Market Economy," *Journal of Consumer Policy* 14, no. 4 (1992): 351–69; Alastair Macgeorge, "Hungarian Consumer Movement," in *Encyclopaedia of the Consumer Movement*, ed. Brobeck *et al.*, 309–10.

41. Janusz Kaliński, *Gospodarka Polski w latach 1944–1989: przemiany strukturalne* (The Polish Economy 1944–1989: structural changes) (Warsaw: Państwowe Wydawnictwo Ekonomiczne, 1995).

42. Edward Wiszniewski, "Potrzebna ochrona konsumenta" (The need for consumer protection), *Życie Gospodarcze* (Economic Life) 4 (1958): 1.

43. Janusz Dąbrowski, "Co dalej z ochronąkonsumenta?" (What next in consumer protection?), *Życie Gospodarcze (Economic Life)* 3 (1981): 5.

44. Krystyna Wojcik, "Federacja Konsumentów w rok po zarejestrowaniu (częśċ II—roczny bilans działalnoŝci)" (The Consumers' Federation one year after its registration: Part 2: balbnce of activities for the year), *Handel Wewnętrzny* (Internal Trade) 5–6 (1982): 49–55; Krystyna Wojcik, "Drugi rok działalnoŝci Federacji Konsumentów" (The second year of the Consumers' Federation activities), *Biuletyn Federacji Konsumentów* (Bulletin of the Consumers' Federation) 1–2 (1983): 11–29.

45. "Sprawozdanie ze spotkania Delegacji Federacji Konsumentów z Przewodniczącym Rady Państwa" (A report on the meeting of the Consumers' Federation's delegation with the chairman of the Council of State), *Biuletyn Federacji Konsumentów* (Bulletin of the Consumers' Federation) 3–4 (1988): I–V (special section).

46. "Uchwała programowa I Zgromadzenia Ogólnego Federacji Konsumentów z 14.11.1981" (The programme approved at the first general assembly of the Consumers' Federation on 14 December 1981), *Biuletyn Federacji Konsumentów* (Bulletin of the Consumers' Federation) 1–2 (1983): 31.

47. Franck Cochoy, "The Industrial Roots of Contemporary Political Consumerism: The Case of the French Standardisation Movement," in *Politics, Products and Markets,* ed. Micheletti *et al.*, 145–60; C. D. Woodward, *BSI: The Story of Standards* (London: British Standards Institution, 1972); Thorelli and Thorelli, *Consumer Information Handbook,* 506–11; International Organisation for Standardisation, *Consumer Standards for Today and Tomorrow* (London: International Organisation for Standardisation, 1976).

48. OECD, *A Global Marketplace for Consumer* (Paris: OECD, 1995); OECD, *Sustainable Consumption and Production* (Paris: OECD, 1997); Committee on Consumer Policy, *Consumer Policy During the Past Ten Years: Main Developments and Prospects* (Paris: OECD, 1983). See also the *Annual Reports on Consumer Policy in OECD Member Countries* published since 1974 (Paris: OECD, various years).

49. Victoria de Grazia, *Irresistible Empire: America's Advance Through Twentieth-Century Europe* (Cambridge, MA: Belknap Press of Harvard University Press, 2005), 372

50. Stephen Weatherill, *EC Consumer Law and Policy* (Longman: London, 1997); Commission of the European Communities, *Consumer Protection and Information Policy: Third Report* (Luxembourg: Office for Official Publications of the European Communities, 1981); Commission of the European Communities, *Consumer Representation in the European Communities* (Luxembourg: Office for Official Publications of the European Communities, 1983); Commission of the European Communities, *Ten Years of Community Consumer Policy: A Contribution to a People's Europe* (Luxembourg: Office for Official Publications of the European Communities, 1986); Economic and Social Consultative Assembly, *The Consumer and the Internal Market* (Brussels: Economic and Social Committee, European Community, 1993); Consumers in the Europe Group, *EU Consumer Protection Policy: A Review of European Union Consumer Programmes, EU Consumer Protection Legislation and European Commission Consumer Initiatives* (London: Consumers in the Europe Group, 1999).

51. Agnès Chambraud, Patricia Foucher, and Anne Morin, "The Importance of Community Law for French Consumer Protection Legislation," *Journal of Consumer Policy* 17, no. 1 (1994): 23–37; Klaus Tonner, "The European Influence on German Consumer Law," *Journal of Consumer Policy* 17, no. 1 (1994): 39–50.

52. Gustavo Ghidini, *Consumer Legislation in Italy: A Study Prepared for the EC Commission* (Wokingham, UK: Van Nostrand Reinhold, 1980); Simonetta Cotterli, Paolo Martinello, and Carlo M. Verardi, "Implementation of EEC Consumer Protection Directives in Italy," *Journal of Consumer Policy* 17, no. 1 (1994): 63–82; Consumers International, *Balancing the Scales, Part 3: Consumer Protection in Greece and Spain* (London: Consumers International, 2000); Manuel-Angel

López Sánchez, "Implementation of the EEC Consumer Protection Directives in Spain," *Journal of Consumer Policy* 17, no. 1 (1994): 83–99. The Italian consumer movement was set back massively in 1974 when the Unione Nazionale Consumatori was suspended from BEUC following the arrest of its secretary-general for "corruption" and for its unrepentant attitude to taking money from industry: Thorelli and Thorelli, *Consumer Information Systems*, 362.

53. David Coen, "The Evolution of the Large Firm as a Political Actor in the European Union," *Journal of European Public Policy* 4, no. 1 (1997): 91–108; David Coen, "The Impact of U.S. Lobbying Practice on the European-Government Relationship," *California Management Review* 41, no. 4 (1999): 27–44.

54. Børge Dahl, "Consumer Protection Within the European Union," *Journal of Consumer Policy* 16, no. 4 (1993): 345–53; H. W. Micklitz and Stephen Weatherill, "Consumer Policy in the European Community: Before and After Maastricht," *Journal of Consumer Policy* 16, nos. 3–4 (1993): 285–322; Economic and Social Committee of the European Communities, "Opinion on the Single Market and Consumer Protection: Opportunities and Obstacles," *Journal of Consumer Policy* 19, no. 2 (1996): 211–44.

55. Consumers in the European Community Group, *Enough Is Enough: The Common Agricultural Policy* (London: Consumers in the European Community Group, 1984); Consumers in the European Community Group, *Commission Reflections on the Development and Future of the Common Agricultural Policy* (London: Consumers in the European Community Group, 1992).

56. Ludwig Krämer, "On the Interrelation Between Consumer and Environmental Policies in the European Community," *Journal of Consumer Policy* 16, no. 2 (1993): 455–67; Klaus Tonner, "Consumer Protection and Environmental Protection: Contradictions and Suggested Steps Towards Integration," *Journal of Consumer Policy* 23, no. 1 (2000): 63–78; Martin Hedemann-Robinson, "EC Law, the Environment and Consumers: Addressing the Challenge of Incorporating an Environmental Dimension to Consumer Protection at Community Level," *Journal of Consumer Policy* 20, no. 1 (1997): 1–43.

57. Commission of the European Communities, *Consumer Policy Strategy, 2002–2006* (Luxembourg: Office for Official Publications of the European Communities, 2002).

58. Gillian K. Hadfield, Robert Howse, and Michael J. Trebilock, "Information-Based Principles for Rethinking Consumer Protection Policy," *Journal of Consumer Policy* 21, no. 2 (1998): 131–69.

59. Ellen Vos, "EU Food Safety Regulation in the Aftermath of the BSE Crisis," *Journal of Consumer Policy* 23, no. 3 (2000): 227–55; Nils Ringstedt, "OECD, Safety and the Consumer," *Journal of Consumer Policy* 9, no. 1 (1986): 57–64.

Chapter 3. Poverty amid Prosperity: Consumer Protest beyond the Affluent West

1. *Utusan Konsumer* 24 (March 1976): 5; *Utusan Konsumer* 25 (April 1976): 2; Consumers' Association of Penang (hereafter CAP), *Pollution: Kuala Juru's Battle for Survival* (Penang: Consumers' Association of Penang, 1976).

2. Michael T. Taussig, *The Devil and Commodity Fetishism in South America* (Chapel Hill: University of North Carolina Press, 1980).

3. James C. Scott, *Weapons of the Weak: Everyday Forms of Peasant Resistance* (New Haven: Yale University Press, 1985), 48.

4. CAP, *Pollution*, 39.

5. CAP, *Kuala Juru: A People's Co-Operative* (Penang: CAP, 1980), 18.

6. Ibid., 28.

7. Lim Teck Ghee, "Nongovernmental organisations in Malaysia and Regional Networking," in *Emerging Civil Society in the Asia Pacific Community: Nongovernmental Underpinnings of the Emerging Asia Pacific Regional Community,* ed. Tadashi Yamamoto (Singapore: Institute for South-East Asian Studies, 1996), 185.

8. CU Archive: Florence Mason Papers (hereafter FM): Box 25: Greta Bergström, "Consumer Problems in a Development Country," report prepared for Swedish Consumer Council, 1963; Jeffrey James, *Consumption and Development* (Basingstoke: Macmillan, 1993); Jeffrey James, *Consumption, Globalisation and Development* (Basingstoke: Macmillan, 2000).

9. Cited in CU Archive: Persia Campbell Papers (hereafter PC): Box 18, Folder "Reports and Speeches, 1969–1973": Karin Himmelstrand, The African Consumer: Does He Have Any Power?" 1970, 5.

10. IOCU Archive: Box 43, File D3.8: Karin Himmelstrand, "Notes on Consumer Problems in Developing Countries," paper presented in Palo Alto, May 1968; IOCU Archive: Box 1, File A2.10: Ruth Simmons Vermeer, "The Consumer Movement in Developing Countries," paper presented to Consumers Association of Bangladesh, April 1979.

11. IOCU Archive: Box 61A, File G5a:10: Anwar Fazal, "The Cost of Living, the Cost of Survival: Women as Consumers," Address to Panel Discussion at the International Women's Year Tribune, Mexico City, 30 June 1975.

12. Troth Wells and Foo Gaik Sim, *Till They Have Faces: Women as Consumers* (Penang: IOCU, 1987), ii.

13. Hans B. Thorelli and Gerald D. Sentell, *Consumer Emancipation and Economic Development: The Case of Thailand* (Greenwich, CT: JAI Press, 1982).

14. Anwar Fazal, "Challenges of the Consumer Movement in Developing Countries," in IOCU, *Consumers in Africa: Meeting the Challenge. Proceedings of the IOCU Confernece for Anglophone Africa, Nairobi, 14–18 June 1988* (The Hague: IOCU, 1988), 11.

15. Consumer Movement Archives, Kansas State University (hereafter KSU): Dorothy K. Willner Papers (hereafter DW): Box 3: N. K. Olembo, "The Kenyan Consumers Organisation," *Contact: Journal of the Kenya Consumers' Organisation*, [no vol. number](1979): 6–7.

16. Josie Fernandez, "Consumer Protection in Asia: The Challenges Ahead," *Journal of Development Communication* 12, no. 1 (2001): 42–52; Josie Fernandez, "Asian-Pacific Consumer Movement," in *Encyclopaedia of the Consumer Movement*, ed. Brobeck et al. (Santa Barbara, CA: ABC-CLIO), 38–42; John T. D. Wood, "Consumer Protection in the Asian-Pacific Region," *Journal of Consumer Policy* 14 (1991) 99–106; CU Archive: PC: Box 18: Folder "Reports and Speeches, 1969–1973": Colston E. Warne, "Trip," 1969; Colston E. Warne, "Summary of Consumer Situation in Countries of the Pacific Area," December 1969; KSU Archives: DW: Box 10: Folder "Philippines': Citizens' Alliance for Consumer Protection, Consumer Handbook" (Manila: Citizens' Alliance for Consumer Protection, 1981); *CACP Journal: A Quarterly Journal of the Citizens' Alliance for Consumer Protection* 1, no. 2 (1981): 1–2; CU Archive: Box 27: Folder 1: Colston E Warne, "The International Growth of Consumer Protective Agencies," memo to K. M. Knight, Charles Hogan and Leslie Woodcock, United Nations, 18 January 1956.

17. Mahmuda Bibi, "A Short Note on the Early History of the Consumer Movement in Malaysia," private papers of Anwar Fazal, 2003.

18. Mohd Hamdan Adnan, *Understanding Consumerism* (Petaling Jaya: FOMCA, 2000), 60.

19. Selangor Consumers' Association (hereafter SCA), *First Conference on Consumer Action in Malaysia, Kuala Lumpur, 24 February 1968* (Kuala Lumpur: SCA, 1968); SCA, *Annual Reports and Accounts, 1967* (Kuala Lumpur: SCA, 1968); SCA, *Consumer Trade Fair, Kuala Lumpur, 7–12 April 1970* (Kuala Lumpur: SCA, 1970); SCA, *Annual Report, 1969* (Kuala Lumpur: SCA, 1970).

20. Barbara Watson Andaya and Leonard Y. Andaya, *A History of Malaysia* (Honolulu: University of Hawaii Press, 2001), 298.

21. Mahathir Mohamad, *The Malay Dilemma* (Kuala Lumpur: Times Books, 2003 [1970]).

22. Syed Hussein Alatas, *The Myth of the Lazy Native: A Study of the Image of the Malays, Filipinos and Javanese from the 16th to the 20th Century and Its Function in the Ideology of Capitalism* (London: Frank Cass, 1977).

23. Andaya and Andaya, *History of Malaysia*; T. N. Harper, *The End of Empire and the Making of Malaya* (Cambridge: Cambridge University Press, 1999); Ziauddin Sardar, *The Consumption of Kuala Lumpur* (London: Reaktion, 2000); Joel S. Kahn and Francis Loh Kok Wah, "Introduction: Fragmented Vision," in *Fragmented Vision: Culture and Politics in Contemporary Malaysia*, ed. Joel S. Kahn and Francis Loh Kok Wah (Sydney: Allen and Unwin, 1992).

24. Mahmuda Bibi, "A Short Note."

25. Anwar Fazal, interview by Jeremy Seabrook, 17 July 1997.

26. T. Rajamoorthy, interview by Jeremy Seabrook, 1994; Anwar Fazal, interview by the author, 13 April 2004.

27. Anwar Fazal, interview by Jeremy Seabrook, 17 July 1997; Ralph Nader, *Unsafe at Any Speed: The Designed-In Dangers of the American Automobile* (New York: Grossman, 1965).

28. Sumit Mandal, "Transethnic Solidarities, Racialisation and Social Equality," in *The State of Malaysia: Ethnicity, Equity and Reform*, ed. Edmund Terence Gomez (London: RoutledgeCurzon, 2004).

29. *The Phoenix: Newsletter of the University of Malaya Graduates Society of Penang* 1, no. 4

(October 1969): 1; University of Malaya Graduates Society of Penang, "Press release," private papers of Anwar Fazal, October 1969; Anwar Fazal, interview by the author, 13 April 2004; CAP, *1st Annual Report, 1969–1970* (Penang: CAP, 1971).

30. S. M. Mohamed Idris, *Reflections on Malaysian Society: Where Do We Go From Here?* (Penang: CAP, 2003), 38; S. M. Mohamed Idris, interview by the author, 16 April 2004.

31. Anwar Fazal, interview by Jeremy Seabrook, 17 July 1997.

32. *Utusan Konsumer* 7 (February–March 1972): 1.

33. Anwar Fazal, interview by Jeremy Seabrook, 17 July 1997.

34. *Utusan Konsumer* 14 (January–February 1974): 2.

35. *Utusan Konsumer* 16 (June–August 1974): 1.

36. *Utusan Konsumer* 17 (September–December 1974): 5.

37. *Utusan Konsumer* 18 (January–March 1975): 2.

38. Jeremy Seabrook, "The Consumers' Association of Penang," unpublished manuscript, private papers of Jeremy Seabrook, 1998.

39. Evelyn Hong, interview by Jeremy Seabrook, n.d.; Mary Assunta, interview by Jeremy Seabrook, 24 March 1998; Subbarow, interview by Jeremy Seabrook, n.d.; Lim Teck Ghee, interview by Jeremy Seabrook, 20 May 1998; Lim Jee Juan, interview by Jeremy Seabrook, 1998.

40. *Utusan Konsumer* 59 (June 1979): 13.

41. Kemkumar Saviour Lopez, "Consumer Associations in Malaysia," in *Proceedings of Law and the Consuemr Conference* (Kuala Lumpur: SCA, 1981), 33; Dexter and Troth Tiranti, *People with a Purpose: The Consumers' Association of Penang* (Penang: CAP, 1985), 15.

42. Tiranti, *People with a Purpose;* CAP, *Crisis in Malaysian Fishing* (Penang: CAP, 1977); CAP, *The Malaysian Fisheries: A Diminishing Resource* (Penang: CAP, 1977); Evelyn Hong, *Natives of Sarawak* (Central Books, 1991); CAP, *Padi Pollution in Kuala Kedah* (Penang: CAP, 1978).

43. CAP, *Look Out! They're After Your Money: A CAP Guide to Sales Tactics and How to Avoid Them* (Penang: CAP, 1987); CAP, *The Hire-Purchase Trap: How You Can Be Cheated and What to Do About It* (Penang: CAP, 1986).

44. CAP, *Selling Dreams: How Advertising Misleads Us* (Penang: CAP, 1986), 103; *Utusan Konsumer* 118 (May 1984): 1; CAP, *The Other Baby Killer* (Penang: CAP, 1981), 14; CAP, *Breastfeeding: The Best Start in Life* (Penang: CAP, 1990); CAP, *Drugs and the Third World: Phenylbutazone and Oxyphenbutazone Sale and Hazards—a Malaysian Study* (Penang: CAP, 1984); CAP, *Pesticide Problems, Legislation and Consumer Action in the Third World: the Malaysian Experience* (Penang: CAP, 1985); CAP, *Battle for the Environment: The Malaysian Experience* (Penang: CAP, 1974); CAP, *The Malaysian Environment in Crisis: Selections From Press Cuttings* (Penang: CAP, 1978); CAP and Institut Masyarakat, *Appropriate Technology, Culture and Lifestyle in Development: Declarations and Resolutions of Seminar, November 1981* (Penang: Institut Masyarakat, 1982); CAP, *Padi Pollution in Kuala Kedah* (Penang: CAP, 1978); Evelyn Hong, ed., *Malaysian Women: Problems and Issues* (Penang: CAP, 1983); CAP, *Rape in Malaysia* (Penang: CAP, 1988).

45. *Utusan Konsumer* 155 (June 1987): 10; S. M. Mohamed Idris, *Malaysian Consumers and Development* (Penang: CAP, 1986).

46. *Utusan Konsumer* 159 (October 1987): 1–14.

47. S. M. Mohamed Idris, *For a Sane, Green Future* (Penang: CAP, 1990), 17, 88–95.

48. Budi Rusindah, *Kampung Diary* (Penang: CAP, 1992), 7; Lim Jee Yuan, *The Malay House: Rediscovering Malaysia's Indigenous Shelter System* (Penang: Institut Masyarakat, 1987); Joel S. Kahn, "Class, Ethnicity and Diversity: Some Remarks on Malay Culture in Malaysia," in *Fragmented Vision,* ed. Kahn and Loh, 158–78.

49. Meena Raman, interview by Jeremy Seabrook, 1998[?]; Meena Raman, interview by the author, 16 April 2004; Committee Against Repression in the Pacific and Asia (CARPA), *Tangled Web: Dissent, Deterrence and the 27 October 1987 Crackdown in Malaysia* (Kuala Lumpur: CARPA, 1988).

50. K. S. Jomo, "Race, Religion and Repression: 'National Security' and the Insecurity of the Regime," in *Tangled Web,* 6; Gordon P. Means, *Malaysian Politics: The Second Generation* (Singapore: Oxford University Press, 1991).

51. Meena Raman, interview by the author, 16 April 2004; Dexter and Troth Tiranti, *People with a Purpose: The Consumers' Association of Penang* (Penang: CAP, 1985), 25–29; Meena Raman and Thayalan Muniandy, "The Legal Centre of the Consumers' Association of Penang: Its History, Activities and Future Programme," paper presented to Third World Network Seminar Ex-

panding Public Interest Legal Activities, 15–19 January 1988; CAP, *Wasted Lives: Radioactive Poisoning in Bukit Merah* (Penang: CAP, 1993).

52. Meena Raman, interview by the author, 16 April 2004; Meena Raman, interview by Jeremy Seabrook, 1998; IOCU Archive: No box number: Folder G23, "Detention of Consumer Activists," G23.21: Anwar Fazal, "Detentions in Malaysia," memo to all members of IOCU Executive, 3 November 1987.

53. CU Archive: Box 161: Folder 25:4, "Greek Council of Consumers': Letters from Haralambos Kouris, President of the Consumers Protection Institute and General Secretary of the Greek Council of Consumers, to IOCU," 19 March and 1 April, 1974; CU, "Greece: Background Note," 5 June 1974; Anon, "Eléments d'information concernant L'Institute Grec pour la protection des consommateurs: interview de H. Kouris," June 1974; IOCU, *Proceeding of the Mediterranean Consumer Conference, Athens, 28–30 March 1976* (The Hague: IOCU, 1976), 9; IOCU Archive: [No box number]: Folder G23, "Detention of Consumer Activists": G23.14: Letter from Linwood Holton, Assistant Secretary for Congressional Relations, U.S. Department of State, to Ogden R. Reid, House of Representatives, 3 July 1974.

54. IOCU Archive: Box 10: Folder B3em, "Minutes of Executive Meetings": various papers relating to 33rd Executive Meeting, 14–15 February 1981, especially Nicky Morales, "Why I Am Where I Am," letter to Julie A. Armago, KMPI President; Anwar Fazal, interview by the author, 13 April 2004.

55. Paul Ekins, *A New World Order: Grassroots Movements for Global Change* (London: Routledge, 1992); Jeremy Seabrook, *Pioneers of Change: Experiments in Creating a New Society* (London: Zed Books, 1993); Tom Woodhouse, ed., *People and Planet: The Right Livelihood Award Speeches* (London: Green Books, 1987).

56. Harold Crouch, "Malaysia: Neither Authoritarian Nor Democratic," in *Southeast Asia in the 1990s: Authoritarianism, Democracy and Capitalism,* ed. Kevin Hewison, Richard Robinson and Garry Rodan (Sydney: Allen and Unwin, 1993); William Case, "Semi-Democracy in Malaysia: Withstanding the Pressures for Regime Change," *Pacific Affairs* 66, no. 2 (1993): 183–205; Zakaria Haji Ahmad, "Malaysia: Quasi-Democracy in a Divided Society," in *Democracy in Developing Countries, Vol. 3,* ed. Larry Diamong, Juan J. Linz and Seymour Martin Lipset (Boulder, CO: Lynne Rienner, 1989); Edmund Terence Gomez and Jomo K. S., *Malaysia's Political Economy: Politics, Patronage and Profits* (Cambridge: Cambridge University Press, 1997), 3; Joel S. Kahn and Francis Loh Kok Wah, "Introduction: Fragmented Vision," in *Fragmented Vision: Culture and Politics in Contemporary Malaysia,* ed. Kahn and Loh Kok Wah (Sydney: Allen and Unwin, 1992), 1–17.

57. Meredith L. Weiss and Saliha Hassan, "Introduction: From Moral Communities to NGOs," in *Social Movements in Malaysia: From Moral Communities to NGOs,* ed. Meredith L. Weiss and Saliha Hassan (London: Routledge, 2003), 4.

58. Lim, "Nongovernmental Organisations"; Bridget Welsh, ed., *Reflections: The Mahathir Years* (Baltimore: Johns Hopkins University Press [School of Advanced International Studies], 2004); Kua Kia Soong, *Malaysian Critical Issues* (Petaling Jaya: Strategic Information Research Development, 2002); Suaram, *Working for Human Rights* (Kuala Lumpur: Suaram, 2003); Kua Kia Soong, "Malaysian Communities Resist: A Critique of Malaysian Development," in *People Before Profits: The Rights of Malaysian Communities in Development,* ed. Kua Kia Soong (Petaling Jaya: Strategic Information Research Department and Suaram, 2001), 1–12.

59. Khoo Boo Teik, *Beyond Mahathir: Malaysian Politics and Its Discontents* (London: Zed, 2003); Vidhu Verma, *Malaysia: State and Civil Society in Transition* (Petaling Jaya: Strategic Information Research Development, 2004); Meredith Weiss, "Malaysian NGOs: History, Legal Framework and Characteristics," in *Social Movements in Malaysia,* ed. Weiss & Hassan, 17–44; Sheila Nair, "Constructing Civil Society in Malaysia: Nationalism, Hegemony and Resistance," in *Rethinking Malaysia,* ed. Jomo K. S. (Kuala Lumpur: Malaysian Social Science Association, 1999), 84–106; Lim, "Nongovernmental Organisations"; Bridget Welsh, ed., *Reflections: The Mahathir Years* (Baltimore: Johns Hopkins University Press [School of Advanced International Studies], 2004); Kua Kia Soong, *Malaysian Critical Issues* (Petaling Jaya: Strategic Information Research Development, 2002); Suaram, *Working for Human Rights* (Kuala Lumpur: Suaram, 2003); Kua Kia Soong, "Malaysian Communities Resist: A Critique of Malaysian Development," in *People Before Profits: The Rights of Malaysian Communities in Development,* ed. Kua Kia Soong (Petaling Jaya: Strategic Information Research Department and Suaram, 2001), 1–12.

60. Martin Khor, *Globalisation and the South: Some Critical Issues* (Penang: Third World Net-

work, 2001); Martin Khor, "The WTO and the South: Implications and Recent Developments," in *Consumer Protection in the WTO Era,* ed. Sothi Rachagan (Louvain-la-Neuve, France: Association Internationale de Droit de la Consommation, 1999), 187–222.

61. Faris Ahmed, *In Defence of Land and Livelihood* (Penang: CAP and Sierra Club of Canada, 1997); CAP, *Land Acquisition: Need for Accountability and Public Participation* (Penang: CAP, 1991); Martin Khor, *Housing for the People: Why Malaysia Has so Far Failed to Meet Housing Needs of the Poor* (Penang: CAP and Southeast Asian Forum on Development Alternatives, 1989); CAP, *Rural Malaysia: Poverty, Basic Needs Problems and Policy Proposals* (Penang: CAP, 1990); IDAC, *Danger School* (Penang: CAP, 1997); CAP, *Key Questions on Malaysian Education: Highlights of the CAP Seminar on Education and Development* (Penang: CAP, 1984); CAP and SAM, *State of the Malaysian Environment: Statement and Conclusions of the CAP-SAM National Conference on the State of the Malaysian Environment 1996* (Penang: CAP and SAM, 1996); Friends of Penang Hill, *Penang Hill: The Need to Save Our National Heritage* (Penang: CAP, 1991); Khor Cheang Kee, *My Island in the Sun: A Penang Perspective* (Penang: Institut Masyarakat, 1995).

62. *And Our Rice Pots Are Empty: The Social Costs of the Economic Crisis* (Penang: Consumers International, Regional Office for Asia and the Pacific 1998); Jomo K. S., *M Way: Mahathir's Economic Legacy* (Kuala Lumpur: Forum, 2003).

63. SCA, *Annual Report, 1969* (Kuala Lumpur: SCA, 1970), 59.

64. *Utusan Konsumer* 3 (August 1971): 2; *Utusan Konsumer* 9 (November 1972—February 1973): 3; *Utusan Konsumer* 10 (March—April 1973): 7.

65. *Utusan Konsumer* 1 (June 1971): 3; Bibi, "A Short Note," 3; *Utusan Konsumer* 2 (July 1971): 3; CU Archive: PC Papers: Box 20: Folder, "Malaysia, 1970–1971": "Discussion papers," First Meeting of the Consumers Association of Penang and the Selangor Consumers' Association, Cameron Highlands, 5–7 June 1970.

66. CU Archive: Box 162: Folder 26.6: Letter from Syed Adam Al-Ja'fri, SCA, to Peter Goldman, IOCU, 19 September 1971; Syed Adam Al-Ja'fri, "The Situation in the Selangor Consumers' Association," memo to IOCU, 20 September 1971.

67. Anwar Fazal, interview by the author, 17 April 2004; Bibi, "A Short Note," 3.

68. Josie M. Fernandez, *Contested Space? FOMCA's Engagement with the Government* (Petaling Jaya: FOMCA, 2004), v; Lim Teck Ghee, "Nongovernmental Organisations in Malaysia."

69. For a full discussion of the Malaysian consumer movement see Matthew Hilton, "The Consumer Movement and Civil Society in Malaysia," *International Review of Social History* 52, no. 3 (2007): 373–406; Matthew Hilton, *Choice and Justice: Forty Years of the Malaysian Consumer Movement* (Penang: Universiti Sains Malaysia Press, 2008).

70. SCA, *The World We Live In: A Closer Look* (Kuala Lumpur: SCA, 1983), foreword.

71. Hamdan Adnan, *Understanding Consumerism,* 15.

72. Bishan Singh, interview by the author, 27 November 2003; *Beritta Pengganu* 2 (1988): 1–12; Sothi Rachagan, interview by the author, 10 November 2003; SCA, *Law and the Consumer: Report of Seminar Proceedings, 10 October 1982, University of Malaya* (Petaling Jaya: SCA, 1982), 8–14; Sothi Rachagan and Tunku Shamsul Bahrin, *Development Without Destruction: The Need for a Pragmatic Forest Policy in Malaysia* (Petaling Jaya: SCA, 1985); M. Nadarajah, interview by the author, 10 April 2004.

73. IOCU, *Knowledge Is Power: Consumer Goals in the 1970s. Proceedings of the 6th Biennial World Conference of the International Organisation of Consumers Unions* (The Hague: IOCU, 1970), 115–17.

74. IOCU, *Report for 1972–1974 to 8th IOCU Congress, Sydney* (The Hague: IOCU, 1975), 30; IOCU, *Five Billion Consumers: Organising for Change. Proceedings of 11th World Congress* (The Hague: IOCU, 1984), 70–74.

75. IOCU Archive: Box 61a: File G5a, "Anwar Fazal": G5a.18: Anwar Fazal, "Consumerism in Southeast Asia," paper presented at International Consumer Seminar, Seoul, 16–19 June 1976.

76. KSU Archives: DW: Box 10: Folder, "Miscellaneous": Katsuko Nomura, *Consumer Movement in Japan* (Tokyo: Information Centre for Public Citizens, 1979); Katsuko Nomura, *Consumer Movement in Japan* (Tokyo: Information Centre for Public Citizens, 1979); Kee-Chon Rhee and Jinkook Lee, "South Korean Consumer Movement," in *Encyclopaedia of the Consumer Movement,* ed. Brobeck *et al.,* 522–25; Jinkook Lee and Kee-Chon Rhee, "Review of Consumer Activism in Korea, 1910–1995: A Political Economic Approach," *Journal of Consumer Policy* 19, no. 3 (1996): 365–92.

77. CI Archive: Box 135: File I7: I17.9: Anuradho Rao, "India Sub-Regional Program: A Re-

port," 28 February 1994; Gurgeet Singh, "Indian Consumer Movement," in *Encyclopaedia of the Consumer Movement,* ed. Brobeck *et al.,* 312–16; CI Archive: Box 49: File E: "Membership Applications: India."

78. CUTS, *State of the Indian Consumer: Analyses of the Implementation of the United Nations Guidelines for Consumer Protection, 1985 in India* (Jaipur: CUTS, 2001), xii. Predeep S. Mehta, *Numbers, at What Cost?* (Jaipur: CUTS, 2002);

79. H. R. Venkatesha, "Consumer Protection in Karnataka: A Diagnostic Study," Ph.D. diss., Karnataka University, 2000; Gurjeet Singh, "Group Actions and the law: A Case Study of Social Action Litigation and Consumer Protection in India," *Journal of Consumer Policy* 18, no. 1 (1995): 25–54; Gurjeet Singh, "Business Self-Regulation and Consumer Protection in India: A Critique," *Journal of Consumer Policy* 16, no. 1 (1993): 1–33; D. P. S. Verma, "Developments in Consumer Protection in India," *Journal of Consumer Policy* 25, no. 1 (2002) 107–23; special issue on "The Consumer," *The Hindu,* 31 October 1999.

80. Ali Qadir, *The State of Consumers in Pakistan: A Foundation Report* (Islamabad: Network for Consumer Protection, 2001); Mizanur Rahman, "Consumer Protection in Bangladesh: Law and Practice," *Journal of Consumer Policy* 17, no. 3 (1994): 349–62.

81. Economic and Social Commission for West Africa (ECSWA), *Consumer Protection Under a Liberalised Trade System in Selected Countries of ECSWA* (New York: United Nations, 2000).

82. CI Archive: Box 36: File C6: C6.18: Martin Abraham, "The Consumer Movement in Nepal: First Impressions," October 1992; Box 133: I13.7: Letter from Sh. Tsendbayar, President, Mongolian Consumers' Association, to CI-ROAP, 17 Marcj 1997; I13.17: CI-ROAP, "Strategic Review and Planning for CI-ROAP," 1997; IOCU, *Behind Our Smiles: Pacific Islands Women's Consumer Education Resource Book* (Wainuiomata: IOCU South Pacific Consumer Protection Programme, 1994).

83. KSU Archives: DW: Box 10: "Yayasan Lembaga Konsumen Indonesia in Brief," 1979; Box 10: "Moves to Protect the Thai Consumer," 1976.

84. KSU Archives: DW: Box 8: Permadi, "The Role of a Consumer Organisation in Indonesia, a Developing Country," 1977; Box 10: "How the Consumer Movement Began in the Philippines', *Philippines Daily Express,* 30 October 1981, 27; Josie Fernadez, "Asia-Pacific Consumer Movement," in *Encyclopaedia of the Consumer Movement,* ed. Brobeck *et al.,* 40; Citizens' Alliance for Consumer Protection, *Consumer Handbook* (Manila: Citizen's Alliance for Consumer Protection, 1981).

85. CAP, *Kuala Juru: A People's Co-Operative* (Penang: CAP, 1980), 24.

86. Rokiah Talib, "Malaysia: Power Shifts and the Matrix of Consumption," in *Consumption in Asia: Lifestyles and Identities,* ed. Chua Beng-Huat (London: Routledge, 2000), 35–60; Antonio L. Rappa, *Modernity and Consumption: Theory, Politics and the Public in Singapore and Malaysia* (Singapore: World Scientific, 2002).

87. CAP has recently published dozens of such pamphlets. See, for instance, CAP, *Fashion That Hurts* (Penang: CAP, 2003); CAP, *Cancer-Causing Chemicals in Cosmetics and Daily Use Products* (Penang: CAP, 2001).

88. "One's Life Has Value so Long as One Attributes Value to the Life of Others, by Means of Friendship, Love, Indignation and Compassion" (Simone de Beauvoir, *The Coming of Age* [New York: Putnam, 1996], 541).

89. Henry Wadsworth Longfellow, *Complete Works* (Boston: Houghton Mifflin, 1922).

90. Khoo Boo Teik, *Beyond Mahathir,* 25; Chandra Muzaffar, *Rights, Religion and Reform: Enhancing Human Dignity through Spiritual and Moral Transformation* (London: Routledge, 2002).

91. Francis Loh Kok Wah, "Towards a New Politics of Fragmentation and Contestation," in *New Politics in Malaysia,* ed. Francis Loh Kok Wah and Johan Saravanamuttu (Singapore: Institute of Southeast Asian Studies, 2003), 253–82 (261); Francis Loh Kok Wah, "Developmentalism and the Limits of Democratic Discourse," in *Democracy in Malaysia: Discourses and Practices,* ed. Francis Loh Kok Wah and Khoo Boo Teik (Richmond, Surrey: Curzon, 2002), 19–50.

92. Lat, *Kampung Boy: Yesterday and Today* (Kuala Lumpur: Berita, 1993).

93. *Utusan Konsumer* 231 (May 1991): 19; *Hansard* (14 June 1994), column 579.

94. Josie Fernadez, interview by the author, 8 December 2003.

95. Private communication with author, 22 September 2006.

Chapter 4. Consumers of the World Unite: Consumption and the New Global Order

1. William Korey, *NGOs and the Universal Declaration of Human Rights: "A Curious Grapevine"* (Basingstoke: Palgrave, 1998), 29–50; Chadwick Alger, "The Emerging Roles of NGOs in the UN System: From Article 71 to a People's Millennium Assembly," *Global Governance* 8, no. 1 (2002): 93–117; Angus Archer, "Methods of Multilateral Management: The Interrelationship of International Organisations and NGOs," in *The US, the UN, and the Management of Global Change*, ed. Toby Trister Gati (New York: New York University Press, 1983), 303–25; Akira Iriye, *Global Community: The Role of International Organizations in the Making of the Contemporary World* (Berkeley: University of California Press, 2002), 42–43; Bill Seary, "The Early History: From the Congress of Vienna to the San Francisco Conference," in *"The Conscience of the World": The Influence of Non-Governmental Organisations in the UN System*, ed. Peter Willets (London: Hurst & Co., 1996), 15–30.

2. Helmut Anheier, Marlies Glasius, and Mary Kaldor, "Introducing Global Civil Society," in *Global Civil Society 2001*, ed. Helmut Anheier, Marlies Glasius and Mary Kaldor (Oxford: Oxford University Press, 2001), 4; Harold K. Jacobson, *Networks of Interdependence: International Organisations and the Global Political System*, 2d ed. (New York: Alfred A. Knopf, 1984); John Boli and George M. Thomas, "INGOs and the Organisation of World Culture," in *Constructing World Culture: International Nongovernmental Organizations Since 1875*, ed. John Boli and George M. Thomas (Stanford, CA: Stanford University Press, 1999), 13–49; Kjell Skjelsbaek, "The Growth of International Nongovernmental Organisation in the Twentieth Century," *International Organisation* 25, no. 3 (1971): 420–42; Kerstin Martens, *NGOs and the United Nations: Institutionalisation, Professionalisation and Adaptation* (Basingstoke: Palgrave, 2005); Peter Willetts, "Consultative States for NGOs at the United Nations," in *"Conscience of the World,"* ed. Willets, 31–62.

3. Bruce Mazlish, *The New Global History* (New York: Routledge, 2006); Bruce Mazlish and Akira Iriye, eds., *The Global History Reader* (New York: Routledge, 2005); Boli and Thomas, *Constructing World Culture;* Iriye, *Global Community.*

4. Ann Marie Clark, Elisabeth J. Friedman, and Kathryn Hochstetler, "The Sovereign Limits of global Civil Society: A Comparison of NGO Participation in UN World Conferences on the Environment, Human Rights and Women," *World Politics* 51, no 1 (1998): 1–35; David A. Snow, Sarah A. Soule, and Hanspeter Kriesi, eds., *The Blackwell Companion to Social Movements* (Oxford: Blackwell, 2004); John Clark, ed., *Globalising Civic Engagement: Civil Society and Transnational Action* (London: Earthscan, 2003); Global Policy Forum, *NGOs and the United Nations: Comments for the Report of the Secretary General* (New York: Global Policy Forum, 1999); John Keane, *Global Civil Society?* (Cambridge: Cambridge University Press, 2003); Ann C. Hudock, *NGOs and Civil Society: Democracy by Proxy?* (Cambridge: Polity, 1999); John Clark, *Worlds Apart: Civil Society and the Battle for Ethical Globalisation* (London: Earthscan, 2003); Håkan Thörn, *Anti-Apartheid and the Emergence of a Global Civil Society* (Basingstoke: Palgrave, 2006).

5. Jacobson, *Networks of Interdependence*, 411–13.

6. Paul Ekins, *A New World Order: Grassroots Movements for Global Change* (London: Routledge, 1992), 130–37.

7. IOCU, *The Consumer and the World of Tomorrow: Report of the Second Conference of the International Organisation of Consumers Union* (The Hague: IOCU, 1962), 7.

8. Ibid.; Eirlys Roberts, *International Organisation of Consumers Unions, 1960–1981* (The Hague: IOCU, 1981); Foo Gaik Sim, *IOCU on Record: A Documentary History of the International Organization of Consumers Unions, 1960–1990* (Yonkers, NY: Consumers Union, 1991), 25–21; IOCU, *Programme of First International Meeting on Consumer Testing* (The Hague: IOCU, 1960).

9. CU Archive: CW: Box 27: Folder "IOCU, 1961": Letter from Elizabeth Schadee to Members of the IOCU Council, 7 February 1961; Jim Murray, "Bureau Européen des Unions de Consommateurs," in *Encyclopaedia of the Consumer Movement*, ed. S. Brobeck, R. N. Mayer, and R. O. Herrmann (Santa Barbara, CA: ABC-CLIO, 1997), 73–76.

10. Sim, *IOCU on Record*, 64; IOCU Archive: Box 1: File A2.9: "Documents re Directorship, 1964."

11. IOCU, *Consumers on the March: Proceedings of the 3rd Biennial Conference of the IOCU* (The Hague: IOCU, 1964), 6.

12. Ibid., 130.

13. Ibid., 136.

14. IOCU, *Knowledge Is Power: Consumer Goals in the 1970s. Proceedings of the 6th Biennial World Conference of the International Organisation of Consumers Unions* (The Hague: IOCU, 1970), 32.

15. Ibid., 8.

16. Ibid., 13.

17. IOCU, *Consumers on the March*, 77.

18. IOCU, *Knowledge Is Power*, 108

19. IOCU, *Five Billion Consumers: Organising for Change Proceedings of 11th World Congress* (The Hague: IOCU, 1984), 61.

20. IOCU, *Consumer Solidarity: For a Better World: Proceedings of 12th Congress* (The Hague: IOCU, 1987).

21. The sheer scale of her correspondence is apparent in the 160 folders devoted to their storage at the archives of Consumers Union in New York: CU Archive: Florence Mason Papers; Sim, *IOCU on Record*, 38; IOCU Archive: Box 1: File A2.10: Florence Mason, Notes on Starting a Consumer Organisation (The Hague: IOCU, 1964); IOCU, *Guidelines for Consumers Organisation: Survey Work* (The Hague: IOCU, 1974); Kansas State University (KSU) Archive: Florence Mason Collection: Biographical sketch.

22. IOCU Archive: Box 68: File G21.5: Colston E. Warne, "An Assessment of Consumer Protective Efforts in Israel, Pakistan, India, Japan, Australia and New Zealand: A Report to the Cultural Exchange Programme of the US Department of State," 23 July 1962; CU Archive: FM: Box 24: Folder 2: CU, "A Digest of the Leading Consumer Movements of the World," 1962; IOCU Archive: Box 43: File D3.7: Letter from Florence Mason to Colston E. Warne, 27 May 1968.

23. Sim, *IOCU on Record*, 42, 46; IOCU Archive: Box 2: File B1.6: "IOCU Constitutional Committee Report," February 1967; B1.8: Letter from Henry Epstein to Colston Warne, 22 February 1967; B1.14: Letter from Peter Goldman to Colston Warne, 7 July 1967; B1.15: Peter Goldman, "IOCU Constitution and Conference," 9 October 1967; *International Consumer* 4 (1968): 6.

24. IOCU, *Knowledge Is Power*, 115–17; IOCU, *Consumer Solidarity*, 6; IOCU, *Report for 1972–1974 to 8th IOCU Congress, Sydney* (The Hague: IOCU, 1974), 44; IOCU, *Report for 1975–1978 to 2nd General Assembly, London* (The Hague: IOCU, 1978), 31; IOCU, *Annual Report, 1982* (The Hague: IOCU, 1983), 5; IOCU, *Annual Report, 1986* (The Hague: IOCU, 1987); IOCU Archive: Box 3: File CM43/4.1: James Firebrace, "Director General Summary Report, 1991–1994," September 1994.

25. Sim, *IOCU on Record*, 60, 73–79; IOCU Archive: Box 3: File B2.1: Summarised Minutes of Council Meetings, 1stt–24th, 1960–1976; Box 130: File I1: Seminar on Consumer Education for Consumer Protection, February 1974, Singapore [various records]; file I2: Establishment of IOCU-ROAP, Singapore [various records]; *International Consumer* 14, no. 4 (1973—74); Anwar Fazal, interview by the author, 13 April 2004; IOCU, *Report for 1975–1978* (The Hague: IOCU, 1978), 2.

26. IOCU, *Report for 1975–1978*, 25–30; IOCU, *Annual Report, 1980* (The Hague: IOCU, 1981), 11–15; IOCU, *Annual Report, 1982* (The Hague: IOCU, 1983), 11–15; IOCU, *Annual Report, 1991* (The Hague: IOCU, 1992), 9–14; IOCU-ROAP, *Study Tour for Consumer Leaders: A Report* (Penang: IOCU-ROAP, 1994); CI-ROAP and Consumer Council of Fiji, *Sub-Regional Consumers' Leader's Forum and Workshop on Food Safety/Codex & Trade Issues, Suva, Fiji Islands, 8–10 April 2002* (Suva: Consumer Council of Fiji, 2002); FOMCA and CI-ROAP, *Southeast Asian Conference on Consumerism in Developing Economies: Agenda for the Future* (Petaling Jaya: FOMCA, 1995); Shanti Ramanathan, "Conditions for Organising," *World Consumer* 202 (July 1992): 4–5.

27. IOCU Archive: Box 11. File B3em: Minutes of Executive Meetings, 36, 12–13 September 1981; Box 17: File B3em: Michel van Hulten, "Proposals for IOCU Publications Policy," 23 August 1989.

28. IOCU Archive: Box 131: File I7.8: *Asia-Pacific Consumer* interviews Anwar Fazal, p. 9.

29. IOCU Archive: Box 131: File I7.4: Julian Edwards, "21stt Anniversary Speech," 27 September 1996; Rhoda Karpatkin, interview by the author, 19 February 2005.

30. IOCU Archive: Box 14: File B3em: Ruth Vermeer, "A Snapshot of the Consumer Movement in Spain," 2 April 1985; IOCU, *Report for 1975–1985*, p. 2; IOCU, *Proceeding of the Mediterranean Consumer Conference, Athens, 28–30 March 1976* (The Hague: IOCU, 1976).

31. IOCU, *Annual Report, 1986* (The Hague: IOCU, 1987), 7, 10–12; IOCU, *Annual Report,*

1985 (The Hague: IOCU, 1986), 22–23; IOCU Archive: Box 15: File B3em: Lars Broch, "UN Regional Seminar for Latin America and the Caribbean," 18 March 1987.

32. IOCU Archive: Box 139: File I23.2: IOCU-ROLAC, *Work Programme*, 1988; Jean Michel Arrighi and Jose Vargas, "Some Accomplishments as a Follow up of March 1987 UN Meeting on Consumer Protection in Latin America," 29 May 1988.

33. IOCU, *Annual Report, 1990* (The Hague: IOCU, 1990), 6; IOCU, *Annual Report, 1991* (The Hague: IOCU, 1991), 16–17, 23–29; IOCU, *Annual Report, 1994* (The Hague: IOCU, 1995), 36–37; IOCU Archive: Box 139: File I23.6: IOCU, *Regional Strategies and Plans of the Regional Office for Latin America and the Caribbean for the Years 1992–1995*, draft copy, 1992; Box 3: File CM48/7(ii): ROLAC, "Summary of Progress Report," 1997; Consumers International, *Annual Report, 1994* (London: Consumers International, 1995), 34–38; *World Consumer* 230 (September 1998): 7; *World Consumer* 233 (June 1999): 14–15.

34. IOCU Archive: Box 142: File I26.1: African Delegation to 12th World Congress, "Consumer Movement in Africa: An Action Agenda," September 1987; I26.2: Ahmed Ndyeshobola and Deborah Engelen-Eigles, "The African Task Force: Discussion and Reassessment," 8 June 1988; I26.4: IOCU Consultative Committee for Africa, *Minutes of First Meeting*, Nairobi, 14–18 June 1988; I27.1: Circular Letter for Africa, June 1991; I27.3: Circular Letter for Africa, December 1991; Box 143: File I28.27: IOCU, *Consumers in Africa: Meeting the Challenge: Proceedings of the IOCU Conference for Anglophone Africa, Nairobi, 14–18 June 1988* (The Hague: IOCU, 1988); Box 144: File I29.92: IOCU and ENDA, *Consommateurs africains face aux politiques de développement: conférence luso-francophone, Dakar, Sénégal, du 21 au 25 novembre 1988* (African consumers and the politics of development: Luso-Francophone Conference) (Dakar: IOCU & ENDO, 1989); Box 147: File I36.3: Amadou Cheilkh Kanouté, "The Next Thirty Years: Emergence of a Consumer Movement in Africa—Challenges and Opportunities," summary to ENDA of an IOCU mini-Congress, The Netherlands, 1–6 May 1990; Box 149: File I40.2: Letter from Michel van Hulten, DG of IOCU to Inter African Union of Lawyers; I40.3: Letter from Rafeeuddin Ahmed, Under-Secretary-General for International Economic and Social Affairs to various governments, 8 January 1991; I40.6Letter from Grada Hellman to various consumer organizations, 21 March 1991; I41.29: Letter from Ngaite Chimbandi and Trudy van Ommeren to IOCU members, 2 June 1992; Box 150: File I43/2.1: Review of CI-ROAF; Box 3: File CM47/3(i): ROAF, "Executive Summary for October 1995 to September 1996"; CM48/7(viii): ROAF, *3 Year Activity Report for the Period January 1995 to September 1997*; Box 183: ROAf Publications: various issues of *Consommation et Développement*, 1989–1999; Box 41: File C17: "Nairobi Declaration," June 1988; Sim, *IOCU on Record*, pp. 69–70; *World Consumer* 230 (September 1998): 14–15; CI-ROAF, *Research Manual for Consumer Organisations* (Harare: CI-ROAF, 2001); CI-ROAF, *Annual Report 2002: Consumer Protection and Quality of Life in Africa* (Harare: CI-ROAF, 2003); Consumers International, *Annual Report, 1997* (London: Consumers International, 1997), 4; IOCU, *Annual Report, 1993* (The Hague: IOCU, 1994), 34–38.

35. IOCU Archive: Box 151: File I44.2: Dick Westendorp, "Some Personal Notes on the 1st Congress of Consumers Organisations in Socialist Countries," May 1989; I45.1: Letter from Grada Hellman & Kevin Cook to IOCU members, February 1990; I45.3: Michel van Hulten, "Mission Report," 14 August 1989; I45.16: Michel van Hulten, Notes on "General Meeting of Representatives from Member Organisations of IOCU and Consumer Organisations in Socialist Countries in Europe and Vietnam, November 1989"; I45.16 [double reference as with above]: "Warsaw Declaration," 16 November 1989; I45.46: Letter from Kevin Cook, IOCU Programme for Eastern Europe, to Alastair Macgeorge, CA, 9 April 1991; IOCU, *Annual Report, 1994* (The Hague: IOCU, 1995), 30–31.

36. IOCU Archive: Box 153: File I52: Correspondence of Alastair Macgeorge, various letters.

37. IOCU Archive: Box 151: File I46.10: Report on First Regional Conference for Central and Eastern Europe, "Creating Consumer Awareness," Bled, Slovenia, 21–24 October 1992, including "The Bled Declaration"; I47.6: *Kontakt* 1 February 1992; PP253; PP254–5; PP321.

38. *World Consumer* 228 (March 1998): 14–15; *World Consumer* 202 (July 1992): 1–3; Consumers International, *Guidelines for Consumer Policy in Central and Eastern Europe* (London: CI, 2000).

39. IOCU, *Report for 1975–1978*, 14; IOCU Archive: Box 8: File B3.2: Minutes of 24th Executive Meeting, 21 April 1976; IOCU Archive: Box 4: File CM29/5: James O'Grady, "IOCU Accounts, Finances and 1982 Budget," 10 June 1981.

40. John Clark, "Introduction: Civil Society and Transnational Action," in *Globalising Civic*

Engagement: Civil Society and Transnational Action, ed. John Clark (London: Earthscan, 2003), 9.

41. IOCU Archive: Box 1: File A2: Ruth Simmons Vermeer, "The Consumer Movement and Developing Countries," paper presented to Consumers' Association of Bangladesh, Dacca, April 1979, 7.

42. Leon Gordenker and Thomas G. Weiss, "Pluralising Global Governance: Analytical Approaches and Dimensions," in *NGOs, the UN, and Global Governance,* ed. Thomas G. Weiss and Leon Gordenker, (Boulder, CO: Lynne Rienner, 1996), 17–47; Global Policy Forum, *NGOs and the United Nations: Comments for the Report of the Secretary General* (New York: Global Policy Forum, 1999); Linda Fasulo, *An Insider's Guide to the UN* (New Haven, CT: Yale University Press, 2004), 6; Antonio Donini, "The Bureaucracy and the Free Spirits: Stagnation and Innovation in the Relationship Between the UN and NGOs," *Third World Quarterly* 16, no. 3 (1995): 421–39; IOCU Archive: Box 54: File F5.2: Marianna Huggard, "Non-Governmental Organisations and the United Nations System: An Examination of Formal and Non-Formal Consultative Relationships," report prepared for the Conference of NGOs in Consultative Status with ECOSOC, April 1981.

43. See, for example, Ramesh Thakur, "Human Rights: Amnesty International and the United Nations," *Journal of Peace Research* 31, no. 2 (1994): 143–60; Irene Tinker, "Introduction: Ideas into Action," in *Developing Power: How Women Transformed International Development,* ed. Arvonne S. Fraser and Irene Tinker (New York: Feminist Press, 2004), xiii–xxx; Ellen Dorsey, "The Global Women's Movement: Articulating a New Vision of Global Governance," in *The Politics of Global Governance: International Organizations in an Interdependent World,* ed. Paul F. Diehl (Boulder, CO: Lynne Rienner, 2001), 436–61.

44. Archer, "Methods of Multilateral Management," 306.

45. KSU Archive: Florence Mason Collection: Box 4: File 4:11: ECOSOC, *Non-Governmental Organisations in Consultative Status with the Economic and Social Council* (September 1963).

46. KSU Archive: Dorothy Willner papers (hereafter DW): Box 5: IOCU, "Reclassification Request," 1976 (UN E/C.2/R.48).

47. KSU Archive: DW: Box 5: Letter from Dorothy Willner to Colston Warne, 1979.

48. CU Archive: Persia Cambell Papers (PC): Box 18: Folder "UN Reports": Persia Campbell, "Review of a Series of UN Documents in Socio-Economic Research with a Bearing on the Consumer Interest," 27 August 1964; Sim, *IOCU on Record,* 95–97; IOCU Archive: Box 60: File G3.8: Remarks of Colston E. Warne at the memorial service held for Persia Campbell at Queens College, New York, 23 March 1974; File G3.10: note on Persia Campbell.

49. John Toye and Richard Toye, *The UN and Global Political Economy: Trade, Finance, and Development* (Bloomington: Indiana University Press, 2004), 2–3; Peter Willets, "From 'Consultative Arrangements' to 'Partnership': The Changing Status of NGOs in Diplomacy at the UN," *Global Governance* 6, no. 2 (2000): 191–212; Alger, "The Emerging Roles of NGOs."

50. Toye and Toye, *The UN and Global Political Economy,* 187–232; Craig N. Murphy, "What the Third World Wants: An Interpretation of the Development and Meaning of the New International Economic Order Ideology," in *Politics of Global Governance,* ed. Diehl, 261–76; Archer, "Methods of Multilateral Management," 309.

51. IOCU, *Biennial Report, 1970–1972* (The Hague: IOCU, 1972), 28–31; Persia Campbell, "The Consumer Role in the Second UN Development Decade," 1971, reprinted in Sim, *IOCU on Record,* 101–7; CU Archive: PC: Box 18: Persia Campbell, "IOCU's Role at the UN, 1970"; KSU Archive: DW: Box 2: ECOSOC Council Committee on NGOs, *Statement Submitted by IOCU on Second United Nations Development Decade, 4 July 1971* (UN E/C.2/749); ECOSOC Council Committee on NGOs, *Statement Submitted by IOCU on Social Development, 8 May 1970* (UN E/C.2/693); ECOSOC Commission for Social Development, *Statement Submitted by IOCU on the Implementation of the International Development Strategy for the Second United Nations Development Decade and the Role of the Commission for Social Development, 17 February 1971* (UN E/CN.5/NGO/100); ECOSOC Commission on Human Rights, *Statement Submitted by IOCU on the Rights of the Consumer and the Question of the Realisation of Economic, Social and Cultural Rights and the Programme of Advisory Services in the Field of Human Rights, 28 February 1972* (UN E/CN.4/NGO/164).

52. Anwar Fazal, interview by the author, 13 April 2004; Rhoda Karpatkin, interview by the author, 19 February 2005.

53. IOCU, *Report for 1975–1978,* 32–43; IOCU, *Annual Report, 1979,* 21–36; IOCU, *Report for 1972–1974,* 28–30, 40–45; IOCU, *Biennial Report, 1970–1972,* 27.

54. KSU Archive: DW: Box 5: Letter from Dorothy Willner to Willy van Rijkeghem, 23 March 1976.

55. KSU Archive: DW: Box 5: IOCU, "Reclassification Request," 1976 (UN E/C.2/R.48); Oral statement on behalf of IOCU on 7 February 1977, by Dorothy Willner to the Economic and Social Council of the UN on Non-Governmental Organisations Updating the Information Provided in the Answers to the Questionnaire re the Application for Reclassification to Category I [from UN E/R 48, pp. 87–96].

56. KSU Archive: DW: Box 5: ECOSOC, *Non-Governmental Organisations in Consultative Status with the Economic and Social Council in 1976*, 14 July 1976 (UN E/INF/154); IOCU Archive: Box 54: File F5.12: ECOSOC, *List of NGOs in Consultative Status with ECOSOC in 1981*, 6 July 1982 (UN E/1982/INF.9).

57. IOCU, *Annual Report, 1981*, 6–9; IOCU, *Annual Report, 1982*, 20–21; IOCU, *The Child as Consumer* (The Hague: IOCU, 1979).

58. IOCU Archive: Box 53: File F3.4: Daphne Grose, "Codex Alimentarius Commission: Report to the Executive Committee," 27 July 1972; IOCU, *Annual Report, 1979*, 27; Consumers International, *Why We Need Labelling of Genetically Engineered Food* (London: CI, 1998).

59. *World Consumer* 221 (March 1996): 1–3; IOCU, *The Food Crisis* (The Hague: IOCU, 1978); Consumers International and Consumentenbond, *Food of the Future: The Risks and Realities of Biotechnology: Conference Proceedings, Oegstgeest, 16–17 November 1995* (London: CI, 1995); Maria Elena Hurtado, *GM Foods: The Facts and the Fiction* (London: CI, 2000); Consumers International, *Food Security: The New Millenium* (Penang: CI-ROAP, 1999); Ratnakar Adhikari, ed., *Food Security in the Global Age: South Asian Dilemma* (Kathmandu and Kuala Lumpur: SAWTEE, Pro Public & CI-ROAP, 2001).

60. IOCU, *Annual Report, 1982*, 22–23; IOCU, *Working Over Time: Triennial Report, 1981–1984* (The Hague: IOCU, 1985), 7; Katherine Gillman, *The Consumer Interpol: A Report to IOCU* (The Hague: IOCU, 1981); IOCU, *Consumer Interpol: Operational Guidelines* (The Hague: IOCU, 1982).

61. IOCU, *Annual Report, 1986*, 15; IOCU, *Annual Report, 1986*, 10; Michael J. Vernon, *Evaluation of the Consumer Interpol: A Report to IOCU* (Penang: IOCU-ROAP, 1984); IOCU Archive: Box 17: File B3em: Martin Abrahams, "Consumer Interpol: A Citizen's Action Approach to Police Corporate Dumping of Hazardous Products," *Project Appraisal* 3, no. 3 (September 1988): 155–58. Consumer Interpol ceased to exist in 1995 as other forms of information about dangerous goods rendered it redundant.

62. IOCU, *Annual Report, 1982*, 1; http://www.rightlivelihood.org; Ekins, *New World Order;* Jeremy Seabrook, *Pioneers of Change: Experiments in Creating a New Society* (London: Zed Books, 1993); Tom Woodhouse, ed., *People and Planet: The Right Livelihood Award Speeches* (London: Green Books, 1987).

63. KSU Archive: DW: Box 9: ECOSOC, *List of Participants to the Sixty-Third Session of the ECOSOC, Geneva, 6 July–5 August 1977*, 19 July 1977 (UN E/INF.161).

64. E. A. Schadee-Hartree, "Harmonisating of Consumer Protecting Laws," in *Consumers on the March*, 28–82.

65. Heather Widdows, "Is Global Ethics Moral Neo-colonialism? An Investigation of the Issue in the Context of Bioethics," *Bioethics* 21, no. 6 (2007): 305–315; Micheline R. Ishay, *The History of Human Rights: From Ancient Times to the Globalization Era* (Berkeley: University of California Press, 2004). See also chapter 7 in this volume.

66. IOCU, *Knowledge Is Power*, 17.

67. KSU Archive: DW: Box 7: Letter from Dorthy Willner to Colston Warne, 2 March 1975; Box 8: IOCU, "Draft Proposal for a Model Code of Consumer Protection for the United Nations," 27 February 1975; Box 10: ECOSOC, *Draft Programme of Work on the Full Range of Issues Relating to Transnational Corporations: Statement Submitted by Dorothy Willner*, 23 February 1976; ECOSOC, *Transnational Corporations: Proposal for Consumer Protection under UN Auspices: Statement Submitted by IOCU*, 19 July 1976 (UN E/NGO/52); Sim, *IOCU on Record*, 97–99; IOCU, *Report for 1975–1978*, 9; IOCU, *Working Over Time*, 9.

68. KSU Archive: DW: Box 9: ECOSOC, *List of Participants to the Sixty-Third Session of the ECOSOC, Geneva, 6 July–5 August 1977*, 19 July 1977 (UN E/INF.161).

69. IOCU Archive: Box 54: File F5.4: Dorothy Willner, "ECOSOC Action on Consumer Protection," 31 October 1977; ECOSOC, *Consumer Protection: A Survey of Institutional Arrangements and Legal Measures*, 8 June 1978 (UN E/1978/81).

70. KSU Archive: DW: Box 4: ECOSOC, *Consumer Protection: Report of the Secretary General,* 14 May 1979 (UN E/1979/65).

71. KSU Archive: DW: Box 7: Letter from Dorothy Willner to consumer organisations in member states of ECOSOC, 8 June 1978.

72. KSU Archive: DW: Box 3: Dorothy Willner, "Progress Report on Consumer Protection at ECOSOC," July 1979.

73. KSU Archive: DW: Box 3: Dorothy Willner, "ECOSOC Progress on Consumer Guidelines," memo to the IOCU Executive Committee, 2–4 January 1981; Box 5: ECOSOC, *Statement Submitted by IOCU on Consumer Protection,* 16 July 1979 (UN E/1979/NGO/17); IOCU, *A World in Crisis: The Consumer Response. Proceedings of the Ninth IOCU World Congress, 10–14 July 1978* (The Hague: IOCU, 1978).

74. IOCU Archive: Box 10: File B3em: *Report of the IOCU Seminar on "The Law and the Consumer," Hong Kong, 6–10 January 1980;* IOCU and University of the Philippines Law Center, *First ASEAN Seminar on Consumer Protection, Quezon City, 1–4 October 1980* (Quezon City: University of the Philippines Law Center, 1981).

75. IOCU, *Annual Report, 1981,* 4; IOCU Archive: Box 54: File No. not given [between F.5.8 and F5.9]: UN Economic and Social Commission for Asia and the Pacific, *Report of the Regional Consultation of Consumer Protection,* 22 June 1981 (UN TRADE/RCCP/8).

76. KSU Archive: DW: Box 10: ECOSOC, *Consumer Protection: Report of the Secretary-General Prepared in Compliance with Economic and Social Council Resolution 1979/74,* 4 June 1981, (UN E/1981/75).

77. IOCU Archive: Box 54: F5.13: UN Economic and Social Council, *International Co-Operation and Co-Ordination Within the United Nations System: Consumer Protection: Report of the Secretary General,* 27 May 1983 (UN E/1983/71); F5.15: Dorothy Willner, "Comments of the International Organisation of Consumers Unions on the UN Draft Guidelines on Consumer Protection to the Senate Committee on Foreign Relations," 6 June 1983.

78. KSU Archive: DW: Box 7: International Chamber of Commerce, "Consumer Protection: Activities of the International Chamber of Commerce," note submitted for consideration by the United Nations meeting of 7–9 November 1979 (Geneva); Box 7: Jacqueline A Keith, Report on November 9th UN Intersecretariat meeting in Geneva, Switzerland to Members of the Committee on Marketing, Advertising and Distribution, United States Council of the International Chamber of Commerce, 12 December 1979; Administrative Committee on Co-Ordination, *Summary of Results of the Ad Hoc Inter-Agency Meeting on Consumer Protection (Geneva, 7–9 November 1979),* 11 February 1980 (UN ACC/1980/5).

79. KSU Archive: DW: Box 7: "Consumer Protection: Meeting of the UN Organisation with NGOs, 9 November 1979: List of Participants."

80. Murray Weidenbaum, "The Case Against the UN Guidelines for Consumer Protection," *Journal of Consumer Policy* 10, no. 4 (1987): 425–32 (425).

81. IOCU Archive: Box 15: File B3em: Minutes of the 45th Executive Meeting, 21–22 April 1985.

82. IOCU Archive: Box 54: File F5.17: Report of Esther Peterson to Lars Broch: "Some Notes Concerning 1983"; David Harland, "The United Nations Guidelines for Consumer Protection," *Journal of Consumer Policy* 10, no. 3 (1987): 245–66; II70; II79.

83. IOCU, *Annual Report, 1986,* 13; CI-ROAP and Consumer Unions and Trust Society, *Consumers in the Global Age: Proceedings of International Conference on Consumer Protection, New Delhi, India, 1997* (Penang and Calcutta: CI-ROAP and CUTS, 1997); UN Department of Economic and Social Affairs, *Consumer Protection for Asia and the Pacific: Report of the International Conference on Consumer Protection* (New York: United Nations, 1998); UN Economic and Social Commission for Western Asia, *Consumer Protection under a Liberalised Trade System in Selected Countries of the ESCWA Region Consumer* (New York: United Nations, 2000); Yujun Mei and George M. Thomas, "The Role of International Nongovernmental Organizations in the Global Construction of Consumer Rights," forthcoming; UN Department of Economic and Social Affairs, *Consumer Protection for Africa: Report of the Africa Conference on Consumer Protection, Harare, Zimbabwe, 28 April–2 May 1996* (New York: United Nations, 1997); Jean Michel Arrighi, "Integration and Consumer Protection: The Case of Latin America," *Journal of Consumer Policy* 15, no. 2 (1992): 179–90.

84. Latest versions available at http://www.un.org/esa/sustdev/publications/consumption_en .pdf; Esther Peterson and Jean M. Halloran, "United Nations Consumer Protections," in

S. Brobeck, R. N. Mayer, and R. O. Herrmann, eds., *Encyclopaedia of the Consumer Movement* (Santa Barbara, CA : ABC-CLIO, 1997), 581–83.

85. KSU Archive: DW: Box 5: "Curriculum Vitae of Dorothy Willner," no date.

86. Helen Laville, *Cold War Women: American Women's Organisations in the Cold War* (Manchester, UK: Manchester University Press, 2002).

87. IOCU Archive: Box 54: File F5.16: various mailgrams between Anwar Fazal and Dorothy Willner, March 1983.

88. Anwar Fazal, interview by the author, 13 April 2004; Rhoda Karpatkin, interview by the author, 19 February 2005.

89. IOCU Archive: Box 66a: File G16c.3: Esther Peterson, "Remarks Before the UN International Business Council," New York, 2 February 1984; Esther Peterson (with Winifred Conkling), *Restless: The Memoirs of Labor and Consumer Activist Esther Peterson* (Washington, DC: Caring, 1995); File G16b.13: Elliot Negin, "Esther Peterson: The Grande Dame of Consumerism," *Public Citizen* (Winter 1985): 17–23; G16b.24: Vicki Kemper, "A Citizen for All Seasons," *Common Cause Magazine* (Spring 1995): 12–17; File G16b.26: Ralph Nader, "In Appreciation of Esther Peterson, Restless Activist," *Multinational Monitor,* December 1997, 29.

90. Iriye, *Global Community;* Mazlish, *New Global History.*

Chapter 5. The All-Consuming Network: The Politics of Protest in an Age of Consumption

1. Up to date information on these issues can be found on the leading anti-baby milk formula websites: http://www.ibfan.org; http://www.babymilkaction.org; http://www.infact.org; http://www.waba.org.my; http://www.lalecheleague.org.

2. Cicely Williams, "Milk and Murder," reprinted in *The Breastfeeding Movement: A Sourcebook,* ed. Lakshi Menon, Anwar Fazal, Sarah Amin, and Susan Siew (Penang: World Alliance for Breastfeeding Action, 2003), 34–36.

3. Naomi Klein, *No Logo* (London: HarperCollins, 2000).

4. Naomi Klein, *Fences and Windows: Dispatches from the Front Lines of the Globalization Debate* (London: Flamingo, 2002), 20.

5. Paul Kingsnorth, *One No, Many Yeses: A Journey to the Heart of the Global Resistance Movement* (London: Free Press, 2003).

6. Marjorie Mayo, *Global Citizens: Social Movements and the Challenge of Citizenship* (London: Zed Books, 2005), 31–33; Michael Hardt and Antonio Negri, Empire (Cambridge, MA: Harvard University Press, 2001).

7. G. Monbiot, *The Age of Consent: A Manifesto for a New World Order* (London: Flamingo, 2003).

8. Noreena Hertz, *The Silent Takeover: Global Capitalism and the Death of Democracy* (London: Heinemann, 2001).

9. Bernard Cassen, "On the Attack," *New Left Review* 19 (January–February 2003): 41–60; Günther Schönleitner, "World Social Forum: Making Another World Possible," in *Globalising Civic Engagement: Civil Society and Transnational Action,* ed. John Clark (London: Earthscan, 2003), 127–49.

10. IOCU Archive: Box 131: File I7.4: Julian Edwards, "Regional Office 21st Anniversary Speech," 27 September 1996.

11. Julian Edwards, interview by the author, 8 September 2004.

12. Rhoda Karpatkin, interview by the author, 19 February 2005.

13. IOCU Archive: Box 61a: File G5a.11: Anwar Fazal, "With *lalang* on Our Minds: A Note on Consumerist Alternatives in Organising to Cope with Changing Material, Social and Psychological Needs and Problems in Malaysia over the Next Quarter Century," paper presented at the conference Malaysia in the Year 2000, Kuala Lumpur, 3–7 August 1975, 26; File G5a.9: Anwar Fazal, "Agenda for Change: An Agenda for Active Citizenship," paper presented at the General Hospital, Johor Baru, Malaysia, 31 May 1975.

14. Anwar Fazal, "Vitality in Diversity," *Malaysian Business,* January 1979, 87–88.

15. IOCU Archive: Box 61a: File G5a.6: Anwar Fazal, "An Outline Strategy for the Promotion and Financing of Consumers Organisations in Developing Countries," paper presented at the IOCU World Congress, 23–27 March 1975, Sydney, 3.

16. IOCU Archive: Box 61a: File G5a.32: Anwar Fazal, "Brave and Angry: The International

Consumer Movement's Response to MNCs," paper presented at the ASEAN Consumer Protection Seminar, 1–4 October 1980, Quezon City, Philippines, 8

17. Scott Lash and John Urry, *The End of Organised Capitalism* (Cambridge: Polity Press, 1987); Thomas Frank, *One Market Under God: Extreme Capitalism, Market Populism, and the End of Economic Democracy* (London: Secker and Warburg, 2000). Chapter 8 will focus more on the debates about economic globalization.

18. Manuel Castells, *The Information Age: Economy, Society and Culture: Vol. I. The Rise of the Network Society* (Oxford: Blackwell, 2000 [1996]).

19. Ibid.; M. Castells, *The Information Age: Economy, Society and Culture: Vol. II. The Power of Identity* (Oxford: Blackwell, 2000 [1997]).

20. John Keane, *Global Civil Society* (Cambridge: Polity, 2003); Mary Kaldor, *Global Civil Society: An Answer to War* (Cambridge: Polity, 2003).

21. Sydney Tarrow, *Power in Movement: Social Movements and Contentious Politics*, 2nd ed. (Cambridge: Cambridge University Press, 1998), 49, 188; Jessica Lipnack and Jeffrey Stamps, The *Networking Book: People Connecting with People* (New York: Routledge and Kegan Paul, 1986); Mario Diani, "Networks and Participation," in *The Blackwell Companion to Social Movements*, ed. David A. Snow, Sarah A. Soule, and Hanspeter Kriesi (Oxford: Blackwell, 2004), 339–59; Mario Diani, "Introduction: Social Movements, Contentious Actions, and Social Networks: 'From Metaphor to Substance'?," in *Social Movements and Networks: Relational Approaches to Collective Action*, ed. Mario Diani and Doug McAdam (Oxford: Oxford University Press, 2003), 1–18; Donatella Della Porta and Mario Diani, *Social Movements: An Introduction* (Oxford: Blackwell, 1998), 110–36.

22. For details on these NGOs, see the Database of Archives of Non-Governmental Organisations at http://www.dango.bham.ac.uk.

23. Cyril Ritchie, "Coordinate? Cooperate? Harmonize? NGO Policy and Operational Coalitions," in *NGOs, the UN, and Global Governance*, ed. Thomas G. Weiss and Leon Gordenker (Boulder, CO: Lynne Rienner, 1996), 177–88.

24. Margaret E. Keck and Kathryn Sikkink, *Activists Beyond Borders: Advocacy Networks in International Politics* (Ithaca, NY: Cornell University Press, 1998).

25. Tarrow, *Power in Movement*, 192

26. John Clark, "Introduction: Civil Society and Transnational Action," in *Globalising Civic Engagement: Civil Society and Transnational Action*, ed. John Clark (London: Earthscan, 2003), 1–28. See also http://www.eltaller.org, http://www.climatenetwork.org, and http://www.social-watch.org.

27. Paolo Grenier, "Jubilee 2000: Laying the Foundations for a Social Movement," in *Globalising Civic Engagement*, ed. Clark, 86–108; Mayo, *Global Citizens*, 172–92.

28. Günther Schönleitner, "World Social Forum: Making Another World Possible," in *Globalising Civic Engagement*, ed. Clark, 127–49.

29. Keck and Sikkink, *Activists Beyond Borders*.

30. Ibid., 59–72

31. Lipnack and Stamps, *Networking Book*, 57.

32. Simon Chapman, *The Lung Goodbye: A Manual of Tactics for Counteracting the Tobacco Industry in the 1980s* (Penang: IOCU-ROAP, 1985); Simon Chapman and Wong Wai Lend, *Tobacco Control in the Third World: A Resource Atlas* (Penang: IOCU-ROAP, 1990); IOCU, *Annual Report, 1986*, 22–23; IOCU, *Annual Report, 1985*, 16–17.

33. IOCU, *Annual Report, 1985*, 16; Vandan Shiva, *Biopiracy: The Plunder of Nature and Knowledge* (Cambridge, MA: South End Press, 1997).

34. IOCU, *Annual Report, 1988*, 6–7; IOCU, *Annual Report, 1985*, 10–11; IOCU Archive: Box 16: File B3em: Minutes of 53rd Executive Meeting, 29 February–1 March 1988; Bishan Singh, "About the Consumer Education Network," in *Consumer Education: A Resource Handbook*, ed. Anwar Fazal and Bishan Singh (Penang: IOCU-ROAP, 1991), ii.

35. Cicely Williams, *Milk and Murder: Address to the Rotary Club of Singapore in 1939* (Penang: IOCU-ROAP, 1986).

36. Kathryn Sikkink, "Codes of Conduct for Transnational Corporations: The Case of the WHO/UNICEF Code," *International Organisation* 40, no. 4 (1986): 815–40; Wolfgang Fikentscher, "United Nations Codes of Conduct: New Paths in International Law," *American Journal of Comparative Law* 30, no. 4 (1982): 590–93; Prakash Sethi, *The Righteous and the Powerful: Corporations, Religious Institutions and International Social Activism—The Case of the Infant For-*

mula Controversy and the Nestlé Boycott (Marshfield, MA: Pitman, 1985). See also http://www
.ibfan.org.

37. IOCU, *Annual Report, 1982,* 24–25; Anwar Fazal, "Brave and Angry," 7–8; Anwar Fazal,
"The Launching of IBFAN," in *Breastfeeding Movement,* ed. Menon et al., 55; Mike Muller, *The
Baby Killer,* 3rd ed. (London: War on Want, 1977); Andrew Chetley, *The Baby Killer Scandal: A
War on Want Investigation into the Promotion and Sales of Powdered Baby Milks in the Third
World* (London: War on Want, 1979).

38. IOCU Archive: Box 98: File H76.3: V. Beardshaw, "HAI Structure Paper," Appendix 1; Box
37: File C11.10: IBFAN, "Battling the Bottle," publicity flier, 1980s; Box 61a: File G5a.62: Anwar
Fazal, "IBFAN: A Force for Happiness," paper presented at opening of IBFAN Forum, Manila, 9
October 1988.

39. IOCU, *Working Over Time,* 8.

40. IBFAN, *Babies, Breastfeeding and the Code: Report of the IBFAN ASIA Conference, Sam
Phran, Thailand, 5–12 October 1986* (Penang: IOCU-ROAP, 1987); IOCU and IBFAN, *Protecting Infant Health: A Health Workers' Guide to the International Code of Marketing of Breastmilk
Substitutes* (Penang: IOCU and IBFAN, 1985); IOCU, *Annual Report, 1981,* 6; IOCU, *Annual Report, 1982,* 14; IOCU, *Working Over Time,* 8; IOCU, *Annual Report, 1986,* 20; Sikkink, "Codes
of Conduct," 832–37; Naomi Baumslag and Dia Michels, *Milk, Money and Madness: The Culture and Politics of Breastfeeding* (Mapusa, Goa: The Other India Press, 1995); Andrew Chetley,
The Politics of Baby Foods: Successful Challenges to an International Marketing Strategy (London:
Frances Pinter, 1986).

41. IOCU, *Annual Report, 1990,* 7; IBFAN, *Breaking the Rules 1991: A Worldwide Report on
Violations of the WHO/UNICEF International Code of Marketing of Breastmilk Substitutes*
(Penang: IBFAN and IOCU-ROAP, 1991); IOCU, *Annual Report, 1985,* 18; IOCU, *Annual Re-
port, 1988,* 9–10; IOCU, *Annual Report, 1989,* 7–8; IBFAN, *Breaking the Rules, Stretching the
Rules 2001: Evidence of Violations of the International Code of Marketing of Breastmilk Substi-
tutes and Subsequent Resolutions* (Penang: IBFAN, 2001); Ellen J. Sokol, *The Code Handbook: A
Guide to Implementing the International Code of Marketing of Breastmilk Substitutes* (Penang: International Code Documentation Centre/IBFAN, 1997).

42. IOCU Archive: Box 91: File H53: "New Links Between IOCU, IBFAN and PAN in Penang,"
9 January 1992; H54.2: "WHO Resolutions and Decisions," 19 January 1989.

43. La Leche League, *The Womanly Art of Breastfeeding,* 6th ed. (Schaumburg, IL: La Leche
League, 1997). For reader comment on this advice literature, see the reviews for *The Womanly Art*
on Amazon.com.

44. James E. Post, "International Consumerism in the Aftermath of the Infant Formula Controversy," in *The Future of Consumerism,* ed. Paul N. Bloom and Ruth Belk Smith (Lexington, MA:
Lexington Books, 1986), 165–78.

45. Rachel Carson, *Silent Spring* (Harmondsworth: Penguin, 1999 [1962]), 31.

46. IOCU Archive: Box 92: File H56.1: E. L. Wheelwright, "Consumers, Transnational Corporations and the Developing World in the 1980s: The Pesticide Industry," paper prepared by the Australian Consumers' Association at the 11th World Consumer Congress, Bangkok, 9–14 December
1984.

47. IOCU and Sahabat Alam Malaysia, *International NGO Workshop on the Global Pesticide
Trade: Background Readings, Penang, 25–28 May 1982* (Penang: IOCU, 1982); IOCU, *The Pesticide Handbook: Profiles for Action* (Penang: IOCU-ROAP, 1984); IOCU, *Annual Report, 1982,*
9, 15; IOCU Archive: Box 37: File C11.11: PAN, "Breaking the Circle of Poison," publicity leaflet,
1980s; Wheelwright, "Consumers, Transnational Corporations," 10.

48. IOCU, *Annual Report, 1982,* 28–29; Wheelwright, "Consumers, Transnational Corporations," 9.

49. IOCU Archive: Box 92: File H56.11: Anwar Fazal, "People, Pests and Pesticides," paper presented at the Nordic Conference on Environment and Development, 3.

50. Wheelwright, "Consumers, Transnational Corporations," 11; IOCU, *The Pesticide Handbook: Profiles for Action* (Penang: IOCU-ROAP, 1984); Foo Gaik Sim, *The Pesticide Poisoning Report: A Survey of Some Asian Countries* (Penang: IOCU-ROAP, 1985).

51. IOCU, *Annual Report, 1985,* 15; Gretta Goldenman and Sarojini Rengam, *Problem Pesti-
cides, Pesticide Problems: A Citizens' Action Guide to the International Code of Conduct on the
Distribution and Use of Pesticides* (Penang: PAN and IOCU-ROAP, 1988); IOCU Archive: Box 92:
File H56.5: PAN, "The 'Dirty Dozen': Report on the Global Campaign Launch," 5 June 1985.

52. IOCU, *Annual Report, 1986,* 16; Gretta Goldenman and Sarojini Rengam, *The Pesticide Code Monitor: A Resource Book for Trainers* (Penang: PAN and IOCU-ROAP, 1989); Gretta Goldenman and Sarojini Rengam, *Pesticides and You: 44 Questions and Answers* (Penang: PAN and IOCU-ROAP, 1989); Michael Hansen, *The First Three Years: Implementation of the World Bank Pesticide Guidelines, 1985–1988* (Mount Vernon, NY: Consumer Policy Institute/Consumers Union, 1990).

53. IOCU, *Annual Report, 1988,* 10; IOCU, *Annual Report, 1990,* 10–11; Michael Hansen, *Escape from the Pesticide Treadmill: Alternatives to Pesticides in Developing Countries* (Penang: PAN and IOCU-ROAP, 1987); RRii55–57; RRii65–67; Sarojini Rengam and Karen Snyder, *The Pesticides Handbook: Profiles for Action,* 3rd ed. (Penang: IOCU and PAN, 1991); IOCU Archive: Box 93: File H57.8: "Tim Lang Memorandum," 31 May 1991; File H57.9: Tenaganita, PAN Asia and the Pacific and IOCU, *Women and Pesticides: A Training Workshop* (Kuala Lumpur: Tenaganita, PAN Asia and the Pacific and IOCU, 1991).

54. Terry Gips, *Breaking the Pesticide Habit: Alternatives to 12 Hazardous Pesticides* (Penang: IOCO-ROAP, 1990).

55. Michael Hansen and Abou Thiam, *Sustainability: The Case for Reducing the Use of Chemical Pesticides* (Penang: PAN, 1987).

56. CI, *Consumer Rights and the Multilateral Trading System: What Needs to Be Done Before a Millennium Round* (London: CI, 1999); CI, *Food Security: The New Millennium* (Penang: CI-ROAP, 1999); Maria Elena Hurtado, *GM Foods: The Facts and the Fiction* (London: CI, 2000); Ratnakar Adhikari, ed., *Food Security in the Global Age: South Asian Dilemma* (Kathmandu and Kuala Lumpur: SAWTEE, Pro Public and CI-ROAP, 2001).

57. David Weir and Mark Schapiro, *Circle of Poison: Pesticides and People in a Hungry World* (Oakland, CA: Food First, 1980).

58. Gunnar Trumbull, *Consumer Capitalism: Politics, Product Markets, and Firm Strategy in France and Germany* (Ithaca, NY: Cornell University Press, 2006), 73.

59. Research Institute for Consumer Affairs, *Clioquinol: Availability and Instructions for Use* (The Hague: IOCU, 1975); IOCU, *Working Over Time,* 6–7; Anwar Fazal, "The Right Pharmaceuticals at the Right Prices: Consumer Perspectives," *World Development* 11, no. 3 (1983): 265–69; IOCU Archive: Box 61a: File G5a.28: Anwar Fazal, "Consumerism: An International Force," Jakarta, 14 May 1979; File G5a.32: Fazal, "Brave and Angry."

60. IOCU, *Working Over Time,* 6–7; IOCU Archive: Box 37: File C11.12: HAI, *"Towards Health for All,"* publicity leaflet, 1980s; Fazal, "The Right Pharmaceuticals," 267–268; Box 96: File H71.21: "Pharmaceuticals," 13; IOCU and BUKO, *Report of the International NGO Seminar on Pharmaceuticals, Geneva, 27–29 May 1981* (Geneva: UN, 1981).

61. IOCU, *Annual Report, 1986,* 17; IOCU, *Annual Report, 1988,* 9; IOCU Archive: Box 96: File H72.41: Letter from Lars Broch to Lena Ekroth, Swedish International Development Agency, 23 April 1987; Box 98: File H76.2: V. Beardshaw, "A New Structure for HAI?" 23 January 1986.

62. IOCU Archive: Box 97: File H74.9: HAI, "The WHO and the Pharmaceutical Industry," briefing paper presented at the 35th World Health Assembly, May 1982; H74.6: HAI, "A Draft International Code on Pharmaceuticals," 1982; Hans-W. Micklitz, "EC Regulation of the Export of Dangerous Pharmaceuticals to Third World Countries: Some Prospects," *Journal of Consumer Policy* 11, no. 1 (1988): 29–53; Andrew Chetley, "Not Good Enough for Us but Good Enough for Them: An Examination of the Chemical and Pharmaceutical Export Trades," *Journal of Consumer Policy* 9, no. 2 (1986): 155–80.

63. IOCU Archive: Box 96: File H71.2: HAI, "EEC Pharmaceutical Exports to Developing Countries," submission to the Environment, Public Health and Consumer Affairs Committee of the European Parliament on a motion for a resolution concerning the rational use of drugs in developing countries, February 1985; File H71.3: Lars Broch, "Consumer Aspects on the Marketing of Drugs in the Third World," April 1985; File H71.10: Charles Medawar, "Principles Involved in the Formulation of a Code of Conduct to Improve the Use of Pharmaceuticals," July 1985.

64. IOCU, *Forty-Four Problem Drugs: A Consumer Action and Resource Kit on Pharmaceuticals* (Penang: IOCU-ROAP, 1981).

65. IOCU, *Annual Report, 1982,* 27; HAI, *The Rational and Economic Use of Drugs in the Third World: A Health Action International Briefing Paper on the Bangladeshi Drug Ordinance of 12 June 1982* (Penang: HAI, 1982); Andrew Chetley, *From Policy to Practice: The Future of the Bangladesh National Drug Policy* (Penang: IOCU-ROAP, 1992).

66. Charles Medawar, *Drugs and World Health: An International Consumer Perspective* (Lon-

don: Social Audit, 1984); Virginia Beardshaw, *Prescription for Change: Health Action International's Guide to Rational Health Projects* (The Hague: IOCU, 1983).

67. Kumariah Balasubramaniam, *Global Marketing of Pharmaceuticals: Prescription for Disaster* (Penang: IOCU-ROAP, 1988).

68. Kumariah Balasubramaniam, *Policy Options in Pharmaceutical Patents for Developing Asian Countries* (Penang: IOCU-ROAP, 1988); Kumariah Balasubramaniam, *Policies and Strategies on Drug Pricing Regulations: International Experiences* (Penang: IOCU-ROAP, 1988).

69. Kumariah Balasubramaniam, *The Rational Use of Drugs: A Universal Concept* (Penang: IOCU-ROAP, 1988), 1; Kumariah Balasubramaniam, ed., *Towards Rational Drug Use: Proceedings of the International Consultation on Rational Drug Use in Undergraduate Medical/Pharmacy Education, Manila, 13–18 August 1988* (Penang: IOCU-ROAP, 1990); Kumariah Balasubramaniam, "Issues of Health Services for the Consumer in Third World countries," *Journal of Consumer Policy* 12, no. 3 (1989): 309–31; Multinational Monitor, "A Healthy Drug Policy for the Third World: An Interview with Kumariah Balasubramaniam," *Multinational Monitor,* December 1992, 25–29; IOCU Archove: Box 97: File H73.1: Kumariah Balasubramaniam, "Pharmaceuticals: Public Health and the Consumer," May 1984; File H73.4: Kumariah Balasubramaniam, paper presented at the Third Meeting of Interested Parties of the Action Programme on Essential Drugs, Geneva, 25–26 May 1989.

70. HAI, *Antibiotics: The Wrong Drugs for Diarrhoea* (The Hague: HAI, 1987); HAI, *The Rational and Economic Use of Drugs in the Third World* (Penang: HAI, 1982).

71. IOCU, *Annual Report, 1985,* 12–13.

72. CI, *Annual Report, 1994* (London: CI, 1995), 18; CI, *Annual Report, 1995* (London: CI, 1996), 16; IOCU Archive: Box 133: File I1.3: IOCU-ROAP, "ROAP Regional Strategy, 1993–1995," 1992, 11KKi53; Box 100: File H84.15: Prem Chandran John, *Assessment of Action for Rational Drugs in Asia (ARDA)* (Madras: Asian Community Health Action Network, 1995).

73. Shila Rani Kaur, Padmaja Padman, and Kumariah Balasubramaniam, eds., *Proceedings of the Asia Pacific Seminar on Implementing National Drug Policies, Sydney, 3–7 October 1995* (Penang: CI-ROAP, 1996); Kumariah Balasubramaniam, *Health and Pharmaceuticals in Developing Countries: Towards Social Justice and Equity* (Penang: CI-ROAP, 1996); Kumariah Balasubramaniam, "National Health Insurance and Financing: The International Scene and Foreign Models," paper presented at the Seminar on The Future of Health Service in Malaysia, Kuala Lumpur, 19–20 October 1996; Kumariah Balasubramaniam, "Health Care: Who Cares? Affordable Quality Health Care for all in Malaysia," paper presented at the Conference on Quality Health Care in Malaysia, Kuala Lumpur, 26–27 August 1996; Kumariah Balasubramaniam, "Towards Affordable Quality Medications for all Malaysians," paper presented at the National Seminar *Towards Affordable Quality Medications for All Malaysians,* Kuala Lumpur, 14 February 1993.

74. CI, *Branding the Cure: A Consumer Perspective on Corporate Social Responsibility, Drug Promotion and the Pharmaceutical Industry in Europe* (London: CI, 2006).

75. IOCU, *Giving a Voice to the World's Consumers* (The Hague: IOCU, 1985), 26.

76. IOCU Archive: Box 98: File H76.1: Ruth Vermeer, "Discussion Document: Working Within Networks—IOCU and IBFAN, HAI and PAN," January 1983; File H77.18: "HAI Working Methods," 29 January 1988.

77. IOCU Archive: Box 16: File B3em: Minutes of 53rd Executive Meeting, 28 February–1 March 1988, 14.

78. IOCU Archive: Box 131: File I7.8: *AP Consumer (25th Anniversary Edition),* 1999, 10.

79. Julian Edwards, interview by the author, 8 September 2004; IOCU Archive: Box 98: File H76.2: V. Beardshaw, "A New Structure for HAI?," 23 January 1986, 2–4.

80. IOCU Archive: Box 98: File H76.1: Ruth Vermeer, "Discussion Document: Working Within Networks—IOCU and IBFAN, HAI and PAN," January 1983.

81. IOCU Archive: Box 61a: File G5a.37: Anwar Fazal, "What the Consumer Movement Is About," paper presented at the seminar Law, Justice and the Consumer, Universiti Sains Malaysia, Penang, 19 November 1982.

82. Anwar Fazal, "People's Watchdogs: Link and Multiply," in *The Fight for Survival: People's Action for Environment,* ed. A. Agarwal and U. Samarth (New Delhi: Centre for Science and Environment, 1987), 231–41 (239).

83. IOCU Archive: Box 61a: File G5a.60: Anwar Fazal, "The Consumer Conscience," opening address at the Asia-Pacific Consumer Congress, Ohmiya City, Japan, 18–22 August 1989, 4.

84. IOCU Archive: Box 63: File G13.5: Rhoda H. Karpatkin, "A Social Agenda for Con-

sumerists: The Legacy of 1985," keynote address at the Consumer Federation of America Consumer Assembly, Washington, DC, 6 February 1986.

85. Geoff Eley, "Historicising the Global, Politicising Capital: Giving the Present a Name," *History Workshop Journal* 63 (2007): 154–88.

86. Klein, *Fences and Windows*.

Chapter 6. Backlash: The Corporate Critique of Consumerism

1. J. B. Matthews, *Odyssey of a Fellow Traveller* (New York: Mount Vernon Publishers, 1938).

2. Norman D. Katz, "Consumers Union: The Movement and the Magazine, 1936–1957," Ph.D. diss., Rutgers University, 1977, 363–99, 125, 136; Helen Sorenson, *The Consumer Movement: What It Is and What It Means* (New York: Harper and Brothers, 1941), 154–78; Kathleen G. Donohue, *Freedom from Want: American Liberalism and the Idea of the Consumer* (Baltimore: Johns Hopkins University Press, 2003), chs. 6 and 7.

3. Matthews, *Odyssey,* 267.

4. Norman Isaac Silber, *Test and Protest: The Influence of Consumers Union* (New York: Holmes and Meier, 1983), 29.

5. CU Archive: Box 238: Folder, "Attacks": various loose papers; Katz, "Consumers Union," 193–201; KSU Archive: Richard L. D. Morse Papers (RM): Box 158: Folder 21: Colston E. Warne, "The Consumer Movement Meets McCarthyism," speech at Kansas State University, 22 February 1977, 5–7.

6. CU Archive: Box 238: Folder, "Dies Committee": "Consumer Groups Organise," 131.

7. CU Archive: Box 99: Folder 4: Arthur Kallet, Press release following J. B. Matthews' statement to Dies Committee, 11 December 1939.

8. CU Archive: Box 266: Folder, "Consumers Union Response": "'Report' by Mr. Matthews"; Katz, "Consumers Union," 399; KSU Archive: RM: Box 158: Folder 21: Colston E. Warne, "The Consumer Movement Meets McCarthyism," speech at Kansas State University, 22 February 1977, 7–9.

9. Silber, *Test and Protest,* 28.

10. CU Archive: Box 89: Folder, "Robert Lynd": Letter from Robert Lynd to Arthur Kallet, 4 February 1942.

11. CU Archive: Box 240: Alan Goodman, "CU History: The First Twenty Years," unpublished manuscript, 14–20; Katz, "Consumers Union," 212–14.

12. CU Archive: Box 238: Folder, "Attacks": Extract from *Guide to Subversive Organisations.*

13. Katz, "Consumers Union," 158–59, 228–36.

14. Silber, *Test and Protest,* 30–31.

15. Ibid., 124; Katz, "Consumers Union," 253–61, 308–55; CU Archive: Box 89: Folder, "Sidney Margolius": Anon, Sidney Margolis, Board Member, 1950–1959," 3.

16. CU Archive: Box 238: Folder, "Attacks": Larston D. Farrar, "Consumers Union: A Red Front," *The Freeman,* 28 July 1952 (offprint); Box 262: Folder, "Publications": CU, "Consumers Union's Answer to an Attack in *The Freeman,*" 21 August 1952; E. F. Tompkins, "Subtle Foe of Free Enterprise," syndicated editorial published in Hearst newspapers; Box 252: "Answer of Consumers Union to Charges Made by Hearst Columnist, E. F. Tompkins, in His Syndicated Column," no date; Katz, "Consumers Union," 172–74.

17. CU Archive: Box 119: Folder 5: Colston E. Warne, "An Answer to Charges Against Consumers Union," 73; Box 99: Folder 4: "Draft Affidavit of Arthur Kallet," 8 June 1953.

18. CU Archive: Box 266: Folder, "Consumers Union Response": "Where Does CU Stand? A Statement by the CU Board of Directors," reprinted from *Consumer Reports,* April 1953.

19. Ibid.; CU Archive: Box 26: Folder, "Minutes 1950–1955": Minutes of the Board of Directors, 4 December 1952; Box 80: Folder 1: Board of Directors, "Policy Resolutions, 1936–1976," 25.

20. CU Archive: Box 262: Folder, "Publications": Extract from Annual Report of the Committee on Un-American Activities, 6 February 1954.

21. Landon R. Y. Storrs, "Red Scare Politics and the Suppression of Popular Front Feminism: The Loyalty Investigation of Mary Dublin Keyserling," *Journal of American History* 90, no. 2 (2003): 491–524.

22. CU Archive: Box 266: Folder, "Consumers Union Response": Walker Sandbach, "Articles About CU," memo to all staff, 24 August 1970.

23. Lucy Black Creighton, *Pretenders to the Throne: The Consumer Movement in the United States* (Lexington, MA: D. C. Heath, 1976), 42–43; Schlesinger Library, Radcliffe Institute, Harvard: MC450: Esther Peterson (hereafter EP) Papers: Box 64: Folder 1240: Consumer Advisory Council, *First Report* (Executive Office of the President, October 1963).

24. Schlesinger Library: EP: Box 66: Folder 1271: Anon. *Consumers' Advisory Council* (1962), 2–5, 22.

25. Schlesinger Library: EP Papers: Box 65: Folder 1246: President's Committee on Consumer Interests, *A Summary of Activities, 1964–1967* (Washington, DC: Executive Office of the President, 1967); Folder 1259: Ralph R. Mueller, "Discussion of Long-Range Goals for the President's Committee on Consumer Interests," Memorandum to Esther Peterson, 19 November 1964; Esther Peterson (with Winifred Conkling), *Restless: The Memoirs of Labor and Consumer Activist Esther Peterson* (Washington, DC: Caring, 1995), 119–35.

26. Thomas Herman, "Betty Furness on Consumer Firing Line," *Wall Street Journal,* 20 September 1967, 18; Mark V. Nadel, *The Politics of Consumer Protection* (New York: Bobs-Merrill, 1971), 50–55; KSU Archive: RM: Box 158: Folder 21: Colston E. Warne, "New Directions in Consumerism, 1953–1966," speech at Kansas State University, 21 March 1977; Schlesinger Library: EP Papers: Box 64: Folder 1239: Office of the White House Press Secretary, "Remarks of the President at the Swearing-In of Betty Furness," 1 May 1967.

27. CU Archive: Box 88: Folder, "Betty Furness": *New York Times* obituary, 4 April 1994.

28. Ralph Nader, *Unsafe at Any Speed: The Designed-in Dangers of the American Automobile* (New York: Grossman, 1965).

29. Linda Charlton, "Ralph Nader's Conglomerate Is Big Business," *New York Times,* 29 January 1978, section IV, 2; Paul Dickson, "What Makes Ralph Run? The Nader Story," *Progressive* 30 (January 1970): 28–32; Eliot Marshall, "St. Nader and His Evangelists," *New Republic,* 23 October 1971, 13–14; Anonymous, "Ralph Nader Becomes an Organization," *Business Week,* 28 November 1970, 86–88; Robert F. Buckhorn, *Nader: The People's Lawyer* (Englewood Cliffs, NJ: Prentice-Hall, 1972); Anon., "The US's Toughest Customer," *Time* 94 (12 December 1969): 89ff.; Patricia Cronin Marcello, *Ralph Nader: A Biography* (Westport, CT: Greenwood Press, 2004), 21–37; Ralph Nader, "The *Safe* Car You Can't Buy . . . ," *The Nation,* 11 April 1959, 310–13.

30. "Meet Ralph Nader: Everyman's Lobbyist and His Consumer Crusade," *Newsweek,* 22 January 1968, 65–73; Nadel, *Politics of Consumer Protection,* 176–87; Creighton, *Pretenders to the Throne,* 51–61; Grant S. McClellan, "The Consumer Interest Movement," in *The Consuming Public,* ed. Grant S. McClellan (New York: H. W. Wilson, 1968), 100–209; Robert N. Mayer, *The Consumer Movement: Guardians of the Marketplace* (Boston: Twayne Publishers, 1989), 41–43.

31. Hays Gorey, *Nader and the Power of Everyman* (New York: Grosset and Dunlap, 1975), 147.

32. David Hapgood, *The Average Man Fights Back* (Garden City, NY: Doubleday, 1977).

33. Anonymous, "The US's Toughest Customer"; Justin Martin, *Nader: Crusader, Spoiler, Icon* (Cambridge, MA: Perseus, 2002); Marcello, *Ralph Nader;* Thomas Whiteside, "Profiles: A Countervailing Force, I," *New Yorker,* 8 October 1973, 50–111; Thomas Whiteside, "Profiles: A Countervailing Force, II," *New Yorker,* 15 October 1973, 46–101; CU Archive: Box 90: Folder, "Ralph Nader 2": "Playboy Interview: Ralph Nader," *Playboy,* 1968, 73–224.

34. Martin, *Nader,* 195.

35. Ibid., 181.

36. Alvin Wolf, *American Consumers: Is Their Anger Justified?* (Englewood Cliffs, NJ: Prentice-Hall, 1977).

37. David Vogel, "The Public-Interest Movement and the American Reform Tradition," *Political Science Quarterly* 95, no. 4 (Winter 1980–81): 607–27, reprinted in David Vogel, *Kindred Strangers: The Uneasy Relationship Between Politics and Business in America* (Princeton, NJ: Princeton University Press, 1996), 141—42.

38. Donald I. Warren, "The Middle American Radicals," *The Nation,* 17 August 1974, 107–10.

39. Susan Gross, "The Nader Network," *Business and Society Review* 13 (1975): 5–15.

40. Edward F. Cox, Robert C. Fellmeth, and John E. Schultz, *The Nader Report on the Federal Trade Commission* (New York: Richard W. Baron, 1969).

41. Bo Burlingham, "Popular Politics: The Arrival of Ralph Nader," *Working Papers for a New Society* 2 (Summer 1974): 5–14.

42. Ronald J. Hrebenar, *Interest Group Politics in America* (Armonk, NY: M. E. Sharpe, 1997),

324–26; CQ Press and The Foundation for Public Affairs, *Public Interest Group Profiles, 2004–2005* (Washington, DC: CQ Press, 2004).

43. Creighton, *Pretenders to the Throne,* 56–61; Ralph Nader, "The Great American Gyp," in *Consumerism: Search for the Consumer Interest,* ed. David A. Aaker and George S. Day (New York: Free Press, 1984), 39–52; Ralph Nader and Mark J. Green, eds., *Corporate Power in America* (New York: Grossman, 1973); Ralph Nader, ed., *The Consumer and Corporate Accountability* (New York: Harcourt Brace Jovanovich, 1973); Ralph Nader and William Taylor, *The Big Boys: Power and Position in American Business* (New York: Pantheon, 1986); Ralph Nader, "Corporate Power in America," *The Nation,* 29 March 1980, 365–67; Ralph Nader, *The Ralph Nader Reader* (New York, NY: Seven Stories, 2000), 80–140; Ralph Nader, *Crashing the Party: Taking on the Corporate Government in an Age of Surrender* (New York: Thomas Dunne, 2002).

44. Ralph Nader, *In Pursuit of Justice: Collected Writings, 2000–2003* (New York: Seven Stories Press, 2004), 13.

45. Ibid.

46. Ralph Nader, "The Megacorporate World of Ronald Reagan," speech given to The National Press Club, Washington, DC, 6 June 1984, reprinted in *The Ralph Nader Reader,* 80–91 (91).

47. Ralph Nader, "We're Still in the Jungle," *The New Republic,* 15 July 1967, reprinted in *The Ralph Nader Reader,* 261–65; Stanley K. Schultz, "The Morality of Politics: The Muckrakers' Vision of Democracy," *The Journal of American History* 52, no. 3 (1965): 527–47.

48. Simon Lazarus, *The Genteel Populists* (New York: Holt, Rinehart and Winston, 1974), xvii

49. Burlingham, "Popular Politics," 6.

50. Ralph Nader, "Keynote Address Presented to the Consumer Assembly," 2 November 1967, in *The Ralph Nader Reader,* 260; Robert D. Holsworth, *Public Interest Liberalism and the Crisis of Affluence: Reflections on Nader, Environmentalism, and the Politics of a Sustainable Society* (Cambridge, MA: Schenkman, 1980).

51. Nader, "Luxury and Excess," in *In Pursuit of Justice,* 432; Ralph Nader, "The Consumer Movement Looks Ahead," in *Beyond Reagan: Alternatives for the '80s,* ed. Alan Gartner, Colin Greer & Frank Riessman (New York: Harper and Row, 1984), 271–85 (284); Ardith Maney and Loree Bykerk, *Consumer Politics: Protecting Public Interests on Capitol Hill* (Westport, CT: Greenwood Press, 1994), 16.

52. Nadel, *Politics of Consumer Protection,* 159; Erma Angevine, "The Consumer Federation of America," *Journal of Consumer Affairs* 3, no. 2 (1969): 152–55; Loree Bykerk and Ardith Maney, *US Consumer Interest Groups: Institutional Profiles* (Westport, CT: Greenwood Press, 1995).

53. David Bollier, *Citizen Action and Other Big Ideas: A History of Ralph Nader and the Modern Consumer Movement* (Washington, DC: Center for the Study of Responsive Law, 1989), 4; Mayer, *Guardians of the Marketplace,* 41; Nadel, *Politics of Consumer Protection,* 42.

54. Nader, "Keynote Address"; CU Archive: Box 90: Folder, "Ralph Nader 1": Ralph Nader, speech at CU Annual Meeting, October 1970.

55. Nader, "Great American Gyp," 39.

56. David Caplowitz, *The Poor Pay More: Consumer Practices of Low-Income Families* (New York: Free Press of Glencoe, 1963); Alan R. Andreasen, *The Disadvantaged Consumer* (New York: Free Press, 1975); Eugene Richards, *Below the Line: Living Poor in America* (Mount Vernon, NY: Consumers Union, 1987).

57. Ralph Nader, "A Citizen's Guide to the American Economy," 1971; "The Burned Kitchen," 1971; "Baby Foods: Can You (and Your Baby) Afford Them?" 1970; "The Toilet Training of Industry: Strategies for the Prevention of Pollution," 1970, all in Nader, *Corporate Accountability,* 4–18, 58–63, 200–205, 206–12; Ralph Nader, "Looting the Medicine Chest: how Bristol-Myers Squib Made Off with the Public's Cancer Research," in *The Ralph Nader Reader,* 159–64.

58. James E. Finch, "A History of the Consumer Movement in the United States: Its Literature and Legislation," *Journal of Consumer Studies and Home Economics* 9, no. 1 (1985): 23–33; KSU Archive: DW: Box 11: Virginia H. Knauer, *President's Committee on Consumer Interests and Office of Consumer Affairs: The Years 1969–1977* (Washington, DC: Office of Consumer Affairs, 1977).

59. David Sanford, *Me & Ralph: Is Nader Unsafe for America?* (Washington, DC: New Republic, 1976).

60. Patrick Anderson, "Ralph Nader, Crusader; or, the Rise of a Self-Appointed Lobbyist," *New York Times,* 29 October 1967, 25, 103.

61. Creighton, *Pretenders to the Throne,* 64–66.

62. Gross, "The Nader Network"; Ralph K. Winter, "Economic Regulation vs. Competition: Ralph Nader and Creeping Capitalism," *The Yale Law Journal* 82, no. 5 (1973): 890–902.

63. Capital Legal Foundation, *Abuse of Trust: A Report on Ralph Nader's Network* (Chicago: Regnery Gateway, 1982).

64. Peter Millones, "Harassment Laid to Consumerism," *New York Times,* 18 February 1970, 1, 59.

65. Melvin J. Grayson and Thomas R Shepard, *The Disaster Lobby: Prophets of Ecological Doom and Other Absurdities* (Chicago: Follett, 1973), 146.

66. Mary Bennett Peterson, *The Regulated Consumer* (Los Angeles, CA: Nash, 1971).

67. Alan Stang, "Consumerism: A Test Report on Consumers Union," *American Opinion,* May 1972, 1–11; Lillian R. Boehme, "The naked consumerist," *Review of the News* 7, no. 49 (8 December 1971): 31–48.

68. David Vogel, "The Power of Business in America: A Reappraisal," *British Journal of Political Science* 13, no. 1 (1983): 19–43.

69. Ibid., 33.; Graham Wilson, "American Business and Politics," in *Interest Group Politics,* 2nd ed., ed. Allan J. Cigler and Burdett A. Loomis (Washington, DC: Congressional Quarterly, 1986), 221–35; Patrick J. Ackard, "Corporate Mobilization and Political Power: The Transformation of US Economic Policy in the 1970s," *American Sociological Review* 57, no. 5 (1992): 597–615; Dan Clawson and Mary Ann Clawson, "Reagan or Business? Foundations of the New Conservatism," in *The Structure of Power in America: The Corporate Elite as a Ruling Class,* ed. Michael Schwartz (New York: Holmes and Meier, 1987), 201–17.

70. Ackard, "Corporate Mobilization," p602; Clawson and Clawson, "Reagan or Business?" 208.

71. Sidney Blumenthal, *The Rise of the Counter-Establishment: From Conservative Ideology to Political Power* (New York: Times Books, 1986).

72. Mark Green, ed., *The Essential Neoconservative Reader* (Reading, MA: Addison-Wesley, 1996).

73. Peter Steinfels, *The Neoconservatives: The Men Who Are Changing America's Politics* (New York: Simon and Schuster, 1979), 10–11.

74. *Regulation,* July/August 1977, front cover.

75. James Allen Smith, *The Idea Brokers: Think Tanks and the Rise of the New Policy Elite* (New York: Free Press, 1991), 270–94; Derk Arend Wilcox, *The Right Guide: A Guide to Conservative and Right-of-Center Organizations* (Ann Arbor, MI: Economics America, 1997).

76. Blumenthal, *Rise of the Counter-Establishment,* 37; Russ Bellant, *The Coors Connection: How Coors Family Philanthropy Undermines Democratic Pluralism* (Somerville, MA: Political Research Associates, 1990); Dan Baum, *Citizen Coors: An American Dynasty* (New York: William Morrow, 2000); William E. Simon, "Foreword: An American Institution," in *The Power of Ideas: The Heritage Foundation at 25 Years,* ed. Lee Edwards (Ottawa, IL: Jameson Books, 1997), xi–xv.

77. John Adams Wettergreen, *The Regulatory Revolution and the New Bureaucratic State, Part II* (Washington, DC: Heritage Foundation, 1989).

78. Rael Jean Isaac and Erich Isaac, *The Coercive Utopians: Social Deception by America's Power Players* (Chicago: Regnery Gateway, 1983), 2; Lee Edwards, ed., *Bringing Justice to the People: The Story of the Freedom-Based Public Interest Law Movement* (Washington, DC: Heritage Foundation, 2004).

79. Ralph K. Winter, *The Consumer Advocate Versus the Consumer* (Washington, DC: American Enterprise Institute, 1972).

80. James T. Bennet and Thomas J. DiLorenzo, *Destroying Democracy: How Government Funds Partisan Politics* (Washington, DC: Cato Institute, 1985), 109.

81. Russell Kirk, *The Popular Conservatives* (Washington, DC: Heritage Foundation, 1988); Russell Kirk, *A Conservative Program for a Kinder, Gentler America* (Washington, DC: Heritage Foundation, 1989).

82. Creighton, *Pretenders to the Throne,* 65.

83. KSU Archive: RM: Box 129: Folder 10: Ronald Reagan, "Few Want Consumer Agency," unidentified newspaper clipping, 1 June 1975.

84. KSU Archive: RM: Box 129: Folder 10: James J. Kirkpatrick, "Agency Would Add to Bureaucracy," unidentified newspaper clipping, 1975.

85. George Schwartz, "The Successful Fight Against a Federal Consumer Protection Agency,"

MSU Business Topics 27, no. 3 (1979): 45–57; Richard J. Leighton, "Consumer Protection Agency Proposals: The Origin of the Species," *Administrative Law Review* 25 (1973): 269–312; Martin, *Nader,* 189; Andrea F. Schoenfeld, "Bill to Create Advocacy Unit Will Be Revived in New Congress," *National Journal* 2 (19 December 1970): 2771–79; Ronald G. Schafer, "Consumer Bill Killed by Words," *Wall Street Journal,* 27 October 1972, 8; Lois G. Wark, "Independent Consumer Agency Bill Moves Toward Election-Year Fight in Senate," *National Journal* 3 (18 December 1971): 2499–504; KSU Archive: RM: Box 129: Folder 8: Consumer Protection Agency Bill, S. 707, 93rd Congress, 2nd Session, Calendar No. 754; Letter from David Fischer, Congress Watch, to Richard Morse, 2 May 1974; Consumer Protection Agency: basic provisions of S.707 (1974); Letter from Ralph Nader to Robert Dole, 3 August 1974; Letter from Senator Bob Dole to The President, 23 August 1974; Folder 9: "Consumer Protection Agency Bill Clears the House Only Slightly Weakened," 5 April 1974; KSU Archive: Roy Kiesling Papers: Box 8: Karen Stein, "A Political History of the Proposal to Create a Federal Consumer Protection Agency," paper presented at the 25th Annual American Council on Consumer Interests Conference, San Antonio, Texas, 27 April 1979.

86. Martin, *Nader,* 189; KSU Archive: RM: Box 129: Folder 10: Ralph Nader, "Battle of the CPA Bill," *Washington Star,* 4 August 1974.

87. Peterson, *Restless,* 160–61.

88. KSU Archive: RM: Box 129: Folder 8: Letter from Richard L. D. Morse to Senator Robert J. Dole, 21 May 1974; Letter from Nancy Chasen and Joan Claybrook, Public Citizen, to supporters of the CPA Bill, 28 June 1974; Letter from Bob Dole to Richard Morse, 17 September 1974; Letter from Joan Claybrook, Public Citizen & Congress Watch, to supporters of the CPA, 8 May 1975; Letter from Richard Morse to Congresswoman Martha Keys, 31 October 1977.

89. Schlesinger Library: EP Papers: Box 94: Folder 1830: Jimmy Carter, "Remarks of the President on the Agency for Consumer Protection," 1 June 1977; Jimmy Carter, "Press briefing," 6 April 1977.

90. Peterson, *Restless,* 162–70; Schlesinger Library: EP Papers: Box 94: Folder 1835: National Coalition for the Consumer Protection Agency, "Public Interest Groups/Union Support," 20 September 1977; Folders 1840–1843: Various letters of support from industry; Box 95: Folder 1849: Letter from Erma Angevine to supportive Congressmen, 14 February 1978; Box 89: Folder 1746: Edward B. Cohen and Davis Wright Tremaine, *Consumer Agency History,* no date .

91. Martin, *Nader,* 191–92; KSU Archive: RM: Box 129: Folder 9: Letter from Ralph Nader to Richard Nixon, 2 April 1974.

92. Mark Green, "Why the Consumer Bill Went Down," *The Nation,* 25 February 1978, 198–201 (198).

93. Schlesinger Library: EP Papers: Box 89: Folder 1746: Cohen and Tremaine, *Consumer Agency History,* 66.

94. Vogel, "Power of Business," 40; KSU Archive: RM: Box 129: Folder 8: "Business Lobbying Against Consumer Protection Agency Bill Intensifies—Grass Roots Support Crucial," 10 May 1974; Schlesinger Library: EP Papers: Box 94: Folder 1839: Jack Anderson & Les Whitten, "Big Business vs. a Consumer Agency," *Washington Post,* 31 October 1977, C23; Chamber of Commerce Consumer Issues Working Group, "Notes," 19 October 1977; Ackard, "Corporate Mobilization," 603–5.

95. Schwartz, "Successful Fight," 48.

96. KSU Archive: RM: Box 129: Folder 11: Tom Low, "Report on the US Chamber of Commerce Campaign Against the Agency for Consumer Advocacy [CPA]," 1977; Schlesinger Library: EP Papers: Box 94: Folder 1839: Letter from Leon Jaworski to Jack Brooks, Chairman of Committee on Government Operations, House of Representatives, 27 April 1977.

97. KSU Archive: RM: Box 129: Folder 12: Morton C. Poulson, "Asking the Rights Questions," *The National Observer,* 17 March 1975.

98. Vogel, "Power of Business," 40; Schwartz, "Successful Fight," 51–52; KSU Archive: RM: Box 129: Folder 12: "Consumer Protection Organisations Acts: Business Responsiveness Kit," 17 January 1972.

99. Schlesinger Library: EP Papers: Box 94: Folder 1839: Jack Anderson & Les Whitten, "Column," *Washington Post,* 22 July 1977.

100. Green, "Why the Consumer Bill," 200.

101. KSU Archive: RM: Box 129: Folder 10: Ralph Nader, "Battle of the CPA Bill," *Washington Star,* 4 August 1974.

102. KSU Archive: RM: Box 129: Folder 9: William E. Timmons, "Consumer Protection

Agency," memorandum for Roy Ash, 8 March 1974; Congress Watch, *Citizen Alert on CPA,* No. 5, April 1974; Ralph Nader, "Battle of the CPA Bill," *Washington Star,* 4 August 1974.

103. Schlesinger Library: EP Papers: Box 94: Folder 1839: Stanley E. Cohen, "The Secret War: Lobbying Against The Consumer Bill," *Advertising Age,* 18 July 1977.

104. Schlesinger Library: EP Papers: Box 95: Folder 1853: Sylvia Porter, "Enemies Endanger Consumer Agency," *Washington Star,* 14 June 1977; Ralph Nader and Mark Green, "A Reply to Jaworski," *Washington Star,* 18 May 1977; Box 84: Folder 1839; CA Special Report, "Agency for Consumer Protection, Parts I and II," *Congressional Action,* 24 June 177 and 18 July 1977; Letter from Alan J. Bayley, CEO, GRT Corporation, to Tina Hobson, National Coalition for the Consumer Protection Agency, 30 June 1977; "Business Roundtable: A Profile"; "Chamber Leads Attack on Consumer Agency," *Washington Report,* 13 June 1977; Folder 1854: William Claiborne, "Consumer Aid Bill Losing Corporate Support," *Washington Post,* 2 August 1977.

105. Schlesinger Library: EP Papers: Box 98: Folder 1901: Esther Peterson, "Future of Legislation to Create an Office of Consumer representation," Memorandum to the President, 30 November 1977; Folder 1904: Max McCarthy, "Lessons Learned from the Charge and the Retreat of the Consumer Forces on Capitol Hill," Memo to Esther Peterson, 14 February 1978; Martin, *Nader,* 192.

106. Peterson, *Restless,* 163.

107. Clawson and Clawson, "Reagan or Business?" 210.

108. Schlesinger Library: EP Papers: Box 98: Folder 1904: Max McCarthy, "The Vote on Wednesday and Lessons to Be Learned from It," Memo to Esther Peterson, 10 February 1978; Esther Peterson, "Seven Point Program for Developing Congressional Majorities for Administration Proposals," Memo to the President, 24 February 1978; Folder 1908: Esther Peterson, "Proposed Schedule Change," Memo to the President, 11 January 1978; Ackard, "Corporate Mobilization"; American Social History Project, *Who Built America? Working People and the Nation's Economy, Politics, Culture and Society, Vol. II: From the Gilded Age to the Present* (New York: Pantheon, 1992); Vogel, "Power of Business," 40.

109. Schlesinger Library: EP Papers: Box 98: Folder 1920: Memo from Esther Peterson to Landon Butler, 13 August 1979; Folder 1927: Esther Peterson, "The Consumer's Executive Order: A New Era Begins For Consumers," *Concerns* 3, no. 7 (1980): 1–3; Jimmy Carter, "Executive Order 12160: Providing for Enhancement and Coordination of Federal Consumer Programs," 26 September 1980; Jimmy Carter, "Executive Order Providing for Enhancement and Coordination of Federal Consumer Programs," 15 January 1981.

110. Michael Pertschuk, *Giant Killers* (New York: W. W. Norton, 1986).

111. Maney and Bykerk, *Consumer Politics,* 1.

112. David S. Broder, "Citizen's Beef," *Washington Post,* 12 December 1976, 37.

113. Martin, *Nader,* 187; Anonymous, "Ralph Nader Takes on Congress as Well as Big Business," *National Journal* 10 (11 March 1978): 388–90.

114. Michael deCourcy Hinds, "A Subdued Nader Works to Organized Consumers," *New York Times,* 27 April 1982, 20.

115. Nader, "The Consumer Movement Looks Ahead," 271–85.

116. Samuel P. Huntington, "The Marasmus of the ICC: The Commission, the Railroads and the Public Interest," *Yale Law Journal* 61, no. 4 (1952): 467–509.

117. Mark V. Nadel, "Introduction," *Symposium on Consumer Protection Policy,* special issue of *Policy Studies Review* 2, no. 3 (1983): 417.

118. CU Archive: Box 719: Folder 1: Sentry Insurance, *Consumerism at the Crossroads: A National Opinion Research Survey of Public, Activist, Business and Regulator Attitudes Toward the Consumer Movement* (1983); Folder 2: Louis Harris and Associates, *Consumerism in the Eighties: A National Survey of Attitudes Toward the Consumer Movement* (1982).

119. Milton and Rose Friedman, *Free to Choose: A Personal Statement* (New York: Harcourt Brace Jovanovich, 1980), 7; Milton Friedman, *Capitalism and Freedom* (Chicago: University of Chicago Press, 1962).

120. Edwards, *Power of Ideas,* 40–51; Joseph A. D'Agostino, "Conservative Spotlight: Heritage Foundation," *Human Events* 58, no. 18 (13 May 2002): 14.

121. Marcello, *Nader,* 95.

122. Michael Schwartz, "Preface," in *Structure of Power,* xii.

123. Graham K. Wilson, *Business and Politics: A Comparative Introduction,* 2nd ed. (Basingstoke: Macmillan, 1990).

124. CU Archive: Box 719: Folder 2: National Consumers' League, *Warning: Reaganomics Is Harmful to Consumers* (Washington, DC: National Consumers' League, 1982), 3.

125. George Black, "The Heritage Foundation Goes Abroad," *The Nation*, 6 June 1987, 747, 760–64.

126. Richard Berryman and Richard Schifter, "A Global Straitjacket," *Regulation*, September/October 1981, 19–28; Kenneth L. Adelman, "Biting the Hand That Cures Them," *Regulation*, July/August 1982, 16–18.

127. Adelman, "Biting," 18; Harry Schwartz, "The UN System's War on the Drug Industry," *Regulation*, July/August 1982, 19–24.

128. Jeane Kirkpatrick, "Global Paternalism: The UN and the New International Regulatory Order," *Regulation*, January/February 1983, 17–22. On the NIEO see Craig Murphy, *Emergence of the NIEO Ideology* (Boulder, CO: Westview Press, 1984); Paul M. Kennedy, *The Parliament of Man: The United Nations and the Quest for World Government* (London: Allen Lane, 2006).

129. Edwards, *Power of Ideas,* 77

130. Burton Yale Pines, ed., *A World Without a UN: What Would Happen If the U.N. Shut Down* (Washington, DC: Heritage Foundation, 1984), vi. See also Ambassador Charles M. Lichenstein, Thomas E. L. Dewey, Juliana Geran Pilon, and Melanie L. Merkle, *The United Nations: Its Problems and What to do About Them: 59 Recommendations Proposed in Response to General Assembly Resolution 40/237* (Washington, DC: Heritage Foundation, 1986).

131. Burton Yale Pines, "Introduction," in *A World Without a UN,* x.

132. Ibid., xi

133. Yonas Deressa, *Subsidizing Tragedy: The World Bank and the New Colonialism* (Washington, DC: Heritage Foundation, 1988).

134. Edwin J. Fuelner, *Searching for Reforms at UNESCO* (Washington, DC: Heritage Foundation, 1989).

135. John M. Starrels, *The World Health Organization: Resisting Third World Ideological Pressures* (Washington, DC: Heritage Foundation, 1988); Doug Bandow, ed., *Protecting the Environment: A Free Market Strategy* (Washington, DC: Heritage Foundation, 1986); "The Us and the UN: The Heritage Foundation Point of View. An Interview with Mark Franz," *Multinational Monitor,* July/August 1989, http://multinationalmonitor.org/hyper/issues/1989/07/franz.html.

136. Alan Woods, *A US Model for Progress in the Developing World* (Washington, DC: Heritage Foundation, 1989); Kim R. Holmes, ed., *A Safe and Prosperous America: A US Foreign and Defence Policy Blueprint* (Washington, DC: Heritage Foundation, 1993).

137. Brett D. Schaefer, *The Bretton Woods Institutions: History and Reform Proposals* (Washington, DC: Heritage Foundation, 2000).

138. Roger A. Brooks, *Multinationals: First Victim of the UN War on Free Enterprise* (Washington, DC: Heritage Foundation, 1982), 1–3; Anon., "Heritage Foundation Slams 'Extremist' Consumer Organizations," *Multinational Monitor,* 4:1, January 1983, 8.

139. Brooks, *Multinationals,* 19.

140. Ibid., 21.

141. Ibid., 23.

142. Ibid., 24.

143. Schlesinger Library: EP Papers: Box 101: Folder 1961: Letter from Charles Sims, American Civil Liberties Union, to Joseph E. Clarkson, Internal Security Section, Criminal Division, Department of Justice, 29 January 1985; Keith B. Richburg, "Esther Peterson, Foreign Agent?" *Washington Post,* 1 November 1984, 23.

144. Peterson, *Restless,* 177; IOCU Archive: Box 54: File F5.17: Report of Esther Peterson to Lars Broch, "Some Notes Concerning 1983."

145. Rhoda Karpatkin, interview by the author, 18 March 2005.

146. IOCU Archive: Box 54: File F5.24: Esther Peterson, "Report of Month to Month Activities in 1984," 1985, 8.

147. Esther Peterson, "The Case Against the UN Guidelines for Consumer Protection," *Journal of Consumer Policy* 10, no. 4 (1987): 433–39 (438).

148. Murray L. Weidenbaum, "The New Wave of Government Regulation of Business," *Business and Society Review* 15 (Fall 1975): 81–86 (83).

149. Ibid.

150. Murray Weidenbaum, "The case against the UN Guidelines for Consumer Protection," 425.

151. Bennet and DiLorenzo, *Destroying Democracy;* Andrew Bacevich, *The New American Mil-*

itarism: How Americans Are Seduced by War (New York: Oxford University Press, 2005); Lucy Williams, *Decades of Distortion: The Right's 30–Year Assault on Welfare* (Somerville, MA: Political Research Associates, 1997).

152. Stefan Halper and Jonathan Clarke, *America Alone: The Neo-Conservatives and the Global Order* (Cambridge: Cambridge University Press, 2004).

153. Lizabeth Cohen, *A Consumers' Republic: The Politics of Mass Consumption in Postwar America* (New York: Alfred A. Knopf, 2003); Gary Cross, *An All-Consuming Century: Why Commercialism Won in Modern America* (New York: Columbia University Press, 2000); Daniel Horowitz, *The Anxieties of Affluence: Critiques of American Consumer Culture, 1939–1979* (Amherst: University of Massachusetts Press, 2004).

154. James B. Twitchell, *Adcult USA: The Triumph of Advertising in American Culture* (New York: Columbia University Press, 1996); James B. Twitchell, *Lead Us Into Temptation: The Triumph of American Materialism* (New York: Columbia University Press, 1999).

155. Maney and Bykerk, *Consumer Politics*, 140.

156. Leslie Sklair, *The Transnational Capitalist Class* (Oxford: Blackwell, 2001).

Chapter 7. Choose Life: Consumer Rights versus Human Rights

1. IOCU Archive: Box 71: File H3.1: John F. Kennedy, "Special Message to the Congress on Protecting the Consumer Interest," 15 March 1962; Jeanine Gilmartin, "An Historical Analysis of the Growth of the National Consumer Movement in the United States from 1947 to 1967," Ph.D. diss., Georgetown University, 1969, 107–32.

2. Anwar Fazal, interview by the author, 13 April 2004.

3. John Rawls, *A Theory of Justice* (Oxford: Clarendon, 1972).

4. Ian Shapiro, *The Evolution of Rights in Liberal Theory* (Cambridge: Cambridge University Press, 1986), 152.

5. Thomas W. Pogge, *World Poverty and Human Rights: Cosmopolitan Responsibilities and Reforms* (Maldon, MA: Polity, 2002), 66.

6. Full text of the Universal Declaration of Human Rights is available at http://www.un.org/Overview/rights.html.

7. T. H. Marshall, *Citizenship and Social Class* (Cambridge: Cambridge University Press, 1950); Peter Saunders, "Citizenship in a Liberal Society," in *Citizenship and Social Theory*, ed. B. S. Turner (London: Sage, 1993), 57–90.

8. Harold K. Jacobson, *Networks of Interdependence: International Organisations and the Global Political System*, 2nd ed. (New York: Alfred A. Knopf, 1984), 294–306; Micheline R. Ishay, *The History of Human Rights: From Ancient Times to the Globalisation Era* (Berkeley: University of California Press, 2004).

9. Nitza Berkovitch, *From Motherhood to Citizenship: Women's Rights and International Organizations* (Baltimore: Johns Hopkins University Press, 1999); Irene Tinker, "Introduction: Ideas into Action," in *Developing Power: How Women Transformed International Development*, ed. Arvonne S. Fraser and Irene Tinker ((New York: Feminist Press, 2004), xiii-xxix.

10. Ramesh Thakur, "Human Rights: Amnesty International and the United Nations," *Journal of Peace Research* 31, no. 2 (1994): 143–60.

11. Amartya Sen, *Human Rights and Asian Values* (New York: Carnegie Council on Ethics and Human Affairs, 1997); Khoo Boo Teik, *Beyond Mahathir: Malaysian Politics and Its Discontents* (London: Zed, 2003); Michael Jacobsen and Ole Bruun, eds., *Human Rights and Asian Values: Contesting National Identities and Cultural Representations in Asia* (London: Routledge Curzon, 2006); Sheldon Garon, "The Transnational Promotion of Saving in Asia: 'Asian Values' or the 'Japanese model'," in *The Ambivalent Consumer: Questioning Consumption in East Asia and the West*, ed. Sheldon Garon and Patricia L. Maclachlan (Ithaca, NY: Cornell University Press, 2006), 163–87; Wm. Theodore de Bary, *Asian Values and Human Rights: A Confucian Communitarian Perspective* (Cambridge, MA: Harvard University Press, 1998); Heather Widdows, "Is Global Ethics Moral Neo-Colonialism? An Investigation of the Issue in the Context of Bioethics," *Bioethics* 21, no. 6 (2007): 305–15.

12. IOCU, *Consumer Rights—A World View: Proceeding of the 5th Biennial Conference of IOCU, 26 June–1 July 1968* (The Hague: IOCU, 1968), 62.

13. IOCU Archive: Box 54: File F5.1: Persia Campbell, "IOCU's Role in the UN," 1970; Box 71: File H3.2: *IOCU Newsletter*, 26, 4 May 1973.

14. CI ROAF, *Annual Report 2002: Consumer Protection and Quality of Life in Africa* (Harare, Zimbabwe: CI-ROAF, 2003), 21.

15. IOCU Archive: Box 71: File H3.3: Michael Dunne, "The Consumer's Right to Choose: Some Thoughts on World Consumer Rights Day," no date.

16. Ibid.

17. IOCU Archive: Box 71: File H3.4: Anwar Fazal, "A Charter for Consumer Action," speech given at opening of UNIDO/IOCU Seminar, Ankara, Turkey, 12 February 1979.

18. IOCU, *Consumer Policy 2000: Seminar Report* (The Hague: IOCU, 1986), 6–8.

19. CU Archive: Box 90: Folder "Ralph Nader 1": Ralph Nader, Speech to CU Annual Meeting, October 1970, 1.

20. KSU Archive: Richard L. D. Morse Papers (RM): Box 158: Folder 24: Colston E. Warne, "The Nader Network," speech to Kansas State University, 18 April 1977, 7.

21. Ibid., 12.

22. Lucy Black Creighton, *Pretenders to the Throne: The Consumer Movement in the United States* (Lexington, MA: D. C. Heath, 1976), 61; Rhoda Karpatkin, interview by the author, 19 February 2005.

23. *Consumer Reports* 40, no. 9 (September 1975): 524–25.

24. KSU Archive: Roy Kiesling Papers: Box 4: Folder "Consumer Assembly": Ralph Nader, "The State of the Consumer," address to the Consumer Federation of America Annual Convention, Washington, DC, 3 January 1975; Ralph Nader, speech to Consumer Assembly, Los Angeles, 5 October 1975.

25. Stewart Lee Richardson, "The Evolving Consumer Movement: Predictions for the 1990s"; and Darlene Brannigan Smith and Paul N. Bloom, "Is Consumerism Dead or Alive? Some Empirical Evidence," in *The Future of Consumerism,* ed. Paul N. Bloom and Ruth Belk Smith (Lexington, MA: Lexington Books, 1986), 17–22, 61–73; Paul N. Bloom and Stephen A. Geyser, "The Maturing of Consumerism," *Harvard Business Review* 59, no. 6 (1981): 130–39.

26. "Memo to Members," *Consumer Reports* 39, no. 3 (March 1974): 188.

27. Rhoda Karpatkin, "Memo to Members," *Consumer Reports* 46, no. 4 (April 1981): 253.

28. CU Archive: Box 256: Folder "Speeches": Rhoda H. Karpatkin, "International Consumer Issues," speech to Consumer Federation of America, Washington, DC, 1985; Rhoda H. Karpatkin, "A Social Agenda for Consumerists: The Legacy of 1985," keynote address to the Consumer Federation of America, Washington, DC, 6 February 1986.

29. Rhoda H. Karpatkin, "Memo to Members," *Consumer Reports* 51, no. 1 (January 1986): 3; Rhoda H. Karpatkin, "Memo to Members," *Consumer Reports* 51, no. 2 (February 1986): 71; Rhoda H. Karpatkin, "Memo to Members," *Consumer Reports* 51, no. 5 (May 1986): 283.

30. Rhoda H. Karpatkin, "Memo to Members," *Consumer Reports* 52, no. 2 (February 1987): 71; Eugene Richards, *Below the Line: Living Poor in America* (Mount Vernon, NY: Consumers Union, 1987).

31. Rhoda H. Karpatkin, "Memo to Members," *Consumer Reports* 56, no. 9 (September 1991): 571; Rhoda H. Karpatkin, "Memo to Members," *Consumer Reports* 57, no. 9 (September 1992): 555; Rhoda H. Karpatkin, "Memo to Members," *Consumer Reports* 58, no. 3 (March 1993): 123; "Wasted Health Care Dollars," *Consumer Reports* 57, no. 7 (July 1992): 435–48.

32. CU Archive: Box 95: Folder 6: Langer Associates, *A Qualitative Study of Consumer Reports Books* (New York, Langer, 1990).

33. CU Archive: Box 94: Folder 1: Benson & Benson, *Survey of Present and Former Subscribers to "Consumer Reports"* (Princeton, NJ: Benson and Benson, 1970).

34. IOCU Archive: Box 11: File B3em: Meeting 36: Dick Smithies, "Some Comments on the Regional Office," 10 September 1981.

35. Sarojeni V. Rengam, interview by the author, 23 April 2004; Dr Kumariah Balasubramaniam, interview by the author, 15 April 2004; Josie Fernandez, interview by the author, 8 December 2003.

36. IOCU Archive: Box 11: File B3em: Meeting 36: Letter from Christopher Zealley to Peter Goldman, 9 September 1981.

37. IOCU Archive: Box 28: File B4.1: Memo from Peter Goldman to CA Council, 8 July 1981.

38. Ibid.

39. IOCU Archive: Box 28: File B4.3: Anwar Fazal, "Role of Headquarters and Regional Office," 30 October 1983; File 4.5a: Telegram from Dick Smithies, New Zealand, to Penang, 18 January 1984; File 4.8: Anwar Fazal, "IOCU Restructuring Exercise," 13 January 1984; Anwar Fazal,

interview by the author, 17 April 2004; CU Archive: Rhoda Karpatkin papers: Box "April 1984–November 1986": Letter from R. J. Smithies to Rhoda Karptakin, 19 April 1984; IOCU Archive: Box 13: File B3em: Consumers' Association, "Some International Developments," October 1982; Box 4: File CM 30/8c: Terms of reference of Director of IOCU, 14 March 1983; File B5.1: John Stork and Partners, *International Organisation of Consumers Unions: Review of International Structure, 1980–1981* (28 November 1980).

40. IOCU Archive: Box 16: File B3em: Minutes of 53rd Executive Meeting, 29 February–1 March 1988, 14.

41. IOCU Archive: Box 28: File B7.1: ROAP internal memo, "The Networks: The Different Scenarios," 1983.

42. IOCU Archive: Box 28: File 7.2: Ruth Vermeer and Virginia Beardshaw, "Review of IOCU Advocacy Work and Strengthening Members' Participation," January 1983.

43. Julian Edwards, interview by the author, 8 September 2004.

44. IOCU Archive: Box 19: File B3em: Minutes of the 61st Meeting of the Executive Committee, 5th and 8th July 1991.

45. IOCU Archive: Box 19: File B3em: Minutes of the 64th Meeting of the Executive Committee, 2–4 November 1991.

46. IOCU Archive: Box 4: File CM 43/2: Minutes of 42nd Council Meeting, 26 April 1993; CM 43/4.1: James Firebrace, "DG Summary Report, IOCU 1991–1994," September 1994; Box 28: File B5.4: The Manitoba Institute of Management, *IOCU Organisation and Management Review Project* (Winnipeg, Manitoba: MIM, 1991).

47. IOCU Archive: Box 28: File B6.7: James Firebrace, "Name Review of IOCU," 30 August 1994; File B6.8: Letter from Erna Witoelar to all IOCU members, 15 November 1994.

48. Julian Edwards, interview by the author, 8 September 2004; Rhoda Karpatkin, interview by the author, 19 February 2005; Foo Gaik Sim, interview by the author, 4 December 2003; Sarojeni V. Rengam, interview by the author, 23 April 2004.

49. Helmut Anheier and Nuno Themudo, "Organisational Forms of Global Civil Society: Implications of Going Global," in *Global Civil Society 2002*, ed. Marlies Glasius, Mary Kaldor, and Helmut Anheier (Oxford: Oxford University Press, 2002), 194.

50. John Keane, *Global Civil Society?* (Cambridge: Cambridge University Press, 2003), 5.

51. IOCU Archive: Box 20: File B3em: Minutes of the 66th Executive Committee Meeting, 23–25 November 1992; Box 68: File G22:4: Peter Cerexhe, "Presidential Hopes: Interview with Erna Witoelar," *Consuming Interest*, January 1993, 14–17; G22.7: "Erna Witoelar: President"; G22.8: Erna Witoelar, "Curriculum Vitae."

52. IOCU Archive: Box 33: File C2.3: IOCU, "Three Year Strategic Plan, 1995–1997."

53. IOCU Archive: Box 36: File C6.13: Martin Abraham, "IOCU at the World Summit/Global Forum," 18 June 1992; IOCU, *Consumers and the Environment: Proceedings of the IOCU Forum on Sustainable Consumption, Rio de Janeiro, 4 June 1992* (Penang: IOCU-ROAP, 1992); IOCU, *Shifting the Balance: Consumer Action for a Green World, Earth Summit Resource Kit, Rio de Janeiro, June 1992* (The Hague: IOCU, 1992).

54. IOCU, *Consumerism: The Green Factor* (Penang: IOCU, 1993); CI, *Green Labels: Consumer Interests and Transatlantic Trade Tensions in Eco-Labelling* (London: CI, 1999); CI, *Green Guidance: How Consumer Organisations Can Give Better Advice on Putting Sustainable Consumption into Practice: An International Study* (London: CI, 1998); CI, *Green Testing: Recyclability, Repairability and Upgradability: A Practical Handbook for Consumer Organisations* (London: CI, 1999).

55. IOCU Archive: Box 20: File B3em: Jeremy Mitchell, "IOCU and the Alternative Consumer Movement," 1992.

56. IOCU Archive: Box 20: File B3em: Minutes of the 66th Executive Committee Meeting: item, 64: membership application: Seikatsu Club, Japan; item 67: ethical shopping.

57. IOCU Archive: Box "Council Meetings, 1996–2003": File B15: CM 49/4.5a: Global Policy and Campaigns Unit, "Progress Report Highlights, 1998"; CM54/5a: "Executive Report," September 2001.

58. Maria Elena Hurtado, *GM Foods: The Facts and the Fiction* (London: CI, 2000).

59. CI, *Why We Need Labelling of Genetically Engineered Food* (London: CI, 1998), 1; CI and Consumentenbond, *Food of the Future: The Risks and Realities of Biotechnology: Conference Proceedings, Oegstgeest, 16–17 November 1995* (London: CI, 1995); IOCU Archive: Box "Council Meetings, 1996–2003": CM51/1: Minutes of 50th Council Meeting, Bath, UK, 31 October 1999.

60. CI and Federation of Consumer Organisations Tamil Nadu, *Privatisation, Quality and Rights: Proceedings of the Asia Pacific Consultation on Quality of Health Care Services, Madurai, South India, 11–14 December 1996* (Penang: CI-ROAP, 1996); IOCU Archive: Box "Council Meetings, 1996–2003": CM54/5c: Regional Office for Africa, "Work Report, October 2000– April 2001," 5.

61. CI, *Empowering Disadvantaged Consumer: World Summit for Social Development, Copenhagen, 6–12 March 1995* (London: CI, 1995); Maria Lourdes B. Suplido, *Empowering Rural Consumers* (Penang: CI-ROAP, 1995).

62. IOCU Archive: Box "Council Meetings, 1996–2003": CM 48/6: "Strategy Proposals: Priorities for 1998 to 2000—and Beyond"; CM51/9: "Consumers, Social Justice and the World Market," statement from Consumers International's 16th World Congress.

63. IOCU Archive: Box "Council Meetings, 1996–2003": CM 48/6: "Strategy Proposals: Priorities for 1998 to 2000—and Beyond."

64. IOCU Archive: Box "Council Meetings, 1996–2003": CM51/3: "Director General's Report, 2000"; CM54/3: "Director General's Report, September 2001"; Box 28: File B4.6: "Reorganising CI's Head Office," 1997.

65. IOCU Archive: Box 76: File H15:10: "Recommendations of the UN Regional Seminar on Consumer Protection for Asia and the Pacific, 19–22 June 1990, Bangkok."

66. IOCU Archive: Box "Council Meetings, 1996–2003": CM 51/10: "Comments and Recommendations Not Included."

67. IOCU Archive: Box "Council Meetings, 1996–2003": CM 54/1: Minutes of 53rd Council Meeting, 20.

68. Ronald Macfarlane, *Green vs. Sustainable Consumption: Choosing Sustainable Consumption* (Penang: CI-ROAP, 1997); Eva Heiskanen and Mika Pantzar, "Toward Sustainable Consumption: Two New Perspectives," *Journal of Consumer Policy* 20, no. 4 (1997): 409–42; Ursula Hansen and Ulf Schrader, "A Modern Model of Consumption for a Sustainable Society," *Journal of Consumer Policy* 20, no. 4 (1997): 443–68; Thomas Wilhelmsson, "Consumer Law and the Environment: From Consumer to Citizen," *Journal of Consumer Policy* 21, no. 1 (1998): 45–70; IOCU Archive: Box "Council Meetings, 1996–2003": CM 47/6: "Extension of UN Guidelines on Consumer Protection," 16 October 1996; JCM 47/8: "A joint Strategy to Develop Environmentally Responsible Citizenship," 1996; CI and UNEP, *Implementing Sustainable Consumption and Production Policies: North-South, South-South and East-West Partnerships. Informal Expert Meeting Report, Paris, 6–7 May 2002* (London and Paris: CI and UNEP, 2002); CI and UNEP, *Tracking Progress: Implementing Sustainable Consumption Policies: A Global Review of Implementation of the UN Guidelines on Consumer Protection* (London and Paris: CI and UNEP, 2002).

69. Kersty Hobson, "Sustainable Consumption in the United Kingdom: The 'Responsible' Consumer and Government at 'Arm's Length'," *Journal of Environment and Development* 13, no. 2 (2004): 121–39.

70. Khoo Boo Teik, *Beyond Mahathir: Malaysian Politics and Its Discontents* (London: Zed, 2003), 25.

71. Chandra Muzaffar, *Rights, Religion and Reform: Enhancing Human Dignity Through Spiritual and Moral Transformation* (London: Routledge, 2002), 45.

72. *Utusan Konsumer* 16, no. 2 (January 1988): 17.

73. *Utusan Konsumer*, 28, no. 1 (January 1998): 3.

74. S. M. Mohamed Idris, *Reflections on Malaysian Society: Where Do We Go From Here?* (Penang: CAP, 2003), 80.

75. Some examples of CAP's promotion of alternative values can be found in CAP, *Natural Wisdom: Stories and Reflections on Nature by the Ancients, Thinkers and Ecologists* (Penang: CAP, 2003).

76. Chitra Nadarajah, *A Biological Management Study of Bukit Larut and Its Surrounding, Perak, Malaysia* (Petaling Jaya: ERA, 1997); ERA, *Annual Report, 1998* (Petaling Jaya: ERA, 1999), 9; *The Sunday*, 24 January 1999, 18; Indrani Thuraisingham, "The Consumers' Perspective: A Brief Overview of the Malaysian Food Security Situation," paper presented at the International Conference on ASEAN Food Security, Hanoi, 3–6 November 1998; ERA, *National Consultation Conference on Food Security, Kuala Lumpur, 25–26 July 1998* (Petaling Jaya: ERA, 1998); Katherine Ann Francis, *Biotechnology—Simplified* (Petaling Jaya: ERA, 2003); ERA, *Awareness Seminar: Introducing Codex Alimentarius* (Petaling Jaya, 2003); G. Umakanthan, ed., *Assessing Food Security: A Micro-Study of 24 Villages in Malaysia* (Petaling Jaya: ERA, 2002);

ERA, *National Agriculture Workshop: For a Successful Food Production Sector in Malaysia* (Petaling Jaya: ERA, 2001); ERA, *Annual Report, 2001* (Petaling Jaya: ERA, 2002); *New Straits Times,* 25 April 1999; [Malaysian] *Sun,* 2 May 1999; ERA, *Annual Report, 2001* (Petaling Jaya: ERA, 2002), 10; Rokiah Alavi, *TRIPS and Pharmaceuticals: The Impact on Malaysian Consumers* (Petaling Jaya: ERA, 2003); Sivananthan Balan, *Direct Selling: An Evaluation* (Petaling Jaya: ERA, 2003); Bishan Singh, *Consumer Education* (Petaling Jaya: ERA, 2002); ERA, *Understanding Malaysian Consumer Redress Mechanisms: Towards Dynamic, Progressive and Responsible Consumer Society* (Petaling Jaya: ERA, 2004).

77. ERA, *Minutes of the Fifteenth AGM, 4 February 2001* (Petaling Jaya: ERA, 2001); ERA, *Annual Report, 2002* (Petaling Jaya: ERA, 2003), 9.

78. ERA, *Proceedings of Forum on Understanding the Human Rights Commission Act 1999* (Petaling Jaya: ERA, 2002); ERA, *Proceedings of the National Consultation on "SUHAKAM: After One Year"* (Petaling Jaya: ERA, 2002); ERA, *National Consultation on Suhakam After 2 Years: "How Has the Commission Played a Role in Promoting and Protecting Human Rights in Malaysia?"* (Petaling Jaya: ERA, 2003).

79. ERA, *A Handbook on Understanding Domestic Violence* (Petaling Jaya: ERA, 2003); ERA, *Understanding Human Rights and Islam: Motivation, Ideology and Relevance in a Contemporary Society* (Petaling Jaya: ERA, 2003).

80. ERA, *Programme: Workshop on the International Criminal Court, 6–8 December 2003* (Petaling Jaya: ERA, 2003)

81. Rokiah Talib, "Malaysia: Power Shifts and the Matrix of Consumption," in *Consumption in Asia: Lifestyles and Identities,* ed. Chua Beng-Huat (London: Routledge, 2000), 35–60; Antonio L. Rappa, *Modernity and Consumption: Theory, Politics and the Public in Singapore and Malaysia* (Singapore: World Scientific, 2002); Ziauddin Sardar, *The Consumption of Kuala Lumpur* (London: Reaktion, 2000).

82. CAP has recently published dozens of such pamphlets. See, for instance, CAP, *Fashion That Hurts* (Penang: CAP, 2003); CAP, *Cancer-Causing Chemicals in Cosmetics and Daily Use Products* (Penang: CAP, 2001).

83. Anwar Fazal, interview by the author, 17 April 2004; Anwar Fazal, *Consumers in the New Millennium: Back to Basics* (Kuala Lumpur: FOMCA, 2001); Sarah Amin, *Nurturing the Future: Our First Five Years* (Penang: WABA, 1996); Lakshmi Menon, *The Breastfeeding Movement: A Sourcebook* (Penang: WABA, 2003); "Backgrounder on Anwar Fazal: 'The Citizen Activist'," Anwar Fazal's private papers; Sustainable Penang Initiative, *Penang People's Report, 1999* (Penang: Socio-Economic and Environmental Research Institute, 1999).

84. F. Josie, "Consumer Protection in Asia: The Challenges Ahead," *Journal of Development Communication* 12, no. 1 (2001): 42

85. M. Nadarajah, "Rethinking Asian Consumerism: Some Preliminary Thoughts," in *Another Malaysia is Possible and Other Essays: Writings on Culture and Politics for a Sustainable World,* ed. M. Nadarajah (Kuala Lumpur: Nohd, 2004), 217; M Nadarajah, interview by the author, 10 April 2004.

86. Bishan Singh, interview by the author, 27 November 2003; Bishan Singh, *The Consumer Movement and the Challenge for the New Millennium* (Kuala Lumpur: FOMCA, 2001).

87. Bishan Singh, *The Quest for Sustainable Development* (Kuantan, Pahang: Sustainable Development Network, 2003); MINSOC, *Learning in MINSOC: Reflecting on Social Change and Sustainable Development* (Kuantan, Pahang: MINSOC, 2002).

88. Marimuthu Nadason, interview by the author, 14 November 2003.

89. Amartya Sen, *On Ethics and Economics* (Oxford: Blackwell, 1988); Amartya Sen, *Rationality and Freedom* (Cambridge, MA: Belknap, 2002); Susan George, *Another World Is Possible If . . .* (London: Verso, 2004); David C. Korten, *When Corporations Ruled the World* (Bloomfield, CT: Kumarian, 2001); Martin Khor, *Globalisation and the South: Some Critical Issues* (Penang: Third World Network, 2001).

90. Pogge, *Global Poverty,* 26.

91. Victoria de Grazia, *Irresistible Empire: America's Advance Through Twentieth-Century Europe* (Cambridge, MA: Belknap Press of Harvard University Press, 2005), 462.

92. "The Final Act of the Conference on Security and Cooperation in Europe," August 1, 1975, 14 I.L.M. 1292 (Helsinki Declaration), http://www1.umn.edu/humanrts/osce/basics/finact75.htm.

93. Rhoda Karpatkin, "Memo to Members: The Reality of Choice," *Consumer Reports* 63, no. 9 (September 1998): 7.Iii14.

94. John Clarke, "Unsettled Connections: Citizens, Consumers and the Reform of Public Services," *Journal of Consumer Culture* 7, no. 2 (2007): 159–78 (166).

Chapter 8. Shopping for Justice: The Freedom of Free Trade

1. UN Department of Economic and Social Affairs, Group of Eminent Persons, *The Impact of Multinational Corporations on Development and International Relations* (New York: UN, 1974, E/5500/Rev.1 ST/ESA/6), 26.

2. E. L. Wheelwright, "The Corporate Response," in *Consumers, Transnational Corporations and Development,* ed. E. L. Wheelwright (Sydney: University of Sydney Transnational Corporations Research Project, 1986), 277–304; Anonymous, "Report of the Group of Experts," *The CTC Reporter* [periodical of the Centre on Transnational Corporations] 1, no. 3 (December 1977): 3.

3. Group of Eminent Persons, *Impact of Multinational Corporations,* 23.

4. Foo Gaik Sim, *IOCU on Record: A Documentary History of the International Organization of Consumers Unions, 1960–1990* (Yonkers, NY: Consumers Union, 1991), 108.

5. KSU Archive: DW Papers: Box 1: International Chamber of Commerce and European Society for Opinion and Marketing Research, *International Code of Marketing and Social Research Practice* (Paris and Amsterdam: International Chamber of Commerce and European Society for Opinion and Marketing Research, 1977); International Chamber of Commerce, *International Code of Direct Mail and Mail Order Sales Practice* (Paris: ICC, 1978); International Chamber of Commerce, *International Codes of Marketing Practice* (Paris: ICC, 1974), 7, 11, 19, 31, 41.

6. Sim, *IOCU on Record,* 111.

7. Group of Eminent Persons, *Impact of Multinational Corporations,* 81.

8. Anonymous, "Background and Activities of the Commission and the Centre on Transnational Corporations," *The CTC Reporter* 1, no. 1 (December 1976): 3–11; L. K. Jha, "The United Nations and the Transnationals," *The CTC Reporter* 1, no. 1 (December 1976): 14; IOCU Archive: Box 101: File H85.2: Nancy Hawkins, "UN Commission and Centre on Transnational Corporations," 1985.

9. United Nations Centre on Transnational Corporations, *Transnational Corporations in South Africa and Namibia: United Nations Public Hearings, Vol. 1: Reports of the Panel of Eminent Persons and of the Secretary-General* (New York: United Nations, 1986, ST/CTC/68); Henry Ford II, "United States Corporate Investment in South Africa," *CTC Reporter* 1, no. 4 (April 1978): 17; "Recommendations Requiring Action by the Economic and Social Council," *CTC Reporter* 1, no. 5 (September 1978): 8; "Fifth Session: Action by the Commission," *CTC Reporter* 1, no. 7 (Autumn 1979): 5–7.

10. KSU Archive: DW: Box 10: Anon., "The Infiltration of the UN System by Multinational Corporations," 1978.

11. IOCU Archive: Box 101: File H87.27: Michael Mortimore, "The UN Code of Conduct on TNCs," presentation at the IOCU Regional Conference, Santiago, Chile, 19–23 November 1990.

12. KSU Archive: DW: ECOSOC Commission on Transnational Corporations, "Completion of the Formulation of the Code of Conduct on Transnational Corporations: Information Paper on the negotiations: Note by the Secretariat," 4 January 1983, E/C.10/1983/S/2, 3–4.

13. Philippe de Seynes, "Transnational Corporations in the Framework of a New International Economic Order," *CTC Reporter* 1, no. 1 (December 1976): 14; Raymond Vernon, "Transnational Corporations in the Development Process," *CTC Reporter* 1, no. 3 (December 1977): 16, 29; Celso Furtado, "The New International Economic Order," *CTC Reporter* 1, no. 3 (December 1977): 17, 30.

14. Intergovernmental Working Group of the Commission on Transnational Corporations, *Transnational Corporations: Views and Proposals of Non-Governmental Interests on a Code of Conduct* (New York: UN, 30 December 1976, E/C.10/20).

15. KSU Archive: DW: Box 8: Dorothy Willner, Statement submitted by IOCU to the Commission on Transnational Corporations, Second session, 1–12 March 1976, Lima, Peru; UN Press Release, Working Group on Code of Conduct, Consumer protection considered for transnational code, 20 September, TNC/134; Letter from Dorothy Willner to Klaus A. Sahlgren, Executive Director, UN Center on Transnational Corporation, 28 September 1978; IOCU Archive: Box 55: File F11.1: Statement by Dorothy Willner, representative to ECOSOC for the IOCVU before the Intergovernmental Working Group of the Transnational Corporations, 22 April 1977.

16. KSU Archive: DW: Box 10: Commission on Transnational Corporations, Statement by

Dorothy Willner, representative of IOCU, 13 February 1978; Statement by Dorothy Willner, IOCU, before the Intergovernmental Working Group of the Transnational Corporation, 22 April 1977; "Consumer Protection," *CTC Reporter* 1, no. 4 (April 1978): 9, 28.

17. ECOSOC Commission on Transnational Corporations, *Completion of the Formulation of the Code of Conduct on Transnational Corporations: Draft Code of Conduct for Transnational Corporations* (New York: UN, 21 January 1983, E/C.10/1983/S/4).

18. Max Weisglas, "International Business and the United Nations Code," *CTC Reporter* 1, no. 12 (Summer 1982): 16–18.

19. "The Code," *CTC Reporter* 16 (Autumn 1983): 10; Arghyrios A. Fatouros, "At the Crossroads: Notes on the Current State of the Negotiations of the United Nations Code of Conduct," *CTC Reporter* 16 (Autumn 1983): 12–13; Patrick L. Robinson, "The Code: The June 1985 Reconvened Special Session On The Code," *CTC Reporter* 20 (Autumn 1985): 11–14; Peter Hansen, "A New Approach to the Code Negotiations," *CTC Reporter* 20 (Autumn 1985): 11–14; IOCU Archive: Box 101: File H87.27: Michael Mortimore, "The UN Code of Conduct on TNCs," presentation at the IOCU Regional Conference, Santiago, Chile, 19–23 November 1990.

20. IOCU Archive: Box 101: File H85.1: Dorothy Willner, "The Consumer Movement and TNCs," 1984; Box 102: File H88.54: "Code of Conduct Project Work," 27 November 1991.

21. "The Code," *CTC Reporter* 24 (Autumn 1987): 31–36; Lars Broch, "The Code of Conduct at the IOCU World Congress," 37–38; IOCU Archive: Box 46: File D16.22: "Consumers and Transnational Corporations," 1986[?]; D16.24: Allan Asher, "Consumers and Internationals: Ideas and Actions," 1986.

22. Wheelwright, *Consumers, Transnational Corporations and Development.*

23. IOCU Archive: Box 46: File D16.24: Statement of IOCU on draft UN Code of Conduct following reconvened session (January 1986) of the Commission on Transnational Corporations, July 1986; D16.26: Esther Peterson, "The United Nations Code of Conduct on TNC's," paper presented at the meeting of the Working Group on Transnational Corporations, 17 September 1986; Box 55: File F11.2: Commission on Transnational Corporations, Completion of the Code of Conduct on Transnational Corporations: Statement by the International Organisations of Consumers Unions, 2 April 1986 (E/C.10/1986/S/CRP.3); F11.4: Esther Peterson, "The United Nations' Role Regarding TNC's," no date; Box 101: H86.14: "Statement of IOCU to the 13th Session of the UN Commission on TNCs," 10 April 1987.

24. IOCU Archive: Box 57: File 16: Letter from Alma Williams to Peter Goldman, 11 November 1973.

25. IOCU Archive: Box 101: File H86.26: "Review of the UN Code of Conduct for Transnational Corporations," hearing before the Subcommittee on Human Rights and International Organizations of the Committee on Foreign Affairs, House of Representatives, 7 May 1987.

26. IOCU Archive: Box 101: File H86.1: Esther Peterson, "Consumers and the UN Code of Conduct for TNCs: Summary Notes," 1988; H86.2: Letter from Esther Peterson to George Bush, Michael Dukakis and Jesse Jackson, 1988; H86.5: Esther Peterson, "The United States Needs to Actively Support a Code of Conduct for Transnational Corporations," 1988; H86.26: "Review of the UN Code," 17–34.

27. All of the citations in this paragraph have been taken from Ted Wheelwright's "The Corporate Response," in *Consumers, Transnational Corporations and Development.*

28. IOCU, *Code of Conduct on Transnational Corporations: A UN Initiative* (The Hague: IOCU, 1990); IOCU Archive: Box 101: File H87.4: Draft decision: Code of Conduct on Transnational Corporations, June 1990; H87.7: Draft Text of the UN Code of Conduct on Transnational Corporations, June 1990.

29. IOCU Archive: Box 103: File H89.57: Elizabeth Hayes, "Meeting Report," 21–23 July 1992, 5; Box 102: File H88.2: Letter from James Firebrace to Allan Asher, 14 January 1991; H88.8: *World Consumer* 2 (1991): 2–3; H88.45: Letter from Peter Hansen, Executive Director, UN Centre on Transnational Corporations, to Elizabeth Hayes, IOCU-ROENA, 11 October 1991; H88.53: Rash Behari, "A Fight to the Finish," *World Consumer*, November 1991, 5–7; Box 103: File H89.10: UN Department of Public Information Press Release, 7 February 1992; H89.15: Memo from James Firebrace to Esther Peterson, 25 February 1992; H89.21: Remarks of Esther Peterson before the 18th Session of the Commission on Transnational Corporations; H89.21–H89.43: Briefing reports; Box 66a: File G16c.23: Esther Peterson, Statement submitted to the 15th session of the Commission on Transnational Corporations, 7 April 1989.

30. IOCU Archive: Box 102: File H88.21: Rhoda Karpatkin and Esther Peterson, "State De-

partment Organizes Disinformation Campaign in US Embassies on UN Consumer Issue," 29 June 1991; Box 101: File H87.21: UN Code of Conduct on Transnational Corporation, Hearing before the Subcommittee on International Economic Policy, Trade, Oceans and Environment of the Committee of Foreign Relations, United State Senate, One Hundred First Congress, Second Session, 11 October 1990, 12–23; Box 102: File H88.6: Telex from US State Department to US Embassies, 26 March 1991.

31. IOCU Archive: Box 103: File H89.65: E. Hayes, "Global Business Project: Summary of Latest Activity," 28 October 1992; Box 104: File H90.11: Allan Asher and Elizabeth Hayes, "Meeting rep kort of the 19th Session of the UN Commission on TNCs," 5–15 April 1993.

32. Consumer Unity and Trust Society (India), *Too Big for Rules: A Report of the IOCU/CUTS International Conference on Fairplay in Global Business, New Delhi, 14–15 February 1994* (Calcutta: CUTS, 1994).

33. Consumers International, *Consumer Charter for Global Business Campaign Kit* (London: CI, 1995).

34. CUTS, *Too Big for Rules,* 7.

35. IOCU Archive: Box 102: File H88.6: Telex from US State Department to US Embassies, 26 March 1991.

36. IOCU Archive: Box 101: H87.21: UN Code of Conduct on Transnational Corporation, Hearing before the Subcommittee on International Economic Policy, Trade, Oceans and Environment of the Committee of Foreign Relations, United State Senate, 101st Congress, 2nd Session, 11 October 1990, 15.

37. Larry Allen, *The Global Financial System, 1750–2000* (London: Reaktion, 2001); Barry J. Eichengreen, *Globalizing Capital: A History of the International Monetary System* (Princeton, NJ: Princeton University Press, 1996); E. A. Brett, *The World Economy Since the War: The Politics of Uneven Development* (Basingstoke: Macmillan, 1985); W. M. Scammell, *The International Economy Since 1945* (Basingstoke: Macmillan, 1980); Herman van der Wee, *Prosperity and Upheaval: The World Economy, 1945–1980* (London: Penguin 1991); CI, *Consumers and Trade: The Consumer Guide to Trade Issues and Agreements* (London: CI, 2001), 25–26; Larry Allen, *The Global Financial System, 1750–2000* (London: Reaktion, 2001); Joseph Stiglitz, *Globalization and Its Discontents* (New York: Norton, 2002).

38. The Economist, *Sisters in the Wood: A Survey of the IMF and the World Bank,* special issue, 12 October 1991; CI, *Consumers and Trade.*

39. Alfred D. Chandler and Bruce Mazlish, eds., *Leviathans: Multinational Corporations and the New Global History* (Cambridge: Cambridge University Press, 2005); Leslie Sklair, *The Transnational Capitalist Class* (Oxford: Blackwell, 2001).

40. James C. Scott, *Seeing Like a State: How Certain Schemes to Improve the Human Condition Have Failed* (New Haven, CT: Yale University Press, 1998).

41. David C. Korten, "The Failures of Bretton Woods," in *The Case Against the Global Economy: And for a Turn Toward the Local,* ed. Jerry Mander and Edward Goldsmith (San Francisco: Sierra Club Books, 1996), 20–31.

42. Stiglitz, *Globalization and Its Discontents,* 209;

43. Heikki Patomäki, *Democratizing Globalization: The Leverage of the Tobin Tax* (New York: Zed, 2001).

44. Anthony McGrew, "Power Shift: From National Government to Global Governance," in *A Globalising World? Culture, Economics, Politics,* ed. David Held (London: Routledge, 2000), 127–67 (157); Jayantai Durai, "Goodbye MAI? Talks on Controversial Investment Accord End in a Stalemate—For Now," *World Consumer* 228 (March 1998): 6–7; "Grassroots Globalisation Grounds MAI," *World Consumer* 229 (June 1998): 8.

45. See, for instance, George Monbiot, *The Age of Consent: A Manifesto for a New World Order* (London: Flamingo, 2003); Susan George, John Cavanagh, Daphne Wysham, and Marcos Arruda, eds., *Beyond Bretton Woods: Alternatives to the Global Economic Order* (Oxford: Pluto Press, 1994); William F. Fisher and Thomas Ponniah, eds., *Another World Is Possible: Popular Alternatives to Globalisation at the World Social Forum* (New York: Zed, 2003); Susan George, *Another World Is Possible If . . .* (New York: Verso, 2004); David Held, *Global Covenant: The Social Democratic Alternative to the Washington Consensus* (Cambridge: Polity, 2004).

46. Ann Pettifor and Romilly Greenhill, "Framework for Economic Justice and Sustainability," in *Real World Economic Outlook: The Legacy of Globalisation: Debt and Deflation,* ed. Ann Pettifor (London: Palgrave, 2003), 211–18.

47. IOCU, *Consumers Call for Urgent Action in Rolling Back Protectionism* (The Hague: IOCU, 1999); OECD, *Consumer Policy and International Trade: Results of the 1984 OECD Symposium and Programme of Action* (Paris: OECD, 1985); IOCU Archive: Box 115: File H125.3: Lars Broch, "Statement at OECD Symposium on Consumer Policy and International Trade," 27–29 November 1984; H125.10: OECD Secretariat, "Consumer Policy and International Trade: Outline for a Symposium to Be Held in 1990," 1 March 1989.

48. IOCU, *Annual Report, 1993* (The Hague: IOCU, 1994), 6.

49. "Legal Texts: The Results of the Uruguay Round of Multilateral Trade Negotiations," http://www.wto.org/english/docs_e/legal_e/legal_texts_e.htm.

50. CI, *Consumers and Trade,* 107.

51. Maria Elena Hurtado, "Making Business Better," *World Consumer* 221 (March 1996): 8–9.

52. IOCU Archive: Box 112: File H116.15: Notes of meeting of IOCU Trade Group, 12 June 1991.

53. IOCU, *The Task Ahead: Recommendations for the Work Programme of the World Trade Organisation* (London: IOCU, 1994); CI, *Annual Report, 1994* (London: CI, 1995), 10.

54. IOCU Archive: Box 113: File H119.9: "Detailed Comments by IOCU and BEUC on Agricultural Trade and the GATT Negotiations," 1988; H119.36: Letter from Mark Ritchie to IOCU, 20 July 1980, Plus Letter Clayton Yeutter, US Department of Agriculture to Ray MacSherry, Commission of the European Communities, July 1989; H119.58: Letter from Mark Ritchie, Minnesota Department of Agriculture, to Atia Scipaanboord, IOCU, 2 January 1990.

55. IOCU Archive: Box 114: File H122.5: Papers relating to a proposed NGO Roundtable on change in the global economic system, April 1991; H122.6: Memo from Atie Schipaanboord to Julian Edwards, April 1991; H122.7: Letter from Atie Schipaanboord to Michael McCoy, 18 April 1991.

56. David Vogel, *Trading Up: Consumer and Environmental Regulation in a Global Economy* (Cambridge, MA: Harvard University Press, 1995).

57. IOCU Archive: Box 18: File B3em: Atia Schipaanboord, "Consumers and the GATT," paper for the 57th Meeting of Executive Committee, March 1990; IOCU, *Consumers call for Urgent Action in Rolling Back Protectionism* (The Hague: IOCU, 1990); Box 21: File Ex68/11k: SAL, "Consumers and GATT: Report of IOCU Delegation to Geneva, 25–27 October 1993," 2 November 1993.

58. IOCU, *Consumer Interests and GATT: The Need for Greater Transparency* (The Hague: IOCU, 1991).

59. IOCU Archive: Box 115: File H127.17: Letter from Atie Scipaanboord to Allan Asher, 14 December 1990.

60. IOCU Archive: Box 114: File H123.40: Letter from Doreen L. Brown, Consumers for World Trade, to Atie Schipaanboord, 28 October 1990; H123.68: Letter from Atie Schipaanboord to Doreen L. Brown, 18 September 1991. For further information on Consumers for World Trade, see http://www.cwt.org.

61. IOCU Archive: Box 83: File H37: Hatch Bill Lobby, various papers.

62. IOCU Archive: Box 84: File H41: Coalition Against Dangerous Exports, various papers.

63. IOCU Archive: Box 1147: File H134.4: Tim Smith, "Notes on Pagan Capitalism," paper presented to the Public Affairs Council, 22 April 1982; H143.5: Rafael D. Pagan, "Carrying the Fight to the Critics of Multinational Capitalism," paper presented to the Public Affairs Council, New York, 22 April 1982.

64. Philip Evans, *Unpacking the GATT: A Step by Step Guide to the Uruguay Round* (London: IOCU, 1994).

65. CI, *Annual Report, 1995* (London: CI, 1996), 14; CI, *Annual Report, 1996* (London: CI, 1997), 24, 34; CI, *Annual Report, 1998* (London: CI, 1999), 24; Phillip Evans, "A Dialogue on World Trade," *World Consumer* 221 (March 1996): 7; Jayanti Durai, "WTO Meeting: Access, Issues," *World Consumer* 223 (December 1996): 2–3, 10.

66. IOCU Archive: Box "Council Meetings, 1996–2003": File CM47/3(v): Global Policy and Campaigns Unit, "Summary Progress Report, November 1995–September 1996."

67. IOCU, *Annual Report, 1993*, 23–37; Allan Asher, *Guidelines for the Global Market* (New Delhi: CUTS and CI-ROAP, 1997); CI-ROAP and CUTS, Consumers in the Global Age: Proceedings of *International Conference on Consumer Protection, New Delhi, India, 1997* (Penang and Calcutta: CI-ROAP and CUTS, 1997).

68. Kumariah Balasubramaniam, *Heads—TNCs Win: Tails—South Loses, or The GATT/ WTO/TRIPs Agreement* (Pennag: CI-ROAP, 1998).

69. IOCU Archive: Box "Council Meetings, 1996–2003": File CM 50/4c: Amadou Kanoute, "Regional Office for Africa Progress Report, October 1998–September 1999"; CM51/5c: "CI-ROAF Work Report, October 1999–November 2000."

70. Bronwen Morgan, "Consuming Without Paying: Stealing or Campaigning? The Civic Implications of Civil Disobedience Around Access to Water," in *Citizenship and Consumption,* ed. Frank Trentmann & Kate Soper (London: Palgrave, 2008); Bronwen Morgan, "Water: Frontier Markets and Cosmopolitan Activism," *Soundings: A Journal of Politics and Culture* 27 (2004): 10–24; CI, *Vital Networks: A Study of Public Utilities in Bulgaria, Macedonia, Czech Republic and Slovakia* (London: CI, 2000); CI-ROAF, *Liberalisation of the Water Sector in Africa: Trends and Impacts* (Harare, Zimbabwe: CI-ROAF, 2001); CI, *Consumers and Competition: Global Competition Report* (London: CI, 2001).

71. CI, *Annual Report, 1997,* 28; IOCU Archive: Box "Council Meetings, 1996–2003": File CM 49/4.1a: "Summary ROLAC progress report, November 1997–November 1998"; CM50/4b: "ROLAC Work Report, October 1998–September 1999"; "Pioneering Work in Public Utilities," *World Consumer* 227 (December 1997): 10–11.

72. CI, *Annual Report, 1997,* 28; Jayanti Durai, "Goodbye MAI?" *World Consumer* 228 (March 1998): 6–7; "Grassroots Globalisation Grounds MAI," *World Consumer* 229 (June 1998): 8.

73. IOCU Archive: Box "Council Meetings, 1996–2003": File CM55/4a: Global Policy and Campaign Unit, "Campaign Directors report," 2003.

74. IOCU Archive: Box "Council Meetings, 1996–2003": File CM54/3: Julian Edwards, "Director General's Report," 2001; CM54/5b: "Council/Executive Report," April 2002; CM55/3: Julian Edwards, "Director General's Report," May 2003.

75. IOCU Archive: Box "Council Meetings, 1996–2003": File CM54/5a: "Executive Report," September 2001, 8.

76. WTO, "Relations with Non-Governmental Organizations/Civil Society," http://www.wto .org/english/forums_e/ngo_e/intro_e.htm.

77. WTO, "WTO Secretariat Activities with NGOs," 12 April 2001, http://www.wto.org/ english/thewto_e/minist_e/min01_e/min01_ngo_activ_e.htm.

78. IOCU Archive: Box "Council Meetings, 1996–2003": File CM55/3: "Director General's Report," May 2003.

79. IOCU Archive: Box "Council Meetings, 1996–2003": File CM51/3: Julian Edwards, "Director General's Report," 2000; CM51/5b: Office for Developed and Transition Economies, "Summary Work Report, November 1999–October 2000"; Jayantai Durai, "Battle in Seattle: WTO Ministerial Collapses," *World Consumer,* 235, December 1999, 2–3; CI, *Consumer Rights and the Multilateral Trading System: What Needs to Be Done Before a Millennium Round* (London: CI, 1999); CI, *Consumers and Trade,* pp. 107–8.

80. IOCU Archive: Box "Council Meetings, 1996–2003": File CM51/5b: "Congress Statement: Consumers, Social Justice and the World Market," 1–2.

81. CI, *Annual Report, 2002* (London: CI, 2003), 29.

82. "Down to the Wire for Doha Ministerial," *World Consumer* 242 (October 2001): 2–8; CI, *The Agreement on Agriculture* (London: CI, 2001); CI, *The General Agreement on Trade in Services* (London: CI, 2001).

83. Jon Barnes, "Consumers International's Recommendations for Cancún and the Future of the Doha Developmental Agenda," *Consumer 21* 14 (Autumn 2003): 8–11; Ian McAuley, *Globalisation for All: Reviving the Spirit of Bretton Woods* (London: CI, 2003); CI, *Consumers, Multilateral Competition Policy and the WTO* (London: CI, 2003); John Marsh and Secondo Tarditi, *Cultivating a Crisis: The Global Impact of the Common Agricultural Policy* (London: CI, 2003); CI, *Putting Consumers at the Heart of Trade* (London: CI, 2005); Phil Evans, *Consumers and the Future Work of the WTO: Where Do We Want to Go from Here?* (London: CI, 2006).

84. IOCU Archive: Box "Council Meetings, 1996–2003": File CM49/4.3a: "PRODEC and PROECT Summary Progress Report, January–October 1998"; CM50/4d: "Programmes for Developed Economies and Economies in Transition summary Progress Report," January–October 1999"; TACD, *Background Briefing for Inaugural Meeting, Washington DC, September 1998* (London: CI, 1998).

85. Sabina Alkire, *Valuing Freedoms: Sen's Capability Approach and Poverty Reduction* (Oxford: Oxford University Press, 2002).

86. CI, *Consumer Charter for Trade: Consumers International's Recommendations for Cancún and the Future of the Doha Development Agenda* (London: CI, 2003).

87. Robert N. Mayer, "Protectionism, Intellectual Property and Consumer Protection: Was the Uruguay Round Good for Consumers," *Journal of Consumer Policy* 21, no. 2 (1998): 195–215; CI, *Consumers and Competition*, 4–5; Phil Evans, *The Consumer Guide to Competition: A Practical Handbook* (London: CI, 2003).

88. UNDP, *Human Development Report 2005* (New York: UNDP, 2005), 34.

89. CI-ROAF, *Impact Assessment of the Agreement on Agriculture and the General Agreement on Trade in Services on Consumers in Africa* (Harare, Zimbabwe: CI-ROAF, 2003).

90. CI-ROAF, *Value of Consuming Indigenous Foods in Africa: Briefing Paper III* (Harare, Zimbabwe: CI-ROAF, 2002). For an early account of the food crisis see: Christopher Robins and Javed Ansari, *The Profits of Doom: A War on Want Investigation into the "World Food Crisis"* (London: War on Want, 1976).

91. IOCU Archive: Box 133: File I13.17: CI-ROAP, "Strategic Review and Planning for CI-ROAP," 1997, 9–10.

92. IOCU Archive: Box 133: File I13.15: Comments and suggestions to draft report of CI-ROAP Strategic Review and Planning, 1997.

93. IOCU Archive: Box 36: File C6.2: "Trip Report on Indonesian Rural Consumers," 27 February 1989.

94. "Consumer Defense Takes Root in War-Torn Colombia," *World Consumer* 237 (September 2000): 2, 22; IOCU Archive: Box 139: File I23.6: IOCU-ROLAC, "Regional Strategies and Plans of the Regional Office for Latin America and the Caribbean for the Years 1992–1995: Draft," 1992.

95. IOCU Archive: Box 142: File I27.5: Africa Circular Letter, February 1993; Box 144: File I29.92: IOCU & ENDA, *Consommateurs africains face aux politiques de dévelopment: conférence luso-francophone, Dakar, Sénégal, du 21 au 25 novembre 1988* (African consumers and the politics of development: Luso-Francophone Conference) (Dakar: IOCU and ENDO, 1989); Box 150: File I43/2.1: "Review of CI-ROAF," 1996.

96. Lezak Shallat, "Linking Gender and Global Trade," *World Consumer* 241 (October 2001): 14–16.

97. IOCU Archive: Box 183: *Consommation et développement,* various editions, 1989–1999; *African Consumer,* various issues, 1995–2003.

98. Cited in Tasneem Mowjee, "Consumers Unite Internationally," in *Globalising Civic Engagement: Civil Society and Transnational Action,* ed. John Clark (London: Earthscan, 2003), 39. See also CUTS, *Too Big for Rules;* CUTS, *We've Been Here Before: Perspectives on the Cancún Ministerial* (Jaipur: CUTS, 2003); CUTS, *Bridging the Differences: Analyses of Five Issues of the WTO Agenda* (Jaipur: CUTS, 2003); Pradeep Mehta, ed., *Competition Regimes in the World: A Civil Society Report* (Jaipur: CUTS, 2005).

99. Paul Blustein, *The Chastening: Inside the Crisis that Rocked the Global Financial System and Humbled the IMF* (New York: Public Affairs, 2001).

100. CI, *. . . And Our Rice Pots Are Empty: The Social Costs of the Economic Crisis* (Penang: CI, 1998).

101. Khoo Boo Teik, *Beyond Mahathir,* 65; Jomo K. S., *M Way: Mahathir's Economic Legacy* (Kuala Lumpur: Forum, 2003); CI, *. . . And Our Rice Pots Are Empty: The Social Costs of the Economic Crisis.*

102. Khoo Boo Teik, *Beyond Mahathir: Malaysian Politics and Its Discontents* (London: Zed, 2003); Vidhu Verma, *Malaysia: State and Civil Society in Transition* (Petaling Jaya: Strategic Information Research Development, 2004); Jomo K. S., *M Way: Mahathir's Economic Legacy.*

103. *Utusan Konsumer* 28, no. 6 (April 1998): 15; *Utusan Konsumer* 28, no. 7 (May 1998): 19; *Utusan Konsumer* 28, no. 7 [error: same number as previous issue] (June 1998): 16; CAP, *Understanding Global Organisations: How They Act Against People's Interests* (Penang: CAP, 2003).

104. *Utusan Konsumer* 28, no. 3 (mid-February 1998): 15 ; Martin Khor, "IMF Policies Leading to Foreign Control of Asian Countries," in *Confronting the Challenges: The Asian Economic Crisis* (Penang: CI, 1998), 12–24.

105. Martin Khor, "Value for People: The Potential Role of a Consumer Movement in the Third World," paper held in archives of Consumers Association of Penang, no date; CAP, *The Consumers Association of Penang* (Penang: CAP, 1987); Meena Raman, "Comparative Analysis of Consumer

Issues in Malaysia and Other Countries," paper presented at a meeting of the Malaysian Consumer Council, 10 December 1994 (private papers of Meena Raman).

106. Martin Khor, *Globalisation and the South: Some Critical Issues* (Penang: Third World Network, 2001).

107. Martin Khor, "Measuring Impact: the Third World Network," in *Measuring the Immeasurable: Planning, Monitoring and Evaluation of Networks*, ed. Marilee Karl (New Delhi: Women's Feature Service, 1998), 124–30. See also its website http://www.twnside.org.sg.

108. Bhagirath Lal Das, *WTO: The Doha Agenda: The New Negotiations on World Trade* (London: Zed, 2003); Bhagirath Lal Das, *Some Key Issues Relating to the WTO* (Penang: TWN, 1996); Bhagirath Lal Das, *Strengthening Developing Countries in the WTO* (Penang: TWN, 1999); Chakravarthi Raghavan, *The New Issues and Developing Countries* (Pennag: TWN, 1996).

109. Martin Khor and Lim Li Lin, eds., *Good Practices and Innovative Experiences in the South, Volume 1: Economic, Environmental and Sustainable Livelihood Initiatives* (London and Penang: UNDP, TWN and Zed Books, 2001); Martin Khor and Lim Li Lin, eds., *Good Practices and Innovative Experiences in the South, Volume 2: Social Policies, Indigenous Knowledge and Appropriate Technology* (London and Penang: UNDP, TWN and Zed Books, 2001); Martin Khor and Lim Li Lin, eds., *Good Practices and Innovative Experiences in the South, Volume 3: Citizen Initiatives in Social Services, Popular Education and Human Rights* (London and Penang: UNDP, TWN and Zed Books, 2001); Martin Khor, "On What the Plot Is for Seattle," text of presentation at Seattle Teach-in, 26 November 1999, http://www.ratical.org/co-globalize/ifg112699MK.pdf; Martin Khor, "Global Economy and the Third World," *International Journal of Rural Studies*, October 1999, http://www.ivcs.org.uk/intaf/intaf8.html; "WTO and the Third World: on a Catastrophic Course. An Interview with Martin Khor," *Multinational Monitor* 20, nos. 10 and 11 (October/November 1999), available at http://multinationalmonitor.org/mm1999/mm9910.10 .html; Martin Khor, "Rethinking Liberalisation and Reforming the WTO," text of presentation made at Davos, 28 January 2000, http://www.twnside.org.sg/title/davos2-cn.htm.

110. CI-ROAF, *Model Law for Consumer Protection in Africa* (Harare, Zimbabwe: CI-ROAF, 1996).

111. CI-ROAF, *Multilateral Framework for Competition Policy: Where do African Consumers Stand?* (Harare, Zimbabwe: CI-ROAF, 2002); CI-ROAF, *Regional Overview on the Impact of Multilateral Trade Agreements on African Consumers* (Harare, Zimbabwe: CI-ROAF, 2001); CI-ROAF, *Liberalisation of the Water Sector in Africa: Trends and Impacts* (Harare, Zimbabwe: CI-ROAF, 2001).

Conclusion: The Poverty of Choice

1. Jimmy Carter, "Energy and the National Goals: A Crisis of Confidence," speech delivered 15 July 1979, http://www.americanrhetoric.com/speeches/jimmycartercrisisofconfidence.htm; Daniel Horowitz, *The Anxieties of Affluence: Critiques of American Consumer Culture, 1939–1979* (Amherst: University of Massachusetts Press, 2004); John Kenneth Galbraith, *The Affluent Society* (London: Penguin, 1999 [1958]).

2. Juliet B. Schor, *Do Americans Shop Too Much?* (Boston, MA: Beacon Press, 2000); Juliet B. Schor, *The Overspent American: Why We Want What We Don't Need* (New York: Basic Books, 1998); Robert Frank, *Luxury Fever: Money and Happiness in an Era of Excess* (Princeton, NJ: Princeton University Press, 1999); Robert Harrison, Terry Newholm, and Deirdre Shaw, *The Ethical Consumer* (London: Sage, 2005); Alex Nicholls and Charlotte Opal, *Fair Trade: Market-Driven Ethical Consumption* (London: Sage, 2005); Daniel Doherty and Amitai Etzioni, eds., *Voluntary Simplicity: Responding to Consumer Culture* (Lanham, MD: Rowman and Littlefield, 2003); Kalle Lasn, *Culture Jam: The Uncooling of America* (New York: Eagle Brook, 1999); J. Elkington and J. Hailes, *Manual 2000: Life Choices for the Future You Want* (London: Hodder and Stoughton, 1998). For an example of the alternative websites, see http://www.newdream.org.

3. John de Graaf, David Wann, and Thomas H. Naylor, *Affluenza: The All-Consuming Epidemic* (San Francisco: Berrett-Koehler, 2001); Oliver James, *Affluenza* (London: Vermilion, 2007); Elaine S. Abelson, *When Ladies Go A-Thieving: Middle-Class Shoplifters in the Victorian Department Store* (New York: Oxford University Press, 1989).

4. See, for example, James B. Twitchell, *Living It Up: Our Love Affair with Luxury* (New York: Columbia University Press, 2002).

5. Simon Schama, *The Embarrassment of Riches: An Interpretation of Dutch Culture in the Golden Age* (New York: Knopf, 1987).

6. "Chinese Growth Heating Up Economy," BBC News, 19 April 2007, http://news.bbc.co.uk/1/hi/business/6570713.stm.

7. I am extremely grateful to Karl Gerth for these statistics, presented in his paper, "Consumption and Politics in Twentieth-Century China," at the Citizenship and Consumption conference, University of Cambridge, 30 March–1 April 2006.

8. Francis Loh Kok Wah, "Towards a New Politics of Fragmentation and Contestation," in *New Politics in Malaysia*, ed. Francis Loh Kok Wah and Johan Saravanamuttu (Singapore: Institute of Southeast Asian Studies, 2003), 253–82 (261); Francis Loh Kok Wah, "Developmentalism and the Limits of Democratic Discourse," in *Democracy in Malaysia: Discourses and Practices*, ed. Francis Loh Kok Wah and Khoo Boo Teik (Richmond, Surrey: Curzon, 2002), 19–50.

9. Timothy Gorringe, *Fair Shares: Ethics and the Global Economy* (London: Thames and Hudson, 1999); John Benton, *Christians in a Consumer Culture* (Fearn, Ross-shire: Christian Focus, 1999); Craig Bartholomew and Thorsten Moritz, eds., *Christ and Consumerism: Critical Reflections on the Spirit of Our Age* (Carlisle: Paternoster Press, 2000); Donald A. Hay and Alan Kreider, eds., *Christianity and the Culture of Economics* (Cardiff: University of Wales Press, 2001); Norwegian Bishops' Conference, *The Consumer Society as an Ethical Challenge* (Oslo: Church of Norway Information Service, 1993).

10. José Bové and Francois Dufour, *The World Is Not for Sale: Farmers Against Junk Food* (London: Verso, 2001).

11. Victoria de Grazia, *Irresistible Empire: America's Advance Through Twentieth-Century Europe* (Cambridge, MA: Belknap Press of Harvard University Press, 2005), 466–73.

12. Matthew Hilton, "The Banality of Consumption," in *Citizenship and Consumption*, ed. Frank Trentmann and Kate Soper (London: Palgrave, 2008), 87–103.

13. See its website http://www.consumerreports.org.

14. Beverley Hooper, "The Consumer Citizen in Contemporary China," Centre for East and South-East Asian Studies Working Paper No. 12, Lund University, http://www.ace.lu.se/images/Syd_och_sydostasienstudier/working_papers/Hooper.pdf; "Complaint Hotline Saves 4.4 Billion Yuan for Consumers During Five Years," *People's Daily*, 26 March 2004, http://english.peopledaily.com.cn/200403/26/print20040326_138603.html; Jing Jian Xiao, "Chinese Consumer Movement," in *Encyclopaedia of the Consumer Movement*, ed. S. Brobeck, R. N. Mayer, and R. O. Herrmann (Santa Barbara: ABC-CLIO, 1997), 104–8; Donald B. King and Tong Gao, *Consumer Protection in China: Development and Recommendations* (Littleton, CO: Rothman, 1991); Tong Gao, "Chinese Consumer Protection Philosophy," *Journal of Consumer Policy* 14, no. 3 (1992): 337–50.

15. UNDP, *Human Development Report, 2005* (New York: UNDP, 2005).

16. Paul Kingsnorth, *One No, Many Yeses: A Journey to the Heart of the Global Resistance Movement* (London: Free Press, 2003), 89; Bronwen Morgan, "Emerging Global Water Welfarism: Access to Water, Unruly Consumers and Transnational Governance," in *Consuming Cultures, Global Perspectives: Historical Trajectories, Transnational Exchanges*, ed. John Brewer and Frank Trentmann (Oxford: Berg, 2006).

17. Manuel Castells, *The Information Age: Economy, Society and Culture, Vol. II. The Power of Identity* (Oxford: Blackwell, 2000 [1997]).

18. Benjamin R. Barber, *Jihad vs. McWorld: Terrorism's Challenge to Democracy* (London: Corgi, 2003 [1995]).

19. de Grazia, *Irresistible Empire*.

INDEX

Action for Rational Drugs in Asia, 146
Action Group to Halt Advertising and Sponsorship of Tobacco, 137
Action on Smoking and Health, 63
Adbusters, 183
Adnan, Mohd. Hamdan, 91
advertising, 7, 30, 39, 42, 86, 120, 157, 207, 218
affluence, 18–19, 23–24, 48, 51–53, 74, 75, 148, 162, 187, 191, 241, 244
Afghanistan, 133
Africa, 3, 11, 74, 75, 92, 104, 107, 109–10, 187, 204–5, 230–31, 234–35, 237–38, 243, 247, 251–52
See also entries for individual nations
Aliran, 89, 96, 207, 209
Al-Ja'fri, Syed Adam, 90
Allende, Salvador, 214–15
Alliance of Consumer Associations (Germany), 61
American Association of Retired Persons, 172
American Council for Capital Formation, 180
American Council on Consumer Interests, 47
American Enterprise Institute, 16, 169–70, 176–80
American Institute for Public Policy Research, 169
Americanization, 24, 35–8, 69, 119, 124–25, 191
American Standards Association, 30

Amnesty International, 99, 111, 115, 149
Anand, Raj, 105
anti-apartheid, 99
anti-communism, 41, 43
anti-globalization, 100, 118, 124–25, 127–28, 135, 150–52, 178, 203, 211, 217, 225–26, 235, 237–38, 246
anti-regulation, 16, 120, 145, 147, 154–57, 161, 166–75, 176–82, 184, 194, 221–23, 247, 249
Anti-Slavery International, 134
Argentina, 136, 223
Asia, 75, 92, 104, 186, 196, 204, 224, 230, 236, 241, 245
See also entries for individual nations
Asian-Pacific Peoples' Environmental Network, 136
Asian values, 84, 95, 170, 188–91, 206–11
Association des Consommateurs (Belgium), 23, 25–26, 33, 36, 46, 56, 103
Association for Consumer Information (Austria), 26, 34, 39, 42, 61, 105
Association Française de Normalisation, 69
Association pour la Taxation des Transactions financiers pour l'Aide aux Citoyens (ATTAC), 129, 135
Australia 53, 92, 106, 222
consumer protection, 63
See also Australian Consumers' Association
Australian Consumers' Association, 26, 33, 35, 37, 42, 45, 103–4, 137, 197

Austria, 9, 22, 107
  consumer protection, 58–59, 61
  trade unions, 56
  See also Association for Consumer Information (Austria)

Baby foods. *See* breast milk substitutes
Baby Milk Action, 126
Balasubramaniam, Kumariah, 146
Bangladesh, 93, 146
Barisan Nasional, 84
Bayer, 141, 143
Becker, Jane E., 223
Belgium, 22, 25–26, 37, 39, 106
  consumer protection, 63
  co-operatives, 55
  women's movement, 57
  See also Association des Consommateurs; Union Féminine pour l'Information et la Défense du Consommateur
Bell, Daniel, 18
Bellamy, Edward, 42
Benin, 238
Bern Third World Action Group, 138
Better Business Bureau, 167
Beveridge, William, 8
Bhopal tragedy, 121, 137, 199
biotechnology, 11, 143, 199, 204
Blair, Tony, 2, 3
Bolivia, 77, 238
Bonino, Emma, 71
Bourdieu, Pierre, 41
Bové, Jose, 246
boycotts, 10, 29, 53, 68, 82, 88, 127, 138–39, 205, 247
Brazil, 109
breast milk substitutes, 11, 16, 86, 117, 126–27, 129, 137–40, 145, 177, 179, 187, 199, 213
Bristol-Myers, 138
British Standards Institute, 57, 69
Broch, Lars, 120–21
Brook, Caspar, 103
Brunei, 108
Buckley, William F., 168Bulgaria, 66, 110
Bureau Européen des Unions de Consommateurs, 69–71, 103
Bush, George H. W., 164, 221
Bush, George W., 2, 3, 156, 164
Bush, Jeb, 170
Business Roundtable, 173, 176

Cameroon, 205
Campbell, Persia, 113–14
Canada, 2, 35, 45, 107, 110
  women's movement, 56
  See also Consumers Association of Canada

Canadian Consumer. See Consumers Association of Canada
Cancún, 232
Caplowitz, David, 166
Care International, 114, 149
Carson, Rachel, 140–41, 147, 162
Carter, Jimmy, 18, 123, 140, 156, 164, 172, 174–75, 180, 241
Casey, William J., 170
Catholic Agency for Overseas Development, 221
Cato Institute, 170, 176
Center for Strategic Tax Reform, 180
Center for the Study of Responsive Law, 63, 164
Center on Transnational Corporation. *See* Commission on Transnational Corporations
Chad, 234
Chamber of Commerce (US), 173, 179
Chapman, Simon, 138
Chase, Stuart, 30, 40, 42–43, 157
Chervet, Hélène, 117
Chifuren, 57, 92
Chile, 214–15, 223, 250
China, 8, 67, 96, 110, 241–42, 247–48, 251
Choice. See Australian Consumers' Association
Chrétien, Jean, 2
Christian Aid, 96, 118, 135, 221
Ciba-Geigy, 141, 143, 144, 146, 218, 221
Citizens International, 210
Climate Action Network, 135
Clinton, Bill, 164, 196
clioquinol, 144, 146
Coalition for a Consumer Protection Agency, 172
Coca-Cola, 4
Code of Conduct on Transnational Corporations, 147, 182, 219–23, 229, 240
Codex Alimentarius, 6, 115, 138
Cold War, 9, 23, 36–37, 65, 68, 124, 178, 213, 250
Columbia, 77, 234–35
Commission on Sustainable Development, 205
Commission on the Status of Women, 115
Commission on Transnational Corporations, 115, 119, 178, 215–23
Common Agricultural Policy, 71, 224
Common Cause, 164
Communist Party, 10, 158
Confucianism, 190
Congress Watch, 63, 173
Consumentenbond, 23, 25–26, 33, 36, 41–42, 46, 57, 65, 103, 118
Consumentengids. See Consumentenbond

Consumer Federation of America, 57, 63, 165, 171
Consumer Interpol, 116–17, 136–37, 145, 179
Consumer Issues Working Group, 173
consumer protection, 5, 16, 51–74, 84, 92, 155, 176, 188–89, 244
 global, 216, 218–23, 228–33
 opposition to, 167–75, 184
 United Nations, 102, 114–25, 180–82
 See also networks; *and entries for individual nations*
Consumer Protection Agency Bill (US), 123, 156, 170–75, 178, 182–84, 195, 213
Consumer Reports. See Consumers Union
Consumer Unity and Trust Society, 235
Consumers Association (UK), 11, 22–23, 25–26, 32, 35–37, 40, 42, 45, 57, 65, 148
 International Organization of Consumers Unions, 103–5, 111, 197, 215
 membership, 46
Consumers' Association of Canada, 26, 37, 45
Consumers' Association of Penang, 78–97, 107, 122, 130, 132, 136, 141, 150, 205–12, 236–37, 245
Consumers Council (Norway), 26, 34, 46, 59
Consumers Council (UK), 6
Consumers for World Trade, 229
Consumers International. *See* International Organisation of Consumers Unions
Consumers' leagues, 2, 10, 29, 57, 63, 160, 183
Consumers' National Federation, 158, 160
Consumers' Research, 10, 21, 149, 153, 157
 early history, 29–32
 efficiency, 40–45
Consumers' Research Bulletin. See Con-ˈsumers' Research
Consumers Union, 10, 11, 21–23, 25–26, 29, 35, 56–57, 63, 131, 148–49, 189, 247
 Americanization, 36–38
 communist charges, 157–61, 167
 Consumer Protection Agency, 171–75
 early history, 29–32
 ideology, 40–45
 International Organization of Consumers Unions, 103–6, 111
 members, 45, 195–98
 opposition to, 153, 167
 Ralph Nader, 165–66, 188, 194–95
Consumers Union of Japan, 61, 92, 141
Consumers Union of Reykjavik, 34
consumption patterns, 27–29, 96
co-operative movement, 1, 9, 19, 21, 34, 38–39, 53, 55, 72–73, 99, 101, 154, 203, 233, 243, 254
 See also entries for individual nations

Coors, Joseph, 170
Corbyn, Jeremy, 96
Cuba, 67, 110
Czechoslovakia, 66

Danish Housewives Consumer Council, 26, 34, 36, 38–39, 43, 60
Darms, Louis, 33
De Beauvoir, Simone, 95
Debord, Guy, 165
Debt Crisis Network, 135
Denmark, 43
 consumer protection, 59–60
 trade unions, 59
 women's movement, 59
 See also Danish Housewives Consumer Council; Home Economics Council (Denmark)
Deutsche Mark, 33, 46
Deutscher Verbraucherbund, 40
Diani, Aldo, 37
Dies, Martin, 153, 156–58, 160
Doha Round (of trade negotiations), 231–32
Dole, Bob, 172
Drop the Debt, 206
Dunne, Michael, 192

Economic and Social Council (UN), 13, 98–99, 112–25, 148, 156, 192, 205, 214–15, 217, 223, 229, 245
Education and Research Association for Consumers, 97, 208–11
Edwards, Julian, 131
efficiency, 40–45
Eisenhower, Dwight D., 133
England. *See* United Kingdom
environmentalism, 11, 14, 41, 46, 86, 89, 99–100, 117, 127, 132–33, 136, 147, 149, 188, 203, 205, 208, 210, 217, 241, 246
 See also pesticides
Environmental Protection Society of Malaysia, 88
Environment and Development Action in the Third World, 110, 235
Epstein, Henry, 45, 104
Erhard, Ludwig, 8
ethical consumption, 10, 20, 41, 100, 128, 152, 183, 189, 203, 217, 233, 246
European Productivity Agency, 36–37
European Recovery Agency, 23
European Round Table, 71
European Social Forum, 89, 129
European Union, 47, 54, 69–72, 103, 110, 117–18, 191, 224

fair trade, 2, 10, 20, 50, 100, 128, 183, 189, 204, 212, 217, 233, 239, 246

Fazal, Anwar, 84–85, 97, 107–8, 117, 122, 130–32, 136, 139, 141–42, 149, 179, 186–88, 192, 195, 198–202, 204, 207, 210, 221, 250
Federal Trade Commission, 164, 166, 176
Federation of Consumers (Poland), 67–68, 110–11
Federation of Malaysian Consumers' Association, 90, 92, 209–10
Fernandez, Irene, 97, 208
Fernandez, Josie, 97, 208, 210
Fiji, 93
Finland, 60
Food and Agriculture Office, 98, 112, 115, 117, 142, 148
food security, 116, 143, 208
Forbruker Rapporten. See Consumers Council (Norway)
Ford, 173
Ford, Gerald, 156, 171–72, 174
Ford Foundation, 169
Foreign Policy Research Institute, 180
Fourastié, Jean, 8
France, 5, 6, 8, 9, 22, 25–27, 29, 37, 44, 144, 235
  consumer protection, 52, 59, 63–64, 70, 72
  co-operatives, 55
  trade unions, 56–58
  women's movement, 57
  See also Institut National de la Consommation; Union Fédérale des Consommateurs
Friedman, Milton, 167, 176
Friends of the Earth, 99, 111, 135, 172, 203
Friends of the Earth Malaysia, 87, 89, 136, 141, 150
Furness, Betty, 160–61

Galbraith, John Kenneth, 6, 18, 42, 106, 164, 241, 243
General Agreement on Trade and Tariffs, 218, 224, 227, 229, 234
General Motors, 161, 164, 173–74
genetically modified (GM) foods. *See* biotechnology,
George, Susan, 211
Germany, 8, 9, 22, 25, 27, 33, 107, 111
  consumer protection, 52, 58–59, 61–62, 64, 70, 72
  German Democratic Republic, 54, 66
  See also Alliance of Consumer Associations; Stiftung Warentest
Ghana, 110, 234
Ghandi, Mahatma, 8, 82, 93, 105, 247
Gingrich, Newt, 170
Gips, Terry, 143
Goldman, Peter, 215
Goldwater, Barry, 170

Goodman, Dorothy and Ray, 22, 32
Greece, 70, 88, 108
Green, Mark, 173
Greenpeace, 99, 111, 133
Grocery Manufacturers' Association, 173
Group of Eminent Persons, 214–19
Guidelines for Global Business, 222
Guidelines on Consumer Protection, 119–25, 179–80, 184, 192, 205, 220, 229
Guyana, 92

Hakam, 208
Hayek, F. A., 167–68, 170
Health Action International, 127, 130, 137, 144–47, 149–52, 179, 201
Hearst, William Randolph, 153, 158–59
Heinz, 4
Helsinki Declaration, 212
Heritage Foundation, 16, 170, 176–80, 221
Himmelfarb, Gertrude, 169
Hinduism, 190
Hittites of Anatolia, 5
Home Economics Council (Denmark), 26, 39, 59
Hong Kong, 88, 92, 232
Hoover Institution, 169
House Un-American Activities Committee, 21, 153, 157–60
human rights, 12–14, 20, 82, 86, 89, 96, 99–100, 113, 119, 128, 133–36, 149, 188–91, 204, 206–12, 252
Hungary, 66–67, 110, 223
Hutchinson, Ruby, 33

Ibrahim, Anwar, 89, 236
Iceland, 22, 34
ICI, 143
ideology of consumerism, 40–45, 50, 89, 96, 151–52, 157, 166, 187, 192, 204
  See also rights
Idris, S. M. Mohamed, 84–85, 87–90, 95–97, 136, 205, 207, 210, 236–37
India, 8, 22, 82, 90, 92, 105, 107, 121, 137, 141, 203, 235, 247
  consumer protection, 93
Indonesia, 82, 92–93, 203, 234
Infant Formula Action Coalition, 138
Institute for Consumer Information (Sweden), 26, 46
Institute for Contemporary Studies, 170
Institute for Informative Labeling (Sweden), 39, 60
Institut National de la Consommation (France), 26, 44, 64
Interfaith Association for Ethical Studies in Economics, 221
Interfaith Center on Corporate Social Responsibility, 138, 145

International Alliance for Sustainable Agriculture, 143
International Baby Food Action Network, 130, 132, 136–40, 142–43, 145, 147–52, 178, 201
International Chamber of Commerce, 37, 99, 100, 120, 218, 220, 222
International Conference of Free Trade Unions, 99
International Co-operative Alliance, 101, 103, 119
International Council of Voluntary Agencies, 100
International Council of Women, 115
International Criminal Court, 209
International Federation of Agricultural Producers, 100
International Labor Organization, 112, 116–17
International Monetary Fund, 17, 90, 117, 224–26, 203, 232, 235–37
International Movement for a Just World, 207
International Organisation of Consumers Unions, 10–11, 13, 36, 76, 92, 97, 156, 246, 250, 252
anti-regulation, 176–82
divisions over trade, 233–40
formation, 33, 37, 103
growth, 102–12, 204–6
Guidelines on Consumer Protection, 119–25
management, 198–202
multinational corporations, 215–23
networks, 127–52
non-governmental organizations, 202–6
rights, 185–213
United Nations, 98–125, 130, 148
International Organization for Standardization, 69, 100, 118
International Telegraph and Telephone Company, 214–15
International Trade Organization, 224
International Union for Conservation of Nature and Natural Resources, 100
International Women's Zionist Organization, 34
International Youth Federation, 143
Iraq, 133
Islam, 89, 190, 207, 209, 234, 253
Israel, 22, 34, 36, 107, 170
Italy, 8, 27, 46, 70, 246
See also Union Nationale Consumatori

Jamaica, 92
Japan, 8, 92, 104, 141, 144, 177, 235
consumer protection, 58–59, 61–62
co-operatives, 55, 61
women's movement, 56–57, 61
See also; Chifuren; Consumers Union of Japan; Seikatsu Consumers' Club Co-operative; Shufuren
Jaruzelski, Wojciech, 68
Jaworski, Leon, 173
Jinnah, Muhammad Ali, 90
Johnson, Lyndon B., 62, 123, 157, 160, 166, 182
Jubilee 2000, 135, 149, 206

Kallett, Arthur, 30–32, 42, 153, 157–60
Karpatkin, Rhoda, 131, 149, 195, 222
Kefauver, Estes, 171
Kellogg's, 4
Kelly, Petra, 117
Kennecott Copper Corporation, 214
Kennedy, John F., 113, 123, 157, 160, 185–86, 188, 191, 210
Kenya, 75, 82, 109, 234
Keyes, Alan, 179–80, 221
Keynes, John Maynard, 224, 226
Keyserling, Mary Dublin, 159–60
Khor, Martin, 80, 87, 89, 203, 211, 237, 239
Khruschchev, Nikita, 9, 79
Kirk, Russell, 168, 170
Kirkpatrick, James J., 171
Kirkpatrick, Jeane, 169, 180
Klein, Naomi, 19, 127–28, 152
Knauer, Virginia, 179
Knights of Labour, 10
Kodak, 4
Konsument. See Association for Consumer Information (Austria)
Korea, 8, 92
Korten, David, 211
Kouris, Haralambos, 88
Kristol, Irving, 169
Kuala Juru, 76–81, 83, 86, 94–95, 132, 141
Kuala Lumpur, 76, 83, 95–96, 107, 131

labor movement, 38–39, 56, 101, 103, 127, 135, 157, 168, 193, 215, 218
See also trade unions
La Leche League, 126, 140
Lasch, Christopher, 18
Latin America, 3, 11, 13, 74, 75, 92, 104, 107–8, 136, 197, 203, 205, 230, 234, 239
See also entries for individual nations
Latvia, 66
Lazzarini, Marilena, 109
League of Arab States, 117
League of Nations, 122
League of Red Cross Societies, 100
League of Women Shoppers, 10, 158, 160, 183
Ledogar, Robert, 109

Lee Kuan Yew, 95, 107, 170, 188, 207
Lichenstein, Charles, 177
Lim Chong Eu, 79, 82
Longfellow, Henry Wadsworth, 95
Lynd, Robert, 40, 43, 158

Macgeorge, Alastair, 110
Mahathir Mohamad, 84, 87–88, 90, 94, 96,
    189, 206–7, 236–37
Malaysia, 13, 76–97, 108, 126, 132–33, 141,
    186, 188, 206–12, 230, 234, 236–37
Malaysian Islamic Youth Movement, 89
Mali, 234–35
Manhattan Institute for Policy Research, 170
Manitoba Institute of Management, 201
Marcuse, Herbert, 12, 165
Marlboro, 4
Marsh, Benjamin, 21
Marshall Plan, 8, 22–23, 35–37, 43, 52, 69,
    159
Marx, Karl, 48, 50, 77, 105, 153, 192
Mason, Florence, 106, 110
Matthews, J. B., 31, 41, 153–55, 157–60
Mauritius, 109
Maviyane-Davies, Chaz, 186
McCarthy, Joseph, 156, 159–60
Medawar, Charles, 145
Médecins Sans Frontières, 149
Mehta, Pradeep, 235
Mexico, 92, 109, 223
Mitchell, Jeremy, 104, 109
Mongolia, 93, 108
Monsanto, 143, 203
Montreal, 56
Morales, Nicky, 88
Moynihan, Daniel Patrick, 169
Multinational Agreement on Investments, 226,
    230, 237
multinational corporations, 11, 16, 23, 86,
    109, 114, 116, 119–20, 155, 164, 166,
    177, 250
  international regulation, 214–23, 238–40
  networks, 126–27, 132, 137–51
  U.S. diplomacy, 178–82
  World Trade Organization, 225–27
  See also Commission on Transnational Cor-
    porations; *and individual corporations*
Mumeo, Oku, 56
Mumford, Lewis, 6
Muskie, Edmund, 140
Muzaffar, Chandra, 89, 207

Nadarajah, M., 210
Nadason, Marimuthu, 210
Nader, Ralph, 2, 12, 13, 16, 29, 44, 62–63,
    84, 145, 156–57, 204, 215, 227, 243–44
  Consumer Protection Agency, 171–75, 184
  opposition to, 167, 170, 179, 181

public interest movement, 161–66
  relationship with Consumers Union, 188,
    194–95
National Association for the Advancement of
    Colored People, 172
National Association of Manufacturers, 158,
    173
National Bureau of Standards (US), 30
National Consumers' League. *See* consumers'
    leagues
National Federation of Consumer Groups
    (UK), 40
nationalism, 8
neoconservatism, 16, 156, 169–70, 173, 176,
    178, 180, 182, 253
Nepal, 93, 108
Nestlé, 4, 127, 138–39, 218, 221
Netanyahu, Benjamin, 170
Netherlands, 22, 25–26, 52, 106, 110–11,
    142, 203, 234
  consumer protection, 65
  trade unions, 56
  women's movement, 57
  See also Consumentenbond
networks, 16, 127–52, 178, 188, 198, 201,
    211–12, 245
New Economic Policy (Malaysia), 76, 80, 84
New International Economic Order, 15, 113,
    125, 177–78, 219, 244
New Zealand, 42, 92, 107
Ngau, Harrison, 87–88, 150
Niger, 235
Nigeria, 92
Nixon, Richard, 9, 79, 157, 166–67, 174,
    182
non-aligned movement, 113, 125
non-governmental organizations, 13, 17, 35–
    36, 68, 87, 89, 96, 107, 110, 176, 179,
    188–91, 253
  International Organization of Consumers
    Unions, 202–6
  Malaysia, 206–12
  multinational corporations, 217–23, 238–
    40
  networks, 127–30, 134
  United Nations, 98–100, 112–18, 124–25
  World Trade Organization, 228–33
Norway, 25, 46
  consumer protection, 59–60
  See also Consumers Council
Novak, Michael, 169
Nyerere, Julius, 81

Ochieng, Samuel, 75
Office of Price Administration, 6
O'Neill, Thomas "Tip," 173
Organization for European Cooperation and
    Development, 36–37, 69, 72

Organization of African Unity, 117
Orwell, George, 43
Oxfam, 114, 118, 135, 138, 142, 145, 149

Pacific Islands, 93, 108
Packard, Vance, 12, 18, 42
Pakistan, 22, 82, 90, 92–93, 107, 121
Papua New Guinea, 93, 108, 234
Patten, Simon, 7
peace movement, 11, 99, 162
Pepsi, 173
Perak Anti-Radioactivity Committee, 88
Peru, 139
Pesticide Action Network, 130, 137, 142–45,
    147–52, 179, 201
pesticides, 11, 16, 86, 93, 116–17, 127–29,
    140–45, 178, 187, 198
Peterson, Esther, 121–14, 160–61, 171–75,
    179–82, 220–22
pharmaceuticals, 11, 16, 86, 116–17, 127–29,
    144–47, 151, 166, 176, 178–79, 187,
    198, 218, 220, 230
Philippines, 82, 88, 93–94, 234
Phillips, Mary, 31
Pines, Burton Yale, 177
Pinochet, Augusto, 214–15
Poland, 54, 67, 100, 223
political action committees, 168
Porritt, Jonathan, 203
Portugal, 70, 108
Preiss, Eva, 105
Procter & Gamble, 173–74
Public Citizen, 63, 164, 173
public interest movement, 145, 156, 161–68,
    172
Public Interest Research Group, 63, 164
Puerto Rico, 92

Que Choisir. See Union Fédérale des Consom-
    mateurs

Råd och Rön. See Institute for Consumer In-
    formation (Sweden)
Råd og Resultater. See Home Economics
    Council (Denmark)
Rahman, Meena, 87–88
Reagan, Ronald, 2, 16, 47, 120, 139, 156,
    164, 169–71, 174–76, 179–80, 184
Research Institute for Consumer Affairs,
    144
Richards, Eugene, 196
rights, 15, 20, 46, 61, 68, 70–71, 114, 119–
    20, 232, 249
    Asian values, 206–12
    International Organization of Consumers
        Unions, 185–206
    See also human rights
Romieu, André, 22, 37, 45–46

Roosevelt, Franklin D., 8, 157–58
Rotary International, 99
Ruskin, John, 30, 43
Russia, 9

Salleh, Pak, 80
Sandbrook, Richard, 203
Sartre, Jean-Paul, 12
Schadee, Elizabeth, 103, 118
Schlink, Frederick J., 30, 40, 42–43, 153,
    157–58
Schui, Hugo, 40
Schweitzer, Walmar, 33
Scrivener, Christiane, 71
Seabrook, Jeremy 96
Seeds Action Network, 137
Seikatsu Consumers' Club Co-operative, 61,
    100, 203
Selangor Consumers' Association, 83, 90–91,
    107, 210
Sen, Amartya, 211
Senegal, 109, 235
Shell, 4, 143
Shiva, Vandana, 137
Shufuren, 56–57, 92
Sinclair, Upton, 6, 42, 165
Singapore, 82, 95, 107, 127, 170, 188
Singh, Bishan, 91, 210
Sisters of the Precious Blood, 138
Slovenia, 110
Social Audit, 145
social movements, 11, 12, 47, 68, 94, 99, 162,
    165, 188, 198, 209
    consumerism as, 13–14, 38–40, 46, 50, 53,
        92, 104–12, 122, 154
    networks, 127, 133–37, 147–52
Social Watch, 135
Sokolsky, George, 158
South Africa, 10, 22, 218, 250, 252
Southeast Asia, 13, 74
    See also entries for individual nations
Soviet bloc, 9, 11, 54, 65–68, 75, 107, 110,
    113, 220, 244
Soviet Union, 9, 66, 110, 178
Spain, 34, 70, 108
Sri Lanka, 92
Stalin, Josef, 9
St. Francis, 95
Stiftung Warentest 11, 23, 25–26, 29, 33, 38,
    40, 42, 46, 49, 64
Stiglitz, Joseph, 226
Stop the War Coalition, 135
structural adjustment programs, 17, 204, 225,
    230, 236, 238
Suaram, 96, 207–9
Suhakam, 208
Sweden, 21, 27, 46, 81, 121
    consumer protection, 59–61

Sweden (*continued*)
    See also Institute for Consumer Informa-
    tion; Institute for Informative Labeling
Switzerland, 6, 138, 218–19

Taenk. *See* Danish Housewives Consumer
    Council
Tagore, Rabindranath, 105
Talib, Rokia, 91
Taller, Ed, 135
Tanzania, 81
Tearfund, 135
Tenaganita, 96–97, 207–8
Test. See Stiftung Warentest.
Test-Achats. See Association des Consomma-
    teurs (Belgium)
Thailand, 82, 92–93, 141, 235
Thalidomide, 144
Thant, U, 113, 125
Thatcher, Margaret, 2, 170
Third World Network, 80, 89–90, 96, 136,
    203, 211, 236–37
Thomas, Norman, 153
Thompson, J. Walter, 7
tobacco, 16, 137, 220
Tobin Tax, 226
Tompkins, E. P., 159
Trade Justice, 135–36, 206
Trade-Related Intellectual Property Rights,
    225, 231, 235, 237
trade unions, 10, 13, 34, 39, 53, 56, 72–73,
    89, 98–99, 105, 115, 149, 151, 157, 174,
    178, 244
    See also labor movement; *and entries for in-
    dividual nations*
Transatlantic Business Dialogue, 232
Transatlantic Consumer Dialogue, 232
transnational corporations. *See* multinational
    corporations.
Transnational Network for Appropriate/Alter-
    native Technologies, 136
Traoré, Aminata Dramane, 235
Trinidad, 92
Trumbull, Gunnar, 58–59
Tugwell, Rexford, 43

Union Fédérale des Consommateurs, 11, 22–
    23, 25–26, 32, 36, 40, 42, 46, 57
Union Féminine pour l'Information et la
    Défense du Consommateur, 25, 39, 56
Union Nazionale Consumatori (Italy), 26, 34,
    37
United Kingdom, 9, 43, 46, 101, 106–7, 170,
    212, 230
    consumer protection, 52, 58–59, 64–65
    consumer revolution, 4
    Consumers' Council, 6

co-operatives, 55
    women's movement, 57
    See also Consumers Association (UK); Na-
    tional Federation of Consumer Groups
United Malays National Organization, 84, 96
United National Industrial Development Or-
    ganization, 115
United Nations, 13, 17, 20, 22, 69, 76, 156,
    203, 237, 245–46
    anti-regulation, 176–82, 184
    consumer protection, 102
    Guidelines on Consumer Protection, 119–
    25
    International Organization of Consumers
    Unions, 98–125, 130, 148
    multinational corporations, 214–23
    networks, 139–40, 142–43, 145
    non-governmental organizations, 98–100,
    112–18, 150
    rights, 190–92
United Nations Conference on Trade and De-
    velopment, 113, 145, 177, 222
United Nations Development Programme,
    234, 251
United Nations Educational, Scientific and
    Cultural Organization, 37, 98, 112, 115,
    178, 221
United Nations Environmental Programme,
    178, 205
United Nations Guidelines on Consumer Pro-
    tection, 102
United Nations International Children's Emer-
    gency Fund, 115, 138
United States, 6–10, 27, 41, 57, 88, 101, 106,
    113, 139, 144, 212, 241
    Americanization 35–38
    "consumer democracy," 55, 72, 185
    consumer movement in, 16, 29–32
    consumer protection, 52, 59–60, 62–63,
    72, 155, 157, 160, 166–75, 195
    Consumer Protection Agency Bill, 123
    multinational corporations, 214–23
    opposition to consumerism, 155–84
    World Trade Organisation, 224–40
    See also Consumers' Research; Consumers
    Union; League of Women Shoppers;
    Nader, Ralph
Universal Declaration of Human Rights, 13,
    15, 20, 82, 190, 193, 212
Uruguay Round (of trade negotiations), 17,
    90, 216, 223, 225, 227–28, 231

Van Miert, Karel, 71
Vargas, Jose, 109
Veblen, Thorstein, 7, 30, 42, 159
Vermeer, Ruth Simmons, 112
Vietnam, 92–93, 113

Warne, Colston E., 21–22, 25, 29, 32–33, 36–37, 42, 45, 66, 88, 103–4, 106, 110, 113, 149, 153, 157–60, 194
War on Want, 138
Weidenbaum, Murray, 120, 180–82
weights and measures, 5
Wheelwright, Ted, 45, 220
Which? See Consumers Association (UK)
Williams, Cicely, 126–27, 137, 147
Williams, Raymond, 192
Willner, Dorothy, 115, 117, 119–24, 220
Witoelar, Erma, 93, 203
women's movement, 10, 11, 13, 34, 39, 53, 56–57, 72–73, 89, 98–99, 103, 113, 115, 122, 127, 133–35, 147, 149, 190, 193, 210, 244
See also entries for individual nations
World Alliance for Breastfeeding Action, 126, 139, 210
World Bank, 17, 112, 117, 178, 224–26, 203, 233, 236–37, 251
World Development Movement, 135

World Economic Forum, 239
World Federation of Trade Unions, 100
World Federation of United Nations Associations, 100
World Health Organization, 98, 112, 115, 117, 126, 137–39, 145, 148, 176, 178, 221, 245
World Rainforest Network, 136
World Social Forum, 89, 129, 135–36, 217, 206, 232, 237, 239
World Trade Organization, 17, 90, 111, 132, 216–27, 223–40
World War I, 6, 30
World War II, 6, 41, 158, 190

Young, Michael, 22, 105
Yugoslavia, 66

Zambia, 234
Zealley, Christopher, 198
Zimbabwe, 109–10
Zola, Émile, 43